The Mammoth Book of
MOVIE DETECTIVES
& SCREEN CRIMES

Also available

The Mammoth Book of Vintage Science Fiction
The Mammoth Book of New Age Science Fiction
The Mammoth Book of Fantastic Science Fiction
The Mammoth Book of Modern Science Fiction
The Mammoth Book of Great Detective Puzzles
The Mammoth Book of True Murder
The Mammoth Book of Short Horror Novels
The Mammoth Book of True War Stories
The Mammoth Book of Modern War Stories
The Mammoth Book of the Western
The Mammoth Book of Ghost Stories
The Mammoth Book of Ghost Stories 2
The Mammoth Book of the Supernatural
The Mammoth Book of Astounding Puzzles
The Mammoth Book of Terror
The Mammoth Book of Vampires
The Mammoth Book of Killer Women
The Mammoth Book of Historical Whodunnits
The Mammoth Book of Werewolves
The Mammoth Book of Golden Age Detective Stories
The Mammoth Book of Contemporary SF Masters
The Mammoth Book of Erotica
The Mammoth Book of Frankenstein
The Mammoth Book of Battles
The Mammoth Book of Astounding Word Games
The Mammoth Book of Mindbending Puzzles
The Mammoth Book of Historical Detectives
The Mammoth Book of Victorian & Edwardian Ghost Stories
The Mammoth Book of Dreams
The Mammoth Book of Symbols
The Mammoth Book of Brainstorming Puzzles
The Mammoth Book of Great Lives
The Mammoth Book of International Erotica
The Mammoth Book of Pulp Fiction
The Mammoth Book of The West
The Mammoth Book of Love & Sensuality
The Mammoth Book of Chess
The Mammoth Book of Fortune Telling
The Mammoth Puzzle Carnival
The Mammoth Book of Dracula
The Mammoth Book of Gay Short Stories
The Mammoth Book of Fairy Tales
The Mammoth Book of New Sherlock Holmes Adventures
The Mammoth Book of Gay Erotica
The Mammoth Book of the Third Reich at War
The Mammoth Book of Best New Horror
The Mammoth Book of Tasteless Lists
The Mammoth Book of Comic Fantasy
The Mammoth Book of New Erotica
The Mammoth Book of Arthurian Legends
The Mammoth Book of True Crime (Second edition)

The Mammoth Book of

MOVIE DETECTIVES & SCREEN CRIMES

Edited by
Peter Haining

Carroll & Graf Publishers, Inc.
NEW YORK

Carroll & Graf Publishers, Inc.
19 West 21st Street
New York
NY 10010–6805

This edition first published in the UK by
Robinson Publishing 1998

First published as two hardback collections, *Crime Movies* and
Crime Movies II by Severn House in 1996 and 1997

A copy of the British Library Cataloguing in Publication
Data is available from the British Library

ISBN 0-7867-0584-1

Contents

Acknowledgements & Sources

The editor and publishers are grateful to the following authors and their publishers or agents for permission to include copyright material in this collection: Victor Gollancz Ltd for "The Dripping" by David Morrell; Davis Publications Inc. for "Nobody's All Bad" by W.R. Burnett and "The Glory Hunter" by Brain Garfield; Linder A. G. for "The Unknown Traitor" by Eric Ambler; Jonathan Cape Ltd for "The Killers" by Ernest Hemingway; Atlas Publishing for "It had to be Murder" by Cornell Woolrich; Scott Meredith Literary Agency for "To Break the Wall" by Evan Hunter; Transworld Publishers Ltd for "Kick it or Kill" by Mickey Spillane; Norman Kark Publications Ltd for "Larger than Life" by Anthony Shaffer; Random House Publishers and Hutchinson for "There are Some Days . . ." by Frederick Forsyth; Virgin Publishing and W. H. Allen Ltd for "Mr Big" by Woody Allen; Hutchinson and Kingsmarkham Enterprises for "A Case of Coincidence" by Ruth Rendell; Magazine Enterprises Inc. for "Reward for Survivors" by George Harmon Coxe; Davis Publications Inc. for "Forbidden Fruit" by Edgar Lustgarten, "The Case of the Howling Dog" by Erle Stanley Gardner and "Inspector Maigret Hesitates" by Georges Simenon; William F. Nolan for his story "Down the Long Night"; London Weekend Television Enterprises for "The Embassy Incident" by Brian Clemens; Weidenfeld & Nicolson Ltd for "Your Appointment is Cancelled" by Antonia Fraser; TV Times

Ltd for "Saint Nick Alas" by Tony Hoare; H.S.D. Publications Inc. for "The End of an Era" by Richard Levinson and William Link; National Broadcasting Company (NBC) Archives for "The Three Garridebs" by Thomas H. Hutchinson, first broadcast 1937; Jay Garon-Brooke Associates for "Old Man Menace" by Louis Joseph Vance, first published in *The Saturday Evening Post*, 1927. While every care has been taken in seeking permission for the use of stories in this anthology, in the case of any accidental infringement interested parties are asked to write to the Editor in care of the publishers.

INTRODUCTION

Playing "armchair detective" is a pastime most people in a cinema audience or watching television enjoy. Indeed, pitting your wits against the investigator on the screen in order to solve the mystery before he or she does is just one of the reasons why films and TV series about crime are so popular. It also goes a long way to explaining why the mystery story is arguably the most popular of all literary genres. For there is surely a bit of the Sherlock Holmes in all of us anxious to find out who-dunnit?

"Sleuths in the Cinema" and "Cops on the Box" are, in fact, what this book is all about. Between them, policemen and detectives of all kinds have provided us with entertainment for most of the twentieth century. Safely out of harm's way, we can enjoy the thrills while others do the dirty work: we just do the thinking. Some might consider the whole business a vicarious and slightly suspect pleasure. But, in fact, it represents one of the oldest themes of all – the triumph of good over evil.

The crime story *per se* is of comparatively modern origin. The American Edgar Allen Poe is credited with writing the first tale of murder and detection, "The Murders in the Rue Morgue" in 1841, in which his pioneer detective C. Auguste Dupin solved the seemingly impossible and brutal murder of two women in a locked room by a process he referred to as "Ratiocination". We now call it "examining the clues" and "damn good detective work". This said, the pursuit of wrong-doers by those trying to uphold the law can be traced back to biblical times and beyond.

In this collection, though, we are concerned with crime stories that have been made into films or television series: specifically, those short stories which have been adapted for the screen or are closely associated with a movie or serial. A quick glance at the Contents will reveal just how many top names in the mystery field have provided material for the two media. That all the films which are featured have already been shown on television – and probably will be again along with re-runs of the various series – is a further indicator of their enduring popularity.

There have been some wonderfully defining moments in crime stories adapted for films and TV. Take, for example, the high drama when Sherlock Holmes confronted Moriarty at the Reichenbach Falls in September 1985 in the British Granada television series, faithfully adapted from the books of Sir Arthur Conan Doyle and starring Jeremy Brett, now widely regarded as the definitive Master of Detectives. The scene of Brett grappling with Eric Porter playing the evil mastermind was described by the *Daily Mirror* as "The most frightening TV sequence ever made" – and though, of course, both men lived to act another day, their plunge into the maelstrom of spray and water at the falls in Switzerland is still breathtaking to watch, no matter how many times it is shown.

I have two favourite film moments. There is the occasion when Humphrey Bogart, playing private eye Sam Spade in *The Maltese Falcon* (1941, based on Dashiell Hammett's novel), growls: "When a man's partner is killed he's supposed to do something about it." Equally, there is the sight of Edward G. Robinson, the tough Chicago gangster in *Little Caesar* (1930, from W.R. Burnett's classic story), mumbling in the picture's closing moments: "Mother of God, is this the end of Little Rico?" In both cases, the answer is a most definite no.

There is another scene in a less-well-known film that has an interesting point to make about watching crime on the screen. The picture is *Bloody Mama*, made in 1970 by legendary American director, Roger Corman. The story concerns Ma Baker (Shelley Winters) and her disturbed sons who go on a machine-gun rampage across America during the Depression era. Based on a true story, the film was condemned for its apparent glorification of the violent rise *and fall* of a female public enemy, and was banned in some US states as well as being prohibited from public exhibition in Britain for some time. Despite its undeniably realistic portrait of merciless blood-letting – tame though it seems compared with recent epics such as *Natural Born Killers* – it does have something important to say about the public fascination with lawlessness.

The point emerges from a scene in which the Baker gang confront the police in a shoot-out. They are hiding in a white, wood-frame house when a fleet of police cars roar into view and surround the building. Almost at once a barrage of gunfire is exchanged between the cops and the family, and as one uniformed figure slumps down behind a patrol car another half-dressed man falls through a pair of net curtains in a window of the house. As the carnage increases, the smoke from the guns becomes almost as thick as the blood pouring from the bodies of dying men. Then, as dramatically as it had begun, the seige ends – leaving a trail of corpses scattered both inside and outside the house which is itself scarred and shattered by bullets.

In the stillness and silence, the camera pans slowly away from this awful scene of death to a small group of people sitting quite calmly about a hundred yards away. Mothers, fathers, even a few children, some eating ice creams and others munching candy bars. They have quite evidently been watching every moment of the slaughter from start to finish.

Now whatever criticism may be levelled at Roger Corman for the way in which he lingers on the excesses of Ma Baker's band of unrepentant criminals, there is no mistaking his point. For those people sitting around are *us* – every man and woman who cannot resist the allure of crime in action. Indeed, it is probably true to say that we *need* our villains to establish any kind of parameter between law and order. It is another reason, I feel, why the crime movie or television series is so popular.

A similar debate has also been going on about the success of "Cops on the Box". Writing recently in *The Mail on Sunday*, the author David Hughes said, "In the days of Stratford Johns, a police show like *Z Cars* made stars but not money. Now the police series is so central to our culture, or rather so popular, that the stars line up. Cop shows are nowadays key shows."

Hughes also makes the point that the careful choice of locations has given these shows an added air of reality that provides viewers with a fresh perspective on where and how we are living. Crime shows can also, of course, tackle the kind of significant issues that affect everyone. They can focus on the perpetrators of crime and their victims. They can look at issues of liberty and the threat to lives. And they can – particularly – discuss the use and abuse of the law.

Although it is true to say that the earliest TV productions treated crime in very black-and-white terms, the increasing sophistication of recent shows and the boldness of their producers have enabled them to address the fallibility of policemen, the weakness of the legal system, and in some cases the corruption of those entrusted with enforcing the law.

It has been argued that at their most basic, crime stories, whether in the cinema or on television, offer escapism in the form of law-breaking, pursuit and capture, and, in the best of them, the viewer's loyalty is alternately switched from one side of the law to the other. With the passage of time they have also reflected changing moral and political climates, ranging from the culture shocks of the Sixties to the violence of the nineties and so on. As David Hughes interestingly concluded his article:

It's all about good and evil made good and funny – and that's what draws the millions. Instead of going to church or into politics or charity, or enlisting as a social worker, we let these programmes be our conscience. Thanks to their efforts we fight society's battles from the fortress of our armchair. Without a flicker of contradiction we become all at once burglars, liars, WPCs, juries, cheats, murderers, the man on the beat.

Ultimately, of course, we enjoy seeing the villain getting his just deserts, and the crime fighters we watch provide a sense of certainty not present in life. We need heroes, too – and most of all in the world of law and order – lest we fear that the very basis of our organized society is under threat. The formula runs through all the top TV police shows such as *Morse, Frost, Taggart, The Bill, NYPD Blue* and *Cracker*. Nor should we forgot Sherlock Holmes, Hercule Poirot, Jane Marple and the other amateur detectives, along with newspaper reporters, television investigators and lawyers who, similarly, turn up with unfailing regularity as the central characters in crime series.

Making a list of favourite films is never easy – and few enthusiasts are ever likely to agree completely. Most would probably include among their top ten, *The Maltese Falcon, Little Caesar, The Mask of Dimitrios, Psycho, Strangers on a Train, Bonnie and Clyde, The Godfather* and *Silence of the Lambs*. Others might feel there should be a place for *Scarface, Rear Window, The Untouchables, Sleuth, The Day of the Jackal* and even *Death Wish* and *Rambo*. The arguments are endless and in the end not really important. What *does* matter is that the crime film has as many different aspects as there are different crimes and it is this diversity in the constant battle between good and evil which makes them all so entertaining.

Obviously in a collection such as this it is only possible to include a representative selection of the stories that have been made into films and television series since the early years of the century. But in making my selections I have tried to pick not only landmark dramas but also those which have a strong literary connection. While not every story herein is the actual basis of a production, all are closely allied to it and are representative of their author's work in the genre. That most of them just happen to be associated with the films and television series which are among *my* favourites I openly admit. If I have missed any of yours, please forgive me.

It was, I believe, Sherlock Holmes who once remarked, "There's a scarlet thread of murder running through the colourless skein of life, and our duty is to unravel it, and isolate it, and expose every inch of it." In the pages that follow you will discover how the media of film and television have "isolated" and "exposed" some of the best short stories of crime and adapted them into outstanding productions. So settle into your armchair and enjoy the moving picture world of crime . . .

PETER HAINING
Boxford, Suffolk

OLD MAN MENACE

Louis Joseph Vance

Adapted to:

ONE DANGEROUS NIGHT

(Columbia, 1943)

Starring: Warren William,

Marguerite Chapman & Victor Jory

Directed by Michael Gordon

Crime stories became a staple of the film industry in its very earliest days. In America, one of the very first movie dramas, The Great Train Robbery, made in 1903, was actually a story of crime, albeit set in the Wild West. A decade later, in 1917, the medium got its first favourite crime character in the person of "The Lone Wolf". This man of disguise had originally appeared in a series of novels begun in 1914 by Louis Joseph Vance and transferred to the screen in The Lone Wolf starring Bert Lytell and directed by David Selznick for Columbia. The crime fighter proved to be of such enduring popularity that in 1958 a television series was produced starring the swashbuckling actor Louis Hayward in 30-minute episodes which opened with a shot of a wolf's-head medallion that for years was one of the most instantly recognized symbols on television. The man behind the persona of "The Lone Wolf" is Michael Lanyard, a reformed criminal who operates on both sides of the law. He moves easily among both the criminal classes and high society, and in the course of his many cases has taken on almost every kind of villain from jewel thieves to organised gangsters. Lanyard's habit of working on his own provided the English language with the expression, "a lone wolf". Among those who later followed Bert Lytell in the screen role were Henry B. Walthall, Jack Holt, Francis Lederer, Warren William, Gerald Mohr and Ron Randell before Louis Hayward introduced the character to TV audiences in what has since become something of a tradition: movie favourites transferring over to television.

New York-born Louis Joseph Vance (1879–1933) initially trained as an artist and illustrator, but later turned to writing crime novels and scored his first success with The Brass Bowl, *published in 1907. The popularity of "The Lone Wolf" novels assured his fame, all the more so when the books were adapted for the screen. Indeed, so popular did Michael Lanyard become that he was recently referred to in the* Encyclopedia of Mystery and Detection *as "one of the most famous rogues in literature" and placed on a par with The Saint, A.J. Raffles and Bulldog Drummond – all of whom have been successfuly portrayed in the cinema and on TV. Vance also wrote another series about a young Secret Service agent named Donlin, though they did not enjoy anything like the success of "The Lone Wolf". However, when the plots of the eight Michael Lanyard novels had been exhausted, a number of Vance's short stories were adapted for the series, including the following Donlin case, "Old Man Menace", which provided the basic theme for* One Dangerous Night *filmed in 1943. "The Lone Wolf" films are, in fact, late night TV favourites in the USA, and there has even been talk recently from Columbia of yet*

*another possible revival of the mysterious man wearing the
wolf's-head medallion . . .*

Donlin says the dick never lived who was too slick to be
taught his trade once in a while by some mug or sucker; and
the sooner the ambitious youngsters finds this out, the fewer
the "bad breaks" he'll have to complain about. Donlin
himself had the lesson to learn on that Winter's day whose
blue dusk saw him waiting at the throat of the railroad Y
outside Savannah – a tired young detective, and a sore one,
and a worried. A string of flops scored on recent assignments
had led him to suspect that maybe he wasn't, after all, God's
gift to the United States Secret Service; and the tone of the
telegram that had brought him abroad on this latest errand
was such as to foster the fear that Washington had begun to
share his suspicion.

Waiting there in the lee of the yardmaster's hutch, Donlin
shivered, hunched up his collar, stamped numbing feet and,
recalling the sense of the message in question, knew a painful
qualm concerning his hold on his job.

And a bride of a year waiting for him back home, too,
fondly proud of and counting on him to distinguish himself
in the Service; and a baby on the way besides; to say nothing
of installments on the mortgage falling due . . .

"Operative answering to name Sap in lower 7 car K-12
Palmetto Ltd southbound today reports ill and may be obliged
to stop off for medical attention before you relieve him. He is
trailing May Gillian sweetheart of Mullethead who is wanted
for mail robbery and believed to be in Florida heading for
Havana. Woman 5 feet 6 about 125 lbs blonde with blue eyes
wears modish black suit with grey pencil stripe. Under no
circumstances uncover yourself but in event of failure to
maintain contact with her and locate Mullethead report back
here in person immediately. – Father."

Or to put it in plain language, it was up to Donlin to land

the Mullethead or post back to the home of the Great White
Father and turn in his papers . . .

He had a morose stare for No. 83 as it shouldered in to
wait, panting, for the right of way into the city; and showing
his pass, the young man of the troubled heart swung aboard
the first car abaft the baggage. The shift to heated aisles was
some comfort; but it was in mounting disconsolation that he
worked back through the Pullmans, spotting on the way no
less than twelve variously fair and blue-eyed nymphs of
middling stature, not one of whom was a modish vision in
pencil-striped black. Sap's reservation, furthermore, was
empty; and the porter could only depose that the gemmun
in lower 1 had suttinly done got off up the line somewhere;
leaving Donlin to believe what he would, that Sap, for all his
distemper a good sleuth, faithful to the scent, had detrained
short of Savannah either (a) to continue dogging the Gillian
dame, or (b) to consult a physician.

It was manifestly, in any event, idiotic to expect anybody –
short of one of those wizard dicks you read about – to be able
to sort out of that dozen, even if she were numbered in it, the
one and only blue-orbed broad who was the light of the
Mullethead's life; so Donlin got off, when the train drew into
the Union Station, of half a mind, if wholly heartsick, to wire
Washington that he was after all but human and was there-
fore tendering his resignation.

But this was reckoning without the luck that makes plain
plodding men well-advertised detectives; and it was the
whim of that luck just then to see that No. 191 should pull
in on the other side of the between-tracks gangway and spout
a spate of its own passengers to mingle with No. 83's and
confuse and clog their flow toward the station outlets.

It resulted that Donlin presently found himself jammed in
between two young things with honey-coloured hair whom
he had first observed through an open door of a compartment
aboard the Limited and had idly sized up as a sister act, one
half demure, the other effervescent. The next thing he knew,
one of his hands was caught and meaningly squeezed, while
breathless accents, for all that freighted with forbidden

fragrance, threw him a caution intended for another.

"Watch your step, honey: if that ain't a cinder dick on the gate this kid's all wet." The speaker saw her mistake and, giggling, jerked her hand away. "Oh excuse *me!*"

"It's all right by *me*." Donlin returned a simple smile – for who was he to know the Underworld's pet name for a railroad detective? – and as guilelessly added: "But what in time's a cinder dick?"

"I hope to tell you it's one of our boy friends that works for the railroad. Get it now – Cinder Dick – don't you?"

"You bet I do."

"Gee! you sure did slip me a jolt. I thought you was my friend."

"All I want to know is," Donlin doggishly retorted: "why ain't I?"

At this stage the sedater sister missed the other, saw her making up to a strange hick, and put a sharp stop to that.

"My gawd, Marge!" she scolded, pinning the offender's wrist and freezing Donlin with eyes like blue ice. "What's the idea? You must be goofy. Next time I leave you alone with a bottle, you'll know it."

Donlin took the snub with the nonchalant pass of a village beau at the brim of his hat, and fell back to take observations which confirmed the evidence of the gay little lady.

The signs are three by which you shall know the run of plain-clothes detectives: the blue-serge bags that seldom boast a coat to match, the shoddy overcoats that they call floggers, the pug-nosed bluchers with pie-crust soles. One figure at the gateman's elbow sported this livery, and so did three more within quick hail; and Donlin took these to mean that the Savannah police had been warned to expect the Mullethead by one of the two trains just in, and had sagely figured that he would never give up without a battle.

He edged over to hug the flanks of 191 and see what might ensue. But the tide ran by without bringing the Mullethead along; and nothing of moment happened till Donlin espied Shortneck Draper alighting from 191 – one of the Mullethead's mob and, for that reason, not improbably enlisted in the efforts to squeeze the mail robber through the meshes. A guess that seemed fair enough when Shortneck, in his turn sighting the bull squad at the exit, reared back and ducked across the platform and into one of 83's day-coaches.

But the man had no more than settled himself on the far side of an almost empty car when Donlin modestly slid into the seat across the aisle.

He caught the flash of Shortneck's sidelong glance, and knew that Shortneck had caught his; but no actual sign of recognition passed. And in point of fact the two had never spoken. Donlin knew the crook only from seeing him in the Mullethead's home-town hang-out – Pete Bove's joint in East Liberty, Pittsburgh – and Shortneck probably remembered seeing Donlin there and, consequently, classed him as a fellow alumnus of the college of crime. But if they had been cronies of old they would naturally, under the circumstances, have refrained from advertising the fact.

Four minutes had passed of the five allotted for the stop at Savannah and the trickle of incoming travellers had filled the coach to a third of its capacity, if with never one who wore any of the earmarks of a menace to a crook's ease of mind, when, with a sounding crash, the door at the far end broke open and upon its threshold Old Man Menace in person awfully appeared.

Tallish, something over six feet and spare as Poverty, he might, but for the absence of knee-boots, have come straight from location work in some movie of the Old South; a starveling Legree ni a full-skirted coat buttoned at the waist, sloppy trousers, a string tie untidily knotted at the notch of an outsize low collar, and a hat that Donlin dubbed at sight a Hymn of Hate – "the sort they wear to keep their hate for humans hot" – a pinched black slouch with a brim like a hell-sent halo for a countenance sallow, cadaverous and mad.

He timed a stage wait in the doorway, spraying the passengers impartially with a scowl fit to curdle the blood in every sinful heart, then began a portentous slow prowl down the aisles, at each stride swinging a cold-drawn stare, now right, now left, of the wight in the nearest seat.

A child up forward gave a whimper of fright, then a howl, and wanted a lot of maternal comforting. An Italian of the labouring class in the second seat ahead on Shortneck's side began to squirm and measure the distance to the door behind him as if wondering whether he could make it before his time came to be bored through and through by those awful eyes. His blanched lips formed the dread word "Lege!" and Donlin masked a twitching mouth. "Every ginny," he reflected, "is guilty of something; and that make-up's enough to throw the fear into a saint."

Wails of "All abo-oo-ard!" were lifted, the bell awoke to toll, the train snorted, groaned, and gathered way; and in by the forward door broke the sister act, the grave blonde and the gay, the last in fits of panting mirth because – obviously – the two had pushed their promenade too far and been obliged to scramble up the steps while the wheels were turning. Their Pullman was aft, and the laughing girl led toward it in a dance that quickly overhauled the sportsman under the Hymn of Hate.

"Pardon me, please."

Her wheedling soprano won from the man no offer to unblock but a halfturn instead with a glare meant to wither. And Marge, making big eyes at that cast-iron mask and finding it more than she could bear, gave one great glad whoop.

"Well – as I live and breath – if it ain't Chief Heavy Static, the Last of the Neutrodynes!"

Before her mark could rally she had risen a-tip-toe as if to kiss the creature and, when he reared back, walling his eyes and pawing the air, one of her hands, its motion so swift and sure that Donlin must have missed if he hadn't been alert for them, flashed into the open coat and fished out an object obling and dark.

In the same breath something happened to sour the jest; the watchful Donlin saw the playful jade start, lose colour, drop her prize, deftly kick it under the seats, then seize the other girl by the wrist.

"Shake a leg, Mam, before this med. show ham starts sellin' us Snake Root. Come on – can't you? – show your speed."

The two sped by at the moment when Donlin was stooping to pick up an oblong dark object that had, only an instant before, nudged his feet – "the leather" of which Marge had despoiled the clown; a worn wallet with a rubber band about its middle.

Its owner, all unaware of his loss, was shaking himself like a dog after a ducking; and not only was it a trick of the trade to make much of short minutes but Donlin had never forgotten the first precept laid down for him by a ranking officer:

"One thing you've got to learn if you want to last in this game, youngster, is to pick up everything you see and look it over. Only, watch yourself if it's a woman."

The leather held a pawn ticket showing that one B. Fyle had lately pledged a suit of clothing in Savannah for $3; an illiterate letter, postmarked Meeks, Ga., and addressed to Mr Beattie Fyle, whose writer, presumably Mrs Fyle, complained that Beattie had left his family to starve in Meeks while he led a gay life in the city; and another, typewritten on the handsome letterhead of the Cosmpolitan Detective Institute of New York. This last opened by informing Mr Fyle that he had passed his final examinations with high marks, his essay entitled "Shadowing a Suspect by Night Through the Streets of Meeks" having won him a rating only a point short of the highest. In view of this showing "the Board" had decided to grant two Gold Badges instead of the one ordinarily awarded the student graduating at the head of his class; and if Mr Fyle would forward a money-order for $2.50 to cover the extra costs, his Gold Badge, with his name engraved on it, would be sent by return mail postpaid. The Board of course assumed that Mr Fyle would start practising his new profession immediately, but ventured none the less to recommend that he take the post-graduate course under the Old Inspector, the fee for which, $15, was trifling in comparison with the value of the Old Inspector's tuition in the subtler nuances of sleuthing. The Board was happy to enclose Mr Fyle's diploma and, as a souvenir of glad college days, a gun-metal cigarette case pressed in the shape of a pistol.

Finally, the wallet yielded a document, all in laborious

longhand, with the heading: "How to Become a Great Detective. 15 Rules Compiled by Mr Beattie Fyle, Meeks, Ga., Graduate Detective of the Cosmopolitan Detective Institute of N. Y. with Gold Badge."

Donlin had time for no more than the first two:

"*Rule No. 1*. Remember a great Detective never Questions a Susspekt he just Tranzfixs him."

This, then, was the meaning of that grim parade down the aisle: one bound by professional ethics to hold all men suspect had been dutifully subjecting the carful to the Ordeal of the Transfixion.

"*Rule No. II*. When you catch a Susspekt but do not Know what Crime he had comited Scarce him all you can Before you Start in Questioning him. This is Very Important as he will likely Break Down and Confes if he Beleives you know All."

At this point Dunlin, with the shadow of the author upon him, hastily refolded the paper and hid it, with the leather, beneath his coat. A wasted precaution: the new-laid sleuth had at last marked the panicky Italian and was proceeding to apply Rule II by planting himself in the opposite seat and slewing sideways to cover his quarry with a baleful countenance.

In vain that unfortunate sought to dissemble his qualms by turning to the window; the night made the glass too good a mirror, he still could see those gimlet eyes searching his soul for its black secret. At length, then, he got up and wove forward – accelerating a bit when the tail of his eye told him Nemesis was hard on his heels; Mr Fyle having been eager to follow and deal with any attempt at evasion.

Donlin watched till the Italian, despairing, halted at the water-cooler and made believe he had wanted only to slake a parched throat. At this juncture Donlin rid himself of the wallet by tossing it over to the seat that the man from Meeks had just vacated. Barely in time, too: with his next breath the victim choked on pure water and, coughing, reeled back to his place – stalked all the way by dour Calamity as by an Apache in war paint.

The long black coat was now unbuttoned and carelessly

thrown open to display that splendid Gold Badge in which Donlin perceived the cause of Marge's abrupt dismay: the hand that lifted the leather having undoubtedly come at the same time in contact with the metal and given the mischief to believe she was getting gay with a legitimate limb of the law.

The Italian pitched feebly into his seat; the graduate detective found the wallet in his and, mystified but grateful, took it back to his fond bosom, then settled to transfix the wretch across the aisle again; and Donlin pulled his hat down over his eyes, and fell into a half-doze.

When, three hours and thirty minutes later, the Palmetto Limited made its last stop at Jacksonville, Donlin, although among the first to leave the train, took such a deliberate pace down the platform that he was passed first by the miserable Italian, scuttling for the station gates like a rabbit to its funk-hole, then by Beattie Fyle, still hot on the tracks of undetected crime, eventually by Shortneck Draper. Donlin inclined to believe that this one had been at loose ends ever since hastily concluding that the air of Savannah was unwholesome for him; he remained, for all that, the only possible clue to the mystery of the Mullethead – a poor straw to catch at, but one that Donlin might not pass up if he hoped to hold on to his job.

He had, however, no more than arrived at this glum conclusion when his heart gave a start as he saw himself overhauled by a trim young person whose yellow hair and cornflower eyes were smartly set off by a suit of black stuff striped with grey.

It needed a second look to make the poor worried wretch sure that this was actually the sober half of the sister act. Set aside her change of costume, she was mysteriously without Marge. Apparently in some haste while anxious not to advertise it, and studiously keeping her eyes to herself, she somehow gave an impression of having all her wits about her, of being prepared for anything, set to let nothing swerve her or hinder. And all at once Donlin's tepid intoxication with the chase was feverish. A break at last!

On the threshold of the common waiting-room the girl made a stop, letting an abstracted gaze travel on toward the street while ostensibly rummaging her mind for some mislaid data. And it might have been, Donlin allowed, sheer coincidence that had caused Shortneck Draper to hold up there in the main entrance while he scanned the headlines of a local newspaper. There might, too, have been no relation whatever between the circumstances that Shortneck presently folded the paper and thrust it into his right-side coat pocket, only to change his mind and shift it to the left, before taking himself off into the night; and that, as soon as this happened, May Gillian snapped out of it and whisked across the waiting-room to the accommodations set aside exclusively for, by the sign on the door, "Women".

Since it was hardly his book to be in sight when she came out, Donlin left the building by a side entrance, doubled round to the front, and took up a stand at a window that commanded a view of the waiting room with the door through which May Gillian had vanished.

The Palmetto Limited had arrived on the do – at 9:05. At 9:25 Donlin still on watch at the window, was asking himself whether or not he had been played for a sucker. But at 9:26 he began to feel better; at 9:26 the elusive Marge emerged alone from the door marked "Women" and – he didn't care how or when she had contrived to get in there – he took this as proof that he hadn't been hornswoggled, that her girl friend was still keeping cover, waiting for Marge to do her some special office.

Marge was now, moreover, a study that posed his wits with a fine puzzle: a changed woman, high spirits all evaporated, a dark mood possessing her instead, Marge was giving a most artistic portrayal of a baggage abroad on nefarious business and in a rare stew about it.

Anxious and mistrustful – in the slang of the crooked side, "screwy" – Marge tarried a minute to size up the waiting-room, then in ostensible relief got under way for the main entrance and darted out with furtive haste that as good as asked for curious attention. And, indeed, if Donlin hadn't been a born sceptic he might have fallen for the invitation; but to his mind Marge was laying it on too thick. It was none of his business what the hussy was up to. It was strictly his business to keep contact with May Gillian till she showed him the way to give the Mullethead the gaff and land him in the hoosegow.

That just had to happen. Or else. . .

He gritted his teeth and doggedly waited.

Nor did his clamped jaws relax till he saw, on the tick of 9:30, the Gillian girl make her long-delayed re-entrance to the general waiting-room and quietly, without the least trace of nervousness, stroll through and out of the station.

Once outside, this one struck a quick step on the street heading straight away from the station. But she passed within arm's-length of Donlin, who couldn't be sure he had escaped her notice, so only his gaze followed her till she rounded the third corner.

It thus became his part to practice for several minutes what goes in his shop by the name of "block tailing". Actually on the move before the woman passed from sight, Donlin jogged down the street that ran on a parallel line with the front of the station, to halt and wait at each intersecting street till May Gillian appeared three blocks away. A ticklish business, as long as it lasted. His heart stood still for seconds at every intersection, and resumed its normal beat only when, at the fourth, he saw the girl cross the street, pull up in front of a corner drug store, and stand a minute studying its windows. Then, sidelong glances presumably having satisfied her that she wasn't being shadowed, she marched boldly into the shop – and left Donlin up in the air again, with three blocks to go.

A ramshackle taxi limped up; and instructing the cabby to drive slowly past the drug store, Donlin made rapid reconnaissance of its interior only to see it completely bare of customers.

Anything was possible: that May Gillian was merely out of sight in a telephone booth; that she passed through to join her lover somewhere back of the prescription counter; that she had found some masked exit to a back alley, and thus definitely balked all pursuit.

Donlin paid off the taxi at the next corner and, as he dejectedly turned back afoot, saw May Gillian dart out of the drug store and in tearing haste retrace her way to the station. Block tailing took Donlin back there as well, and in good time: when he took up his post at the window again, May Gillian was openly waiting near the main entrance. It was then 9:49. At 9:51 a cab lolloped up and discharged two passengers who made getting out an awkward if understandable, business, seeing they were handcuffed to each other. One was the Mullethead, all crestfallen and disgusted; the other, with his hard-boiled hat, shabby flogger and unshined bluckers, was the plain-clothes man complete. The two walked into the station like friends arm-in-arm, with the overcoat thrown over their linked wrists; but that camouflage was old stuff.

By every sign, however, May Gillian didn't mind. She welcomed her man with a warm smile, kissed him while all the waiting-room looked on, found something not too sour to say to his captor, and followed to the ticket window. There the officer who had the Mullethead in charge took two tickets to Chicago and a drawing-room on the Seminole. May Gillian then bought one ticket and a section in the same car. Donlin the defeated stood at her elbow the while, but she never heeded him; the strain of uncertainty was no more, her manner said, the man-hunt ended, she had no longer to worry about possibly ill-intentioned strangers. You might almost have thought her glad her lover had been captured.

It was different with Donlin. He saw the trio through the gates to the Seminole, which left at 10, and saw his last hope go glimmering with them. Tough enough to have been denied the chance to make the arrest himself. But to have been beaten to it by a hick cop! He well knew Washington wouldn't forget that.

"Love!" he mused as he trudged off in disgust – "love sure is funny. Wonder what a guy does to get dames dippy about him, the way that frail is about the Mullethead? Just to be with him was enough for her, no matter if the heel was in handcuffs and headed for the pen. . . Funny!"

*   *   *

Donlin turned leaden feet toward the cheap hotel he had in mind; down in the mouth enough, in all conscience, but even beyond that vexed by a sense of dissatisfaction with the undramatic end of the Mullethead affair. After all that sinister intrigue which so many had conspired to weave for the confusion of the law, it did seem that a livelier dénouement had been in order, that tame scene in the station seemed somehow anticlimatic.

His way led through streets of poor shops for the most part dark, with here and there an eating place bravely lighting a patch of mean sidewalk. It was thus easy to mark and identify at some distance a long, lank, lonesome shape at halt in front of one such window.

He closed up quietly on Mr Fyle of Meeks, wondering what was on the mind of his colleague.

Colleague was right. He guessed that as comic-strip sleuths there was little to choose between them.

If his first supposition was the obvious one, something more than hunger was manifestly bothering Beattie Fyle. The eyes were sad instead of searching that gazed from under the Hymn of Hate at the display of meats and pastry and fruits in season; Donlin fancied something pathetic in the set of the mouth whose cast had been so stern on board the Limited; and the man since last seen had been in a minor accident of some description – a shoulder of the long black coat was dusty and so were the knees of his trousers, and he sported a scraped bruise on one cheekbone.

All too plainly indecision preyed on his mind: he hungered, yet he hesitated, while knobby fingers fumbled in his waistcoat pocket – Donlin could surmise how few the coins were that they counted.

But belly need in the end prevailed: Mr Fyle shuffled into the restaurant, chose a place at its beggarly array of empty tables, and gave his order in two short phrases and without looking at the bill-of-fare. Then he rested, big gnarled red hands spread out on the bare board before him, head thrown back, sunken eyes fixed on some bleak remoteness – all his air breathing a vast disconsolation.

Unconsidered impulse drove Donlin into the place and seated him opposite the graduate detective. Misery, he reminded himself, loves company.

"Good evening, Mr Fyle," he cried in response to a repellant stare. "And how'd you leave the folks in Meeks? Well, I trust, and happy in the knowledge that the head of the family is launched at last upon the career for which his gifts so conspicuously fit him."

A pause for reply won no more than a blank glare and an inarticulate croak from tremulous dry lips.

"I see you're surprised to find I know you. But it's nothing to be wondered at, Mr Fyle, really. Permit me to introduce myself" – Donlin offered a hand – "*ex*-Inspector Donlin of the United States Secret Service, at present the 'Old Inspector' of the Cosmopolitan Detective College of New York, and happy to make the acquaintance of one of our most brilliant graduates."

"The Old Inspector!" Beattie Fyle took Donlin's hand as gingerly as if it had been a sainted relic. "My stars! Mister Inspector, I suttin'ly am proud to meet ye – proud and glad. I never did reckon to have sich reel pleasure!" He looked it, too: a man transfigured by happy excitement, with new sparkle in his lacklustre eyes, a sudden flush in his sallow cheeks. "But what beats me is how ye come to know me when we ain't never met ner spoken ner nothin'."

"It's quite simple, Mr Fyle," Donlin protested with a smile wise beyond words, "but – forgive me – a professional secret; a feature of my post-graduate course not to be divulged until preliminary lessons have prepared your mind to grasp it. Enough that I do know you and am here to shake you by the hand and beg you to be my guest tonight. Do me the honour, I beg, to countermand the order you have just given, and let me order a dinner that will do justice to this happy occasion."

Neither would Donlin hear a word against his wishes; and beckoning the waiter, he commanded a meal, on a foundation of double porterhouse and fried onions, that caused the features of his guest to glisten.

"You probably don't realize the warm interest the Cosmopolitan Detective College takes in its graduates," Donlin resumed. "It has long been an unadvertised custom of ours to look up our Gold Badge in person and do everything we can to see that they get a good start in their life work. Some are self-starters like yourself, of course, Mr Fyle; the ambition and enterprise you show, the way you do get around, gave me some trouble when it came to locating you. But a good detective – I don't have to tell you – never quits till he gets his man. Now tell me: How goes it?"

"Not so good," Mr Fyle glumly confessed. "Ye've got me wrong, Mister Inspector; I ain't got started right yit, not reely. Ye see, I figger it like this: Folks ain't goin' to have no reel confidence in a detective, Gol' Badge or no Gol' Badge, unless'n he's pulled some big coop and shown 'em he's as smart as he lets on. So I been just kind of lookin' round, to begin with, keepin' my eyes peeled and sizin' up suspecks. I put in quite some time, off and on, shadderin' suspecks, but – lan's sake! – it turned out every time they hadn't done nothin' to speak of. Now tonight it was dif-run . . . But the luck was agin me."

Mr Fyle looked back on the night with wistful eyes and absently rubbed his bruised cheek.

"Why, what happened, Mr Fyle?"

"Nothin' that was my fault, Mister Inspector. It was the cops put the kibosh on it, like they allus do when they're up agin a good detective. Anyway, that's how it always is in the books."

"It was like this: I picked out the likeliest suspeck I seen yit on the train comin' down from Savannah. He was some sort of furriner, and ye never did see nobody that had all the marks of a crook stickin' out more prominent. So I shaddered him all the way, and when we got out of the depot here he started runnin', and that's one of the surest signs of guilt there is, of course; so I up and arrested him and took him to the station house and told them they had better look him up before he had time to commit some crime or other. So the sergeant asked me what charge they was to lock him up on, and I said 'Actin' screwy', and instead of doin' their duty they all started laughin' and called me out of my name and said I hadn't no right to arrest anybody only on suspicion. And they took the furriner to the door and told him beat it, and when I pertested they threw me out."

"That's always the way!" Donlin declared. "I tell all my pupils every good detective ought to paste this precept of our noble profession in his hat: 'The less a detective asks of the police the less risk he runs of having them crab his biggest coups and steal his glory.' "

"That's a great rule, Mister Inspector," Mr Fyle protested. "Wud ye mind if I copied it off with mine?"

"Not at all, Mr Fyle. But am I to understand you have already formulated a set of rules for your own guidance?"

"Yes, suh. That's one of the very first things I done when I set out to make me a reputation shadderin' suspecks." The man from Meeks reached for his wallet. "Mebbe ye'd keer to listen to them."

"I should be only too glad."

Mr Fyle sorted out the paper, unfolded it, and in quavers of pride began to recite his commandments. But Donlin hardly listened. He was not only repenting the soft-hearted impulse that had committed him to such punishment, he was good and sore on himself for playing such a cheap trick on a simp. Who was he, anyway, to think himself a better man than Beattie Fyle of Meeks? Hadn't he lost himself a job by being less than half as smart as he thought he was?

All at once a turn of words recited in a nasal drone captured his interest and, as soon as he seized an inkling of their general sense, treated him to a cruel but electrifying kick in the intelligence . . .

"What was that, Mr Fyle?" he broke in. "Would you mind reading that last again?"

"Sure will!" Mr Fyle consented, deeply gratified. " 'Rule Nine: Remember that a woman, no matter how low she has fallen, will always break down when she sees her man in manacles.' "

"Just a minute, please." Donlin thrust his chair back. "I'm afraid you'll have to excuse me for a few minutes. You have just reminded me of a matter I was in danger of overlooking. In fact, Mr Fyle, you have done the Old Inspector a great service; you have taught him a great lesson."

He seized and warmly shook the graduate's hand.

"I hope to be back, Mr Fyle; but on the off-chance of anything turning up to detain me, I'll settle for the dinners as I go out."

Donlin left five dollars with the cashier and told him to give the waiter the change. He hadn't any time to waste, with the vast volume of business he would have to transact by telegraph and long distance telephone at the earliest possible instant if he were to repair an oversight that might have cost him his job if he hadn't had his mind opened to it by Rule IX of the Code of Graduate Detective Fyle of Meeks.

May Gillian most decidedly had not broken down, in the Jacksonville railway station.

Donlin arrived by airplane in Columbia the next morning in time to accompany the United States Marshall and the posse of police detectives who met the Seminole and removed in manacles not only Peter ("Mullethead") McGonigle, but another and a longwanted offender, Charles ("Pud") Morse – holding this last, against the arrival of warrants charging him with graver crimes, for impersonating a police officer.

And this time, Donlin was interested to observe, Rule IX worked like a charm. When she saw the handcuffs snapped on her man's wrists, May Gillian threw a fit of hysterics whose violence didn't even begin to abate till she had been given a shot in the arm by an ambulance surgeon.

The Secret Service man walked his way to the telegraph office, then, to report his success to Washington – gravely grateful for the lesson he had learned from his colleague of Meeks. A good dick, he insists, is a guy wise enough to realize that there are times when even a cuckoo can teach him his business.

THE GHOST
OF JOHN HOLLING

Edgar Wallace

Adapted to:

MYSTERY LINER

(Monogram, 1934)

Starring: Noah Beery,

Astrid Allwyn & Gustav von Seyffertitz

Directed by Roy William Neill

In the early years of this century British audiences were also enjoying films about crime, most tending to be fictionalised accounts of the careers of real-life villains such as Charlie Peace, the Victorian cracksman who was also a master of disguise and featured in a silent short, The Life of Charlie Peace, *made in 1901. It was not, in fact, until the mid-Twenties that English studios began to produce crime movies in any number when they started to cash in on the best-selling novels of Edgar Wallace, already being described as "The King of Thrillers" and whose books were selling in their millions. In the next quarter of a century, literally hundreds of pictures, both silent and talkies, black and white and technicoloured, were made from Wallace's stories, including such box office hits as* The Green Archer *(1925) starring Allene Ray and Walter Miller;* The Terror *(1928) with Louise Fazenda and Edward Everett Horton;* The Ringer *(1928), featuring Leslie Farber and Annette Benson which had already been a very successful London stage production;* The Flying Squad *(1929) co-starring Wyndham Standing and Dorothy Bartlam – plus Edgar's son, Bryan, and Carol Reed playing two small-time crooks – not forgetting* The Menace *(1932) which featured H.B. Warner and a youthful Bette Davis. After scripting and even directing a number of his stories for the screen, Wallace was lured to Hollywood in the Thirties where he worked on the script of one of the most famous horror movies of all time,* King Kong *(1933). Since his death, a series of short screen adaptations were made by Jack Greenwood in the Sixties and then followed almost a decade later by* The Edgar Wallace Mystery Theatre *for television. Many of Wallace's crime dramas are still being re-shown on late night TV for the benefit of crime movie aficionados.*

Edgar Wallace (1875–1932) was a publishing phenomenon: the illegitimate son of an actress, who became a journalist and then mystery writer after the success of his first book, The Four Just Men *(1906), which he actually published himself! His work later became so popular with the reading public that it was claimed by his publishers that every fourth book sold in the UK bore the name of Edgar Wallace. His output was certainly prodigious and he maintained he could compose a 75,000 word manuscript in 36 hours with the aid of a dictaphone and a team of secretaries! Although many of his stories are unreadable today, the best of his mystery fiction has ensured him a permanent place in the crime fiction genre. "The Ghost of John Holling" was just one of Edgar Wallace's short stories to be adapted for the screen as* Mystery Liner *and tells a story of murder at sea which was made all the more memorable on screen through a brilliantly sinister performance by the German actor, Gustav von Seyffertitz. This 1934 movie has been screened at least twice on British television in the last decade, and it offers a typical example of the kind of picture that helped to launch the crime movie genre in Britain over 70 years ago . . .*

"There are things about the sea that never alter. I had a writing gentleman in one of my suites last voyage who said the same thing, and when writing people say anything original, it's worth jotting down. Not that it often happens.

" 'Felix,' he said, 'the sea has got a mystery that can never be solved – a magic that has never been and never will be something-or-other to the tests of science.'

"(I'm sure it was 'tests of science,' though the other word has slipped overboard).

"Magic – that's the word. Something we don't understand, like the mirror in the bridal suite of the *Canothic*. Two men cut their throats before that mirror. One of 'em died right off, and one lived long enough to tell the steward who found him that he'd seen a shadowy sort of face looking over his shoulder and heard a voice telling him that death was only another word for sleep.

"That last fellow was Holling – the coolest cabin thief that ever travelled the Western Ocean. And what Holling did to us when he was alive was nothing to what he's done since, according to certain stories I've heard.

"Spooky told me that when the mirror was taken out of the ship and put in the stores at Liverpool, first the storekeeper and then a clerk in his office were found dead in the storeroom. After that it was carried out to sea and dropped into fifty fathoms of water. But that didn't get rid of Holling's ghost.

"The principal authority on Holling was the steward who worked with me. Spooky Simms his name was, and Spooky was so called because he believed in ghosts. There wasn't anything in the supernatural line that he didn't keep tag on, and when he wasn't making tables rap he was casting horror-scopes – is that the way you pronounce it?

" 'I certainly believe in Holling's ghost,' said Spooky, on this voyage I'm talking about now, 'and if he's not on this packet at this minute, I'm no clairvoyager. We passed right over the spot where he died at three-seven this morning, and I woke up with the creeps. He's come aboard – he always does when we go near the place he committed suicide.'

"There was no doubt that Spooky believed this, and he was a man with only one delusion: that he'd die in the poorhouse and his children would sell matches on the street. That accounts for the fact that he hoarded every cent he made.

"Personally, I don't believe in spooks or anything, but I do admit that there is one magical thing about the sea – the way it affects men and women. Take any girl and any man, perfect strangers and not wanting to be anything else, put them on the same ship and give them a chance of talking to one another, and before you know where you are, his wastepaper basket is full of poetry that he's torn up because he can't find a rhyme for 'love,' and her wastepaper basket's top-high with bits of letters she's written to the man she was going to marry, explaining that they are unsuitable for one another, and that now she sees in a great white light the path that love has opened for her.

"I know, because I've read 'em. And the man hasn't got to be handsome or the girl a doll for this to happen.

"There was a gang working the *Mesopotamia*, when I served in her a few years ago, that was no better and no worse than any other crowd that travels for business. They used to call this crowd 'Charley's'. Charley Pole being the captain. He was a nice young fellow, with fair, curly hair, and he spoke London English, wore London clothes and had a London eyeglass in his left eye.

"Charley had to work very carefully, and he was handi-capped, just as all the other gangs were handicapped, by the

Pure Ocean Movement, which our company started. Known card-sharps were stopped at the quayside by the company police and sent back home again – to America if they were American, to England if they were English. About thirty of our stewards were suspended, and almost every bar steward in the line, and it looked as if the Western Ocean was going to be a dull place. Some of the crowds worked the French ships, and nearly starved to death, for though the French are, by all accounts, a romantic race, they're very practical when it comes to money.

"So the boys began to drift back to the English and American lines, but they had to watch out, and it was as much as a steward's place was worth to tip them off. Charley was luckier than most people, for he hadn't got the name that others had got, and though the company officials looked down their noses every time he carried his grip ashore at Southampton, they let him through.

"Now the Barons of the Pack (as our old skipper used to call them) are plain business men. They go travelling to earn a living, and have the same responsibilities as other people. They've got wives and families and girls at the high school and boys at college, and when they're not cutting up human lamb, they're discussing the high cost of living and the speculation in theatre seats, and how something ought to be done about it.

"But on one point they're inhuman: they have no ship-board friendships that can't pay dividends. Women – young, old, beautiful, or just women – mean nothing in their lives. So far as they are concerned, women passengers are in the same category as table decorations – they look nice, but they mean nothing. Naturally they meet them. A sucker is a sucker because he wants to look important. That's the why of it. A mean man who doesn't care a darn how mean he looks, never really gets into the sucker class.

"But the others, the fellows that are dying to overhear somebody say, 'Ain't he grand?' are ready to flash anything from bank notes to a wife to push home the impression that they're grander than you thought they were at first. But beyond a 'Glad to meet you, Mrs So-and-so,' the big men of the big crowds never bother with women. That was why I was surprised when I saw Charley walking the boat deck with Miss Lydia Penn for two nights in succession. I wasn't surprised at her, because I've given up being surprised at women.

"She had suite 107 on C deck, and Spooky Simms and I were her room stewards – we shared that series – so that I knew as much about her as anybody. She was a gold and tortoise-shell lady, and had more junk on her dressing-table than anybody I've known. Silver and glass and framed photographs, and manicure sets, and all her things were in silk, embroidered with rosebuds and blue birds. A lady.

"From what she told me she was travelling for a big woman's outfitters in Chicago. She had to go backward and forward to London and Paris to see new designs, and by the way she travelled it looked as if no expenses were spared.

"As a looker Miss Lydia Penn was in the *de luxe* class. I've never been a good hand at describing women, and have got in bad at home often and often owing to my not being able to say what women are wearing, and how they looked – especially film stars that we've brought home. But this Miss Penn was easy. She had golden hair, just dull enough to be genuine, and a complexion like a baby's. Her eyebrows were dark and so were her eyelashes – black and long.

"I admire pretty girls. I don't mean that I fall in love with them. Stewards don't fall in love, they get married between trips and better acquainted when the ship's in dry dock. But if I was a young man with plenty of money and enough education to pass across the line of talk she'd require, I shouldn't have gone further than Miss Penn.

"But she wasn't everybody's woman – being a little too clever to suit the average young business man.

"The day before we made Nantucket Lightship, Spooky Simms came to me just as I was going off watch.

" 'Remember me telling you about Holling?' he said.

"As a matter of fact, I'd forgotten all about the matter.

" 'He's on board – saw him last night as plain as you – if it's possible, plainer. He was leaning up against No. 7 boat, looking white and ill. Plain! Why, I can see him now. There will be trouble!'

"And he was right. Mr Alex McLeod of Los Angeles took his bag from the purser's safe that night to save himself trouble first thing in the morning. He locked the bag in a big trunk and locked the door of his cabin, and wanted to give the key to Spooky, who was his steward. But Spooky was dead scared.

" 'No, sir, you'd better keep it. And if you'll allow me to say so, sir. I shouldn't leave any valuables lying about to-night if I was you.'

"This he said in my hearing.

"When Mr McLeod went to his bag the next morning, three thousand dollars and a gold watch and chain were gone.

" 'Holling,' said Spooky, and you couldn't budge him. He was one of those thin, bald men that never change their opinions.

"The Central Office people investigated the case, but that's where it ended.

"It wasn't much of a coincidence that Miss Penn and Charley were on the ship when it turned round. Charley was on business, and so was she. I saw them together lots of times, and once he came down with her and stood outside her cabin whilst she dug up some photographs of the South Sea Islands.

"Charley's side-partner was a fellow named Cohen, a little fellow with the biggest hands I've ever seen. They say he could palm a whole pack and light a cigarette with the hand they palmed in without the sharpest pair of eyes spotting it.

"One morning I took Cohen in his coffee and fruit, and I thought he was sleeping, but just as I was going away he turned round.

" 'Felix,' he said, 'who is that dame in the private suite?' (She travelled that way).

"I told him as much as I thought necessary.

" 'She's got Charley going down for the third time,' he

said, worried, 'and he's side-stepping business. We're eight hundred dollars bad this trip unless somebody comes and pushes it into my hand – and that only happens in dreams.'

" 'Well, it's your funeral, Mr Cohen,' I said.

" 'And I'll be buried at sea,' he groaned.

"Cohen must have talked straight to Charley, because that same night the smoke-room waiter told me that Charley had caught an English Member of Parliament for a thousand dollars over a two-handed game that this bird was trying to teach him.

"We got to Cherbourg that trip early in the morning, and I had to go down to lock up the lady's baggage, because she was bound for Paris. She was kneeling on the sofa looking out of the porthole at Cherbourg, which is about the same thing as saying that she was looking at nothing, for Cherbourg is just a place where the sea stops and land begins.

" 'Oh, steward,' she said, turning round, 'do you know if Mr Pole is going ashore? He wasn't certain last night.'

" 'No, Miss,' I said, 'not unless he's going ashore in his pyjamas. The tender is coming alongside, and when I went into his cabin just now he was asleep.'

"She looked very thoughtful at this.

" 'Thank you,' she said, and that was all.

"She went off in the tender and left me the usual souvenir. She was the only woman I've met that tipped honest.

"There was some delay after the tender left, and I wondered why, till I heard that a certain English marquis who was travelling with us discovered that his wife's jewel-case had been lifted in the night, and about twenty thousand pounds' worth of pearls had been taken.

" 'It is very unpleasant for everybody when a thing like that happens, because the first person to be suspected is the bedroom steward. After that, suspicion goes over to the deck hands, and works its way round to the passengers.

"The chief steward sent for all the room-men, and he talked straight.

" 'What's all this talk of Holling's ghost?' he said, extremely unpleasant. 'I want to tell you that the place where

Holling's gone, money – especially paper money – would be no sort of use at all, so we can rule spirits out entirely. Now, Spooky, let's hear what you saw.'

" 'I saw a man go down the alleyway toward Lord Crethborough's suite,' he said, 'and I turned back and followed him. When I got into the alleyway there was nobody there. I tried the door of his cabin and it was locked. So I knocked, and his lordship opened the door and asked me what I wanted. This was at two o'clock this morning – and his lordship will bear out my words.'

" 'What made you think it was a ghost?' asked the chief steward.

" 'Because I saw his face – it was Holling.'

"The chief steward thought for a long time.

" 'There's one thing you can bet on – he's gone ashore at Cherbourg. That town was certainly made for ghosts. Go to your stations and give the police all the information you can when they arrive.'

"On the trip out, Miss Penn was not in the passenger list, and the only person who was really glad was Cohen. When he wasn't working, I used to see Charley moping about the alleyway where her cabin had been, looking sort of miserable, and I guessed that she'd made a hit. We had no robberies, either; in fact, what with the weather being calm and the passengers generous, it was one of the best out-and-back trips I've had.

"We were in dock for a fortnight replacing a propeller, and just before we sailed I had a look at the chief steward's list, and found I'd got Miss Penn again, and to tell you the truth, I wasn't sorry, although she was really Spooky's passenger.

"I don't think I've ever seen a man who looked happier than Charley Pole when she came on board. He sort of fussed round her like a pet dog, and for the rest of the voyage he went out of business. Cohen felt it terribly.

" 'I've never seen anything more unprofessional in my life, Felix,' he said bitterly to me one day. 'I'm going to quit at the end of this trip and take up scientific farming.'

"He was playing patience in his room – the kind of

patience that gentlemen of Mr Cohen's profession play when they want to get the cards in a certain order.

"What poor old Holling said about Charley is right – a college education is always liable to break through the skin.

" 'Did you know Holling?' I asked.

" 'Did I know him? I was the second man in the cabin after Spooky found him. In fact, I helped Spooky get together his belongings to send to his widow.' He sighed heavily. 'Holling did some foolish things in his time, but he never fell in love except with his wife.'

" 'Have you heard about his ghost?' I asked.

"Cohen smiled.

" 'Let us be intelligent,' he said. 'Though I admit that the way Charley goes on is enough to make any self-respecting cardman turn in his watery tomb.'

"Two days out of New York we struck a real ripsnorting south-wester, the last weather in the world you'd expect Holling to choose for a visit. At about four o'clock in the morning, Spooky, who slept in the next bunk to me, woke up with a yell and tumbled out on to the deck.

" 'He's aboard!' he gasped.

"There were thirty stewards in our quarters, and the things they said to Spooky about Holling and him and everything were shocking to hear.

" 'He's come on board,' said Spooky, very solemn.

"He sat on the edge of his bunk, his bald head shining in the bulkhead light, his hands trembling.

" 'You fellows don't think as I think,' he said. 'You haven't got my spiritual eyesight. You laugh at me when I tell you that I shall end my days in the poorhouse and my children will be selling matches, and you laugh at me when I tell you that Holling's come aboard – but I know. I *absolutely* know!'

"When we got to New York the ship was held up for two hours in the Hudson, whilst the police were at work, for a lady passenger's diamond sunburst had disappeared between seven o'clock in the evening and five o'clock in the morning, and it was not discovered.

"Miss Penn was a passenger on the home trip, and this

time Charley wasn't as attentive. He didn't work either, and Cohen, who was giving him his last chance, threw in his hand and spent his days counting the bits of gulf weed we passed.

"As I've said before, there's one place on a ship for getting information, and that's the boat deck after dark. Not that I ever spy on passengers – I'd scorn the action. But when a man's having a smoke between the boats, information naturally comes to him.

"It was the night we sighted England, and the Start Light was winking and blinking on the port bow, and I was up there having a few short pulls at a pipe, when I heard Charley's voice. It wasn't a pleasant kind of night – it was cold and drizzling, and they had the deck to themselves, he and Miss Penn. He put down a Mackintosh coat on one of the chairs and covered her with a rug he was carrying. I couldn't see that, but I guessed what was happening.

" 'You're landing at Cherbourg?' said Charley.

" 'Yes,' said Miss Penn's voice, and then: 'What has been the matter with you all this voyage?'

"He didn't answer at once. I could smell the scent of his Havana. He was thinking things over before he spoke.

" 'You generally get off a boat pretty quick, don't you?' he asked, in his drawling voice.

" 'Why, yes,' she said. 'I'm naturally in a hurry to get ashore. Why do you say that?'

" 'I hope Holling's ghost isn't walking this trip,' he said.

"I heard her gasp.

" 'What do you mean?' she asked.

"And then he said in a low voice:

" 'I hope there'll be no sunbursts missing to-morrow. If there are, there's a tug full of police meeting us twenty miles out of Cherbourg. I heard it coming through on the wireless to-night – I can read Morse – and you'll have to be pretty quick to jump the boat this time.'

"It was such a long while before she answered that I wondered what had happened, and then I heard her say:

" 'I think we'll go down, shall we?' And then the creak of her chair as she got up.

"It was six o'clock the next morning, and I was taking round the early coffee, when I heard the squeal. There was a Russian count, or prince, or something, travelling on C deck, and he was one of the clever people who never put their valuables in the purser's safe. Under his pillow he had a packet of loose diamonds that he'd been trying to sell in New York. I believe that he couldn't comply with some Customs' regulations, and had to bring them back. At any rate, the pocket-book that held them was found empty in the alley-way, and the diamonds were gone. I had to go to the purser's office for something and I saw him writing out a radio, and I knew that this time nothing was being left to chance, and that the ship would be searched from the keel upwards.

" 'They can search it from the keel downwards,' said Spooky, very gloomily, when I told him. 'You don't believe in Holling, Felix, but I do. Those diamonds have left the ship.'

"And then, what I expected happened. The ship's police took charge of the firemen's and stewards' quarters; nobody was allowed in or out, and we were ordered to get ready to make a complete search of passengers' baggage. The tug came up to us about nine o'clock, and it was crowded, not with French police, but with Scotland Yard men who had been waiting at Cherbourg for something like this to happen.

"The police interviewed the Russian and got all they could get out of him, which was very little, and then the passengers were called to the main saloon and the purser said a few words to them. He apologised for giving them the trouble, but pointed out that it was in their interests as much as in the interests of the company that the thief should be discovered.

" 'We shan't keep you long, ladies and gentlemen,' he said. 'There is an adequate force of detectives on board to make the search a rapid one, but I want every trunk and every bag opened.'

"The ship slowed down to half-speed, and then began the biggest and most thorough search I've ever seen in all my experience of seagoing. Naturally, some of the passengers kicked, but the majority of them behaved sensibly and helped the police all they knew how. And the end of it was, as a lot of people had foreseen, that nothing that looked like a loose diamond was brought to light.

"There was only one person who was really upset by the search, and that was Charley. He was as pale as death, and could hardly keep still for a second. I watched him, and I watched Miss Penn, who was the coolest person on board. He kept as close to the girl as he could, his eyes never leaving her, and when the search of the baggage was finished and the passengers were brought to the saloon again, he was close behind her. This time the purser was accompanied by a dozen men from headquarters, and it was the chief of police who addressed the crowd.

" 'I want, first of all, to search all the ladies' handbags, and then I wish the passengers to file out – the ladies to the left, the gentlemen to the right, for a personal search.'

"There was a growl or two at this, but most of the people took it as a joke. The ladies were lined up and a detective went along, opened each handbag, examined it quickly and passed on to the next. When they got to Miss Penn, I saw friend Charley leave the men's side, and, crossing the saloon, stand behind the detective as he took the girl's bag in his hand and opened it. I was close enough, anyway, to see the officer's changed expression.

" 'Hullo, what's this?' he said, and took out a paper package.

"He put it on the table and unrolled it. First there was a lot of cotton wool, and then row upon row of sparkling stones. You could have heard a pin drop.

" 'How do you account for having these in your possession, madam?' asked the detective.

"Before she could reply, Charley spoke.

" 'I put them there,' he said. 'I took them last night, and placed them in Miss Penn's handbag, in the hope that the bag would not be searched.'

"I never saw anybody more surprised than Miss Penn.

" 'You're mad,' she said. 'Of course you did nothing of the sort.'

"She looked round the saloon. The stewards were standing in a line to cover the doors, and after a while she saw Spooky.

" 'Simms,' she called.

"Spooky came forward. As he came, Miss Penn spoke in a low voice to the detective, and showed him something in her hand.

" 'Simms, do you remember that I sent you down to my cabin for my bag?'

" 'No, Miss,' he said, 'you never asked me for a bag.'

"She nodded.

" 'I didn't think you'd remember.' And then: 'That is your man, Inspector.'

"Before Spooky could turn the police had him, and then Miss Penn spoke.

" 'I am a detective in the employment of the company, engaged in marking down card-sharpers, but more especially on the Holling case. I charge this man with the wilful murder of John Holling on the high seas, and with a number of thefts, particulars of which you have,' she said.

"Yes, it was Spooky who killed Holling – Spooky, half mad with the lunatic idea that he'd die in the poorhouse, who had robbed and robbed and robbed, and when he was detected by Holling, who woke up and found Spooky going through his pocket-book, had slashed him with a razor, and invented the story of the face in the mirror. Whether he killed the other man I don't know – it is very likely. One murder more or less wouldn't worry Spooky, when he thought of his children selling matches on the streets. Was he mad? I should say he was. He had no children.

"I never saw Miss Penn again until she came out on her honeymoon trip. There was a new gang working on the ship – a crowd that had been pushed off the China route, and weren't very well acquainted with the regulars that worked the Western Ocean. One of them tried to get Miss Penn's husband into a little game.

" 'No, thank you,' said Charley. 'I never play cards in these days.'

NOBODY'S ALL BAD

W. R. Burnett

Adapted to:

LITTLE CAESAR

(First National, 1930)

Starring: Edward G. Robinson,

Douglas Fairbanks, Jr. & Glenda Farrell

Directed by Mervyn LeRoy

It was the rise of organised crime in America after the end of the First World War fueled by Prohibition which was to prove a major source of inspiration for the US film industry's pioneer crime movies. The gangsters, hoods, bootleggers, petty thieves and corrupt officials who made up the criminal elements in the big cities of the nation and were rarely off the front pages of the newspapers, were soon being transposed in thinly-disguised fictional form into books and on to the screen. In just a few years in the early thirties the gangster picture became arguably the biggest draw in the cinema, and its influence has been evident right through to the present day, pre-eminently in such blockbusters as The Godfather *(1972)*. *It was the rise of the new "robber barons" like Al Capone which especially caught the attention of writers and film makers – and starting with* Underworld *screened in 1927, and W. R. Burnett's novel,* Little Caesar, *published in 1929, a new storyform was born. Their impact on the public consciousness was further enhanced by the new crime and detective "pulp" magazines which introduced hardboiled writers like Dashiell Hammett, Raymond Chandler and Erle Stanley Gardner, plus movies whose titles said everything about the content,* The Public Enemy *(1931),* Scarface *(1932),* The Gang Buster *(1933),* "G" Men *(1935) and so on.*

The importance of Little Caesar *by William Riley Burnett (1899–1982) as a book and movie cannot be understated. It has been described as the first, best and most authentic native American crime novel – no mean achievement for a writer who had previously written five novels, several plays and over 100 short stories all of which he had been unable to get published before the amazing success of his gangster story. Born in Springfield, Ohio where he did all his unsuccessful writing, Burnett moved to Chicago in the late Twenties and there found the theme of the rise and fall of a tough local gangster, Cesare "Rico" Bandello, which became a best-selling book and the inspiration of the movie which was directed by Mervyn LeRoy with a consummate sense of atmosphere and language.* Underworld, *its only predecessor, had been a silent picture: so the impact of Edward G. Robinson's opening speech growling menacingly, "When, I get in a tight corner, I'll shoot my way out of it . . . sure, sure, I'll shoot first and argue afterwards" was unforgettable. Buoyed by the success of the book and the picture, Burnett wrote several more novels and short stories which further enhanced his status in crime fiction. Amongst these works which were also filmed were* Scarface *(1932) starring Paul Muni, Karen Morley and George Raft;* King of the Underworld *(1939) with Humphrey Bogart and Kay Francis;* High Sierra *(1941) also with Bogart and Ida Lupino; and* The

Asphalt Jungle (1950) which was initially a movie featuring Sterling Hayden, Louis Calhern and Marilyn Monroe and later in the sixties a popular TV series starring Jack Warden. "Nobody's All Bad" is something of a landmark among Burnett's short stories in that although it features another small time criminal who wants to make it big, the background here is the Wild West which would later be displaced as the heartland of wrongdoers by the urban jungles of the big cities. Intriguingly, too, it was written in the same year as Little Caesar . . .

I'm convinced there's a heap of nonsense wrote about this here so-called Golden West. I ain't what you'd call a reading man, but since I been old and infirm, as you might say, I been kind of doing some perusing, and I don't find no truth in books nohow. Leastways in books I know something about.

Take these here Western novels now. Hogwash! Plain, unadulterated hogwash. There's always a vilyun black as ink, and a hero white as snow, and a sweet little schoolmarm or sech a matter in the offing, as you might say, and that there's a Western novel. Even a Mexican'd laugh himself sick. I'm telling you, life in this here Golden West didn't go by no formulas. It was a lot better and a lot worse than most people knows about.

Take that Lincoln County War where Billy the Kid done his high, wide and handsome riding. Let one of these here writing fellers take it up and what do you reckon he'd make of it? A massacre or a holy war, yes, sir, and Billy the Kid'd be a poor misunderstood angel or a demon with a forked tail, spitting fire. 'Tain't in the cards that-a-way, gents. 'Tain't all one way or another; it's mixed. Howsomever, that ain't what I starts out to say. I starts out to tell you about Billy the Kid.

Well, personally, I could never see nothing to get excited about in this here Billy the Kid. Good enough boy, as they grew 'em out here in them days, and as fine a shot as ever used a six-shooter. Kind of a bashful acting boy, somehow, though he was always a-laughing and a-kicking up his heels, as you might say. Nerve? Yes, sir; that boy had nerve and lots of it. But still there was a God's plenty of men with nerve in these parts, gents. It wasn't no outstanding virtue like sobriety would have been; far from it. But what I'm getting at is this, even if I am shying away from it like a yearling: the truth ain't never been told about young William Bonney, which was The Kid's rightful name, nor never will be.

The Mexicans around these parts are locoed over Billy, El Cheevito, they calls him, and they talks nonsense and rubbish till it gives an oldtimer the bellyache. Good enough boy; but no demon and no angel, that's my contention. Maybe there was a hundred boys in this here Southwest as nervy and as plucky as The Kid, but they wasn't put in The Kid's circumstances, as you might say, and so you never hear tell of them.

There's a heap of chance in this world. Things goes by chance a whole lot. I'm telling you, and I've seen plenty. How about that time down to old Alex McSween's adobe in Lincoln when the Murphy boys burnt the McSween boys out and peppered 'em with lead when they come through the door? Yes, sir. Old McSween steps out and, bang! down he goes first pop with his Bible in his hand. So I've heard tell; though a Bible was a queer instrument to be a-carrying in the Lincoln County War.

Out steps a couple more boys and down they go, full of shot. Yes, sir. Then out steps The Kid and his chances was the slimmest of the lot, as there wasn't a feller in the Murphy faction that wouldn't't've give his trigger finger to let some daylight into Billy. What happens? Nothing. Positively nothing. They bangs away at The Kid and nary a bullet does he get in his young hide. Nary a bullet from guns fired at ten yards. Now that's chance, gents. You can't make me believe nothing different nohow.

Other day I was a-talking things over with an old messmate of mine and somehow we got to jawing about Billy the

Kid and the Lincoln County War. "There's a special Providence looking after critters like The Kid," says this here old longhorn.

"Hell," I says, "your mind must be a-failing."

"Nothing like it," says my old matey, "I'm telling you I know what I'm a-saying."

Then he relates to me how down Tombstone way old Wyatt Earp, and, gents, there never was a nervier and straighter-shooting feller, walks right up to a passel of Curly Bill's rustlers and bangs away at 'em, and them with rifles at fifteen yards a-peppering at him in broad daylight, and never a crease nor a scratch does he get.

"Howsomever," I says, "that's just luck, like filling an inside straight."

"No, sir," says this stubborn old hombre, "some men has got something on their side excepting luck."

And you couldn't make him believe different effen you argued till doomsday.

No, sir. Books ain't telling the truth, and no wonder when an old hombre like my matey begins talking about a special Providence for bad men. An old hombre that's been every place, from Dodge City, when she was a ripsnorting town, to San Francisco; down the Pecos and 'cross the Rio, lived in Tombstone when she was roaring and in Lincoln when they shot a man a day.

I'll tell you a little story being's you got time to listen, and maybe it'll kind of open your eyes about the Golden West, you being strangers, and maybe it'll amuse you some likewise. Effen not, don't stand on ceremony, as Sheriff Brady used to say, but bust right out with yawns. When a man gets old he gets garrulous with the past and no mistake nohow.

Well, when I was a sight younger than I am at this sitting, with black hair and not this dead white stuff, I was working for a man named Riddle over Lincoln way. Riddle was tangled up with the Murphy faction 'count he was in business with Murphy some; but he wasn't no man for wars and did a lot of lamenting about sech goings-on; a peaceable-like man. But in them days effen you lived in Lincoln County you was in the war whether you liked it or not, as you might say. Neutrality was looked on by both parties as a sight suspicious.

Howsomever, Riddle never actually got in any of the ructions till one day he was over in Lincoln and bumped plumb into The Kid, who was coming out of a bar as old man Riddle went in.

"Asking your pardon," says old man Riddle, who didn't know Billy the Kid from Lucifer.

The Kid laughed and batted him one with the flat of his hand.

"That'll learn you to go around asking pardons, you old snake," says The Kid. Then he turns his back and goes on calm as you please.

That was Billy the Kid, turning his back on a man he'd just whacked across the face, which wasn't healthy in them days nohow. Old Riddle, peaceable-like, as I say, just stood there and looked at this blustering kid, who wasn't no more than nineteen nor twenty, maybe less. And the longer he looked the madder he got, so he ups with his rifle and is all for shooting The Kid when a feller of the name of Willis struck the gun from his hands and planted a knife in him.

"Shooting The Kid in the back, was you!" says this here Willis party.

But old man Riddle don't say nothing. He just climbs up on his horse and rides for home, holding his side. Nervy old crow, he was. When he pulls in I was standing over by the corral, whittling or something, and he says: "War is declared for good and all, boys, and we'll fight till there ain't a McSween varmint left in the county no how."

Then he kind of gets a funny look on his face and falls off his pony. That knife went deeper than he calculated and 'fore nightfall he was a dead cattleman.

Well, we buries him over back of the ranch house. There wasn't no cemetery in Lincoln in them days; they usually just buried 'em where they lay effen it was feasible. And we puts up a board, saying: "Elias Riddle. Killed in the Lincoln County War."

Well, we was some inflamed, being as how Riddle was a good man to his hands, and when his brother come in from Santa Fe to take the ranch over we was r'aring to go, which didn't anger the brother none, as he was a fire-eating kind of feller, noways like the old man. Them that didn't have rifles was supplied by old man Riddle's brother, and he 'lows as how they can start shooting any time.

Lem Cowan was my matey then and a mighty square feller he was, though apt to get full of nose paint and shoot things up some. He used to be friendly with this here Billy the Kid and rustled cattle with him a whole lot in Old Mexico, but since the killing of old man Riddle he was dead set against him and went around saying he'd pay off that slinking varmint as soon as he got square with Willis, the feller that got old man Riddle.

Well, Lem Cowan sure enough made good on the Willis end of the deal. He shot him so full of holes out on the Riddle range one day that he wouldn't hold water nor liquor neither no more than a sieve. But Lem got sort of overconfident and boastful, as you might say, and one day he ran square into The Kid on the streets of Lincoln and 'fore you could chalk your cue he was shot by The Kid, who shot first and talked afterwards. The Kid could pull a six-gun and shoot accurate 'fore you could get your hand towards your gun. He was sure hell for quickness.

Well, some Murphy boys took Lem into the Murphy store and propped him up on the counter to die, but he didn't die none, which fooled everybody, including himself, and when he got a little better they moved him out to the ranch and put him in the bunkhouse.

That bullet had sure raised the devil in Lem. He couldn't sleep nor eat for thinking about that Billy the Kid person, and him and the new Riddle boss used to spend hours in the bunkhouse a-taking turns cussing The Kid and 'lowing what they'd do to him. Well, the rest of the hands was a little lukewarm about the matter by now, and wise they was, though I'm including myself in that category. What was the sense in a bunch of cowhands getting themselves shot up over a fight that didn't pay no dividends to them neither way?

'Course they got pretty riled up at first over the killing of the old man, but time sort of dulls things and as they begin to forget about the old man tumbling from his saddle and all, they begin to think more about their own hides and less about shooting things up. As I say, I was lukewarm. I was saving my money, figuring I'd go a-prospecting over Little Mesa way, and I was aiming to keep from getting planted effen I could help it. But this here devil of a Cowan, flat on his back in the bunkhouse, called us forty kinds of cowards and he had such a lashing tongue and such a way with him that it wasn't long till we begin to get all het up again, being young fellers and warmblooded and not particularly relishing being called cowards nohow. But we was playing in luck 'cause things kind of settled up without us horning in.

One evening up rides a Mexican of the name of Romero, or some such name, all shot up and bleeding, and he says that Billy the Kid has been run out of town, that McSween is dead, that the troops is a-camping at the edge of the town, and that the Lincoln County War is practically over. We take the Mexican back to the bunkhouse to palaver with Lem and get himself tied up and respectable, and we lights out for town.

Sure enough what the Mex says is right. The Murphy boys have done burned old man McSween's house down and killed him, which is a pity, as he was a decent, Godfearing man, effen he was a lawyer, and two or three of the McSween boys is stretched out in the street, dead as might be, and these here Murphyboys is drunk as loons and sashaying and capering about among the dead like a passel of Apaches. Well, we stayed to watch the excitement, being's we had been pretty quiet of late and longing to work off our energy some place, and then we rides home, singing.

Might be a week later, gents, and we're still a sight joyful over the end of the Lincoln County War, and riding in from town full of nose paint and contentment. It was a mighty fine night with a full moon and a nice breeze, and we was just kind of idling along, when up the trail comes some feller, hell bent for election, rides past us like a cyclone, and yells: "Ketch me, you sons-of-guns. I'm Billy the Kid, and I'm looking for excitement!" Well, he got it. We all blazed away at once with six-shooters and rifles and down went his horse, but up he got and 'fore we knowed what the play was he'd winged two of our horses, including mine, and had vanished, clean vanished, gents, like as if he'd flew away.

I was so cussing mad I extricates myself from my horse, which is kicking up a big fuss and getting ready to die, and starts after Billy the Kid. I hear him thrashing his way down a hillside where he'd vanished and I bangs away at the noise, then goes after him.

Well, the boys shout for me to come back and raise almighty hell yelling and whooping in that quiet night, but I'm that mad and locoed 'cause I lost my pony I don't know a thing excepting to get the brazen varmint that done the shooting. I'm getting farther and farther away from the boys all the time, and pretty soon I can't hear them noways and all I can hear is a feller running like holy hell and a-thrashing through the brush. I don't know how long I kept hot foot after that Billy person, but by the time the east began to get light I'd lost him. I was still on the Riddle range but way over to the eastward, and I had heard some talk lately about some Mescaleros that had got disgruntled-like and left their reservation, but that was way off to the south, so I just rolled up in my coat to sleep some 'fore I made tracks for the ranch.

It might have been two hours later or such a matter when I wakes up with a start, hears some yelling and carrying on, and sees a man hotfooting it down a little ridge not a quarter of a mile off. It's this here Billy the Kid. I can recognise him easy, and he's in a almighty big hurry about something, and I see what it is when a couple of Injuns stick their nobs up over the edge of the ridge. Yes, sir. Here I was right in the middle of that passel of locoed Mescaleros which had skipped their reservation.

I was cold and chilled, and I wasn't looking for any such

ructions this early in the morning. But I seen I was in for it, so I looks to my rifle and yells to The Kid. He sees and kind of stops and considers for a spell. He ain't in such a good fix nohow. Injuns on one side of him and one of old man Riddle's men on t'other, but blood is thicker than water, and Injuns is Injuns, so he joins up with me, ducking and running.

The Injuns is holding a powwow up at the edge of the ridge and they don't interrupt themselves none excepting to take a pot shot at The Kid or me once in a while just to keep us interested. But Injuns can't shoot nohow and that far away it's plumb ridiculous. Up comes this Billy the Kid, his face red from running and showing his big teeth.

"How many Injuns is they?" I says.

"Seven or eight," says Billy. "Was that a good pony of yourn?"

"It surely was," I says, "and I don't thank you none for your gunplay."

"I was loaded up with jig-juice," says Billy, "and my blood was up; I'm plumb sorry."

Well, we crawled up into the hills just across from the Injuns and got our backs up against a rock wall and a big boulder in front of us. The Injuns was still powwowing over on the ridge and popping at us every now and then just to relieve their feelings, I reckon, 'cause they wasn't doing nothing but wasting powder.

"Looky here, pardner," says The Kid, "you're a Riddle man, ain't you."

"I am," I says, "and I been chasing you all over hell and gone."

"Well," says The Kid, grinning, "here I be."

He was a danged ingratiating feller and I kind of took a shine to him.

"Looky here," he says, "let me take that rifle and dust some of them Injuns."

"Nope," I says, "use your six-gun."

"Can't," he says, "the range ain't right and I dropped my rifle some place or another."

"Pretty careless, ain't you?" I said.

"Right smart," he said and picked up my rifle and was sighting it when I took it away from him.

"Use your own gun," I says. But, gents, effen he didn't talk me out of that gun I'm a shoemaker, and good thing he did, too, 'cause while we was arguing a couple of young bucks started veering off to the right, figuring to flank us, I reckon. Effen he didn't get 'em both with two quick shots!

Yes, sir, mighty good shooting it was and him grinning and a-smiling all over his face with his big hat pushed back.

"Good gun," he says, handing it back to me.

Them Injuns 'peared to lose heart, as you might say, after that snap shooting and snuck over, not taking no chances, and picked up their comrades and disappeared over the hill.

Well, we sat there behind that boulder till round noontime, kind of expecting them Injuns to come back or do something and not wanting to walk into no ambuscade, but they never showed up.

"Well," says Billy, "I'm getting powerful hungry and a little water wouldn't hurt none."

So we footed it down across the valley and made Seven Mile Spring towards evening. We just walked along side by side and not saying a word, mind you, but me thinking plenty how I ought to take this desperate character, as they say, and turn him over to the proper authorities. But I don't know. I kind of took a shine to The Kid and, besides that, being's I'm a truthful man and ain't got no reputation to keep up now that I'm about ready for eternity, this Billy person wasn't the kind that you march off to jail nohow and a gun in his face didn't mean much to that hombre; and effen you understand me, I kind of lost my ill feeling towards this Billy person since him and me fought off them Injuns together, yes, sir.

Well, after we'd soaked ourselves with water down at the waterhole, Billy says: "I'm on my way, mister; so long."

"So long," I says.

And there he goes, turning his back on me and walking off as unconcerned as you please just as effen him and me was the best friends in the world and I hadn't been chasing him all over hell and back the night before. At the top of the ridge he looks back and sort of nods, and that's the last I ever see of that so-called bad hombre, Billy the Kid.

Well, gents, that's the last of Billy the Kid in person in this here chronicle but it ain't the last of him in another form, as you might say. It was two hours later and dark; I was hoofing it for the ranch when I hears a sight of horsemen coming across the vega and me not knowing whether it be Injuns, McSween remnants nor what, till Tom Kane opens his big mouth and yawns, then I yells to 'em.

"By God," says Riddle, "we thought you was done for sure enough; been a-hunting you since sun-up."

"I had a brush with some hostiles," I says, "and it delayed me a whole lot."

So Tom Kane took me up behind and we made tracks for the ranch, talking and jesting about them Mescaleros and such, till one of the hands says: "Did you ketch up with that varmint, Billy the Kid?"

This here hand was just joking, you see. Well, I didn't know what to say, but being, generally speaking, a truthful man, I says: "Yep, me and The Kid stood off a bunch of Mescaleros meaning no good, killing two."

"What!" screams Riddle. "Where is this Billy person?"

"Done gone on," I says.

"Gone on!" yells Tom Kane. "Effen that don't beat all with your matey Lem Cowan still laid up with The Kid's bullet."

"Well," I says, "I 'lows as how since we fought off them Injuns they ain't no sense nor profit in us being nasty with each other."

"You draws your pay tonight," says Riddle.

Well, I wasn't none too popular around that ranch, gents, as I reckon you can figure out for yourselves. Riddle pays me off and tells me to cut myself out a pony besides 'cause he owes me a bonus, and Tom Kane brings me my saddle that he brung in offen my dead pony.

In the morning I'm out saddling my pony when I see Lem Cowan coming out of the ranch house where he's been sleeping lately 'count it's quiet and he's pale and staggery, but he's got a six-gun in his hand and he says: "I'll learn you to go consorting with that killing varmint, you Judas!" And he bangs away at me, but being weak and shakylike, he misses me by a mile and then the boss comes up and takes the gun away from him and carries him in the house, 'cause he don't weigh no more than a hundred pounds. But he kicks and squeals mighty lifelike.

I gets on my pony right spry 'cause I know that gunplay is contagious, like measles, and I don't want no well men taking shots at me 'cause some of them Riddle boys can shoot.

"Goodby," I says, waving my arms and off I go galloping, hell bent for election.

Well, that's about all of my story, gents, excepting that Lem Cowan and me turns out to be pardners after all and goes a-prospecting together over Little Mesa way and finds the old Red Cougar Mine, where we made our pile. Yes, sir. And Billy the Kid got himself shot up a whole lot over Sumner way by Pat Garrett, sheriff in them days, who used to be his bosom friend, and nobody was a-looking for him to be the feller to get The Kid nohow.

Well, as I was saying, there's been a heap of rubbish wrote about this so-called Golden West. There's no truth in books, gents, and little knowledge in the heads of them that writes 'em. Wasn't a matter of vilyuns and heroes and herowines in these parts. No, sir. It was all jumbled up so bad it would take God almighty Himself to cut His own cattle and leave the rest to the devil. Do you see how I'm aiming?

THE THREE GARRIDEBS

Thomas H. Hutchinson

> ⊟
>
> Script for:
>
> ### *The Three Garridebs*
>
> (NBC TV, 1937)
>
> Starring: Louis Hector,
>
> William Podmore & James Spottswood
>
> Directed by Eustace Wyatt

"Sherlock Holmes sleuthed around the television cameras at Radio City during the past weekend and stalked out across the ultra-short wave-lengths in the most ambitious experiment in tele-showmanship so far attempted in the air over New York." With this report on Sunday, 28 November 1937, the New York Times *announced the arrival of the world's most famous fictional detective on the new medium of television via an adaptation of Sir Arthur Conan Doyle's short story, "The Adventure of the Three Garridebs" (1926) starring Louis*

Hector as the Great Detective and William Podmore as the faithful Dr Watson. The story was performed "live" with several brief, pre-filmed inserts of London scenes, and three sets – one of Holmes' flat in Baker Street, Nathan Garrideb's study and the office of Inspector Lestrade. Despite all the limitations of this production requiring actors to move quickly from one set to another during fades and scenes to be re-dressed by prop men even as the action went on, it was well received by critics and the comparatively small number of people with sets. It has since proved to be the first in a long line of TV versions of the Holmes' cases which has continued into the nineties with the definitive performances of the late Jeremy Brett. (Sherlock Holmes in fact made his début on the cinema screen as early as 1903 in the brief silent film, Sherlock Holmes Baffled, *produced by American Mutoscope in which a group of unknowns enacted a drama about a vanishing visitor to Baker Street which left the great man for once completely mystified.) Sir Arthur Conan Doyle did not live long enough to see his detective on the small screen, although experiments with television were already underway when he died in 1930. It was, in fact, on 1 October 1936 that the BBC inaugurated the world's first television service from Alexandra Palace in London. Although the outbreak of the Second World War slowed down this development and caused the service to be closed until peace was restored, once TV broadcasting restarted in 1946, other detectives from literature were not long in becoming popular with viewers on both sides of the Atlantic.*

Thomas H. Hutchinson (1896–1970), the man who adapted "The Three Garridebs" for television, was a New York scriptwriter who had worked for NBC Radio for almost a decade. He had been associated with a number of radio series featuring characters from mystery fiction including Holmes, Hercule Poirot and Father Brown. He was also briefly associated with NBC's Mr Keen, Tracer of Lost Persons *which started on the air in 1937 and opened with the theme tune, "Someday I'll Find You". Hutchinson's knowledge of the Holmes stories made him an obvious choice to script "The Three Garridebs" for the network, and fortunately a copy of this has survived, thanks to television historian, Lennon R. Lohr, and can be reprinted here in an anthology for the first time. In fact the dialogue reads as easily as a story, and it will be of especial interest to Sherlockians who have not seen it before, enabling a comparison to be made with Conan Doyle's original tale. "The Three Garridebs" represents a landmark in the saga of "Cops on the Box" and, as the* New York Times *put it, represents "The first televised representation of the Baker Street scene". It was also the first television representation of* any *crime scene, for that matter!*

SCENE I

Dr Watson is standing looking out of the window in Sherlock Holmes' flat at Baker street below. Door at left opens, and Holmes enters in dressing gown with a foolscap document in his hand.

HOLMES: Friend Watson. Have you ever heard of Garrideb?

WATSON: Garrideb? What on earth is it?

HOLMES: A name – a man's name – Garrideb. If you can lay your hand on a Garrideb, Watson, there's money in it.

WATSON: In heaven's name, Holmes, what are you talking about?

HOLMES: (*Crossing down to table center. Fills pipe at tobacco jar on table.*) Oh, that's a long story – rather a whimsical one too. I don't think in all our explorations of human complexities we have ever come upon anything more singular.

WATSON: (*Turning to stand right of door*.) Sounds interesting.

HOLMES: The fellow will be here presently for cross-examinations, so I won't open the matter up until he comes, but meanwhile that's the name we want.

WATSON: (*Looks through telephone directory on stand as Holmes lights his pipe*.) Holmes! (*Crossing down to Holmes*) Here it is in the telephone book.

HOLMES: (*Taking book from Watson. Reading*.) Garrideb, No. 136 Little Ryder Street, West. (*Putting book back*.) Sorry to disappoint you, my dear Watson, but this is the man himself. That is the address on his letter. We want another to match him.

WATSON: Match him?

HOLMES: Exactly. (*Knock on door center*.) Come in. (*Sits left of table*.)

MRS HUDSON: (*Entering with card*) There is a gentleman here to see you, Mr Holmes.

WATSON: (*Taking card from tray. Amazed*.) Why, here he is. But this is a different initial. John Garrideb, counsellor-at-law, Moorville, Kansas, USA. (*Hands card to Holmes*.)

HOLMES: I'm afraid you must make another effort, Watson. Show him in, Mrs Hudson.

MRS HUDSON: Yes, sir. (*Exits center*.)

WATSON: But why if he's here now –

HOLMES: (*Rising crosses to right of table*.) This gentleman is also in the plot already, though I certainly didn't expect to see him this morning. However, he is in a position to tell us some of the things we want to know.

MRS HUDSON: (*Entering door center.*) Mr John Garrideb.

JOHN: (*Entering door center and crossing to table.*) Mr Holmes? (*Mrs Hudson exits. Looking from one to the other.*) Oh, yes. (*Crossing to left of table.*) Your pictures are not unlike you, sir, if I may say so.

HOLMES: Thank you.

JOHN: I believe you have had a letter from my namesake Mr Nathan Garrideb, have you not?

HOLMES: Pray sit down. (*Indicating chair left of table.*) May I introduce my colleague Dr Watson?

WATSON: How do you do? (*Back of table.*)

JOHN: (*Sitting left of table.*) How do you do.

HOLMES: I fancy we have a good deal to discuss. (*Looking at letter.*) You are, of course, the Mr John Garrideb mentioned in this letter?

JOHN: Yes, I am.

HOLMES: But surely you have been in England some time.

JOHN: (*Suspiciously.*) Why do you say that, Mr Holmes?

HOLMES: Your whole outfit is English.

JOHN: (*Forcing a laugh.*) I have read of your tricks, Mr Holmes, but I never thought that I would be the subject of them. Where do you read that?

HOLMES: The shoulder cut of your coat, the toes of your boots – could anyone doubt it?

JOHN: Well, I had no idea I was so obviously English. Business brought me over here some time ago, and so, as you say, my outfit is nearly all London made. (*Brusquely*.) However, I guess your time is of value, and we did not meet to talk about the cut of my socks. What about getting down to that paper you hold in your hand?

HOLMES: Dr Watson would tell you that these digressions of mine sometimes prove in the end to have bearing on the matter in hand. But why did Mr Nathan Garrideb not come with you?

JOHN: (*With sudden anger*.) Why in thunder did he draw you into it at all? A bit of professional business between two gentlemen.

HOLMES: There is no reflection upon you, Mr Garrideb. He knew that I had means of getting information, and it was only natural that he should apply to me.

JOHN: Forgive me, Mr Holmes. When I went to see him this morning he told me that he had called in a detective, and I don't want police butting into a private matter. But if you are willing just to help us find the man, I would be very happy to have you.

HOLMES: Thank you. And now, we would like a complete account from your own lips. My friend here knows nothing of the details.

JOHN: (*Looking at Watson*.) Does he need to know?

HOLMES: We usually work together.

JOHN: Well, there is no reason it should be kept a secret. I'll give you the facts as concisely as I can. (*John sits.*) If you came from Kansas I would not need to explain to you who Alexander Hamilton Garrideb was. He made his money in the wheat pit in Chicago, but he spent it in buying up as much land as would make one of your counties, lying along the Arkansas River, west of Fort Dodge. He had no kith or kin – or if he had, I never heard of them. But he took a kind of pride in the queerness of his name. That was what brought us together. I was practicing law in Topeka, and one day I had a visit from the old man.

HOLMES: Alexander Hamilton Garrideb?

JOHN: Right. He was tickled to death to meet (*Holmes moves chair down and to center.*) another man with his own name. It was his pet fad, and he was dead set to find out if there were any more Garridebs in the world and wanted me to find him another. I told him I was too busy to spend my life hiking around the world in search of Garridebs. But that's just what you will do, he said, if things pan out as I have planned. I thought he was joking, but I soon discovered that he wasn't. He died within a year and left behind him the queerest will that has ever been filed in the state of Kansas. Under its terms, his property was divided into three parts, and I was to have one on condition that I found two Garridebs who would share the remainder. It's five million dollars for each of us if it's a cent, but we can't lay a finger on it until we all three stand in a row.

WATSON: A sort of a 15-million dollar game of tit-tat-toe.

JOHN: It was so big that I let my legal practice slide and began looking for Garridebs. There's not one in the United States. I went through it with a fine-tooth comb. Then I tried the old country. In the London telephone directory I found a Garrideb. I went to see him two days ago and explained the whole matter to him. But he is a lone man like myself with some women relatives but no men. It says three adult men in the will, so you see we still have a vacancy; and if you can help to fill it, we will be willing to pay your charges.

HOLMES: Well, Watson, I said it was rather whimsical didn't I? (*To John.*) I should have thought that your obvious course of procedure was to advertise in the paper.

JOHN: I have done that, Mr Holmes, with no replies.

HOLMES: Well, Mr Garrideb, it certainly is an interesting little problem. I may take a glance at it. By the way, it's curious that you should have come to me from Topeka. I used to have a correspondent there – he's dead now – old Dr Lysander Starr. He was a mayor in the nineties.

JOHN: Did you know Dr Starr? That is a coincidence. He's still talked about in Topeka. (*Rising.*) Well, Mr Holmes, I suppose all we can do is to report to you and let you know how we progress. I reckon you'll hear within a day or two.

HOLMES: We will be expecting your call. You can find your way out?

JOHN: Of course. (*Crossing to door.*) Good day, Mr Holmes. (*Exits door center.*)

WATSON: Well. (*Crosses to Holmes who is seated in chair center.*)

HOLMES: I'm wondering, Watson, just wondering.

WATSON: At what? (*Crossing to back of table.*)

HOLMES: I'm wondering, Watson, what on earth could be the object of this man in telling us such a rigmarole of lies. I nearly asked him, but I judged it better to let him think he had fooled us.

WATSON: How did you know he was lying? (*Sits left of table.*)

HOLMES: Elementry, my dear Watson, elementry. Here is a man with an English coat – frayed at the elbow and trousers bagged at the knee with a year's wear – and yet by this letter and by his own account, he is a provincial American lately landed in London. There have been no advertisements in the paper. I never knew a Dr Lysander Starr of Topeka. Touch him where you would, he was false. I think the fellow is really an American, but he has worn his accent smooth with years in London.

WATSON: What's his game then, and what motive lies behind this preposterous search for Garridebs? (*Rise to window.*)

HOLMES: That's the question, Watson, and it's worth our attention, for, granting that the man is a rascal, he is certainly a complex and ingenious one. We must now find out if our other correspondent is a fraud also.

WATSON: But how?

HOLMES: Ring him up.

WATSON: (*Crossing to telephone on table. Getting number from book. Picks up phone.*) Newgate 6583 – Hello – Mr Nathan Garrideb? Sherlock Holmes calling. Just a moment please. (*To Holmes.*) He wants to talk to you. (*Holmes crosses to phone*).

HOLMES: (*At phone.*) Yes. Yes, he's been here. Will you be at home this evening, Mr Garrideb? I suppose your namesake will not be? Very well, we'll come round then, for I'd rather have a chat with you without him. Dr Watson will come with me. About six. You needn't mention our visit to the American lawyer.

SCENE II

Holmes and Watson riding in hansom cab. Cab coming to stop at curb. Close shot of men and cab as it stops.

HOLMES: Well, Watson, we seem to have arrived.

WATSON: Right. Little Ryder Street West and there is number 136. (*Looking at house.*)

HOLMES: (*Looking at watch.*) And right on time. Six o'clock to the minute. (*They get out of cab. Watson pays cabby.*)

WATSON: (*To driver.*) You needn't wait.

(*Cabby touches his hat and drives off. Shot of house from curb. Holmes and Watson start into house.*)

HOLMES: Let's see if our friend Mr Garrideb is at home.

WATSON: Right.

SCENE III

Hallway outside Garrideb's door.

WATSON: Apparently we are in the right house. Here's his name plate.

(Close shot of name plate reading "Nathan Garrideb")

HOLMES: That name plate has been up some years, Watson.

WATSON: I deduced that myself from the condition of the discoloured brass surface.

HOLMES: Splendid, Watson. And it's his real name, anyhow. That is something to note. (*He rings the door bell.*)

SCENE IV

Bell heard ringing.

Interior of Nathan Garrideb's room. To all appearances a small museum. Cupboards and cabinets on all walls. Cases of butterflies, stuffed birds. Table center with microscope. Case of ancient coins. Plaster skulls. Fossil bones and debris on table. Chairs right and left of table. Door left, large window center. Nathan seated at right of table center studying object through microscope. As bell rings third time he rises, crosses to door, and opens it.

Door bell.

NATHAN: Yes?

HOLMES: (*Outside door.*) Mr Nathan Garrideb?

NATHAN: Yes, and you are Sherlock Holmes?

HOLMES: I am. And this is Dr Watson.

NATHAN: Come in, gentlemen. (*They come into the room.*)

HOLMES: Well, Mr Garrideb, quite an interesting place you have here.

NATHAN: Yes, I have around me all my little interests in life.

HOLMES: (*Crossing down to back of table and picking up coin.*) Ah, Syracusan, isn't it?

NATHAN: (*Coming to his left.*) Of the best period. They degenerated greatly toward the end. At their best I hold them supreme, though some prefer the Alexandrian school. (*Indicating chair right of table.*) Take that chair, Mr Holmes, and pray allow me to clear these bones. (*To Watson who is examining skull at left of table.*) You find that interesting, doctor?

WATSON: Very.

NATHAN: If you don't mind, I'll remove that vase, doctor. (*Indicating vase in chair left of table. Nathan takes vase from chair and places it on cabinet up left and stands center. Watson sits left.*)

HOLMES: I take it you spend a great deal of your time in this room, Mr Garrideb.

NATHAN: I do. My doctor lectures me about never going out, but why should I go out when I have so much to interest me here? I can assure you that the adequate cataloguing of one of these cabinets would take me three good months.

HOLMES: Do you mean to tell me that you never go out?

NATHAN: Very seldom. But you can imagine, Mr Holmes, what a terrific shock – pleasant but terrific – it was for me when I heard of this unparalleled good fortune. It only needs one more Garrideb to complete the matter, and surely we can find one. I had a brother, but he is dead; but there surely must be others in the world. I had heard that you handled strange cases, and that was why I sent for you.

HOLMES: I think you acted very wisely. But are you anxious to acquire an estate in America?

NATHAN: Certainly not, sir, nothing would induce me to leave my collection. But this gentleman has assured me that he will buy me out as soon as we have established our claim. Five million dollars. There are a dozen specimens in the market which fill gaps in my collection that I am unable to purchase for want of a few hundred pounds. Just think what I could do with five million dollars. Why, I will have the nucleus of a National Collection.

HOLMES: (*Rising and crossing up center.*) I merely called to make your acquaintance, as I prefer to establish personal touch with those with whom I do business. I understand that up to this week you were unaware of our American friend's existence. (*Watson rises and crosses left and examines cabinet.*)

NATHAN: (*Crossing up center to Holmes.*) Yes, he called for the first time last Tuesday.

HOLMES: Did he tell you of our interview this morning?

NATHAN: Yes, he came straight back to me. He had been very angry.

HOLMES: Why should he be angry?

NATHAN: He seemed to think that it was some reflection on his honor! But he was quite cheerful again when he returned.

HOLMES: Did he suggest any course of action?

NATHAN: No, sir. He did not.

HOLMES: Has he ever asked for any money from you?

NATHAN: No, sir, never.

HOLMES: You see no possible object he has in view?

NATHAN: None, except what he states.

HOLMES: Did you tell him of our telephone appointment?

NATHAN: Yes, sir, I did.

HOLMES: (*Looking about room.*) Have you any articles of great value in your collection?

NATHAN: No, sir, I am not a rich man. It's a good collection but not a very valuable one.

HOLMES: You have no fear of burglars.

NATHAN: Not the least.

HOLMES: How long have you been in these rooms?

NATHAN: Nearly five years.

Door bell. Bell is heard on door left.
Watson crosses extreme right. Nathan crosses to door and opens it. John enters greatly excited with newspaper in his hand. He crosses to center.

JOHN: (*To Nathan who follows him center.*) Here you are. I thought I'd be in time. Mr Nathan Garrideb, my congratulations. You are a rich man. Our business is finished, and all is well. As to you, Mr Holmes, we can only say we are sorry if we have given you any useless trouble.

NATHAN: But what is it? What do you mean?

JOHN: This. This advertisement in a Birmingham newspaper. (*Holmes, Watson, and Nathan look at paper.*)

HOWARD GARRIDEB
Binders, reapers, steam and hand plows,
drills, harrows, farmer's carts, buckboards
and all other appliances.
Estimates for Artesian Wells
Apply Grosvenor Building, Aston.

NATHAN: That makes our third man. How did you find it? (*Holmes hands paper to Watson on his right.*)

JOHN: I had opened up inquiries in Birmingham, and my agent there sent me this advertisement from a local paper. We must hustle and put this thing through. I have written to this man and told him that you will see him in his office tomorrow afternoon at four o'clock.

NATHAN: You want me to see him?

JOHN: What do you say, Mr Holmes? Don't you think it would be wiser? Here I am, a wandering American with a wonderful tale. Why should he believe what I tell him? But you are a Britisher with solid references, and he is bound to take notice of what you say. I could go with you, but I have a very busy day tomorrow, and I could always follow you if you get in any trouble.

NATHAN: I haven't made such a journey in years. (*Crosses to chair left of table and sits.*)

JOHN: It's quite simple, Mr Garrideb; I have figured out your train connections. You leave at twelve and should be there shortly after two. Then you can be back the same night. All you have to do is to see this man, explain the matter, and get an affidavit of his existence. Considering that I have come all the way from the center of America it surely is little enough if you go a hundred miles to put this matter through.

NATHAN: (*Disconsolately.*) Well, if you insist, I shall go. It certainly is hard for me to refuse you anything, considering the glory of hope that you have brought into my life.

HOLMES: Then that is all agreed, and no doubt you will let me have a report as soon as you can.

JOHN: I'll see to that. Well, (*Looking at watch.*) I'll have to get on. (*Nathan rises. Crosses to door.*) I'll call tomorrow, Mr Garrideb, and see you off to Birmingham. (*At door.*) Coming my way, Mr Holmes?

HOLMES: Not just yet.

JOHN: Well, good-bye then, and we may have good news for you tomorrow night. (*Exits door left.*)

NATHAN: Five million dollars.

HOLMES: I wish I could look over your collection, Mr Garrideb. In my profession all sorts of odd knowledge is useful, and this room of yours is a storehouse of it.

NATHAN: I have always heard, sir, that you were a very intelligent man. I'd be glad to show it to you now, if you have the time.

HOLMES: Unfortunately I haven't. But these specimens of yours are so well labelled and classified that they hardly need your personal explanation. If I should be able to look in tomorrow, I presume you would have no objection to my glancing over them.

NATHAN: None at all. You are most welcome, Mr Holmes. The place, of course, will be shut up, but Mrs Saunders is in the basement up to four o'clock and will let you in with her key.

HOLMES: Thank you. I happen to be clear tomorrow afternoon; and if you would say a word to Mrs Saunders, I would appreciate it. By the way, who is your house agent?

NATHAN: House agent?

HOLMES: Yes.

NATHAN: Holloway and Steele in the Edgware Road. But why do you ask?

HOLMES: (*Laughing.*) I am a bit of an archaeologist myself when it comes to houses. I was wondering if this place was Queen Anne or Georgian.

NATHAN: Georgian, beyond a doubt.

HOLMES: (*At door left with Nathan.*) Really, I should have thought a little earlier. Come Watson. (*Watson is seated at table examining object through microscope in same attitude as Nathan was in opening scene.*)

WATSON: Oh, yes, of course. (*Crossing to Holmes at door.*) Excellent microscope you have there, Mr Garrideb.

NATHAN: Yes, isn't it?

HOLMES: Well, good-bye, Mr Garrideb, may you have every success in your Birmingham journey. (*Opens door. They exit.*)

NATHAN: One million pounds. (*Crossing down to camera for close-up.*)

SCENE V

Table center is covered with white tablecloth, Holmes right of table and Watson left are just finishing dinner. Mrs Hudson is serving demitasse, cheese, and crackers. Clock strikes seven.

MRS HUDSON: And will you be wantin' anything else, Mr Holmes?

HOLMES: No thanks, Mrs Hudson. This repast should satisfy the cravings of the inner man until breakfast time tomorrow morning, eh Watson?

WATSON: Undoubtedly, and if you will permit me, Mrs Hudson, I would like to state a deduction I have just made.

MRS HUDSON: Of course, Dr Watson.

WATSON: After eating this dinner I am convinced without a doubt that Mrs Hudson is the best cook in all London.

MRS HUDSON: (*Beaming.*) I think it's a bit of the blarney you're handing me, Dr Watson. (*Exits door center*)

HOLMES: (*Sipping coffee.*) Well, Watson, our little problem draws to a close. No doubt you have outlined the solution in your own mind.

WATSON: Solution? I can make neither head nor tail of the case.

HOLMES: The head is surely clear enough, and the tail we should see tomorrow. Did you notice anything curious about that advertisement in the Birmingham paper?

WATSON: I saw that the word plough was misspelled P-L-O-W – instead of P-L-O-U-G-H as it should have been.

HOLMES: Oh, you noticed that, did you? Watson, you improve all the time. Yes, it was bad English but good American. The printer had set it up as received. Then the buckboards. That is American also. And artesian wells are commoner with them than with us. It was a typical American advertisement, but purporting to be from an English firm. What do you make of that?

WATSON: I can only suppose that this American lawyer put it in himself. What his object was I fail to understand.

HOLMES: Well, there are alternative explanations. Anyhow, he wanted to get this good old fossil up to

Birmingham. That is very clear. I might have told him that he was clearly going on a wild-goose chase, but, on second thought, it seemed better to clear the stage by letting him go. Tomorrow, Watson – well tomorrow will speak for itself.

SCENE VI

Interior of Inspector Lestrade's office. Inspector seated at desk. Desk clock shows 9.45.

Telephone rings at opening of scene.

LESTRADE: (*Picking up phone.*) Scotland Yard. Yes – Speaking – Yes. I'll send a man over. (*Hangs up phone. Door opens and Holmes enters with photograph in his hand. Comes to front of desk and sits.*) Ah, Holmes, find what you were looking for?

HOLMES: I think so, Inspector.

LESTRADE: Well, that's a nice way to start the day. To have found what you were looking for by ten o'clock in the morning.

HOLMES: I enjoy the early morning hours but I still have some way to go before I find what I'm looking for.

LESTRADE: And that is?

HOLMES: I have been trying to learn something about Mr John Garrideb, counsellor-at-law.

LESTRADE: Never heard of him.

HOLMES: Neither had I until yesterday. But from the gentleman's actions I thought it might be possible that you had met him under another name.

LESTRADE: And you found this Mr Garrideb in the Rogues' Gallery.

HOLMES: Either him or his twin brother. What do you think of my chubby-faced friend? (*Passing photograph to Lestrade.*)

LESTRADE: (*Looking at it.*) James Winter, alias Morecroft, alias Killer Evans. (*Turning photograph over – reading*) Age 44. Native of Chicago. Known to have shot three men in the States. Escaped from penitentiary through political influence. Came to London in 1893. Shot a man over cards in a night club in Waterloo Road. January, 1895. Man died but was shown to have been the agressor. Dead man identified as Roger Prescott famous as forger and coiner in Chicago. Killer Evans released in 1901. Has been under police supervision since but so far as known has led an honest life. Very dangerous man – usually carries arms and is prepared to use them. (*To Holmes.*) You have found that our friend Killer Evans has decided to stop leading an honest life?

HOLMES: I'm not sure, but I must admit that I am rather anxious to find out.

LESTRADE: Well, if we can be of any service, Mr Holmes –

HOLMES: You have been, Inspector, in letting me look over your Rogues' Gallery.

LESTRADE: If we can be of any further assistance –

HOLMES: (*Rising.*) I'll call you. Thank you, Inspector, and good day. (*Exits.*)

SCENE VII

Watson enters door of Holmes' study followed by Mrs Hudson.

MRS HUDSON: Mr 'Olmes ain't in, doctor. He went out after breakfast and I ain't seen 'ide nor 'air of him since.

WATSON: I'll wait if you don't mind.

MRS HUDSON: Of course not. You know, doctor, Mr 'Olmes' 'ome is almost your 'ome.

WATSON: Do you mind, Mrs Hudson?

MRS HUDSON: Oh, Dr Watson.

HOLMES: (*Entering door center.*) Oh, doctor, good afternoon. Just in time for luncheon. How about it, Mrs Hudson?

MRS HUDSON: I'll have it ready in a jiffy, sir. (*Exits.*)

WATSON: Well?

HOLMES: This is a more serious matter than I had expected, Watson. (*Sits up right near window.*)

WATSON: Then I'll see it through to the finish with you.

HOLMES: I expected that, but there is danger, and you should know it. Sit down. (*Watson sits facing him.*) This morning I paid a visit to Inspector Lestrade of Scotland Yard and learned that our friend Mr John Garrideb is pictured in the Rogues' Gallery as Killer Evans.

WATSON: But what's his game?

HOLMES: It begins to define itself. From Scotland Yard I paid a visit to Holloway and Steele, Mr Nathan Garrideb's agents.

WATSON: Why on earth did you go there?

HOLMES: Another elementry step in the problem, Watson. They confirmed our client's statement that he had occupied his present quarters for the past five years. It was unlet for a year before that. The previous tenant was a gentlemen named Waldron who was well remembered at the office. He had suddenly vanished and nothing more was heard of him. He was a tall bearded man with very dark features. Now our friend, John Garrideb alias Killer Evans, shot a man named Prescott, and Prescott was a tall dark man with a beard. As a working hypothesis I think we may take it that Prescott, an American criminal, used to live in the very room which our innocent friend now devotes to his museum. So at last we get a link.

WATSON: And the next link?

HOLMES: Well, we must go and look for that. (*Rises. Takes revolver from table drawer which he hands to Watson.*)

WATSON: What's this for?

HOLMES: You may need it. I have an old favourite with me. If our wild west friend tries to live up to his nickname we must be ready for him. We'll have luncheon and perhaps a short siesta, and then, Watson, I think it will be time for our Ryder Street adventure.

SCENE VIII

Close shot of Mrs Saunders. She is obviously anxious to get away. She has hat and coat on. She looks through microscope – sniffs disdainfully – crosses up and looks out window.

MRS SAUNDERS: So there's the things he spends all his time looking at. (*Distant clock strikes four.*) Four o'clock and he ain't here yet. (*Door bell rings.*)

MRS SAUNDERS: (*She crosses to door and opens it.*) If you'd been a bit later, sir, you'd have missed me altogether as I'm just this minute off for the day.

HOLMES: Yes, Mr Garrideb said you left at four o'clock.

MRS SAUNDERS: If you'll just close the door when you leave, sir, it has a spring lock.

HOLMES: I'll be sure to do that, Mrs Saunders.

MRS SAUNDERS: Well then, good day to you, sir. (*She exits closing door.*)

WATSON: Now what's the plan?

HOLMES: (*Moving about the room.*) I'm definitely certain, Watson, that our American friend was determined to get Mr Garrideb out of this room, and as the collector never left it, it took some deliberate planning to accomplish it.

WATSON: But what did he want?

HOLMES: That's what we're here to find out. The whole of this Garrideb invention was devised for that one reason. There is a certain devilish ingenuity about it. Even if the queer name of the tenant did give him an opening which he could hardly have expected, he wove his plan with remarkable cunning. Has Mrs Saunders left the house?

WATSON: (*At window.*) Yes, she just went down the street.

HOLMES: Good. Whatever the reason was for him to want to get our client out of this room, I am convinced it had nothing to do with our friend Nathan Garrideb.

WATSON: You mean it is something connected with the man he murdered, the man who used to live here?

HOLMES: Yes, a man who may have been his confederate in crime. There is some guilty secret in this room.

WATSON: But this collector may have something in his collection more valuable than he knows.

HOLMES: No, Watson, I believe that the fact that Roger Prescott lived here points to some deeper reason. (*A key is heard in the door. In whisper.*) Quick, Watson, behind this curtain. (*They cross down behind curtain extreme left. They crouch behind curtain down left as John enters door left. He closes door softly, looks around room, and removes overcoat. He feels over wall up left for secret button. Finds it – cupboard up left center swings open. John looks down. Goes to center table – strikes match and lights stub of candle. He exits behind cupboard. Holmes and Watson with drawn revolvers come out from behind curtain and creep slowly toward open door left center and Holmes looks down. Shot of cellar. John is seen descending ship's ladder with light entirely from above. Halfway down John suddenly turns as . . .*)

HOLMES: (*Out of picture.*) Where are you going, Mr Garrideb? (*With drawn revolver.*) Keep your hands up,

John Garrideb, alias James Winter, alias Killer Evans.
We seem to have you trapped in your lair.

JOHN: (*Coming up from behind trap door with his hands in the air.*) Well, I guess you have been one too many for me, Mr Holmes. You saw through my game, I suppose, and played me for a sucker from the start. Well, sir, I hand it to you; you've beaten me.

HOLMES: Search him, Watson. (*Turning to open door. Watson takes candle from John. As Watson turns away, John draws revolver from breast and fires twice. Watson cries out in pain and falls. Holmes strikes John on head with revolver. John crumples in chair. Holmes takes John's revolver from him and turns to Watson.*)

HOLMES: You're not hurt, Watson, for God's sake say you're not hurt.

WATSON: It's nothing, Holmes, a mere scratch. (*He sits in chair right. Raises coat sleeve.*) Only seared the flesh.

HOLMES: (*Examining wound.*) Yes, it's quite superficial which is particularly fortunate for you, Evans, for if you had killed Watson, you wouldn't have got out of this room alive. (*Crossing up stage. Looking down trap door.*) Let's see what's in the cellar. Watson, look. (*Holmes covering Evans with revolver looks down through trap with Watson.*) A printing press – a counterfeiter's outfit.

JOHN: Yes, the greatest counterfeiter London ever saw. That's Prescott's machine, and those bundles on the table are two thousand of Prescott's notes worth a hundred each and fit to pass anywhere.

　　Help yourselves, gentlemen. Call it a deal and let me beat it.

HOLMES: (*Laughing.*) We don't do things like that, Mr
   Evans. There is no bolthole in this country. You shot
   this man, Prescott, did you not?

JOHN: (*Sitting.*) Yes, sir, and got five years for it. Five
   years – when I should have had a medal the size of a
   soup plate. No living man could tell a Prescott from a
   Bank of England, and if I hadn't put him out, he would
   have flooded London with them. I was the only man in
   the world who knew where he made them. Do you
   wonder that I wanted to get to the place? Do you
   wonder that when I found this crazy book of a bug-
   hunter with the queer name squatting right on the top
   of it and never quitting his room, I had to do the best I
   could to get him out? It would have been easier if I had
   put him away, but I'm a soft-hearted guy, Mr Holmes,
   and I can't begin shooting unless the other man has a
   gun. But say, what have I done wrong, anyhow? I
   haven't used this plant. I didn't hurt the old stiff.
   Where do you get me?

HOLMES: (*On John's left.*) Only for attempted murder, as
   far as I can see. But that's not our job. They take that
   up at the next stage. (*Nathan bursts in door right.*)

NATHAN: Say, what are you all doing here? And Mr
   Garrideb? There wasn't any Garrideb in Birmingham at
   all. You must have made a mistake.

HOLMES: I think he did. Permit me to introduce you to
   Killer Evans.

NATHAN: Killer Evans. Then he ain't a Garrideb?

HOLMES: No – he's not a Garrideb.

NATHAN: And there ain't no five million dollars?

HOLMES: Yes, there's five million dollars all right. Downstairs in your cellar.

NATHAN: Downstairs?

HOLMES: But it's all counterfeit.

NATHAN: Counterfeit? Why – why – (*to John*) Why, you crook, you.

HOLMES: Yes, Mr Garrideb, I'm afraid he is. Watson, give Scotland Yard a call. It won't be entirely unexpected.

Fade to credits.

THE UNKNOWN TRAITOR

Eric Ambler

Adapted to:

EPITAPH FOR A SPY

(RKO, 1944)

Starring: James Mason,

Herbert Lom & Raymond Lovell

Directed by Lance Comfort & Max Greene

The espionage thriller – which was also a part of the crime movie genre from its early days with a silent adaptation of William Le Queux's Guilty Bonds *in 1912 and the first of several versions of* The Thirty Nine Steps *by John Buchan made by Alfred Hitchcock in 1935 – achieved another landmark in the Thirties as a result of a series of ground-breaking novels by Eric Ambler, who is numbered among the most influential and admired English crime and adventure writers. For it was in 1936 that Ambler wrote the very first non-patriotic spy novel,* The Dark

Frontier. *Crime historian, H.R.F. Keating has explained the importance of what he did in these words, "He [Ambler] initiated a new phase in the history of the spy novel by choosing a hero, not an operative with right and the Establishment on his side, but a person caught up in the machinations of the Great Powers." In subsequent books such as* Background to Danger *(1937),* Epitaph for a Spy *(1938) and* The Mask of Dimitrios *(1939) all of which have been filmed, he presented agents who were victims of circumstances — men who attempted to extricate themselves from situations of danger without any undue displays of courage or putting themselves at much risk. These members of the "anti-hero movement", as they have been called, were the forerunners of the characters who now people the books of such stars of the genre as Len Deighton, John Le Carré and Frederick Forsyth.*

Born in London, Eric Ambler (1909–) gave up an initial career in engineering to write sketches for vaudeville and then worked in an advertising agency until the outbreak of the Second World War. (He is credited with having dreamed-up the famous breakfast cereal jingle, "Snap, Crackle and Pop".) After a brilliant Army career in the Royal Artillery during which he rose to be a Lieutenant Colonel, Ambler went into the film industry and later wrote the scripts for a number of very successful films including The Cruel Sea *(1951) for which he received an Oscar nomination. But despite a long period working in Hollywood, he remains best known as a crime and adventure novelist, with his more recent books including* Topkapi *(1964) and* The Intercom Conspiracy *(1970) also having been filmed. Ambler's use of exotic locations and unforgettable criminal characters has deservedly won him honours from both the UK Crime Writers Association and the Mystery Writers of America who have made him a Grand Master. "The Unknown Traitor" is a rare short-short story, written for the now defunct* Strand *magazine in December 1948, in which Ambler once again uses the theme of the unwilling agent as exemplified in* Epitaph for a Spy *and* The Mask of Dimitrios. *The ending is as surprising as anything the master of the unexpected has ever pulled off . . .*

Mr Robinson lifted the lid of the dustbin and peered out.

The rising moon was becoming visible through the trees, and the Representative of the Plutocratic West (for so the grey-haired man was described in Mr Robinson's orders) had stopped pacing to and fro and looking at his watch. He was standing at the top of the path leading down from the gardens of the hotel to the lake. He was listening intently.

Mr Robinson's heart beat faster and he forgot the cramp in his legs. He, too, could hear the sound – the drone of a fast motor-boat coming from the eastern shore of the lake.

The Unknown Traitor was on his way to the rendezvous.

Lieutenant Lubin (to give Mr Robinson his real name) had not until now been happy in the Secret Police. For some time he had suspected that the Chief had a low opinion of his intelligence and that he was being passed over for promotion. Now he had been given this really important mission and the days of unhappiness were over.

The Chief had taken him into his confidence.

Information had been received from foreign sympathisers that a highly placed and important official was about to go over to the West. His name was not known, but the exact place appointed for his reception on Western territory was. The Traitor must be killed before he could talk. The Chief had selected Lieutenant Lubin to do the job.

He had been given a forged Scandinavian passport in the name of Robinson and a suit of Western civilian clothes.

"You have been chosen," the Chief had said, "for your loyalty and for your implicit and unquestioning obedience to orders. Do not forget it."

As if he could forget! Try he might wonder why the Chief should lay it down that he must conceal himself at the rendezvous in a dustbin – it had called for careful planning to plant the dustbin there successfully – but such idle questionings would not prevent obedience.

The Chief knew best.

The motor launch had reached the landing-stage and its engine stopped. There was silence for awhile. Then the Lieutenant saw the Representative of the Plutocratic West take a pace forward and look down the path. There was the sound of approaching footsteps. The Unknown Traitor had arrived.

He was a thick-set man in a long, loose raincoat and a felt hat. He went up to the Representative and shook hands with him. Then the Traitor said something quickly in an undertone and began to walk towards the dustbin.

The Chief's orders had said that the Traitor must be positively identified before he was shot, but the moon was behind the man and his face was in shadow as he advanced. The Lieutenant peered out at him uncertainly.

Suddenly the Traitor stopped, took a pistol out of his raincoat pocket and, pointing it at the dustbin, pulled the trigger.

He fired eight shots, and as the heavy bullets tore through the dustbin and thudded into his body and legs, the Lieutenant tried to get his own pistol out. But a kind of paralysis was stealing over him. Dimly he became aware of the lid being taken off the dustbin and of something being said.

"I couldn't get in touch with you to change the rendezvous and I had to take some action to avoid suspicion, so I sent the stupidest man I had. Myself, I am a bad shot. He had to be kept still and visible or I would have missed. Well, there he is. At six paces even I can hit a dustbin."

The Lieutenant scarcely heard the words but he recognized the voice. It was the Chief. Then, mercifully, at the moment of disillusion, death came to Mr Robinson.

THE KILLERS

Ernest Hemingway

📽️

Adapted to:

THE KILLERS

(Universal, 1946)

Starring: Burt Lancaster,

Edmond O'Brien & Ava Gardner

Directed by Robert Siodmak

The Killers *is another landmark American crime film also on a theme of the vulnerable hero. The original story by Ernest Hemingway written in 1923 is important, too, in the crime story genre because its terse, atmospheric style of storytelling is believed to have been a source of inspiration to the tough school of crime writers whose work first burst on to an unsuspecting world in the pages of the legendary pulp magazine* Black Mask *from 1926 onwards. Though, as the reader will find, the story of "The Killers" is little more than a vignette, when it was*

*adapted for the screen by Robert Siodmak, the central role
played by Burt Lancaster became – in the words of critic Ian
Cameron – "that of one of the most elaborate losers in the whole
dark genre". The film undoubtedly had a tremendous influence
on all its audience – and one fan, Hollywood producer-director,
Don Siegel, remade it again in 1964 with Lee Marvin, John
Cassavetes, Ronald Reagan and Angie Dickinson. Intended for
television, the remake was instead shown in cinemas – probably
because the violence in it was considered too strong then for
family viewing – but it has since become something of a favourite
in late night TV seasons of crime movies.*

*Ernest Hemingway (1898–1961), famous for his depiction of
violent action and sudden death, prided himself on being a
"hard-boiled" character and this is very evident in his early
writing. Born in Oak Park, Illinois, he worked first as a
newspaperman covering every sort of news story from crime
to local sporting events, and many of his experiences at this time
later found their way into his fiction. His supreme gift of
staccato, vernacular dialogue and technique of understatement
– particularly in stories such as "The Killers" – can be seen now
to have heralded a revolution in writing. Themes of physical
courage run through most of the books that built his legandary
reputation including* The Sun Also Rises *(1926),* A Farewell
to Arms *(1929) and* For Whom The Bell Tolls *(1940).
Today Ernest Hemingway is rightly held in high regard for
his influence on so many aspects of modern fiction – not the least
of these being the crime story, for reasons which will be immediately apparent when reading the next few pages . . .*

The door of Henry's lunch-room opened and two men came
in. They sat down at the counter.

"What's yours?" George asked them.

"I don't know," one of the men said. "What do you want
to eat, Al?"

"I don't know," said Al. "I don't know what I want to eat."

Outside it was getting dark. The street-light came on outside the window. The two men at the counter read the menu. From the other end of the counter Nick Adams watched them. He had been talking to George when they came in.

"I'll have a roast pork tenderloin with apple sauce and mashed potatoes," the first man said.

"It isn't ready yet."

"What the hell do you put it on the card for?"

"That's the dinner," George explained. "You can get that at six o'clock."

George looked at the clock on the wall behind the counter.

"It's five o'clock."

"The clock says twenty minutes past five," the second man said.

"It's twenty minutes fast."

"Oh, to hell with the clock," the first man said. "What have you got to eat?"

"I can give you any kind of sandwiches," George said. "You can have ham and eggs, bacon and eggs, liver and bacon, or a steak."

"Give me chicken croquettes with green peas and cream sauce and mashed potatoes."

"That's the dinner."

"Everything we want's the dinner, eh? That's the way you work it."

"I can give you ham and eggs, bacon and eggs, liver –"

"I'll take ham and eggs," the man called Al said. He wore a derby hat and a black overcoat buttoned across the chest. His face was small and white and he had tight lips. He wore a silk muffler and gloves.

"Give me bacon and eggs," said the other man. He was about the same size as Al. Their faces were different, but they were dressed like twins. Both wore overcoats too tight for them. They sat leaning forward, their elbows on the counter.

"Got anything to drink?" Al asked.

"Silver beer, bevo, ginger-ale," George said.

"I mean you got anything to *drink?*"

"Just those I said."

"This is a hot town," said the other. "What do they call it?"

"Summit."

"Ever hear of it?" Al asked his friend.

"No," said the friend.

"What do you do here nights?" Al asked.

"They eat the dinner," his friend said. "They all come here and eat the big dinner."

"That's right," George said.

"So you think that's right?" Al asked George.

"Sure."

"You're a pretty bright boy, aren't you?"

"Sure," said George.

"Well, you're not," said the other little man "Is he, Al?"

"He's dumb," said Al. He turned to Nick. "What's your name?"

"Adams."

"Another bright boy," Al said. "Ain't he a bright boy, Max?"

"The town's full of bright boys," Max said.

George put the two platters, one of ham and eggs, the other of bacon and eggs, on the counter. He set down two side-dishes of fried potatoes and closed the wicket into the kitchen.

"Which is yours?" he asked Al.

"Don't you remember?"

"Ham and eggs."

"Just a bright boy," Max said. He leaned forward and took the ham and eggs. Both men ate with their gloves on. George watched them eat.

"What are *you* looking at?" Max looked at George.

"Nothing."

"The hell you were. You were looking at me."

"Maybe the boy meant it for a joke Max," Al said.

George laughed.

"*You* don't have to laugh," Max said to him. "*You* don't have to laugh at all, see?"

"All right," said George.

"So he thinks it's all right." Max turned to Al. "He thinks it's all right. That's a good one."

"Oh, he's a thinker," Al said. They went on eating.

"What's the bright boy's name down the counter?" Al asked Max.

"Hey, bright boy," Max said to Nick. "You go around on the other side of the counter with your boy friend."

"What's the idea?" Nick asked.

"There isn't any idea."

"You better go around, bright boy," Al said. Nick went around behind the counter.

"What's the idea?" George asked.

"None of your damn business," Al said. "Who's out in the kitchen?"

"The nigger."

"What do you mean the nigger?"

"The nigger that cooks."

"Tell him to come in."

"What's the idea?"

"Tell him to come in."

"Where do you think you are?"

"We know damn well where we are," the man called Max said. "Do we look silly?"

"You talk silly," Al said to him. "What the hell do you argue with this kid for? Listen," he said to George, "tell the nigger to come out here."

"What are you going to do to him?"

"Nothing. Use your head, bright boy. What would we do to a nigger?"

George opened the slip that opened back into the kitchen. "Sam," he called. "Come in here a minute."

The door to the kitchen opened and the nigger came in. "What was it?" he asked. The two men at the counter took a look at him.

"All right, nigger. You stand right there," Al said.

Sam, the nigger, standing in his apron, looked at the two men sitting at the counter. "Yes, sir," he said. Al got down from his stool.

"I'm going back to the kitchen with the nigger and bright boy," he said. "Go back to the kitchen, nigger. You go with him, bright boy." The little man walked after Nick and Sam, the cook, back into the kitchen. The door shut after them. The man called Max sat at the counter opposite George. He didn't look at George but looked in the mirror that ran along back of the counter. Henry's had been made over from a saloon into a lunch-counter.

"Well, bright boy," Max said, looking into the mirror, "why don't you say something?"

"What's it all about?"

"Hey, Al," Max called, "bright boy wants to know what it's all about."

"Why don't you tell him?" Al's voice came from the kitchen.

"What do you think it's all about?"

"I don't know."

"What do you think?"

Max looked into the mirror all the time he was talking.

"I wouldn't say."

"Hey, Al, bright boy says he wouldn't say what he thinks it's all about."

"I can hear you, all right," Al said from the kitchen. He had propped open the slit that dishes passed through into the kitchen with a catsup bottle. "Listen, bright boy," he said from the kitchen to George. "Stand a little further along the bar. You move a little to the left, Max." He was like a photographer arranging for a group picture.

"Talk to me, bright boy," Max said. "What do you think's going to happen?"

George did not say anything.

"I'll tell you," Max said. "We're going to kill a Swede. Do you know a big Swede named Ole Andreson?"

"Yes."

"He comes here to eat every night, don't he?"

"Sometimes he comes here."

"He comes here at six o'clock, don't he?"

"If he comes."

"We know all that, bright boy," Max said. "Talk about something else. Ever go to the movies?"

"Once in a while."

"You ought to go to the movies more. The movies are fine for a bright boy like you."

"What are you going to kill Ole Andreson for? What did he ever do to you?"

"He never had a chance to do anything to us. He never even seen us."

"And he's only going to see us once," Al said from the kitchen.

"What are you going to kill him for, then?" George asked.

"We're killing him for a friend. Just to oblige a friend, bright boy."

"Shut up," said Al from the kitchen. "You talk too goddam much."

"Well, I got to keep bright boy amused. Don't I, bright boy?"

"You talk too damn much," Al said. "The nigger and my bright boy are amused by themselves. I got them tied up like a couple of girl friends in the convent."

"I suppose you were in a convent."

"You never know."

"You were in a kosher convent. That's where you were."

George looked up at the clock.

"If anybody comes in you tell them the cook is off, and if they keep after it, you tell them you'll go back and cook yourself. Do you get that, bright boy?"

"All right," George said. "What you going to do with us afterwards?"

"That'll depend," Max said. "That's one of those things you never know at the time."

George looked up at the clock. It was a quarter past six. The door from the street opened. A street-car motorman came in.

"Hello, George," he said. "Can I get supper?"

"Sam's gone out," George said. "He'll be back in about half-an-hour."

"I'd better go up the street," the motorman said. George looked at the clock. It was twenty minutes past six.

"That was nice, bright boy," Max said. "You're a regular little gentleman."

"He knew I'd blow his head off," Al said from the kitchen.

"No," said Max. "It ain't that. Bright boy is nice. He's a nice boy. I like him."

At six-fifty-five George said: "He's not coming."

Two other people had been in the lunch-room. Once George had gone out to the kitchen and made a ham-and-egg sandwich "to go" that a man wanted to take with him. Inside the kitchen he saw Al, his derby hat tipped back, sitting on a stool beside the wicket with the muzzle of a sawed-off shotgun resting on the ledge. Nick and the cook were back to back in the corner, a towel tied in each of their mouths. George had cooked the sandwich, wrapped it up in oiled paper, put it in a bag, brought it in, and the man had paid for it and gone out.

"Bright boy can do everything," Max said. "He can cook and everything. You'd made some girl a nice wife, bright boy."

"Yes?" George said. "Your friend, Ole Andreson, isn't going to come."

"We'll give him ten minutes," Max said.

Max watched the mirror and the clock. The hands of the clock marked seven o'clock, and then five minutes past seven.

"Come on, Al," said Max. "We better go. He's not coming."

"Better give him five minutes," Al said from the kitchen.

In the five minutes a man came in, and George explained that the cook was sick.

"Why the hell don't you get another cook?" the man asked. "Aren't you running a lunch-counter?" He went out.

"Come on, Al," Max said.

"What about the two bright boys and the nigger?"

"They're all right."

"You think so?"

"Sure. We're through with it."

"I don't like it," said Al. "It's sloppy. You talk too much."

"Oh, what the hell," said Max. "We got to keep amused, haven't we?"

"You talk too much, all the same," Al said. He came out from the kitchen. The cut-off barrels of the shotgun made a slight bulge under the waist of his too tight-fitting overcoat. He straightened his coat with his gloved hands.

"So long, bright boy," he said to George. "You got a lot of luck."

"That's the truth," Max said. "You ought to play the races, bright boy."

The two of them went out the door. George watched them, through the window, pass under the arc-light and cross the street. In their tight overcoats and derby hats they looked like a vaudeville team. George went back through the swing-ing-door into the kitchen and untied Nick and the cook.

"I don't want any more of that," said Sam, the cook. "I don't want any more of that."

Nick stood up. He had never had a towel in his mouth before.

"Say," he said. "What the hell?" He was trying to swagger it off.

"They were going to kill Ole Andreson," George said. "They were going to shoot him when he came in to eat."

"Ole Andreson?"

"Sure."

The cook felt the corners of his mouth with his thumbs.

"They all gone?" he asked.

"Yeah," said George. "They're gone now."

"I don't like it," said the cook. "I don't like any of it at all."

"Listen," George said to Nick. "You better go see Ole Andreson."

"All right."

"You better not have anything to do with it at all," Sam, the cook, said. "You better stay way out of it."

"Don't go if you don't want to," George said.

"Mixing up in this ain't going to get you anywhere," the cook said. "You stay out of it."

"I'll go see him," Nick said to George. "Where does he live?"

The cook turned away.

"Little boys always know what they want to do," he said.

"He lives up at Hirsch's rooming-house," George said to Nick.

"I'll go up there."

Outside, the arc-light shone through the bare branches of a tree. Nick walked up the street beside the car-tracks and turned at the next arc-light down a side-street. Three houses up the street was Hirsch's rooming-house. Nick walked up the two steps and pushed the bell. A woman came to the door.

"Is Ole Andreson here?"

"Do you want to see him?"

"Yes, if he's in."

Nick followed the woman up a flight of stairs and back to the end of the corridor. She knocked on the door.

"Who is it?"

"It's somebody to see you, Mr Andreson," the woman said.

"It's Nick Adams."

"Come in."

Nick opened the door and went into the room. Ole Andreson was lying on the bed with all his clothes on. He had been a heavyweight prize-fighter and he was too long for the bed. He lay with his head on two pillows. He did not look at Nick.

"What was it?" he asked.

"I was up at Henry's," Nick said, "and two fellows came in and tied up me and the cook, and they said they were going to kill you."

It sounded silly when he said it. Ole Andreson said nothing.

"They put us out in the kitchen," Nick went on. "They were going to shoot you when you came in to supper."

Ole Andreson looked at the wall and did not say anything.

"George thought I better come and tell you about it."

"There isn't anything I can do about it," Ole Andreson said.

"I'll tell you what they were like."

"I don't want to know what they were like," Ole Andreson said. He looked at the wall. "Thanks for coming to tell me about it."

"That's all right."

Nick looked at the big man lying on the bed.

"Don't you want me to go and see the police?"

"No," Ole Andreson said. "That wouldn't do any good."

"Isn't there something I could do?"

"No. There ain't anything to do."

"Maybe it was just a bluff."

"No. It ain't just a bluff."

Ole Andreson rolled over towards the wall.

"The only thing is," he said, talking towards the wall, "I just can't make up my mind to go out. I been in here all day."

"Couldn't you get out of town?"

"No," Ole Andreson said. "I'm through with all that running around."

He looked at the wall.

"There ain't anything to do now."

"Couldn't you fix it up some way?"

"No. I got in wrong." He talked in the same flat voice. "There ain't anything to do. After a while I'll make up my mind to go out."

"I better go back and see George," Nick said.

"So long," said Ole Andreson. He did not look towards Nick. "Thanks for coming around."

Nick went out. As he shut the door he saw Ole Andreson with all his clothes on, lying on the bed looking at the wall.

"He's been in his room all day," the landlady said downstairs. "I guess he don't feel well. I said to him: 'Mr Andreson, you ought to go out and take a walk on a nice fall day like this,' but he didn't feel like it."

"He doesn't want to go out."

"I'm sorry he don't feel well," the woman said. "He's an awfully nice man. He was in the ring, you know."

"I know it."

"You'd never know it except from the way his face is," the woman said. They stood talking just inside the street door. "He's just as gentle."

"Well, good-night, Mrs Hirsch," Nick said.

"I'm not Mrs Hirsch," the woman said. "She owns the place. I just look after it for her. I'm Mrs Bell."

"Well, good-night, Mrs Bell," Nick said.

"Good-night," the woman said.

Nick walked up the dark street to the corner under the arc-light, and then along the car-tracks to Henry's eating-house. George was inside, back of the counter.

"Did you see Ole?"

"Yes," said Nick. "He's in his room and he won't go out."

The cook opened the door from the kitchen when he heard Nick's voice.

"I don't even listen to it," he said and shut the door.

"Did you tell him about it?" George asked.

"Sure. I told him, but he knows what it's all about."

"What's he going to do?"

"Nothing."

"They'll kill him."

"I guess they will."

"He must have got mixed up in something in Chicago."

"I guess so," said Nick.

"It's a hell of a thing."

"It's an awful thing," Nick said.

They did not say anything. George reached down for a towel and wiped the counter.

"I wonder what he did?" Nick said.

"Double-crossed somebody. That's what they kill them for."

"I'm going to get out of this town," Nick said.

"Yes," said George. "That's a good thing to do."

"I can't stand to think about him waiting in the room and knowing he's going to get it. It's too damned awful."

"Well," said George, "you better not think about it."

REWARD FOR SURVIVORS

George Harmon Coxe

Adapted for:

CRIME PHOTOGRAPHER

(CBS, 1951–52)

Starring: Darren McGavin,

Cliff Hall & Jan Miller

Directed by Sidney Lumet

Curious as it may seem, the earliest group of heroes in crime series on television were not detectives or policemen, but reporters, who dominated the genre in America in the late forties and early fifties. In 1948 what its producers, NBC, claimed was the very first regularly scheduled mystery series, Barney Blake: Police Reporter, appeared: a live show starring Gene O'Donnell as a formidable newspaperman who, with his secretary, Jennifer Allen (Judy Parrish), specialized in solving murder cases – all in less than 30 minutes! Although the series only lasted thirteen weeks before being cancelled, this did not deter rival network, ABC, from screening Photocrime, *a year later with Chuck Webster as an investigator with the unlikely name of Hannibal Cobb. In 1951, however, CBS hit the jackpot with* Crime Photographer *based on a popular series of novels and short stories about Jack "Flashgun" Casey, the tough cameraman of the* Boston Express. *Written by George Harmon Coxe, the tales of Casey had first appeared in* Black Mask *magazine in 1934, and later been transferred to the cinema in 1936 (starring Stuart Erwin) and then formed the basis for a long-running radio series,* Casey, Crime Photographer *(from 1946 with Stats Cotsworth) before making the transition to the TV screen in April 1951. Like its predecessors,* Crime Photographer *was broadcast live, and most episodes were set in the Blue Note Café where Casey recounted his triumphs to his girlfriend, Ann Williams (Jan Miller), also a reporter, and a barman with the extraordinary name of Ethelbert (Cliff Hall). In the early episodes of the series, Casey was played by Richard Carlyle, but he was replaced by Darren McGavin who would later become famous as Mike Hammer in the TV version of the Mickey Spillane novels. The series ran successfully for two years and undoubtedly helped to establish crime stories as popular viewing with audiences. The quality of acting and general stylishness of the series owed a lot to the rapidly developing talent of its director, Sidney Lumet, who later became one of the most famous directors in Hollywood.*

George Harmon Coxe (1901–89), the creator of Flashgun Casey, had himself been a newspaper reporter in Santa Monica, Los Angeles and New York, before starting to write crime stories for the pulp magazines in the thirties. It was Coxe's own interest in photography that led to his creation of Casey to fill a gap in the fictional detective field – previously there had been plenty of reporter-sleuths, but never a cameraman who took pictures and solved crimes. Later, Coxe created another newspaperman, Kent Murdock, who also enjoyed great popularity with readers. The success of these two characters resulted in Coxe becoming a contract scriptwriter for MGM in Hollywood – although he did find time to help in adapting the first Casey story for the screen, Women are Trouble *(1936), and then a decade later when the radio series was launched on CBS. His contributions to the crime story genre earned him a Grand Master Award from the Mystery Writers of America in 1964. "Reward for Survivors" is a typical Flashgun story in which he has to solve the double mystery of a missing judge and the murder of a reporter – it was adapted for the TV series by producer Charles Russell and screened in May 1952.*

Casey, number one camera, for the *Express,* filled the exposed film holder from his camera and shoved it into the bulky plate-case at his feet. He took out a fresh holder, slipped it into the camera, fastened the case and swung the strap over his shoulder; then he leaned his stomach against the fire rope and watched the blaze.

There was not much to it; the very nature of the source limited the spectacle. A three-storey, wooden tenement; old, crumbling, dilapidated even for Kaley Street. A kindling wood structure which seemed to glory in the display and nourish the broad spearheads of fire belching from the windows along the front and one side, and rapidly making the ground floor a continuous spread of flame.

The hot, yellow glow made a glistening bronze mask of Casey's rugged face, and after a minute or so he became aware of what felt like an acute attack of sunburn.

He said, "What the hell," irritably, as though disgusted at his rapt attention, and ran his hand over the soft fabric of his ulster.

It was hot to the touch and he grunted, turned away and began to look for Wade, his fellow cameraman, in the crowd behind the fire lines.

A white helmet caught his eye. He bucked through to a battalion chief whose name escaped him, but whose face was familiar. He saw then that the chief was talking to Jim Trask.

Trask said: "Hi, Flashgun."

Casey grunted an answer, let the plate-case slide from his shoulder, spoke to the chief.

"I hear there was a guy caught in there."

"If he was," the chief growled, "he's still there."

"Well," Casey said, "it won't be long, anyway. In an hour you can wet down the foundation and go home."

"If it don't spread and wipe out the block." The chief's tone was annoyed and he cursed as his eyes swept the adjoining buildings.

Casey fell silent and followed the chief's gaze. A half dozen fat hose lines criss-crossed on the street, continued to drench the side walls of the adjacent brick tenements which, fortunately, were set back from the flaming structure. A derricklike water tower had waddled into position in the middle of the pavement and was alternately wetting down every nearby roof.

Casey glanced at Trask. "You eat it up, huh?"

Trask shrugged. One of the city's leading criminal lawyers, he was a nut on fires. Given an honorary appointment to the fire department, he had promptly ordered a gold replica of the official badge. A flash of that got him into the front row at every blaze.

Trask shrugged thick, overcoated shoulders. He was a heavy-set man with an imposing mien, a course, brutal face and a contradictory, booming voice that was nurtured for courtroom use.

"I get a kick out of it, yes," he admitted defiantly. "Liked fires as a kid and never got over it."

Casey said: "Must be a complex," and then turned around in response to a tug on his arm.

Tom Wade was doing a dance, the routine of which consisted mainly of hopping from one foot to the other so that his chunky body bounced his plate-case in and out from his hip. His round, good-natured face looked strangely aggravated and he said: "We got enough. Let's go."

"Why?" Casey said. "It's warm here, ain't it?"

"Warm hell! It's hot – all but my feet. They're froze."

Casey hesitated, glanced down the street again. The side opposite the blaze was, with one exception, made up of third-rate apartment houses and tenements. The exception was a four-storied, brick loft building with a plumbing supply house on the ground floor. His glance slid up the dingy facade, focused on the roof and he said:

"Okey. One more shot. There's an alley back of that loft building. If there's a fire-escape I can get to the roof. It oughta make a good shot from there – and I might catch her when the walls go."

He started through the crowd. Wade stopped hopping and grinned. "I'll go with you."

"You stay here," Casey grunted. "You'd never make it with those cold feet of yours."

Once one of the crowd, Casey broke into a trot. He swung right at the corner, jogged into thick shadows. The mouth of the alley was an opaque black curtain, and to eyes accustomed to the glare of the fire, the alley, itself, was an inky crevasse with no end, no floor.

He jogged on, keeping to what he thought was the middle of the cobblestone paving. He kept his head down, squinting vainly for guidance. He must have looked directly at that box-like obstruction. But he did not see it; did not know it was there until his toe caught it.

He was off balance, his weight was all wrong. That right foot, just starting its step, stopped short and the rest of him kept on going. One knee hit the paving first; then he went flat on the cobblestones and slid along on the camera which had caught under his chest. The bulky plate-case, slung around one shoulder, plopped down on the back of his neck.

It took Casey several seconds to collect himself. The complete suddenness of the fall seemed to aggravate the jar. The wind was knocked from his body and he had to roll off the camera before he could get his breath. Once he got it he began to swear.

He got to his feet, retrieved his hat and plate-case, and as he groped for the camera, his hand touched the box-like object responsible for his fall. Seizing this outlet for his outraged feelings with savage delight, he caught one corner of the box and knocked it to the side of the alley with a combined heave and sweep of his arm.

Again he groped for his camera, snatched it up; then, as he turned to continue down the alley, his foot caught a second unseen object.

This time he did not fall; he merely stumbled. But the shock was greater; a cold, nervous shock that yanked his muscles taut and made his breath stick in his throat.

The object was soft, yielding.

Casey pulled his foot back. The complete blackness of the alley defied him. He shrugged off the plate-case and went quickly to one knee, his left hand groping. Stiff fingers touched cloth, found the buttons of an overcoat and as he bent close the fumes of whiskey tickled his nose.

He said, "Oh, a drunk, huh?" and there was relief in his hushed tones. He let his pent-up breath out slowly and found a match.

The little burst of flame threw a weird orange glow at his feet, picked up the outlines of a man who lay on his side. The hat had fallen off and he saw the profile of a thin face, hair that looked reddish and tousled. He pulled the man on his back, said: "Jeeze! Shorty Prendell," softly.

The match went out. Casey tore another from the paper packet and his mind found temporary acceptance in a satisfactory answer.

Shorty Prendell was a photographer for the *News*, a happy-go-lucky fellow, an habitual souse, good-natured, well-liked in spite of his irresponsible character. Casey had saved him his job more than once by covering an assignment for him, when he passed out; apparently he was running true to form.

Casey struck the second match and again the feeble glow settled upon the inert form. This time Casey's peering gaze slid down to Prendell's overcoat, slid down as far as the chest and stopped; and he sucked air and forgot about the whiskey breath.

There was an irregular round stain in the worn fabric of the grey overcoat – a reddish stain with frayed threads showing in the centre.

For one brief moment Casey knelt there with his gaze riveted on the stain, and grappled with his thoughts while the stiff cold wind of the early March night swept the floor of the alley and tugged at his nerve ends. Then the match flame singed thumb and finger and he dropped it. Blackness wrapped around him, spurred him to action.

He left his case and camera, spun quickly and raced for the mouth of the alley, conscious of a dryness, a thickness in his throat.

There were three or four hundred people on Kaley Street, crowding the fire lines, hanging from windows, warming themselves and enjoying the blaze. There were firemen everywhere; but not policemen, not that Casey could see.

He found Wade right where he had left him. Wade was still dancing and he came up behind him and jerked him around.

Wade took one look at the white, grim lines of Casey's face and went wide-eyed and said: "What the –"

"Shorty Prendell," Casey flung out. "Shot. I stumbled over him in the alley. Get on a phone and –"

"Dead?"

"Call Logan!" Casey rapped, ignoring the question. "Tell him to bring a doctor. Save time. He oughta make it in five minutes." He hesitated while Wade battled his surprise, added: "Snap into it! I'm goin' back."

In the alley again, Casey moved cautiously forward until he reached Prendell's body. He struck another match, glanced at the thin face. Then he wiped a damp palm on his coat and reached for a limp wrist. He held his breath while he felt for a pulse; then he let it out in a silent blast and gently eased the lifeless hand back on the cobblestones.

Casey was hunched there in the darkness, sitting on his heels smoking a cigarette when Wade came into the alley. Casey called to him, directed his steps and Wade crouched beside him and said:

"Is he –"

"Yeah," Casey said wearily. "A slug in the chest."

Wade whispered an awed oath, fell silent, finally said: "Why? What's it all about? What –"

"How do I know?" Casey clipped and his voice was angry,

irritable from reaction. "I stumbled over him – over his plate-case. Maybe he came back for the same reason I did. Maybe he came back to sneak a couple snifters out of his bottle. Somebody let him have it. Somebody might've had it in for him, or –" He broke off in a curse. "How the hell do I know?"

Wade said: "Jeeze. He was a swell guy."

"Yeah," Casey said. "And he's got a wife. And he was a souse and that made it tough for her. But he was a good guy. I'd like to get a crack at the punk that did it."

The two photographers were crouched there in silence when the police car jerked to a stop at the mouth of the alley. Two men swung to the sidewalk and became running silhouettes against the faint background of reflected light. A yellow cone from a flashlight swept the floor and sides of the alley, focused on Casey's face and Lieutenant Logan's voice flared: "Dead?" sharply.

Casey said: "Yeah."

The man with Logan, a vague, unrecognisable figure to Casey knelt beside Shorty Prendell, unbuttoned the coat, slid hands and fingers about in the semi-darkness.

"Shot twice," he said finally and stood up. "It's the examiner's job all right and he's still warm."

Logan said: "Thanks, Doc. Tell the driver to take you home and then come back here."

When the doctor withdrew Logan turned to Casey. "Let's have it."

Casey told him what he knew, and was bitterly conscious that he had but little to tell. Logan began a search of the alley.

"Well," Wade's voice was hesitant, guilty. "Er – hadn't we ought to get a couple pictures?"

Casey said, "Yeah," wearily. "With your box. I can't use mine till I look it over in the light."

Both ends of the alley were guarded by plain-clothes men. The examiner's physician had just finished his examination and he had but little to offer in the way of additional information.

"In the back," he said as he snapped his bag shut. "Looks like he was running, from the way he fell. One slug still in him; I'll turn it over to ballistics and give you a report tomorrow."

The little group around the body fell silent as the examiner left. Feet shuffled on the cobblestone floor and cigarette ends glowed and vaguely illuminated masklike faces. Logan spoke first and his voice was sullen, jerky.

"Not a thing. Not a damned thing but two empty shells."

He turned to the lieutenant from the precinct house, and Casey whispered to Wade:

"You better beat it. The couple of shots I got of the fire ain't worth a damn alongside this. Take my case with you and –"

"But what're you gonna do?" Wade asked dubiously.

"Me?" Casey grunted. "Me – I'm gonna stick with Logan."

"Then why can't I –"

"Will you quit arguin"? You took the pictures – develop 'em. It ain't my job, is it? G'wan, now. Take my case. If they need my two shots, develop 'em. But they probably won't."

"All right, all right," Wade grumbled. He groped around in the darkness, shouldered the two plate-cases and started down the alley.

Logan said: "Listen, Flash, don't you know if Prendell was working on something that –"

"How would I know?" Casey hesitated. "Why don't you get those other *News* guys in here?"

"I will," Logan jerked out. And he did not have to go far. He found the men he sought trying to argue their way past the plain-clothes man at the alley's entrance, and brought them back.

With the help of the flashlights, Casey recognised them both. Beardsley, a photographer, and Kelly, a legman. Logan gave them a few seconds to get used to the atmosphere of death, then he said:

"Come on, now. Gimme a lead. We ain't got to first base yet. What was he workin' on?"

"Nothing that I know of," Kelly said. "The three of us came down here in a taxi. Shorty'd had a couple of drinks, and he still had the bottle. I didn't see him again after we got out of the cab."

"But wasn't he workin' on something else – before this, maybe?" Logan pressed. "Think, damn it!"

Kelly hesitated. Casey heard Beardsley opening his camera, and the *News* photographer seemed to do his work, instinctively, automatically. It was apparent his mind was elsewhere because he kept saying: "Jeeze!" Then, "What would they kill him for? He never hurt a fly. Jeeze!"

Kelly seemed to shake himself, spoke regretfully. "I don't know. He wasn't workin' on anything that I know of." He turned there in the darkness and spoke to Casey. "You know, Flash. He was a swell little guy when he was sober. But the bottle was gettin' him. He was slippin', never got any big assignments any more. I don't think he was working on anything."

"Well, hell!" Logan exploded. "Can't I get any co-operation? What am I, a magician or something? Somebody better know something or it'll go down in the books as a bust. A newspaper guy gets knocked off and every sheet in town'll yell its head off. But that's all. Yell and take it out on the department."

"We'll find something," Casey said and there was a certain grim conviction in his tone.

"Talk," Logan snorted. "You find him dead. With that fire nobody'd pay any attention to this alley. Nobody saw him come in here. How the hell –"

The fading wail of a siren stopped him. An ambulance lurched slowly into the alley, its headlights exploding light over the cobblestones. Two white-coated internes swung off the rear step with a stretcher, set it down beside Shorty Prendell.

Casey watched the thin form being lifted to the canvas and his fingers flexed and he became conscious of that tightening of the throat. A dull, gnawing resentment smoldered deep within him. A bitter sense of frustration, born under the goading of his helplessness, warped his thoughts.

Murdered. A harmless little guy like Shorty. But something would come to light that would help. There'd be a break some place. And Logan could weave the breaks together if anyone could. He watched the stretcher disappear, heard the doors slap shut. The ambulance backed down the alley and its bell clanged jarringly to clear a path across the sidewalk.

He turned quickly then spoke brusquely to hide his feelings.

"You'd better take his camera and case when you go, Beardsley. And" – he hesitated, continued hurriedly – "if they take up some dough for his wife or anything, count me in."

Casey rolled over in bed, tucked his head under the covers for a moment, then stuck his nose out and blinked angry eyes at the insistently shrilling telephone on the bedside table. Each strident burst jarred the back of his head and in self defence he reached out, removed the receiver, dropped it.

He growled an oath, rolled over on his back. He stretched himself awake; for a second or two he enjoyed the luxury of a completely relaxed brain; then the thoughts of the previous night, and Shorty Prendell's death, flooded his mind and he sat up, scowling, at once troubled and resentful.

Reaching for the telephone, he pulled it over to his chest, fumblingly retrieved the dangling receiver, growled: "Yeah?"

The answering terse, incisive voice belonged to Blaine, city editor of the *Express*. This surprised him because he thought it was early and Blaine did not come on the desk until after lunch.

"What's the matter with you?" Blaine said.

"Matter with who?" Casey growled.

"You, dammit. Why didn't you bring that picture in yourself, develop it yourself, tell somebody about it?"

"What picture?" Casey said wonderingly.

"It looks like the biggest thing in months," Blaine went on crisply. "But that don't excuse you for running out on the job. Now, get down here – and in a hurry. Logan's waiting."

"Listen," Casey rapped, "what –" He listened, said "Hello," jiggled the receiver arm and finally slapped the telephone back on the stand and made noises in his throat.

Reaching under his pillow, he got his watch, saw that it was only ten after nine. He knew he was not due at the office for a couple of hours and he said, "What's eatin' him? What the hell picture is he squawkin' about?"

He swung his feet to the floor, ran thick fingers through a shock of curly dark hair that was streaked with grey at the temples. For a moment he sat there on the edge of the bed, scowling, his stiff arms angling out at his sides, propping him up. He reached for the telephone, then changed his mind about calling Blaine back.

"Now that he's got me up," he grumbled, "I might as well go down. Boy, what a job!"

He pulled his pyjama top off over his head, stood up and stepped out of the pants. For a moment he remained poised there, a big, naked, thick-chested figure, and grappled with Blaine's words.

He had gone back to the paper last night. Wade had the necessary pictures, and he, Casey, had stuck with Logan for an hour or so, until he saw that further developments in the murder case were unlikely until morning. It was nearly two o'clock then and he had stopped in an all-night coffee shop for sandwiches before coming home.

"Nerts", he said finally and went into the bathroom.

He took a quick shower and a shave. Within ten minutes he was fully dressed, and he had just picked up his ulster when the knock came at the door.

The knock annoyed him for some reason, and he put on his ulster and glared at the door without answering. The knock was repeated, vigorously, sharply.

Casey growled, "In a minute," then crossed the room, snapped back the lock and turned the knob.

There were two men in the hall. Casey knew one of them: a small, skinny fellow with a pale, wedge-shaped face and small shifty eyes. Sid Glasek. The other fellow, a thick-necked bruiser with a flat nose and scarred brows was a stranger.

Glasek pushed back his derby, said: "Hello, Flash," nodded to the thick-necked fellow and the two of them stepped across the threshold.

Casey frowned, stepped back, trying to figure things out. Glasek was a petty larceny politician, a punk and – He said: "I was just goin' out – and I'm in a hurry."

Glasek was warily apologetic. "It won't take a minute. He just wants to know if you got your camera and plate-case here."

"Yeah?" Casey's brows lifted sceptically and his voice got thin. "Why?"

The thick-necked fellow closed the door and put both hands in the pockets of his worn blue overcoat. Glasek shrugged, pushed his derby still farther back.

"We wanta take a look."

"You'd better beat it," Casey said and his brows came down. "I'm in a hurry."

Glasek's shifty eyes spied the camera on the centre table. "There's no use gettin' tough about it. Show us the camera and case and we'll beat it."

"You'll beat it anyway," Casey clipped, "or maybe you wanta –"

"We wanta look around," the thick-set man cut in hoarsely. Casey glanced at him, watched the fellow take a heavy automatic from his coat pocket, deliberately turn it over in his hand and replace it so that the muzzle jutted threateningly forward. "And maybe you'd better pull in your neck while we do it."

Casey's eyes flared behind narrowed lids, but he made his voice disgusted. "Maybe you're right."

He stepped to the davenport, perched on the edge. The camera had nothing in it, was probably broken although he had not looked. And Wade had taken the plate-case to the office. The thick-necked fellow stood by the door and watched him, and Glasek searched the room, went into the bedroom, came back and spread his hands.

"Okey," he said, but he said it regretfully. "If it ain't here, it ain't here. You see? We didn't want any trouble." He moved to the door. "Nothing to get het up about. No hard feelings."

"Oh, no," Casey said and his lip curled. "No. Come in an' look around any time – any time you got some punk with a gun."

"Don't get smart!" the thick-necked fellow blustered.

Glasek said, "Come on," and opened the door.

Casey watched it close and he glared at the panels for a moment as he reached for a cigarette. "That kind of stuff burns me up," he fumed. "And I hate riddles."

He crossed to the two front windows, glanced up at the heavy, sullen sky, down at the bleak and sunless street. Glasek and his hood were just getting into a taxi. Casey saw that it was a Blue and White. He noticed the number – T36746 – and repeated it absently, half aloud.

Farrar, a rewrite man, was on the desk when Casey swung into the nearly deserted *Express* city room at nine-fifty, and he glanced up, said:

"Blaine's in Magrath's office. He's waiting for you."

"Yeah," Casey said. "I had an idea he was." He moved into a corridor behind the desk, turned into an office whose frosted glass panel said: T.A. Magrath, Managing Editor.

Blaine was sitting at the desk. Logan, opposite Blaine, turned and spoke over his shoulder before Casey got the door shut.

"You didn't hurry, did you?" he leered. Then, with a voice that snapped: "Hours we waste, you cluck. And all the time you –"

"Wait a minute," Casey barked. "What –"

"Sit down," Blaine said, "and listen."

Casey unbuttoned his ulster, made two more attempts to break through Logan's rush of words. Finally he muttered an oath, dropped into a chair beside the desk, and remained scowlingly silent, aware that some mistake had been made, but stubbornly unwilling now to try and explain until he heard the rest of the story.

Blaine, sitting stiffly behind the desk, his clothing immaculate, his grey hair smoothly parted, watched Casey and there was condemnation in his cold, grey eyes.

Casey watched Logan as he listened to his story and he saw that the lieutenant's handsome, smooth-shaven face was tense, a bit grim, that the black eyes were sharp and glaring.

"I don't know if it hooks up with Prendell or not," he was saying. "But this line we've got on Judge Ottleib is plenty hot."

Ottleib. Judge Ottleib had been missing for more than a month. The name jerked Casey's thoughts from Logan.

At first the police had gone on the theory that his disappearance was a straight kidnapping job. But there had been no ransom notes, no demands of any kind. The theory shifted. For a short time it was thought he might have been murdered by some criminal he had sentenced and who sought vengeance. Then some investigator turned up information that clouded the issue still further.

Judge Ottleib received a salary of 17,500 dollars a year. But in the past four years he had, in different banks, made deposits of nearly a hundred thousand dollars. And these deposits were almost entirely made of cash. With something to get their teeth into, the District Attorney's office began to unearth irregularities of other types. Certain criminal lawyers – Arnostein – Myers – Trask – had been thoroughly questioned. A record of cases tried under Ottleib showed a preponderance of decisions in their favor. Trask particularly had been fortunate in his verdicts under Ottleib.

But proof was lacking. And the disappearance of the Judge became a matter of personal opinion – that and nothing more. He was kidnapped, he was murdered, he intentionally disappeared.

"But I didn't have a lead," Logan broke in on Casey's thoughts. "No lead, no nothing; so I checked up on the guy that burned up in that tenement."

"It was straight, then, huh?" Casey said.

"Not so straight," Logan drawled sardonically. "But a guy burned up, yeah. The inspectors think the fire was set, but they can't be sure because the blaze wiped out everything. There's nothing left of this guy except bone ashes and teeth and a ring and a key – one of them law fraternity keys."

Logan grunted, stared at Casey and his eyes narrowed.

"The ring and the key were Judge Ottleib's."

Casey whistled and his eyes widened and Logan said: "We don't know how long he lived in that shack. Nobody in the neighborhood remembers him much until about a week ago. I showed 'em a picture of Ottleib. He's the guy that's been living there and the way it looks he's been there all the time. But he laid low at first when his picture was in the papers and everything, just started comin' out when the thing died down.

Logan pushed back in his chair. "The thing's a natural,

huh? No mystery. The Judge hides out and gets burned to death. Only you and that bull-headed luck of yours run smack into a break again and knock the layout all to hell." Logan leaned forward. "Now, by gawd, I wanta know why you get a picture like that and then –"

"Wait a minute," Casey blasted, and anger flushed his face. "I'm gettin' fed up with these riddles. Where'd you get the picture?"

"Out of your plate-case," Blaine said and his tone was sarcastically polite. "Wade brought it in, but all he developed was his own stuff. That's about all I could expect from him. But you –"

"I've probably heard it before," Casey said caustically. "What's the rest of it?"

"Wade forgot about your shots. He didn't remember until early this morning. Then he called in about a quarter of eight and told Farrar maybe we'd better see what you had."

"That's not his fault," Casey said. "I told him he didn't need to bother with my stuff. I didn't have anything but a couple of routine shots that –"

"Routine?" grated Logan. "Why you held out on me, you louse."

Casey stood up. "Let's see this masterpiece of mine," he said quickly.

Blaine opened a drawer, took out a four-by-five print, handed it to Casey. The big photographer stared at it and his eyes went wide. He jerked his glance away from the print, looked at Blaine, wet his lips. Then he looked back at the picture again and the eyes narrowed.

The camera had caught three men moving down what looked like an alley. All three men were back to the camera, but two of them, apparently attracted by some noise, were looking over their shoulders. Both faces were distinct. The man in the centre was Judge Ottleib; the big man at his right was Brad Shannon. The third man could not be recognised.

Logan's voice was harsh, accusing. "One of your friends gets knocked off and –"

"And," Casey clipped, "you think I'd have a picture like

this and hold out on you? That's the kind of a punk you think I am, huh?"

"Well," Logan pressed.

"You took it, didn't you?" Blaine whipped.

"No."

"Then," choked Logan, "who —"

"I never saw it before," Casey said.

"Where'd it come from?" Blaine exploded. "Who took it?"

"Shorty Prendell," Casey said grimly and then stared sightlessly at the picture and tried to figure out definite and logical reasons to substantiate his conviction.

Casey placed the telephone back on the desk and straightened up.

He looked at Blaine, then at the scowling and uncomprehending Logan. He took off his brown felt, wiped the sweatband, jammed it back on his head again.

"That's it," he said. "Beardsley says he tried to get me last night. There wasn't a single plate in my plate-case."

Logan took a deep breath and his nostrils dilated as he snuffed it out again. "He musta just taken it," he said thoughtfully. "He was tryin' to get away with it and somebody put the slug on him — twice. But I can't figure how —"

"Listen," Casey said and slid a thick thigh across the edge of the desk. "Suppose Shorty was out there sneakin' a drink. While he was standing there these three came along — came out of one of those back doors, maybe. Somehow he gets a look at 'em, recognises Ottleib. He knew what he had, and he took a flash of 'em and tried to run.

"Maybe he took a few steps before they got him. He went down on his face and the camera and case flopped out in front of him. Whoever shot him knew he had a picture —"

"Then why the hell —" Logan began.

"Because I musta come along," Casey said slowly, trying to visualise just what he had done the night before. "They were probably looking for the plate-case. I came along and they ducked into a doorway or something to wait until I went past. But I fell over the plate-case — Shorty's.

"And when I got up I knocked it clear over to the side of

the alley. Then I found him. And I left my case right there beside him. They thought it was his. It's gotta be that way. They were there all the time and they opened my case by mistake, took out all the plates."

Silence greeted this. Blaine rubbed a lean jaw nervously, swivelled his eyes to Logan, back to Casey, "All right," he said. "What's the rest of it?"

"I can guess for you," Casey said. "Logan moved my case to one side. I told Wade to bring that case to the office. But Wade didn't know, or didn't think, about there being two cases besides his own. He picked up the first one – Shorty's – and brought it in. Beardsley took mine.

"I fell on my camera – would not risk using it. If it hadn't been for that I'd probably opened the case and then there would not've been any mix-up. But –" He broke off, continued as though talking to himself. "Shorty was good. He must've jerked that plate from his camera as soon as he snapped it; must've slipped it into the case as he ran and –"

Logan stood up with a savage grunt. "Talk about your breaks," he said. "I should've had this dope last night."

"You're lucky to get it at all," Blaine said. "If there hadn't been two cases, Ottleib would've got the plate and you'd still be thinking he burned to death."

Logan began to pace the floor, talking as he moved. "All right. We know why Prendell got it. One of those three guys shot him. We gotta find Ottleib or Shannon. And the hook-up between 'em fits."

Casey knew what Logan meant. Brad Shannon was the sort of private investigator who worked exclusively for lawyers. He could be found almost any day hanging around the City Hall corridors, or the Court House rotunda. On two occasions he had been forced to stand trial for jury fixing. And in one instance Jim Trask had been implicated.

"Shannon used to work for Trask," Logan said. "And with this picture of him and Ottleib, we know which way we're going. I'll have a talk with Trask, too."

"He was at the fire," Casey said and told of the conversation.

"We'll get a story from him," Logan grunted. "Only it

probably won't be much. Trask is plenty smart and he knows the law. Nothing but facts'll work with him. It's Shannon we want – or Ottleib."

"And Glasek," Casey said. He mouthed a curse, told of what happened at his apartment that morning.

"We got something," Logan said when Casey finished. "They know how they muffed the picture." He turned to Blaine. "Don't run it until I okay it. Let 'em worry about it and –"

"It's not ours, anyway," Casey charged. "It's a *News* beat."

"I'll take care of that," Blaine said coldly.

"Yeah?" Casey said. "Well, Shorty Prendell took it, and he oughtta get credit, even if it won't do him any good."

Blaine's eyes blazed. "If it hadn't been for you, and a pot full of luck, nobody'd have it. But at that, I don't steal pictures." His lips curled as he finished, and he reached for the telephone, asked for Murphy, managing editor of the *News*.

Casey thought about just one thing while Blaine talked: Shorty Prendell – and his wife. Casey had met Mrs Prendell and he recalled her now. A small, quiet, tired-looking woman who seemed to accept the negative lot life had cast for her.

Beardsley had not been quite right about Shorty. He had never harmed anyone maliciously, and he had the sort of personality that made you like him even when he was wrong. But he had harmed his wife. Irreparably, it seemed, by incessant drinking. She worked in an office to offset his expenditures on liquor. Casey brooded about all this, and more, before he finally remembered something that gave a new and hopeful twist to his reverie.

Blaine hung up, spoke sardonically. "It's okey with Murphy. We'll both run it. Satisfied, Casey?"

Casey stood up. "There was a reward, wasn't there?" he asked, ignoring Blaine's comment. "When Ottleib was first missing."

"There still is," Logan said dryly. "Twenty-five hundred." He looked curiously at Casey and there was an undertone of disdain, unusual in his relations with the photographer, in his voice, "Lookin' for your cut already?"

Casey caught Logan's gaze, held it as he moved to the door. His lips dipped at the corners and his eyes brightened and narrowed. "My pal, huh?" he grunted, and left the room.

Casey was slouched in a broken down chair in the photographic department a half hour later, his feet cocked on the desk top, a cigarette in his lips, when Wade came in.

The young photographer's guileless blue eyes were wide with interest and there was a breathless, eager quality about his stance as he stopped beside Casey.

"Hey," he flung out, "you know this guy Glasek that —"

"Yeah," Casey said.

"Well," Wade hurried on, "he and some hood come up to my place a little while ago and want to know about my camera and plate-case. They searched —"

Casey jerked erect in his chair, listened to Wade tell a story similar to his own.

"Now how the hell can you figure that out?" Wade wanted to know.

Casey stood up without answering, picked up his hat and shrugged into his ulster. "Come on," he said.

"Where?"

"Come on," Casey urged, starting for the door. "You remind me of an idea I've been too dumb to develop. It might be good."

"Yeah," Wade said, perplexed, "but where? Do I take the box or —"

"Why not?" Casey said. "We might need it. I want to check up on the Blue and White cab that carted Glasek and his hood around."

Casey and Wade were in luck. From the taxi office they found the driver had a stand on Providence and Boylston; and he was parked there when they reached the intersection. All this took but twenty minutes, and ten minutes after that they stood on Marlborough Street surveying the ancient vine-covered facade of a four-storied structure that had the appearance of a private house which had been remodelled into small apartments.

Casey had related the incidents of the morning, had told about the mix-up in plate-cases. Wade made brief awkward apologies for his failure to pick the right case and to develop Casey's supposed plates the night before, and, reassured by Casey's manner, promptly forgot about everything but the job at hand.

"It's a break the driver remembered where Glasek went," he said.

"There was nothing to it," Casey said. "He went from my place to yours, and then here. Let's have a look."

They went up worn stone steps, flanked by a stone railing, stepped into a gloomy vestibule. There were more than a dozen name cards tacked over mail-boxes along the wall, cards which identified the house or both a residential and business place, furnishing studios for two music teachers, an artist, an interior decorator.

Casey looked at the names twice, grunted disgustedly: "All we draw is a blank."

Wade looked glum, "What do you want to do?"

"I want to find out who lives in each one of these apartments."

"You don't know any of 'em, do you?"

"My gawd," Casey growled, "do you always give your right name?"

Wade grinned and said, "Oh," and then went out to the top step, stood there a moment while Casey took out a cigarette. When he lighted it and inhaled, he said:

"Go down to that drugstore on the next corner and call Logan. I oughtta pass him up after what he said, but I don't trust some of those Headquarters guys. You give 'em a tip and they freeze you out on the pay-off."

"What'll I tell him?" Wade asked dubiously.

Casey sighed wearily and shook his head. "What the hell do you think? Tell him to get down here. Let him dope up a way of going through the building."

Wade was gone about five minutes. The frown on his

round, good-natured face told Casey the answer before he said:

"He ain't there. Just stepped out."

"Yeah," Casey stormed. "Stepped out with his foot on a rail." He scowled, looked up the facade of the building. "I don't want to take a chance on anybody else."

"Why don't we go through the place ourselves," Wade said.

"Sure," Casey sniffed. "And tip our mitt if anybody recognises us."

"Well," Wade scratched behind his ear and his brows knotted, "then why don't we get your car, park it across the street and watch the place. We could get a pint and –"

"Lay off," growled Casey. "You're wearin' me down." He flipped his cigarette away. "What we need is somebody to –" He broke off in a grunt of satisfaction and the scowl vanished as an idea caught in his brain, began to blossom. He said, "You wait across the street," and ran down the steps.

At the corner drugstore, he walked to the telephone booths, called the *Express* and a minute later was talking with Gowan, the City Circulator.

"Mac – Flash Casey. You got any solicitors in the office? Yeah, the guys that go around from house to house and ask if they want to take the *Express*. Yeah. Well send one to –" Casey gave the Marlborough Street address. "What? No, nobody wants to subscribe, dammit. I just want the guy to go through a house for me. I might get a lead on the Prendell job. If I do the circulation department might peddle a couple extra sheets. And listen, connect me with Jerry – in the morgue – our morgue. I'll have him bring some pictures down to this subscription guy."

The circulation solicitor was a hoarse-voiced, red-faced fellow with a faded black coat, a dusty derby and glasses.

Casey said: "Did you bring the pictures I told Jerry to give you?"

"Yeah. What do you want I should do?"

"Take a good look at those pictures," Casey said and waited

while the fellow took them from his pocket and studied the faces of Ottleib, Shannon and Glasek. "Then go through this house just like you was selling subscriptions. If you see any of these guys beat it back here. I wanta know if –"

"How about orders?" the man wheezed. "I work on commission and if I can sell a coupla names –"

"Sell 'em, then," snorted Casey. "But shake it up and don't stop to gas with everybody in the building."

The man looked dubious and shook his head from side to side. Then he took a folded copy of the *Express* from his pocket and stepped through the vestibule and into the hallway beyond.

Wade, top-heavy with admiration, said: "Hey, Flash. That's a swell idea."

Casey said: "Sure," and stepped down in the areaway under the steps.

All through the noon hour they waited and the stiff, March wind swept the street and whirled and eddied about the areaway. Casey stamped his feet in a monotonous rhythm, and kept his hands in the ulster pockets, hunched the collar around his ears. Wade sat on his plate-case and hugged his overcoat, and pulled his neck in like a turtle.

Traffic in the street was swift, sporadic, flowing and ebbing with the signal light on the Avenue. Some time after one, two young girls with brief cases ran up the steps, giggling. A long-haired man with a flowing black tie came out.

A small truck with *Quinn's Trucking* lettered on its side pulled up to the curb. Two men got out of the enclosed cab. As they came up the steps one of them saw Casey in the areaway. He said "Hi, Flashgun."

Casey grunted, "How's it, Spike?"

The two men came out a few minutes later, carrying an old-fashioned, squarish trunk. Casey cursed softly, said: "I'll bet that subscription guy's sellin' the whole building." He stepped out on the sidewalk and lit a cigarette as he watched the trunk being loaded on the truck.

"This ain't so soft as drivin' a hack, Spike," he said.

Spike Largo, a former second-rate boxer who had put on weight and drifted to taxi-driving, and then to trucking, grinned at Casey, said:

"But I'm gettin' three squares now, son. I'd starve, hackin' in these times."

Heels clicking on the steps behind Casey checked a reply. He turned, saw the red-faced solicitor and forgot Spike Largo. He said, "Who'd you find?"

"Him," the man said, and showed Glasek's picture. He sucked at his teeth, grunted and spoke in an injured voice. "This is gettin' to be a tough racket. There was another guy in the room; I didn't get a chance to see him because this first guy acts like he's got a grudge against me, or something. I ask him, does he want to take the *Express* and he –"

"Where?" chafed Casey.

"Apartment 3-D."

"Here." Casey thrust a dollar bill at the fellow. "Here's some expense money. I'll tell Gowan you're a wizard."

While the man stood there looking at the bill, Casey grabbed Wade's shoulder. "Listen," he ordered. "Go back to the drugstore. Call Logan again. If you can't get him this time, get Judson – or Orcutt. But get somebody, tell 'em where to come; then come back here and wait."

"What're you gonna do?" Wade argued.

"I'm goin' upstairs and –"

"You ain't gonna try and take those guys by yourself?"

"Hell, no. But I'm takin' no chances of their slippin' out the back way, either. I'm goin' up in the hall and wait there until Logan or somebody comes. But if Glasek *should* come out I can throw a bluff and –" He broke off. "Oh, hell! Will you quit givin' me an argument?"

Casey shoved Wade, watched him hesitate, then break into a reluctant trot, the plate-case banging his hips. He climbed to the vestibule and went into a dim entrance hall that seemed strangely hot and stuffy. Opposite doors opened from the hall in front of the stairs, and adjoining this was a corridor which stretched to the rear. In one of the lower rooms, someone was banging out an exercise on the piano. From above came the muted shrill of a soprano trilling up and down a scale.

Casey climbed the carpeted stairs, unbuttoning his coat as he went. The practicing soprano became steadily louder, formed a background for thoughts that were expectant, yet apprehensive.

He did not know just how much good he was doing by following up his hunch and tracing the taxi; he was not sure what Logan would find when he went into the apartment. But it was at least a lead. The police would look for Shannon and Ottleib through the regular channels. This was on his own. And action, any kind of action, was better than sitting around and thinking about Shorty Prendell with the slugs in his back and a red-hot picture in his plate-case.

At the third floor landing the soprano was much louder, but still above him. Casey moved slowly along the corridor, found Apartment 3-D was about halfway down. He stopped in front of the door, leaned close to listen. But the soprano defied him and he scowled at the ceiling, cursed softly.

He moved to the opposite wall, leaned against it and lit another cigarette. It was probably an unnecessary precaution, his coming up here. But after this much trouble, there was no use taking a chance. Logan – and he hoped to hell it would be Logan – should be here in another five or ten minutes and –

A lock clicked. Casey's eyes jerked to the doorknob of Apartment 3-D, saw it turn. He stuck the cigarette in one corner of his mouth, wiped his palms on his coat. The door opened. Then he stepped forward so that, as the door swung wide, he met Glasek in the opening.

He stepped back, acted surprised and uncertain. But his eyes shot over Glasek's shoulder and got hard and shiny as they fastened on the big, overcoated figure beyond, Brad Shannon.

Glasek's surprise was genuine. He stammered, "Why–what"

Shannon grunted and stepped forward, brushing Glasek out of the way. Then Casey saw the gun in Shannon's hand and he blinked, said:

"Hey. What the –"

Shannon stepped aside, motioned with the gun. "Come on in."

Casey moved into the well-furnished living room and closed the door by backing against it. He kept his eyes on Shannon, kept them wide and surprised.

Shannon watched Casey for a moment in silence. He was a big man, as tall as Casey and just as heavy; good-looking in a gross, swarthy way, he had a pointed moustache and hard, metallic eyes that seemed too small for his face. At the moment the eyes were suspicious, speculative; and his low voice had a snarl in it.

"Nosey, huh? Well, speak your piece."

"I was lookin' for Glasek," Casey said flatly.

"You wouldn't kid me, would you?"

"I was lookin' for Glasek," Casey went on and glanced at the little man's wedge-shaped face which was still overwritten with surprise. "He busted in on me this morning and I wanta know the set-up."

"How'd you find this place?" Shannon said slowly.

"Taxi-driver."

Shannon seemed to accept this, but with the acceptance, the eyes narrowed and his moustache drew back against his teeth. Reaching into his coat pocket, he took out a blackjack, weighed it in his palm, slipped the gun into the pocket.

"I'm gonna enjoy this," he muttered. "I'm kinda hot; maybe you know it. And this Glasek gag won't rub. There's a picture out that's put the pressure on me. Right now I got only one out. I gotta run for it till I find out where I stand. And you're the guy that got me in the jam."

Shannon moved slowly forward. "I should've let you have it in the alley last night. Then there wouldn've been any picture. But we made a mistake. You've got nothing on Glasek; but me – I'm spotted. So for hornin' in last night – and now"

Shannon came forward swiftly, his left fist doubled, the right hand holding the blackjack, cocked.

Casey said: "Now wait –"

He knew what to expect; he shifted his weight and got

ready for Shannon. And he had time to think that perhaps this was a good break, that the more time he could waste, the better it would be; and he was glad now, that he had taken the precaution to come up to the third floor hall and wait.

He poised on the balls of his feet, put up his hands. Shannon jabbed with his left, slashed out with the blackjack. Casey took the left, on his hunched chin, kept his eyes on Shannon's right, blocked the swing and stepped close, hooking his right. Shannon grunted, clinched, began to swing with blackjack as his left arm hugged Casey close.

Casey took two glancing blows – painful, but not too damaging – to the shoulder before he could counter. Then he got his chin over Shannon's shoulder, gained momentary safety from the blackjack, and slammed away with both hands; short, powerful punches that ripped into Shannon's stomach and solar plexus.

Shannon could not stand up under such an attack. Lacking the cast-iron stomach muscles of a fighter in condition, he doubled, gasped, fell back. Casey jabbed him away with a left and then whipped over a right to the face. The punch missed the jaw by an inch. Shannon went over backwards. Casey followed him. Then Glasek was at his back, raining blows on the back of his head and neck.

Casey cursed, spun angrily. Glasek's eyes mirrored fear and he jumped back with catlike quickness as Casey lashed out. His left was short, and he took a step forward to follow up; then Glasek yelled:

"No! For gawd's sake, no!"

Casey froze at the almost hysterical tone; saw that Glasek's wide-eyed gaze was not on him, but to one side. He glanced over his shoulder and went cold. Shannon was on his knees, his swarthy face a mask of hate. The gun was in his right hand and the trigger finger was tensed.

Glasek saved his life. Casey knew that. But he had no feeling of gratitude then; it was all over in two or three seconds, and his only sensation was one of surprise and stark, momentary fear, followed by relief as Glasek wheezed:

"The noise! You can run for it if you don't spoil it!"

Shannon's pitiless gaze shifted to Glasek. That did it. The gun hand seemed to relax, and he got to his feet.

"Okey," he said. "This can wait a while." He picked up the blackjack, cocked one eyebrow, moved around behind Casey and said: "If you turn around, you get it anyway."

Casey half turned in spite of the warning. Then the blackjack crashed on his head. His legs sagged. Pain exploded in his brain, in his ears, and he went down on his hands and knees. He did not entirely lose consciousness, but he was helpless for a long minute while he rocked there on his knees, his head hanging between braced arms.

When he got to his feet again, Glasek had a length of rope. Shannon, grinning now, covered him with the gun while Glasek tied Casey's wrists behind his back.

"This'll do," Shannon said. "Hands and feet. By the time you get loose I'll be on my way and before I go I'll give you something to remember me by."

Casey fought the panic in his head, glanced about the room and wondered about Logan. He did not know how much time had elapsed since he had left Wade, but in another couple of minutes it would be too late. Once Shannon and Glasek left the house, there would be small chance of finding them again. His glance stopped on the suitcase at the end of the davenport. He had not seen it before and it served to verify his contention: Shannon had a definite plan of escape.

Glasek stepped from behind Casey. Shannon said: "Down on your belly now while we get the ankles."

Casey hesitated. Shannon started for him. He did not repeat the command and he took but one step, because in the next moment a loud knocking shook the apartment door.

Casey stiffened. Glasek gasped audibly and Shannon glanced wildly about the room, back at Casey. His gun came up then, and he stepped close, whispered:

"I don't stop now. I ain't got much to lose. Grab this and by gawd I'll let you have it." He looked at Glasek. The knock was repeated. Shannon prodded Casey with the gun. "Say, 'Just a minute'."

Casey repeated the command in a thick dry voice; then

Shannon pulled him to the door, stationed him two feet in front of it. He motioned Glasek to one side.

Shannon flattened himself against the opposite wall, lifted the blackjack in his right hand and covered Casey with the gun in his left. He motioned again to Glasek, who reached forward and slowly opened the door, keeping behind it.

Lieutenant Logan, one hand making a suspicious bulge in the pocket of his new-looking Chesterfield, said: "What the hell were you doing?" and stepped into the room.

Casey's teeth clicked together. His hands clenched behind his back and he shook his head wildly in spite of his danger. Logan sensed the mute warning, but there was not time enough to do much about it. Shannon's blackjack slammed down on his grey felt before he could turn and he took one more step and folded over on his face, his hat rolling out in front of him.

Logan pulled himself to his feet three or four minutes later and said: "What'd he hit me with?" He rubbed the top of his head gingerly and his handsome face twisted in a scowl. "I'll bet you got a kick out of it, too, you louse."

"Nerts!" rapped Casey. "I got a lump behind my ear I'll stack up against yours. If my hands hadn't been tied I might've taken a chance." He hesitated. "But he was hot – and he knew it. He had the gun on me and if he started to blast – and he would if he got cornered – he'd 'a' got us both."

Logan punched his hat back in shape, cursed bitterly. "That part's all right," he grated. "I can take it. But he's clear again. How the hell we gonna pick him up? What the hell kind of a set-up did you frame?"

Casey said: "Untie my hands," and told the lieutenant what had happened.

"Why didn't you wait for me?" Logan said.

"How'd I know they wouldn't go out the back way? I had to stall 'em, didn't I? Why weren't you in when Wade called you the first time?" Casey rubbed his wrists when Logan untied them, turned as a new thought struck him. "Hey. Where's Wade? I told him to wait outside."

"He was outside," Logan said. "He followed me in and I told him he'd better wait downstairs."

Casey muttered an oath, jerked open the door. The hall was deserted and he ran down the stairs. At the front door he saw a police sedan at the curb and went to it, spoke to the driver.

"You know Brad Shannon?" The driver said he did and Casey continued: "He didn't come out?"

"Would I be sittin' here if he did?"

"Where's Tom Wade?"

"He went in with Logan. I ain't seen him since." The driver, a young, ruddy-faced fellow, pushed over on the seat. "Say, what the hell's up? What —"

"Plenty," Casey clipped and ran up the steps. He went through the lower corridor to the back door, looked out into the little courtyard. He stood for a moment, grumbling to himself, then went back upstairs. The soprano was still practicing the same scale on the floor above.

Logan was on his knees in the centre of the floor, inspecting a dark spot in the middle of the light brown rug. The spot was about three inches across and as he stepped close, Casey saw that it had a reddish cast.

Logan said: "That's blood just as sure as hell." He looked up at Casey. "It ain't yours." Casey shook his head. "Did Shannon or Glasek look like they'd been bleeding?"

"No."

Logan stood up, rubbed the lump on his head again, scratched his nape thoughtfully. When he spoke his voice was sharp, jerky.

"I don't know how old that stain is, but if it's fairly new, if it was made today —" He broke off, gave Casey a steady, narrowed glance. "The way I dope it, there's four guys mixed up in this act. Whose blood is it?"

Casey's brow drew down but he did not answer and Logan said:

"It ain't Shannon's, it ain't Glasek's; it ain't Trask's because we had him down for questioning and I only left him a half hour ago. So who does it leave?"

"Ottleib?" Casey wheezed. "Hell, you mean –"

"I don't know what I mean," Logan said grimly. "I'm just askin' myself questions. If –"

The sudden shrill ring of a telephone stopped the sentence. Casey and Logan both turned towards the instrument on the little stand near an opposite doorway. Casey reached it first, swept the receiver into his hand.

The voice was Wade's, and even in his present tense state, Casey sensed the excited, breathless quality in the tone.

"Where are you?" Casey flashed. "Where'd you go?"

"I was in the downstairs hall," Wade said hurriedly. "I heard somebody running down, so just for fun I ducked under the stairs. It was Glasek and Shannon. They went to the front door, saw the police car and ran out the back way.

"I didn't know what had happened to you and Logan, but I thought I'd better follow 'em. So I did. They went over to Newbury, to a garage. I went down to the corner and got a cab. When they came out in a car, I followed 'em –"

"Where?" Casey cut in excitedly. "Where the hell are you?"

"In a drugstore on Westland: Glasek went up in an apartment house; Shannon's hiding on the floor in the back of the car. I ain't seen a cop and I thought I could call you and –"

"We'll be right over," Casey rapped. "Stick –"

"They're comin' out," Wade gasped. "Gasek – and Jim Trask."

"Wait!" Casey shouted. "Wait and –"

"I gotta go," Wade said. "They're gettin' in the car. I gotta go. I gotta follow 'em, ain't I? Call you back."

Casey slammed down the receiver as the line went dead. "Call me back," he jeered. "How the –" He straightened up, knocked his head against Logan's who was standing over him, trying to get the gist of the conversation.

Casey told him what Wade had done and Logan said:

"Wait? Wait, hell! We can't wait. You said they took a suitcase. They'll blow out of town and –"

Casey didn't hear the rest of the sentence. One word stuck in his brain, flashed a driving association. Suitcase. In the stress of action he had forgotten an incident that might possibly be important – damn' important. Grabbing for the telephone directory, he pawed through it, found a number and again scooped up the telephone.

"Quinn's Trucking?" he bellowed a moment later. "Police business. Lieutenant Logan speaking. You had a call for a trunk at – Marlborough. Spike Largo was drivin'. What apartment number was it?"

He waited, thumping one heel against the floor. "Yeah?" he said a few seconds later. "Where were you supposed to take it? Where? Okey. Okey."

Logan grabbed Casey's arm and jerked him around as he hung up. "What've you got?" he clipped. "You been holdin' out again? You know where they're goin'?"

"Yeah," Casey said and told about seeing Spike Largo and the trunk. "That trunk came from here," he finished bitterly.

"Where's it goin'?"

Casey started to speak, checked himself as a sudden calmness settled over him and he found room amid his racing thoughts for a new and forgotten perspective.

He put his fists on his hips, sweeping the tails of his ulster aside as he did so; he leaned forward slightly and took special pains with his words.

"Maybe you and I are workin' on different angles. Shorty Prendell was a friend of mine. I don't give a good – damn about Judge Ottleib, except for one thing. There's a reward out. If we get lucky and pull something out of a hat, I wanta be damn' sure Shorty's wife gets it all."

"You're not sure now, huh?" Logan asked caustically. "You think maybe I'm chiselin' in on widows now, huh?"

"You made a sweet crack about it to me this morning," Casey said. "I want to get you straight on it."

For a moment Logan's dark eyes snapped their irritation and resentment. Then he seemed to relax and a wry grin tugged at the corners of his mouth.

"Just when I think you'd like a slap in the mouth for yourself, you pull something that makes me like you. You want me to write out an assignment now, or can you wait till we earn the dough?"

"I'll wait, and we'll earn it. That trunk went out to the Norwell airport. We oughta make it in time."

It was past mid-afternoon when the driver kicked the motor of the police touring car to life. Logan sat in front, and Casey braced himself in the middle of the seat and hung on to a door with one hand, his hat with the other.

They went through traffic which was normal and not yet snarled by the five o'clock home-going parade.

Outside of Dedham they were doing seventy and Logan hunched over and said: "Shake it up, Eddy."

"We're doin' seventy," Eddy said.

"Sure," Logan said. "But we're in a hurry. Step on it."

Casey held on. The chilled wind whipped in on him from both sides.

He let go of the door and leaned over on the back of the front seat. This was better and he wiped his eyes and watched the road. He saw the approaching truck about a mile this side of Norwell, had time to get a fleeting glance of Spike Largo in the cab.

"That's the truck," he yelled in Logan's ear. "Comin' back."

Logan nodded, yelled something in the driver's ear. The car held its pace for another minute, then braked suddenly and swung into a macadam feeder road in a dry skid. They roared up a half mile rise, reached the level ground again, and the landing field spread out before them under the dull and low-hung sky.

A heavy-looking cabin plane stood a hundred yards or so from the office, its wheels blocked, its propeller idling. Opposite the office, on the road, was a black sedan; a quarter of a mile behind this, a taxi crawled along, seemed on the verge of stopping.

Three men got out of the sedan as Casey watched. A figure stepped out of the office and walked to meet them. Even at a distance of a half mile Casey recognised the three men from the sedan. Faces were but vague ovals in the dusky light, but the figures – Glasek's, the towering Shannon, the burly stockiness of Jim Trask – furnished identification.

Casey yelled in Logan's ear again and the lieutenant pulled his coat open and reached for his gun. Then Glasek saw the onrushing police car; it was evident from the way he pointed.

For an instant all four men stared. The police car whipped past the loafing taxi and Casey saw Wade's face pressed to the side of the window. The man in the helmet started to run for the plane; the other three followed and strung out behind him.

Ten seconds later the police car slammed to a stop, its rear end yawing towards the ditch. Momentum slapped Casey against the front seat and he bounced back on the floor. By the time he got the rear door open, Logan was twenty feet in front of him with Eddy at his heels.

The taxi squealed to a stop. Casey saw Wade pile out and start to run and he yelled: "Stay back," and then set out after Logan.

The pilot was about ten yards from the plane. Glasek was about twenty yards behind him, Shannon followed, and Trask was still farther back, only fifteen yards ahead of Logan.

The lieutenant yelled a command, then Casey saw his right arm come stiffly up. His wrist kicked upward and the wind swept back the report of the shot.

Trask turned, stopped abruptly and whipped up his arm. He and Logan fired together; the police chauffeur fired. Logan went down as though one leg had been cut from under him. Trask staggered, fired again wildly; he went to one knee, pulled himself to a crouch, then fell over on his face.

Shannon fired over his shoulder, but kept running and the pilot had reached the plane, was tugging at the cabin door. Logan was trying to get to his feet when Casey raced past without slowing down. Then Eddy fired again; so did Shannon who was still ten yards shy of the plane.

Casey, weighted down by his bulky coat, was wheezing and puffing by the time he reached Trask's crumpled form; then he saw the automatic on the ground beside the outstretched fingers, and with no preconceived idea, he stooped, snatched it up without breaking his stride.

As he straightened, he saw Shannon jerk to a stop and spin about. Ignoring Eddy, who was five feet closer, Shannon swung his automatic towards the photographer.

Casey dropped to one knee as Shannon fired – and missed. He was close enough to hear Shannon's curses, close enough to see the desperate, twisted expression on the swarthy face, to see the black hole of the muzzle as Shannon brought the automatic down after the recoil of the first shot.

This time Shannon aimed deliberately. So did Casey. And a curiously fleeting thought of Shorty Prendell helped him, as he squeezed the trigger, felt the slap of recoil at his wrist an instant before he saw Shannon's automatic jump.

Two shots, Shannon's and Eddy's, roared out a fraction of a second after his own. Shannon's big body jerked sideways. Casey did not know whether it was his shot or Eddy's which had found the target, and he held his gun steady, waited stiffly on one knee.

Shannon's arm came down, hung limply and he took a step to brace himself. The gun slipped from loose fingers. Casey stood up and started forward, the police chauffeur moving at his side.

Death was streaking Shannon's swarthy face before Casey reached him. He seemed to crumple and go over backward, as though he were trying to sit down in a chair which had been jerked from under him.

Casey yanked his gaze away. At the side of the plane, Glasek and the pilot stood stiffly erect, their arms stretched rigidly perpendicular.

Logan limped to the side of the plane and Casey said: "You scared hell out of me. You went down so damn' quick I –"

"In the thigh," Logan said thickly. "I thought I lost a leg." He pulled his coat aside, glanced down and felt the side of his thigh where red was staining the blue fabric of his trousers. "It'll be okey when it stops bleeding."

Wade, who had run up and was standing at Casey's

shoulder, whispered: "I'll be right back," and started across the field.

The police chauffeur had searched Glasek and the white-faced pilot and Logan said: "Where do you fit?"

"I don't know," the pilot said and his shaky voice sounded convincing. "That fellow" – he pointed to Glasek – "hired me to take him and two other guys to Richmond."

"What'd you run for?"

"Somebody yelled, 'Run' and I ran. I was rattled and –"

"It's gonna be tough for you if you can't prove it, buddy," Logan said.

He turned to Glasek. "You wanta talk?"

"I wasn't in on it," Glasek wailed. "I didn't know a thing about it till this morning. Trask told me to hire a plane, told me to see if I could turn up that picture and –"

"You didn't know about Prendell, maybe," Logan said. "But you damn' well knew about Ottleib. He couldn't stand the gaff and Trask couldn't either if Ottleib was caught. So the Judge hid out, doped out the plan to get himself burned to death. Who was it that got burned?"

"Shannon got somebody to claim an unidentified man in the morgue – some guy that drowned and was about Ottleib's size."

"And Ottleib," Logan went on grimly, "or maybe Trask – he was there – set that tenement on fire. Ottleib yelled from the window for a fake and beat it down the back way. Then what?"

"I tell you I wasn't there," wheezed Glasek. "How do I –"

Logan limped forward a step and slapped the fellow in the mouth so hard he knocked his hat off. It bounced on the frozen turf and Glasek yelped, staggered. He put his hand to lips that welled blood.

"Maybe you weren't there," Logan leered, "but you know."

"Shannon and some other guy was waiting in a place down the street. Ottleib beat it around there and when the fire got going good they sneaked out the back way to get a car and –"

"Prendell saw 'em," rapped Casey. "And he had guts

enough to try a picture – and they shot him in the back." He stepped forward, cocking his wrist.

Logan grabbed him, said: "Lay off, I'm doin' the slappin' on this job." He pulled Glasek towards him. "What happened to Ottleib?"

Glasek's face went dead white and a fit of trembling seized him. Logan said: "He had a run-in with Trask or Shannon, huh?"

"He went all to pieces when they killed Prendell," Glasek whimpered. "Murder scared him. He said he'd give himself up and say Trask had him kidnapped. He tried to fight himself out of the Marlborough Street place." Glasek's voice became faint. "Shannon shot him."

Glasek's head came up and his voice got sharp. "But that was early this morning. I wasn't there."

"You could be right," Logan said. He hesitated, pressed his lips together, looked at the plane, then at the pilot. "The trunk loaded in there?" The pilot nodded nervously and Logan said: "Well, I suppose we gotta take a look," grimly.

Casey knew what Logan meant. He'd had the same idea in the back of his head all the time, but other things had kept the thought submerged.

"Come on," Logan snapped. "You" – he pointed at the pilot – "and you, Flash."

They lowered the trunk to the ground.

Logan found it locked and the police chauffeur eventually found the key on Shannon.

Logan opened the lid, sucked in his breath. Casey took one quick look. That was enough to see that the body which lay face down inside, was tightly wedged with wadded newspapers, that there was quite a bit of blood, that the legs did not seem to be in the right place. He looked away and wiped cold sweat from his face as Logan slammed the lid.

"What were they gonna do with it?" Logan asked the stiff-lipped pilot.

"I don't –" the fellow said and Glasek interrupted.

"They were gonna dump it in the ocean – way out. Shannon was goin' to Miami, get a Pan-American to Trinidad. Trask was comin' back if it worked – you had nothin' on him."

Logan looked steadily at the pilot. "What a break for you, son."

Wade stumbled up then, fell over his plate-case as he slipped it from his shoulder.

Casey had forgotten that Wade had taken the camera with him from the office. Now he said: "You been luggin' that thing all this time?"

"Sure," said Wade, opening the camera and fooling with the shutter and focus.

His pop-eyed gaze fell on the trunk. "You find Ottleib? Is he in there?" Casey nodded and Wade said: "Then open it up and let me –"

Casey and Logan said: "No," together. Wade looked hurt. Then his tone brightened. "Ain't there a reward or something for finding Ottleib?"

"Yeah," Casey said. He looked at Logan, who met his gaze with steady eyes and nodded slowly; then he added: "There's a reward, but it's all sewed up. And don't give me an argument," he growled, but the hint of a smile in his eyes belied the growl. "Just get busy with that box. Get pictures enough for both of us and I'll take you in to Steve's and buy the drinks."

"Hah," Wade said. "I knew there was a reward in it some place."

IT HAD TO BE MURDER

Cornell Woolrich

Adapted to:

REAR WINDOW

(Paramount, 1954)

Starring: James Stewart,

Grace Kelly & Wendell Corey

Directed by Alfred Hitchcock

Alfred Hitchock is recognized as one of the greatest directors of crime movies – and Rear Window *has been described by many critics as one of his finest achievements. By the time he came to make this adaptation of a short story by Cornell Woolrich, Hitchcock was at the peak of his powers and had proved himself to be a master of suspense and mystery by providing for the cinema a whole string of small masterpieces adapted from crime stories and including* The Lodger *(1926), based on Marie Belloc Lowndes'* Jack the Ripper *story;* The Secret Agent

(1936) from Somerset Maugham's Ashenden spy stories; Rope *(1948), a version of the classic Patrick Hamilton stage play;* Strangers on a Train *(1951) adapted from the best-selling novel by Patricia Highsmith; and* Dial M for Murder *(1954) also derived from a play by Frederick M. Knott. Hitchcock knew the moment he read Woolrich's story of a man immobilized in an apartment who sees all life through his rear window – and perhaps even murder – that here was perfect material for him. The tale was adapted for the screen by Michael Hayes and Hitchcock encouraged marvellous performances from James Stewart as the invalid and Grace Kelly as his attentive girl-friend who, initially, does not share his suspicions about what might be happening. Playing the mystery man of the story was Raymond Burr later, of course, to become famous on television as the great lawyer sleuth, Perry Mason, and then the wheel-chair bound, Chief Robert T. Ironside. Critics have found the concept of the invasion of privacy in* Rear Window *both shocking and compulsive, with Hitchcock's style a mixture of the funny, the macabre and the terrifying. It is a picture as compulsive to watch today as it was when made almost half a century ago.*

Cornell Woolrich (1903–68) was a tortured, near-reclusive writer for most of the closing years of his life and set many of his stories in the seamy side of New York which surrounded the sparse hotel room where he lived. Although Woolrich was born of affluent parents and spent much of his childhood travelling between Latin America where his father worked as an engineer and New York where his mother was a leading socialite, his character grew increasingly morbid and he started pouring his anxieties and frustrations into novels and short stories, espe-cially The Bride Wore Black *(1940),* Phantom Lady *(1942) and* Night Has A Thousand Eyes *(1945). After a brief marriage, he chose to live with his increasingly domineering mother in New York and, after her death in 1957, his already unstable character declined into despair and alcoholism. Wool-rich died less than ten years later, sick and alone, still in the last hotel room he had occupied with his mother. In recent years, his work has come in for new evaluation and his major contribution to the crime genre fully appreciated. Apart from the twenty odd films based on his work, dozens of his short stories have also been adapted for television anthology series. None, however, has enjoyed quite the fame and prestige of* Rear Window *adapted from this next story which was first published in* Dime Detective, *February 1942. Whether you have seen the movie or not, it is a chilling and rivetting piece of storytelling.*

I

I didn't know their names. I'd never heard their voices. I didn't even know them by sight, strictly speaking, for their faces were too small to fill in with identifiable features at that distance. Yet I could have constructed a timetable of their comings and goings, their daily habits and activities. They were the rear-window dwellers around me.

Sure I suppose it was a little bit like prying, could have been even mistaken for the fevered concentration of a Peeping Tom. That wasn't my fault, that wasn't the idea. The idea was, my movements were strictly limited just around this time. I could get from the window to the bed, and from the bed to the window, and that was all. The bay window was about the best feature my rear bedroom had in the warm weather. It was unscreened, so I had to sit with the light out or I would have had every insect in the vicinity in on me. I couldn't sleep, because I was used to getting plenty of exercise. I'd never acquired the habit of reading books to ward off boredom, so I hadn't that to turn to. Well, what should I do, sit there with my eyes tightly shuttered?

Just to pick a few at random. Straight over, and the windows square, there was a young jitter couple, kids in their teens, only just married. It would have killed them to stay home one night. They were always in such a hurry to go, wherever it was they went, they never remembered to turn out the lights. I don't think it missed once in all the time I was watching.

But they never forgot altogether either. I was to learn to call this delayed action, as you will see. He'd always come skittering madly back in about five minutes, probably from all the way down in the street, and rush around killing the switches. Then fall over something in the dark on his way out. They gave me an inward chuckle those two.

The next house down, the windows already narrowed a little with perspective. There was a certain light in that one that always went out each night too. Something about it, it used to make me a little sad. There was a woman living there with her child, a young widow I suppose. I'd see her put the child to bed, and then bend over and kiss her in a wistful sort of way. She'd shade the light off her and sit there painting her eyes and mouth. Then she'd go out. She'd never come back till the night was nearly spent. Once I was still up and I looked and she was sitting motionless there with her head buried in her arms. Something about it, it used to make me a little sad.

The third one down no longer offered any insight, the windows were just slits like in a medieval battlement, due to foreshortening. That brings us around to the one on the end. In that one frontal vision came back full-depth again, since it stood at right-angles to the rest, my own included, sealing up the inner hollow all these houses backed on. I could see into it, from the rounded projection of my bay-window, as freely as into a doll-house with its rear wall sliced away. And scaled down to about the same size.

It was a flat-building. Unlike all the rest it had been constructed originally as such, not just cut up into furnished rooms. It topped them by two stories and had rear fire escapes, to show for this distinction. But it was old, evidently hadn't shown a profit. It was in the process of being modernized.

Instead of clearing the entire building while the work was going on they were doing it a flat at a time in order to lose as little rental income as possible. Of the six rearward flats it offered to view, the topmost one had already been completed but not yet rented. They were working on the fifth-floor one now, disturbing the peace of everyone all up and down the "inside" of the block with their hammering and sawing.

I felt sorry for the couple in the flat below. I used to wonder how they stood it with that bedlam going on above their heads. To make it worse the wife was in chronic poor health too. I could tell that even at a distance by the listless way she moved about over there, and remained in her bathrobe without dressing.

Sometimes I'd see her sitting by the window, holding her head. I used to wonder why he didn't have a doctor in to look her over but maybe they couldn't afford it. He seemed to be out of work. Often their bedroom light was on late at night behind the drawn shade, as though she were unwell and he was sitting up with her.

And one night in particular he must have had to sit up with her all night, it remained on until nearly daybreak. Not that I sat watching all that time. But the light was still burning at three in the morning when I finally transferred from chair to bed to see if I could get a little sleep myself. And when I failed to and hopscotched back again around dawn it was still peering wanly out behind the tan shade.

Moments later, with the first brightening of day, it suddenly dimmed around the edges of the shade and then shortly afterward not that one, but a shade in one of the other rooms – for all of them alike had been down – went up, and I saw him standing there looking out.

He was holding a cigarette in his hand. I couldn't see it but I could tell it was that by the quick, nervous little jerks with which he kept putting his hand to his mouth, and the haze I saw rising around his head. Worried about her, I guess. I didn't blame him for that. Any husband would have been. She must have only just dropped off to sleep, after night-long suffering. And then in another hour or so at the most, that sawing of wood and clattering of buckets was going to start in over them again. Well, it wasn't any of my business, I said to myself, but he really ought to get her out of there. If I had an ill wife on my hands . . .

He was leaning slightly out, maybe an inch past the window frame, carefully scanning the back faces of all the houses abutting on the hollow square that lay before him. You can tell, even at a distance, when a person is looking fixedly. There's something about the way the head is held.

And yet his scrutiny wasn't held fixedly to any one point, it was a slow, sweeping one, moving along the houses on the opposite side from me first. When it got to the end of them I knew it would cross over to my side and come back along there. Before it did I withdrew several yards inside my room to let it go safely by. I didn't want him to think I was sitting there prying into his affairs. There was still enough blue nightshade in my room to keep my slight withdrawal from catching his eyes.

When I returned to my original position a moment or two later he was gone. He had raised two more of the shades. The bedroom one was still down. I wondered vaguely why he had given that peculiar comprehensive semicircular stare at all the rear windows around him. There wasn't anyone at any of them at such an hour. It wasn't important, of course. It was just a little oddity, it failed to blend in with his being worried or disturbed about his wife.

When you're worried or disturbed, that's an internal preoccupation, you stare vacantly at nothing at all. When you stare around you in a great sweeping arc at windows, that betrays external preoccupation, outward interest. One doesn't quite jibe with the other. To call such a discrepancy trifling is to add to its importance. Only someone like me, stewing in a vacuum of total idleness, would have noticed at all.

The flat remained lifeless after that as far as could be judged by its windows. He must have either gone out or gone to bed himself. Three of the shades remained at normal height, the one masking the bedroom remained down. Sam, my day houseman, came in not long after with my eggs and morning paper and I had that to kill time with for a while. I stopped thinking about other people's windows and staring at them.

The sun slanted down on one side of the hollow oblong all morning long, then it shifted over to the other side for the afternoon. Then it started to slip off both alike and it was evening again – another day gone.

The lights started to come on around the quadrangle. Here and there a wall played back, like a sounding board, a snatch of radio program that was coming in too loud. If you listened carefully you could hear an occasional clink of dishes mixed in, faint, far off. The chain of little habits that were their lives unreeled themselves.

They were all bound in them tighter than the tightest straitjacket any jailer ever devised, though they all thought themselves free. The jitterbugs made their nightly dash for the great open spaces, forgot their lights, he came careening back, thumbed them out and their place was dark until the early morning hours. The woman put her child to bed, leaned mournfully over its cot, then sat down with heavy despair to redden her mouth.

In the fourth-floor flat at right angles to the long interior "street" the three shades had remained up and the fourth shade had remained at full length all day long. I hadn't been conscious of that because I hadn't particularly been looking at it or thinking of it until now. My eyes may have rested on those windows at times during the day but my thoughts had been elsewhere at those times.

It was only when a light suddenly went up in the end room behind one of the raised shades, which was their kitchen, that I realized that the shades had been untouched like that all day. That also brought something else to my mind that hadn't been in it until now. I hadn't seen the woman all day. I hadn't seen any sign of life within those windows until now.

He'd come in from outside. The entrance was at the opposite side of their kitchen, away from the window. He'd left his hat on so I knew he'd just come in from the outside.

He didn't remove his hat. As though there was no one there to remove it for any more. Instead he pushed it farther to the back of his head by pronging a hand to the roots of his hair. That gesture didn't denote removal of perspiration, I knew. To do that a person makes a sidewise sweep – this was up over his forehead. It indicated some sort of harassment or uncertainty. Besides, if he'd been suffering from excess warmth, the first thing he would have done would be to take off his hat altogether.

She didn't come out to greet him. The first link, of the so-strong chain of habit, of custom, that binds us all, had snapped wide open.

She must be so ill she had remained in bed, in the room behind the lowered shade, all day. I watched. He remained where he was, two rooms away from there. Expectancy became surprise, surprise incomprehension. Funny, I thought, that he doesn't go in to her. Or at least go as far as the doorway, look in to see how she is.

Maybe she was asleep and he didn't want to disturb her. Then immediately – but how can he know for sure she's asleep without at least looking in at her? He just came in himself.

He came forward and stood there by the window as he had at dawn. Sam had carried out my tray quite some time before and my lights were out. I held my ground. I knew he couldn't see me within the darkness of the bay window. He stood there motionless for several minutes. And now his attitude was the proper one for inner preoccupation. He stood there looking downward at nothing, lost in thought.

He's worried about her, I said to myself, as any man would be. It's the most natural thing in the world. Funny, though, he should leave her in the dark like that without going near her. If he's worried, then why didn't he at least look in on her on returning? Here was another of those trivial discrepancies between inward motivation and outward indication. And just as I was thinking that, the original one that I had noted at daybreak repeated itself.

His head went up with renewed alertness and I could see it start to give that slow circular sweep of interrogation around the panorama of rearward windows again. True, the light was behind him this time, but there was enough of it falling on him to show me the microscopic but continuous shift of direction his head made in the process. I remained carefully immobile until the distant glance had passed me safely by. Motion attracts.

Why is he so interested in other people's windows, I wondered detachedly and of course an effective brake to dwelling on that thought too lingeringly clamped down almost at once. *Look who's talking. What about you yourself?*

An important difference escaped me. I wasn't worried about anything. He presumably was.

Down came the shades again. The lights stayed on behind their beige opaqueness. But behind the one that had remained down all along the room remained dark.

Time went by. Hard to say how much – a quarter of an hour, twenty minutes. A cricket chirped in one of the backyards. Sam came in to see if I wanted anything before he went home for the night. I told him no I didn't – it was all right, run along. He stood there for a minute, head down. Then I saw him shake it slightly, as if at something he didn't like. "What's the matter?" I asked.

"You know what that means? My old mammy told it to me, and she never told me a lie in her life. I never once seen it to miss either."

"What, the cricket?"

"Any time you hear one of them things, that's a sign of death – some place close around."

I swept the back of my hand at him. "Well, it isn't in here so don't let it worry you."

He went out, muttering stubbornly, "It's somewhere close by though. Somewhere not very far off. Got to be there."

The door closed after him and I stayed there alone in the dark.

It was a stifling night, much closer than the one before. I could hardly get a breath of air even by the open window at which I sat. I wondered how he – that unknown over there – could stand it behind those drawn shades.

Then suddenly, just as idle speculation about this whole matter was about to alight on some fixed point in my mind, crystallize into something like suspicion, up came the shades again and off it flitted, as formless as ever and without having had a chance to come to rest on anything.

He was in the middle windows, the living-room. He'd taken off his coat and shirt, was bare-armed in his undershirt. He hadn't been able to stand it himself, I guess – the sultriness.

I couldn't make out what he was doing at first. He seemed to be busy in a perpendicular, up-and-down way rather than lengthwise. He remained in one place, but he kept dipping down out of sight and then straightening up into view again, at irregular intervals. It was almost like some sort of calisthenic exercise except that the dips and rises weren't evenly timed enough for that. Sometimes he'd stay down a long time, sometimes he'd bob right up again, sometimes he'd go down two or three times in rapid succession.

There was some sort of a wide-spread black V railing him off from the window. Whatever it was, there was just a sliver of it showing above the upward inclination to which the window-sill deflected my line of vision. All it did was strike off the bottom of his undershirt to the extent of a sixteenth of an inch maybe. But I hadn't seen it there at other times, and I couldn't tell what it was.

Suddenly he left it for the first time since the shades had gone up, came out around it to the outside, stooped down into another part of the room, and straightened again with an armful of what looked like varicoloured pennants at the distance at which I was. He went back behind the V and allowed them to fall across the top of it for a moment, and stay that way. He made one of his dips down out of sight and stayed that way a good while.

The "pennants" slung across the V kept changing color right in front of my eyes. I have very good sight. One moment they were white, the next red, the next blue.

Then I got it. They were a woman's dresses and he was pulling them down to him one by one, taking the topmost one each time. Suddenly they were all gone, the V was black and bare again and his torso had reappeared. I knew what it was now and what he was doing. The dresses had told me. He confirmed it for me. He spread his arms to the ends of the V, I could see him heave and hitch as if exerting pressure, and suddenly the V had folded up, become a cubed wedge. Then he made rolling motions with his whole upper body and the wedge disappeared off to one side.

He'd been packing a trunk, packing his wife's things into a large upright trunk.

He reappeared at the kitchen window presently, stood still for a moment. I saw him draw his arm across his forehead, not once but several times, and then whip the end of it off into space. Sure, it was hot work for such a night. Then he reached up along the wall and took something down. Since it was the kitchen he was in my imagination had to supply a cabinet and a bottle.

I could see the two or three quick passes his hand made to his mouth after that. I said to myself tolerantly, That's what nine men out of ten would do after packing a trunk – take a good stiff drink. And if the tenth didn't, it would only be because he didn't have any liquor.

Then he came closer to the window again and standing edgewise to the side of it, so that only a thin paring of his head and shoulder showed, peered watchfully out into the dark quadrilateral along the line of windows, most of them unlighted by now once more. He always started on the left-hand side, the side opposite mine, and made his circuit of inspection from there on around.

That was the second time in one evening I'd seen him do that. And once at daybreak, made three times altogether. I smiled mentally. You'd almost think he felt guilty about something. It was probably nothing, just an odd little habit, a quirk he didn't know he had himself. I had them, everyone does.

He withdrew into the room again and it blacked out. His figure passed into the one that was still lighted next to it, the living-room. That blacked next. It didn't surprise me that the third room, the bedroom with the drawn shade, didn't light up on his entering there. He wouldn't want to disturb her, of course – particularly if she was going away tomorrow for her health, as his packing of her trunk showed. She needed all the rest she could get, before making the trip. Simple enough for him to slip into bed in the dark.

It did surprise me, though, when a match-flare winked sometime later, to have it still come from the darkened living-room. He must be lying down in there, trying to sleep on a sofa or something for the night. He hadn't gone near the bedroom at all, was staying out of it altogether. That puzzled me frankly. That was carrying solicitude almost too far.

Ten minutes or so later there was another match-wink, still from that same living-room window. He couldn't sleep.

The night brooded down on both of us alike, the curiosity-monger in the bay window, the chain-smoker in the fourth-floor flat, without giving any answer. The only sound was that interminable cricket.

II

I was back at the window again with the first sun of morning. Not because of him. My mattress was like a bed of hot coals. Sam found me there when he came in to get things ready for me.

"You're going to be a wreck, Mr Jeff," was all he said.

For awhile there was no sign of life over there. Then suddenly I saw his head bob up from somewhere down out of sight in the living-room, so I knew I'd been right, he'd spent the night on a sofa or easy chair in there. Now, of course, he'd look in at her, to see how she was, find out if she felt any better. That was only common ordinary humanity. He hadn't been near her, so far as I could make out, since two nights before.

He didn't. He dressed, and he went in the opposite direction, into the kitchen, and wolfed something in there, standing up and using both hands. Then he suddenly turned and moved offside, in the direction in which I knew the flat-entrance to be, as if he had just heard some summons, like the doorbell.

Sure enough, in a moment he came back and there were two men with him in leather aprons. Expressmen. I saw him standing by while they laboriously maneuvered that cubed black wedge out between them in the direction they'd just come from. He did more than just stand by. He practically hovered over them, kept shifting from side to side, he was so anxious to see that it was done right.

Then he came back alone and I saw him swipe his arm across his head, as though it was he, not they, who was all heated up from the effort.

So he was forwarding her trunk, to wherever it was she was going. That was all.

He reached up along the wall again and took something down. He was taking another drink. Two. Three. I said to myself, a little at a loss, yes, but he hasn't just packed a trunk this time. That trunk has been standing packed and ready since last night. Where does the hard work come in? The sweat and the need for a bracer?

Now at last, after all those hours, he finally did go in to her. I saw his form pass through the living-room and go beyond into the bedroom. Up went the shade that had been down all this time. Then he turned his head and looked around behind him. In a certain way, a way that was unmistakable, even from where I was. Not in one certain direction as one looks at a person. But from side to side and up and down and all around, as one looks at – *an empty room.*

He stepped back, bent a little, gave a fling of his arms and an unoccupied mattress and bedding upended over the foot of a bed, stayed that way, emptily curved. A second one followed a moment later.

She wasn't in there.

They use the expression "delayed action." I found out then what is meant. For two days a sort of formless uneasiness, a disembodied suspicion, I don't know what to call it, had been flitting and volplaning around in my mind like an insect looking for a landing place.

More than once, just as it had been ready to settle, some slight reassuring thing, such as the raising of the shades after they had been down unnaturally long, had been enough to keep it winging aimlessly, prevent it from staying still long enough for me to recognise it.

The point of contact had been there all along, waiting to receive it. Now, for some reason, within a split second after he tossed over the empty mattress, it landed – *zoom!* And the point of contact expanded – or exploded, whatever you care to call it – into a certainty of murder.

In other words the rational part of my mind was far behind the instinctive subconscious part. Delayed action. Now the one had caught up to the other. The thought-message that sparked from the synchronisation was, *He's done something to her!*

I looked down and my hand was bunching the goods over my kneecap, it was knotted so tight. I forced it to open. I said to my self, steadyingly, *Now wait a minute, be careful, go slow. You've seen nothing. You know nothing. You only have the negative proof that you don't see her any more.*

Sam was standing there, looking over at me from the pantry way. He said accusingly, "You ain't touched a thing. And your face looks like a sheet."

It felt like one. It had that needling feeling, when the blood has left it involuntarily. It was more to get him out of the way and give myself some elbow room for undisturbed thinking than anything else, that I said, "Sam, what's the street address of that building down there? Don't stick your head too far out and gape at it."

"Somep'n or other Benedict Avenue." He scratched his neck helpfully.

"I know that. Chase around the corner a minute and get me the exact number on it, will you?"

"Why you want to know that for?" he asked as he turned to go.

"None of your business," I said with the good-natured firmness that was all that was necessary to take care of that once and for all. I called after him just as he was closing the door, "And while you're about it step into the entrance and see if you can tell from the mailboxes who has the fourth-floor rear. Don't get me the wrong one. And try not to let anyone catch you at it."

He went out, mumbling something that sounded like, "When a man ain't got nothing to do but just sit all day he sure can think up the blamest things –" The door closed and I settled down to some good constructive thinking

I decided to compute what I had to go on. 1. The lights were on all night the first night. 2. He came in later than usual the second night. 3. He left his hat on. 4. She didn't come out to greet him – she hadn't appeared since the evening before the lights were on all night. 5. He took a drink after he finished packing her trunk. But he took three stiff drinks the next morning, immediately after her trunk went out. 6. He was inwardly disturbed and worried. Yet superimposed upon this was an unnatural external concern about the surrounding rear windows that was off-key. 7. He slept in the living-room, didn't go near the bedroom, during the night before the departure of the trunk.

Very well. If she had been ill that first night and he had sent her away for health, that automatically cancelled-out points 1,2,3,4. It left points 5 and 6 totally unimportant and unincriminating. But when it came up against 7 it hit a stumbling-block.

If she went away immediately after being ill that first night, why didn't he want to sleep in their bedroom *last night*? Sentiment? Hardly. Two perfectly good beds in one room, only a sofa or uncomfortable easy chair in the other. Why should he stay out of there, if she was already gone? Just because he missed her, was lonely? A grown man doesn't act that way. All right, then she was still in there.

Sam came back parenthetically at this point and said, "That house is Number five twenty-five Benedict Avenue. The fourth-floor rear, it got the name of Mr and Mrs Lars Thorwold up."

"Sh-h," I silenced and motioned him backhand out of my ken.

"First he want it, then he don't," he grumbled philosophically, and retired to his duties.

I went ahead digging at it. But if she was still in there, in that bedroom last night, then she couldn't have gone away to the country, because I never saw her leave today. She could have left without my seeing her in the early hours of yesterday morning. I'd missed a few hours, been asleep. But this morning I had been up before he was himself, I only saw his head rear up from that sofa after I'd been at the window for some time.

To go at all, she would have had to go yesterday morning. Then why had he left the bedroom shade down, left the mattresses undisturbed, until today? Above all, why had he stayed out of that room last night? That was evidence that she hadn't gone, was still in there. Then today, immediately after the trunk had been dispatched, he went in, pulled up the shade, tossed over the mattresses and showed that she hadn't been in there. The thing was like a crazy spiral.

No, it wasn't either. *Immediately after the trunk had been dispatched he had–*

The trunk.

That did it.

I looked around to make sure the door was safely closed between Sam and me. My hand hovered uncertainly over the telephone dial a minute. Boyne, he'd be the one to tell about it. He was on Homicide. He had been, anyway, when I'd last seen him. I didn't want to get a flock of strange dicks and cops into my hair. I didn't want to be involved any more than I had to. Or at all, if possible.

They switched my call to the right place after a couple of wrong tries and I got him finally.

"Look, Boyne? This is Hal Jeffries –"

"Well, where've you been the last sixty-two years?" he started to enthuse.

"We can take that up later. What I want you to do now is, take down a name and address. Ready? Lars Thorwald. Five twenty-five Benedict Avenue. Fourth-floor rear. Got it?"

"Fourth-floor rear. Got it. What's it for?"

"Investigation. I've got a firm belief you'll uncover a murder there if you start digging at it. Don't call on me for anything more than that – just a conviction. There's been a man and wife living there until now. Now there's just the man. Her trunk went out early this morning. If you can find someone who saw *her* leave herself –"

Marshalled aloud like that and conveyed to somebody else, a lieutenant of detectives above all, it did sound flimsy, even to me. He said hesitantly, "Well, but –" Then he accepted it as was. Because I was the source. I even left my window out of it completely. I could do that with him and get away with it because he'd known me years, he didn't question my reliability. I didn't want my room all cluttered up with dicks and cops taking turns nosing out of the window in this hot weather. Let them tackle it from the front.

"Well, we'll see what we see," he said. "I'll keep you posted."

I hung up and sat back to watch and wait events. I had a grandstand seat. Or rather a grandstand seat in reverse. I could only see from behind the scenes but not from the front. I couldn't watch Boyne go to work. I could only see the results when and if there were any.

Nothing happened for the next few hours. The police work that I knew must be going on was as invisible as police work should be. The figure in the fourth-floor windows remained in sight, alone and undisturbed. He didn't go out. He was restless, roamed from room to room without staying in one place very long but he stayed in. Once I saw him eating again – sitting down this time – and once he shaved and once even tried to read the paper but he didn't stay with it long.

Little unseen wheels were in motion around him. Small and harmless as yet, preliminaries. If he knew, I wondered to myself would he remain there quiescent like that, or would he try to bolt out and flee? That mightn't depend so much upon his guilt as upon his sense of immunity, his feeling that he could outwit them. Of his guilt I myself was already convinced, or I wouldn't have taken the step I had.

At three my phone rang. Boyne calling back. "Jeffries?

Well, I don't know. Can't you give me a little more than just a bald statement like that?"

"Why?" I fenced. "Why do I have to?"

"I've had a man over there making inquiries. I've just had his report. The building superintendent and several of the neighbours all agree she left for the country, to try and regain her health, early yesterday morning."

"Wait a minute. Did any of them *see* her leave, according to your man?" I asked.

"No."

"Then all you've got is a second-hand version of an unsupported statement by him. Not an eyewitness-account."

"He was met returning from the depot, after he'd bought her ticket and seen her off on the train."

"That's still an unsupported statement, once removed."

"I've sent a man down there to the station to try and check with the ticket agent if possible. After all, he should have been fairly conspicuous at that early hour. And we're keeping him under observation, of course, in the meantime, watching all his movements. The first chance we get we're going to jump in and search the place."

I had a feeling that they wouldn't find anything even if they did.

"Don't expect anything more from me. I've dropped it in your lap. I've given you all I have to give. A name, an address, and an opinion."

"Yes, and I've always valued your opinion highly before now, Jeff —"

"But now you don't, that it?"

"Not at all. The thing is we haven't turned up anything that seems to bear out your impression so far."

"You haven't got very far along, so far."

He went back to his previous cliche. "Well, we'll see what we see. Let you know later."

Another hour or so went by and sunset came on. I saw him start to get ready to go out. He put on his hat, put his hand in his pocket and stood still looking at it for a minute. Counting change, I guess. It gave me a peculiar sense of suppressed excitement, knowing they were going to come in the minute he left. I thought grimly, as I saw him take a last look around, *If you've got anything to hide, brother, now's the time to hide it*.

He left. A breath-holding interval of misleading emptiness descended on the flat. A three-alarm fire couldn't have pulled my eyes off those windows. Suddenly the door by which he had just left parted slightly and two men insinuated themselves, one behind the other. There they were now. They closed it behind them, separated at once and got busy.

One took the bedroom, one the kitchen, and they started to work their way toward one another again from those extremes of the flat. They were thorough. I could see them going over everything from top to bottom. They took the living-room together. One cased one side, the other man the other.

They'd already finished before the warning caught them. I could tell that by the way they straightened up and stood facing one another frustratedly for a minute. Then both their heads turned sharply, as at a tip-off by doorbell that he was coming back. They got out fast.

I wasn't unduly disheartened, I'd expected that. My own feeling all along had been that they wouldn't find anything incriminating around. The trunk had gone.

He came in with a mountainous brown-paper bag sitting in the curve of one arm. I watched him closely to see if he'd discover that someone had been there in his absence. Apparent he didn't. They'd been adroit about it.

He stayed in the rest of the night. Sat tight, safe and sound. He did some desultory drinking. I could see him sitting there by the window and his hand would hoist every once in awhile but not to excess. Apparently everything was under control, the tension had eased now that – the trunk was out.

Watching him across the night I speculated, *Why doesn't he get out? If I'm right about him, and I am, why does he stick around – after it?* That brought its own answer: *Because he doesn't know anyone's on to him yet. He doesn't think there's any hurry. To go too soon, right after she has, would be more dangerous than to stay awhile.*

III

The night wore on. I sat there waiting for Boyne's call. It came later than I thought it would. I picked the phone up in the dark. He was getting ready to go to bed over there now. He'd risen from where he'd been sitting drinking in the kitchen and put the light out. He went into the living-room, lit that. He started to pull his shirt tail up out of his belt. Boyne's voice was in my ear as my eyes were on him over there. Three-cornered arrangement.

"Hello, Jeff? Listen, absolutely nothing. We searched the place while he was out –"

"I know you did, I saw it," I nearly said and checked myself in time.

"– and didn't turn up a thing But –" He stopped as though this was going to be important. I waited impatiently for him to go ahead.

"Downstairs in his letterbox we found a postcard waiting for him. We fished it up out of the slot with bent pins –"

"And?"

"And it was from his wife, written only yesterday from some farm up-country. Here's the message we copied – 'Arrived okey. Already feeling a little better. Love, Anna.' "

I said, faintly but stubbornly, "You say written only yesterday. Have you proof of that? What was the post-mark-date on it?"

He made a disgusted sound down in his tonsils. At me, not it. "The postmark was blurred. A corner of it got wet and the ink smudged."

"All of it blurred?"

"The year-date," he admitted. "The hour and the month came out okay. August. And seven thirty p.m., it was mailed at."

This time I made the disgusted sound, in my larynx. "August, seven thirty p.m. – nineteen thirty-seven or thirty-nine or forty. You have no proof how it got into that mailbox, whether it came from a letter-carrier's pouch or from the back of some bureau-drawer!"

"Give up, Jeff," he said. "There's such a thing as going too far."

I don't know what I would have said. That is, if I hadn't happened to have my eyes on the Thorwald flat living-room windows just then. Probably very little. The postcard *had* shaken me, whether I admitted it or not. But I was looking over there. The light had gone out as soon as he'd taken his shirt off. But the bedroom didn't light up. A match-flare winked from the living-room, low down, as from an easy chair or sofa. With two unused beds in the bedroom he was *still staying out of there.*

"Boyne," I said in a glassy voice. "I don't care what postcards from the other world you've turned up. I say that man has done away with his wife! Trace that trunk he shipped out. Open it up when you've located it – and I think you'll find her!"

And I hung up without waiting to hear what he was going to do about it. He didn't ring back, so I suspected he was going to give my suggestion a spin after all, in spite of his loudly proclaimed scepticism.

I stayed there by the window all night, keeping a sort of death-watch. There were two more match-flares after the first at about half-hour intervals. Nothing more after that. So possibly he was asleep over there. Possibly not. I had to sleep sometime myself and I finally succumbed in the flaming light of the early sun. Anything that he was going to do he would have done under cover of darkness and not waited for broad daylight. There wouldn't be anything much to watch for awhile now. And what was there that he needed to do any more, anyway? Nothing, just sit tight and let a little disarming time slip by.

It seemed like five minutes later that Sam came over and touched me but it was already high noon. I said irritably, "Didn't you lamp that note I pinned up, for you to let me sleep?"

He said, "Yeah, but it's your old friend Inspector Boyne. I figured you'd sure want to –"

It was a personal visit this time. Boyne came into the

room behind him without waiting and without much cordiality.

I said to get rid of Sam, "Go inside and boil a couple of eggs."

Boyne began in a galvanized-iron voice, "Jeff, what do you mean by doing anything like this to me? I've made a fool of myself thanks to you. Sending my men out right and left on wild-goose chases. Thank God, I didn't put my foot in it any worse than I did and have this guy picked up and brought in for questioning."

"Oh, then you don't think that's necessary?" I suggested dryly.

The look he gave me took care of that. "I'm not alone in the department, you know. There are men over me I'm accountable to for my actions. That looks great don't it, sending one of my fellows one-half-a-day's train ride up into the sticks to some God-forsaken whistle-stop or other at departmental expense –"

"Then you located the trunk?"

"We traced it through the express agency," he said flatly.

"And you opened it?"

"We did better than that. He got in touch with the various farm-houses in the immediate locality and Mrs Thorwald came down to the junction in a produce-truck from one of them and opened it for him herself with her own keys!"

Very few men have ever got a look from an old friend such as I got from him. At the door he said, stiff as a rifle-barrel, "Just let's forget all about it, shall we? That's about the kindest thing either one of us can do for the other. You're not yourself and I'm out a little of my own pocket-money, time and temper. Let's let it go at that. If you want to telephone me in future I'll be glad to give you my home number."

The door went *whopp!* behind him.

For about ten minutes after he stormed out my numbed mind was in a sort of straitjacket. Then it started to wriggle its way free. *The hell with the police. I can't prove it to them, maybe but I can prove it to myself, one way or the other, once and for all. Either I'm wrong or I'm right. He's got his armour on against them. But his back is naked and unprotected against me.*

I called Sam in. "Whatever became of that spyglass we used to have when we were bumming around on that cabin-cruiser that season?"

He found it someplace downstairs and came in with it, blowing on it and rubbing it along his sleeve. I let it lie idle in my lap first. I took a piece of paper and a pencil and wrote six words on it – *What have you done with her?*

I sealed it in an envelope and left the envelope blank. I said to Sam, "Now here's what I want you to do and I want you to be slick about it. You take this, go in that building five twenty-five, climb the stairs to the fourth-floor rear and ease it under the door. You're fast, at least you used to be. Let's see if you're fast enough to keep from being caught at it. Then when you get safely down again, give the outside doorbell a little poke to attract attention."

His mouth started to open.

"And don't ask me any questions, you understand? I'm not fooling."

He went, and I got the spyglass ready.

I got him in the right focus after a minute or two. A face leaped up, and I was really seeing him for the first time. Dark-haired but unmistakably Scandinavian ancestry. Looked like a sinewy customer although he didn't run to much bulk.

About five minutes went by. His head turned sharply profilewards. That was the bell-poke right there. The note must be in already.

He gave me the back of his head as he went back toward the flat door. The lens could follow him all the way to the rear, where my unaided eyes hadn't been able to before.

He opened the door first, missed seeing it, looked out on a level. He closed it. Then he dipped, straightened up. He had it. I could see him turning it this way and that in his hands.

He shifted in, away from the door, nearer the window. He thought danger lay near the door, safety away from it. He didn't know it was the other way around, the deeper into his own rooms he retreated the greater the danger.

He'd torn it open, he was reading it. God, how I watched his expression. My eyes clung to it like leeches. There was a sudden widening, a pulling – the whole skin of his face seemed to stretch back behind the ears, narrowing his eyes to Mongoloids. Shock. Panic. His hand pushed out and found the wall and he braced himself with it. Then he went back toward the door.

I could see him creeping up on it, stalking it as though it were something alive. He opened it so slenderly you couldn't see it at all, peered fearfully through the crack. Then he closed it and came back, zig-zag, off-balance from sheer reflex dismay. He toppled into a chair and snatched up a drink. Out of the bottle-neck itself this time. And even while he was holding it to his lips his head was turned looking over his shoulder at the door that had suddenly thrown his secret in his face. I put the glass down.

Guilty! Guilty as all hell and the police be damned!

My hand started toward the phone, came back again. What was the use? They wouldn't listen now any more than they had before. "You should have seen his face, etc." And I could hear Boyne's answer. "Anyone gets a jolt from an anonymous letter, true or false. You would yourself." They had a real live Mrs Thorwald to show me – or thought they had. I'd have to show them the dead one to prove that they both weren't one and the same. I, from my window, had to show them a body.

Well, he'd have to show me first.

It took hours before I got it. I kept pegging away at it, pegging away at it, while the afternoon wore away. Meanwhile he was pacing back and forth there like a caged panther. Two minds with but one thought, turned inside-out in my case. How to keep it hidden, how to see it wasn't kept hidden.

I was afraid he might try to light out but if he intended doing that he was going to wait until after dark, apparently, so I had a little time yet. Possibly he didn't want to himself, unless he was driven to it – still felt that it was more dangerous than to stay.

The customary sights and sounds around me went on unnoticed while the main stream of my thoughts pounded like a torrent against that one obstacle stubbornly damming them up – how to get him to give the location away to me so that I could give it away in turn to the police.

I was dimly conscious, I remember, of the landlord or somebody bringing in a prospective tenant to look at the sixth-floor apartment, the one that had already been finished. This was two over Thorwald's. They were still at work on the in-between one. At one point an odd little bit of synchronization, completely accidental of course, cropped up. Landlord and tenant both happened to be near the living-room windows on the sixth at the same moment that Thorwald was near those on the fourth.

Both parties moved onwards simultaneously into the kitchen from there and, passing the blind spot of the wall, appeared next at the kitchen windows. It was uncanny, they were almost like precision-strollers or puppets manipulated on one and the same string. It probably wouldn't have happened again just like that in another fifty years. Immediately afterwards they digressed, never to repeat themselves again.

The thing was, something about it had distrubed me. There had been some slight flaw or hitch to mar its smoothness. I tried for a moment or two to figure out what it had been and couldn't. The landlord and tenant had gone now and only Thorwald was in sight. My unaided memory wasn't enough to recapture it for me. My eyesight might have if it had been repeated but it wasn't.

It sank into my subconscious, to ferment there like yeast while. I went back to the main problem at hand.

I got it finally. It was well after dark and I finally hit on a way. It mightn't work, it was cumbersome and roundabout, but it was the only way I could think of. An alarmed turn of the head, a quick precautionary step in one certain direction, was all I needed. And to get this brief, flickering, transitory give-away, I needed two phone calls and an absence of about half an hour on his part between them.

I leafed a directory by match-light until I'd found what I wanted:

Thorwald, Lars. 525 Benedict. Swansea 52114.

I blew out the match, picked up the phone in the dark. It was like television. I could see to the other end of my call, only not along the wire but by a direct channel of vision from window to window.

He said, "Hullo?" gruffly.

I thought, *How strange this is I've been accusing him of murder for three days straight and only now I'm hearing his voice for the first time.*

I didn't try to diguise my own voice. After all, he'd never see me and I'd never see him. I said, "You got my note?"

He said guardedly, "Who is this?"

"Just somebody who happens to know."

He said craftily, "Know what?"

"Know what you know. You and I, we're the only ones."

He controlled himself well. I didn't hear a sound. But he didn't know he was open another way too. I had the glass balanced there at proper height on two large books on the sill. Through the window I saw him pull open the collar of his shirt as though its stricture was intolerable. Then he backed his hand over his eyes like you do when there's a light blinding you.

His voice came back firm. "I don't know what you're talking about."

"Business, that's what I'm talking about. It should be worth something to me, shouldn't it? To keep it from going any further." I wanted to keep him from catching on that it was the windows. I still needed them, I needed them now more than ever. "You weren't very careful about your door the other night. Or maybe the draft swung it a little open."

That hit him where he lived. Even the stomach-heave reached me over the wire. "You didn't see anything. There wasn't anything to see."

"That's up to you. Why should I go to the police?" I coughed a little. "If it would pay me not to."

"Oh," he said. And there was relief of a sort in it. "D'you want to – see me? Is that it?"

"That would be the best way, wouldn't it? How much can you bring with you for now?"

"I've only got about seventy dollars around here."

"All right, then we can arrange the rest for later. Do you know where Lakeside Park is? I'm near there now. Suppose we make it there." That was about thirty minutes away. Fifteen there and fifteen back. "There's a little pavilion as you go in."

"How many of you are there?" he asked cautiously.

"Just me. It pays to keep things to yourself. That way you don't have to divvy up."

He seemed to like that too. "I'll take a run out," he said, "just to see what it's all about."

I watched him more closely than ever, after he'd hung up. He flitted straight through to the end room, the bedroom, that he didn't go near any more. He disappeared into a clothes-closet in there, stayed a minute, came out again. He must have taken something out of a hidden cranny or niche in there that even the dicks had missed. I could tell by the piston like motion of his hand, just before it disappeared inside his coat, what it was. A gun.

It's a good thing, I thought, I'm not out there in Lakeside Park, waiting for my seventy dollars.

The place blacked and he was on his way to the Park.

I called Sam in. "I want you to do something for me that's a little risky. In fact, damn risky. You might break a leg or you might get shot or you might even get pinched. We've been together ten years and I wouldn't ask you anything like that if I could do it myself. But I can't and it's got to be done." Then I told him, "Go out the back way, cross the backyard fences and see if you can get into that fourth-floor flat up the fire escape. He's left one of the windows a little down from the top."

"What do you want me to look for?"

"Nothing." The police had been there already, so what was the good of that? "There are three rooms over there. I want you to disturb everything just a little bit in all three, to show someone's been in there. Turn up the edge of each rug a little, shift every chair and table around a little, leave the closet doors standing out. Don't pass up a thing. Here, keep your eyes on this."

I took off my own wristwatch, strapped it on him. "You've got twenty-five minutes, starting from now. If you stay within those twenty-five minutes nothing will happen to you. When you see they're up don't wait any longer, get out and get out fast."

"Climb back down?"

"No." He wouldn't remember in his excitement, if he'd left the windows up or not. And I didn't want him to connect danger with the back of his place, but with the front. I wanted to keep my own window out of it. "Latch the window down tight, let yourself out the door and beat it out the front way."

"I'm just an easy mark for you," he said ruefully but he went.

He came out through our own basement door below me, and scrambled over the fences. If anyone had challenged him from one of the surrounding windows I was going to backstop for him, explain I'd sent him down to look for something. But no one did. He made it pretty good for anyone his age. He isn't so young any more. Even the fire escape backing the flat, which was drawn up short, he managed to contact by standing up on something. He got in, lit the light, looked over at me. I motioned him to go ahead and not weaken.

I watched him at it. There wasn't any way I could protect him now that he was in there. Even Thorwald would be within his rights in shooting him down – this was break and entry. I had to stay in back behind the scenes like I had been all along. I couldn't get out in front of him as a lookout and shield him. Even the dicks had had a lookout posted.

He must have been tense doing it. I was twice as tense watching him do it. The twenty-five minutes took fifty to go by. Finally he came over to the window, latched it fast. The lights went and he was out. He'd made it. I blew out a bellyful of breath that was twenty-five minutes in my lungs.

I heard him keying the street-door and when he came up I said warningly, "Leave the light out in here. Go and build yourself a great big two-story whiskey-punch. You're as close to white as you'll ever be."

Thorwald came back twenty-nine minutes after he'd left for Lakeside Park. A pretty slim margin to hang a man's life on. So now for the finale of the long-winded business, and here was hoping. I got my second phonecall in before he had time to notice anything amiss. It was tricky timing but I'd been sitting there with the receiver ready in my hand, dialling the number over and over, then killing it each time. He came in on the 2 of 52114, and I saved that much time. The ring started before his hand came away from the light switch.

This was the one that was going to tell the story.

"You were supposed to bring money, not a gun, that's why I didn't show up." I saw the jolt that threw into him. The window still had to stay out of it. "I saw you tap the inside of your coat, where you had it, as you came out on the street." Maybe he hadn't but he wouldn't remember by now whether he had or not. You usually do when you're packing a gun and aren't an habitual carrier.

"Too bad you had your trip out and back for nothing. I didn't waste my time while you were gone though. I know more now than I knew before." This was the important part. I had the glass up and I was practically fluoroscoping him. "I've found out where – it is. You know what I mean. I know now where you've got – it. I was there while you were out."

Not a word. Just quick breathing in my ear.

"Don't you believe me? Look around. Put the receiver down and take a look for yourself. I found it, all right."

He put it down, moved as far as the living-room entrance and touched off the lights. He just looked around him once in a sweeping, all-embracing stare that didn't come to a head on any one fixed point, didn't centre at all.

He was smiling grimly when he came back to the phone.

All he said softly and with malignant satisfaction was, "You're a liar."

Then I saw him lay the receiver down and take his hand off it. I hung up at my end.

The test had failed. And yet it hadn't. He hadn't given the location away as I'd hoped he would. And yet that, "You're a liar," was a tacit admission that it was there to be found, somewhere around him, somewhere on those premises. In such a good place that he didn't have a worry about it, didn't even have to look to make sure.

So there was a kind of sterile victory in my defeat. But it wasn't worth a damn to me.

He was standing there with his back to me and I couldn't see what he was doing. I knew the phone was somewhere in front of him but I thought he was just standing there pensive behind it. His head was slightly lowered, that was all. I'd hung up at my end. I didn't even see his elbow move. And if his index finger did I couldn't see it.

He stood like that a moment or two, then finally he moved aside. The lights were out over there. I lost him. He was careful not even to strike matches, like he sometimes did in the dark.

My mind no longer distracted by having him to look at, I turned to trying to recapture something else – that troublesome little hitch in synchronization that had occurred this afternoon, when the renting agent and he both moved simultaneously from one window to the next.

The closest I could get was this – it was like when you're looking at someone through a pane of imperfect glass, and a flaw in the glass distorts the symmetry of the reflected image for a second until it has gone on past that point. Yet that wouldn't do, that was not it. The windows had been open and there had been no glass between. And I hadn't been using the lens at the time.

My phone rang. Boyne, I supposed. It wouldn't be anyone else at this hour. Maybe, after reflecting on the way he'd jumped all over me – I said, "Hello," unguardedly in my own normal voice.

There wasn't any answer.

I said, "Hello? Hello? Hello?" I kept giving away samples of my voice.

There wasn't a sound from first to last.

I hung up finally. It was still dark over there, I noticed.

IV

Sam looked in to check out. He was a bit thick-tongued from his restorative drink. He said something about "Awri' if I go now?" I half-heard him. I was trying to figure out another way of trapping *him* over there into giving away the right spot, I motioned my consent absently.

He went a little unsteadily down the stairs to the ground-floor and after a delaying moment or two I heard the street-door close after him. Poor Sam, he wasn't much used to liquor.

I was left alone in the house, one chair the limit of my freedom of movement.

Suddenly a light went on over there again, just momentarily, to go right out again afterwards. He must have needed it for something, to locate something he had already been looking for and found he wasn't able to put his hands on readily without it. He found it, whatever it was, almost immediately and moved back at once to put the lights out again. As he turned to do so I saw him give a glance out the window. He didn't come to the window to do it, he just shot it out in passing.

Something about it struck me as different from any of the others I'd seen him give in all the time I'd been watching him. If you can qualify such an elusive thing as a glance, I would have termed it a glance with a purpose. It was certainly anything but vacant or random, it had a bright spark of fixity in it. It wasn't one of those precautionary sweeps I'd seen him give either. It hadn't started over on the other side and worked its way around to my side, the right. It had hit dead-centre at my bay-window for just a split second while it lasted, then was gone again. And the lights were gone. He was gone.

Sometimes your senses take things in without your mind translating them into their proper meaning. My eyes saw that look. My mind refused to smelter it properly. "It was meaningless," I thought. "An unintentional bull's-eye that just happened to hit square over here as he went toward the lights on his way out."

Delayed action. A wordless ring of the phone. To test a voice? A period of bated darkness following that, in which two could have played at the same game – stalking one another's window-squares, unseen. A last-moment flicker of the lights that was bad strategy but unavoidable. A parting glance, radio-active with malignant intention. All these things sank in without fusing. My eyes did their job, it was my mind that didn't – or at least took its time about it.

Seconds went by in packages of sixty. It was very still around the familiar quadrangle formed by the back of the houses. Sort of a breathless stillness. And then a sound came into it, starting up from nowhere, nothing. The unmistakable spaced clicking a cricket makes in the silence of the night. I thought of Sam's superstition about them, that he claimed had never failed to fulfill itself yet. If that was the case it looked bad for somebody in one of these slumbering houses around here –

Sam had been gone only about ten minutes. And now he was back again, he must have forgotten something. That drink was responsible. Maybe his hat or maybe even the key to his own quarters uptown. He knew I couldn't come down and let him in and he was trying to be quiet about it, thinking perhaps I'd dozed off.

All I could hear was this faint jiggling down at the lock of the front door. It was one of those old-fashioned stoop houses with an outer pair of storm doors that were allowed to swing free all night, then a small vestibule, and then the inner door, worked by a simple iron key. The liquor had made his hand a little unreliable although he'd had this difficulty once or twice before, even without it. A match would have helped him find the keyhole quicker but then Sam doesn't smoke. I knew he wasn't likely to have one on him.

The sound had stopped now. He must have given up, gone away again, decided to let whatever it was go until tomorrow. He hadn't got in, because I knew his noisy way of letting doors coast shut by themselves too well, and there hadn't been any sound of that sort, that loose slap he always made.

Then suddenly it exploded. Why at this particular moment I don't know. That was some mystery of the inner workings of my own mind. It flashed like waiting gunpowder which a spark has finally reached along a slow train. Drove all thoughts of Sam and the front door and this and that completely out of my head. It had been waiting there since midafternoon to-day and only now – More of that delayed action. Damn that delayed action.

The renting agent and Thorwald had both started even from the living-room window. An intervening gap of blind wall and both had reappeared at the kitchen window, still one above the other. But some sort of a hitch or flaw or jump had taken place right there that bothered me. The eye is a reliable surveyor. There wasn't anything the matter with their timing, it was with their parallel-ness, or whatever the word is. The hitch had been vertical, not horizontal. There had been an upward "jump".

Now I had it, now I knew. And it couldn't wait. It was too good. They wanted a body? Now I had one for them.

Sore or not Boyne would *have* to listen to me now. I didn't waste any time, I dialed his precinct-house then and there in the dark, working the slots in my lap by memory alone. They didn't make much noise going around, just a light click. Not even as distinct as that cricket out there –

"He went home long ago," the desk sergeant said.

This couldn't wait. "All right, give me his home phone number."

He took a minute, came back again. "Trafalgar," he said. Then nothing more.

"Well? Trafalgar what?" Not a sound.

"Hello? Hello?" I tapped it. "Operator, I've been cut off. Give me that party again." I couldn't get her either.

I hadn't been cut off. My wire had been cut. That had been too sudden, right in the middle of – And to be cut like that it would have to be done somewhere right here inside the house with me. Outside it went underground.

Delayed action. This time final, fatal, altogether too late. A voiceless ring of the phone. A direction-finder of a look from over there. "Sam" seemingly trying to get back in a while ago.

Sure, death was somewhere inside the house here with me. And I couldn't move, I couldn't get up out of this chair. Even if I had got through to Boyne just now it would have been too late. There wasn't time enough for one of those camera-finishes in this. I could have shouted out the window to that gallery of sleeping rear-window neighbors around me, I supposed. It would have brought them to the windows. It couldn't have brought them over here in time. By the time they had even figured which particular house it was coming from it would stop again, be over with. I didn't open my mouth. Not because I was brave but because it was so obviously useless.

He'd be up in a minute. He must be on the stairs now, although I couldn't hear him. Not even a creak. A creak would have been a relief, would have placed him. This was like being shut up in the dark with the silence of a gliding cobra.

There wasn't a weapon in the place with me. There were books there on the wall in the dark within reach. Me, who never read. The former owner's books. There was a bust of Rousseau or Montesquieu, I'd never been able to decide which, one of those gents with flowing manes, topping them. It was a monstrosity, bisque clay, but it too dated from before my occupancy.

I arched my middle upward from the chair-seat and

clawed desperately up at it. Twice my fingertips slipped off
it, then at the third raking I got it to teeter and the fourth
brought it down into my lap, punching me down into the
chair. There was a steamer-rug under me. I didn't need it
around me in this weather, I'd been using it to soften the seat
of the chair.

I tugged it out from under and mantled it around me like
an Indian brave's blanket. Then I squirmed far down in the
chair, let my head and one shoulder dangle out over the arm,
on the side next to the wall. I hoisted the bust to my other,
upward shoulder, balanced it there precariously for a second
head, blanket tucked around its ears. From the back, in the
dark, it would look – I hoped.

I proceeded to breathe adenoidally, like someone in heavy
upright sleep. It wasn't hard. My own breath was coming
nearly that laboured anyway, from tension.

He was good with knobs and hinges and things. I never
heard the door open and this one, unlike the one downstairs,
was right behind me. A little eddy of air puffed through the
dark at me. I could feel it because my scalp, the real one, was
all wet at the roots of the hair right then.

If it was going to be a knife or head-blow the dodge might
give me a second chance, that was the most I could hope for,
I knew. My arms and shoulders are hefty. I'd bring him
down on me in a bear-hug after the first slash or drive, and
break his neck or collarbone against me. If it was going to be
a gun he'd get me anyway in the end. A difference of a few
seconds. He had a gun, I knew, that he was going to use on
me in the open, over at Lakeside Park I was hoping that here,
indoors, in order to make his own escape more practicably –

Time was up.

The flash of the shot lit up the room for a second, it was so
dark. Or at least the corners of it, like flickering, weak
lightning. The bust bounced on my shoulder and disinte-
grated into chunks.

I thought he was jumping up and down on the floor for a
minute with frustrated rage. Then when I saw him dart by
me and lean over the window-sill to look for a way out the

sound transferred itself rearwards and downwards, became a
pummeling with hoof and hip at the street-door. The finish
after all. But he still could have killed me five times.

I flung my body down into the narrow crevice between
chair-arm and wall but my legs were still up and so was my
head and that one shoulder.

He whirled, fired at me so close that it was like looking a
sunrise in the face. I didn't feel it, so – it hadn't hit.

"You –" I heard him grunt to himself. I think it was the
last thing he said. The rest of his life was all action, not
verbal.

He flung over the sill on one arm and dropped into the
yard. Two-story drop. He made it because he missed the
cement, landed on the sod-strip in the middle. I jacked
myself up over the chair-arm and flung myself bodily forward at the window, nearly hitting it chin-first.

He went all right. When life depends on it you go. He took
the first fence, rolled over that bellywards. He went over the
second like a cat, hands and feet pointed together in a spring.
Then he was back in the rear yard of his own building. He
got up on something, just about like Sam had –

The rest was all footwork, with quick little corkscrew-
twists at each landing-stage. Sam had latched his windows
down when he was over there but *he'd* re-opened one of them
for ventilation on his return. His whole life depended now on
that casual, unthinking little act –

Second, third. He was up to his own windows. He'd made
it. Something went wrong. He veered out away from them in
another pretzel twist, flashed up toward the fifth the one
above. Something sparked in the darkness of one of his own
windows where he'd been just now and a shot thudded
heavily out around the quadrangle-enclosure like a big bass
drum.

He passed the fifth, the sixth, got up to the roof. He'd
made it a second time. Gee, he loved life! The guys in his
own windows couldn't get him, he was over them in a
straight line and there was too much fire escape interlacing
in the way.

I was too busy watching him to watch what was going on around me. Suddenly Boyne was next to me, sighting. I heard him mutter, "I almost hate to do this, he's got to fall so far."

He was balanced on the roof parapet up there with a star right over his head. An unlucky star. He stayed a minute too long, trying to kill before he was killed. Or maybe he was killed and knew it.

A shot cracked, high up against the sky, the window pane flew apart all over the two of us and one of the books snapped right behind me.

Boyne didn't say anything more about hating to do it. My face was pressing outward against his arm. The recoil of his elbow jarred my teeth. I blew a clearing through the smoke to watch him go.

It was pretty horrible. He took a minute to show anything, standing up there on the parapet. Then he let his gun go, as if to say, "I won't need this any more." Then he went after it. He missed the fire escape entirely, came all the way down on the outside. He landed so far out he hit one of the projecting planks, down there out of sight. It bounced his body up, like a springboard. Then it landed again – for good. And that was all.

I said to Boyne: "I got it. I got it finally. The fifth-floor flat, the one over his, that they're still working on. The cement kitchen-floor, raised above the level of the other rooms. They wanted to comply with the fire laws and also obtain a dropped living-room effect as cheaply as possible. Dig it up –"

He went right over then and there, down through the basement and over the fences, to save time. The electricity wasn't turned on yet in that one, they had to use their torches. It didn't take them long at that, once they'd got started. In about half an hour he came to the window and wigwagged over for my benefit. It meant yes.

He didn't come over until nearly eight in the morning, after they'd tidied up and taken them away. Both away, the hot dead and the cold dead. He said, "Jeff, I take it all back.

That damn fool that I sent up there about the trunk – well, it wasn't his fault, in a way. I'm to blame.

"He didn't have orders to check on the woman's description, only on the contents of the trunk. He came back and touched on it in a general way. I go home and I'm in bed already, and suddenly pop! into my brain – one of the tenants I questioned two whole days ago had given us a few details and they didn't tally with his on several important points. Talk about being slow to catch on!"

"I've had that all the way through this damn thing," I admitted ruefully. "I call it delayed action. It nearly killed me."

"I'm a police officer and you're not."

"That how you happened to shine at the right time?"

"Sure, we came over to pick him up for questioning. I left them planted there when we saw he wasn't in and came on over here by myself to square it up with you while we were waiting. How did you happen to hit on the cement floor?"

I told him about the freak synchronization. "The renting agent showed up taller at the kitchen window in proportion to Thorwald, than he had been a moment before when both were at the living-room windows together. It was no secret that they were putting in cement floors, topped by a cork composition, and raising them considerable. But it took on new meaning. Since the top floor one has been finished for some time, it had to be the fifth. Here's the way I have it lined up, just in theory. She's been in ill health for years and he's been out of work, and he got sick of that and of her both –"

"She'll be here later today, they're bringing her down under arrest."

"He probably insured her for all he could get and then started to poison her slowly, trying not to leave any trace. I imagine – and remember this is pure conjecture – she caught him at it that night the light was up all night. Caught on in some way or caught him in the act. He lost his head, and did the very thing he had wanted all along to avoid doing. Killed her by violence – strangulation or a blow. The rest had to be hastily improvised.

"He got a better break than he deserved at that. He thought of the apartment upstairs, went up and, looked around. They'd just finished laying the floor, the cement hadn't hardened yet and the materials were still around. He gouged a trough out of it just wide enough to take her body, put her in it, mixed fresh cement and recemented over her, possibly raising the general level of the flooring an inch or two so that she'd be safely covered. A permanent odourless coffin.

"Next day the workmen came back, laid down the cork surfacing on top of it without noticing anything. I suppose he'd used one of their own trowels to smooth it. Then he sent his accessory upstate fast, near where his wife had been several summers before but to a different farmhouse where she wouldn't be recognized, along with the trunk keys. Sent the trunk up after her and dropped himself an already-used postcard into his mailbox with the year-date blurred.

"In a week or two she would have probably committed 'suicide' up there as Mrs Anna Thorwald. Despondency due to ill health. Written him a farewell note and left her clothes beside some body of deep water. It was risky but they might have succeeded in collecting the insurance at that."

By nine Boyne and the rest had gone. I was still sitting there in the chair, too keyed up to sleep. Sam came in and said, "Here's Doc Preston."

He showed up rubbing his hands, in that way he has. "Guess we can take that cast off your leg now. You must be tired of sitting there all day doing nothing."

I just gave him a look.

FORBIDDEN FRUIT

Edgar Lustgarten

Adapted for:

SCOTLAND YARD

(BBC, 1955–1957)

Starring: Edgar Lustgarten,

Russell Napier & Ken Henry

Directed by Jack Greenwood

It was perhaps no surprise that the first popular crime series on British television should feature Scotland Yard. In 1954, the headline-making career of the great thief-taker Inspector Robert Fabian was adapted by BBC TV for a series entitled Fabian of the Yard – *with the commanding character actor Bruce Seton in the title role – and the thirty-minute, pre-filmed episodes quickly built up a large UK audience before being syndicated with similar success in the USA.* Fabian *was still on the air when the noted criminologist and author, Edgar*

Lustgarten, became the host of Scotland Yard *(also known as* Case Histories of Scotland Yard*), which fictionalized real cases from the Yard's huge files of robberies, blackmailings and murder. It featured as regular characters Inspector Duggan (Russell Napier) and Inspector Ross (Ken Henry). Arthur Mason who appeared as the gruff Sergeant Mason was something of a prototype for Sergeant Flint (Arthur Rigby) who in 1955 co-starred with Jack Warner in the classic Bobby-on-the-beat series* Dixon of Dock Green, *which has subsequently become one of the benchmarks for all police shows on television. (Hard on the heels of these series in 1956 came* Charlesworth *with the authoritarian Metropolitan police officer, Chief Detective Inspector Charlesworth, played initially by John Welsh and later by Wensley Pithey, which also ran for over two years.)*

The landmark show, Cases of Scotland Yard, *remembered for its many scenes of police cars, bells clattering, rushing from the Yard into the streets of London, was produced by Jack Greenwood, but the driving force behind the success was undoubtedly Edgar Lustgarten (1907–78) who combined a profound knowledge of crime with a gift of oratory which he had begun to develop while at Oxford University.*

Born in Manchester, the son of a prosperous lawyer, he naturally enough entered the law and graduated to the bar in 1932. Although he was soon running a very successful practice, Lustgarten was also keen to write and in the mid-Thirties began to contribute short stories to magazines and plays to radio. After working with the BBC in counter-propaganda during the Second World War, he started broadcasting on radio himself and made the transition just as easily into television when the BBC began transmitting once again in the late Forties. His book A Case to Answer *(1947), a novel about the sordid murder of a Soho prostitute, was a best-seller and led to a string of other novels and works of non-fiction all dealing with crime and criminals. He was a natural to front* Scotland Yard, *and such was his success at describing murders and mysteries, by making full use of his hooded eyes and sepulchral voice, that he became widely known by the epithet, "Mr Murder". Following the success of the* Scotland Yard *programme, he appeared in several more series with similar themes and titles like* Prisoner at the Bar, Accused in the Box, *and* Famous Trials. *"Forbidden Fruit", the story of a young man's infatuation with a beautiful model and its tragic outcome (written by Lustgarten in 1953), was daring for its time and serves as an excellent reminder of one of the men who helped to pioneer the crime series on British television . . .*

The very first moment he came in last night I guessed from his face exactly what he had to say. Only a half-wit could have missed it. He's not a bad old stick, quite soft-hearted in his way, but I'd swear he only wears that particular expression – as if he were nursing some secret sorrow of his own – in circumstances such as those that made him visit me.

I wouldn't admit to myself, though, that the look of him told me all. There are mental defenses one keeps manned to the last. I quickly thought up some other possible reasons for his coming: my mother was ill, or a message from friends, or pure humdrum routine. For a split second I even half kidded myself that he'd brought good news, that everything was okay. Then he turned his eyes towards me, and I let that idea drop.

"I'm sorry, Holt," he said.

"Yes," I said, fatuously.

I realize now I was trying hard to detach myself from the scene, to escape being emotionally involved in what would follow.

"I'm sorry, very sorry indeed," he said.

We had been playing dominoes when he arrived. I fixed my gaze on the double-blank, the last piece I had played.

"It's my duty," he said, and hesitated, "my unhappy duty –"

That got through all right. My defenses cracked on the instant, and I met reality.

I knew then for certain that a reprieve had been refused. I knew then that mortal power could do no more on my behalf. I knew then that the day after tomorrow I should hang.

It is only now, though, when those shocks have been in part absorbed, that I also realize there is no longer any reason why I should not tell, in these last hours of my life, the whole truth about Marian and me . . .

The first time I actually set eyes on Marian I had gone to her home as a reporter to get an interview. She had recently been voted Top Model of the Year by one of the countless panels that bestow suchlike distinctions, and it was reckoned she would rate a couple of pars on an evening when we were running short of West End stuff. I always got what the Features boys thought not quite worth their while, so this assignment was a natural for me.

When the office gave me her address I remember querying it, and as I pressed the doorbell I still wondered if they had it right. I am not sure exactly what sort of set-up I expected, what sort of background I pictured, for the Top Model of the Year. A flat, I suppose, in a fashionable district; on the small side, possibly, but up-to-date and chic. Certainly not an old-fashioned house with French windows and a garden, tucked away at the foot of a cul-de-sac with a railway running by. It couldn't have been more than a one-and-sixpenny ride from the bright lights, but it was the sort of place that made you tell the taxi-man to wait.

I wasn't kept long in doubt, though. She opened the door herself.

Our picture editor had already had her photographed, and I had judged from the pictures that she was quite a dish. I was ready for the great dark eyes, the mass of raven hair, the faultless curve of the slightly pouting lips. What the pictures didn't – couldn't – catch was the light in those dark eyes, the soft coils of that hair, the provocation in that pout.

She stood still, as if waiting to be admired. I admired her.

"Bob Holt's my name. *Evening Post*. You're expecting me, I think?"

"Of course," she said. "Come in."

She led the way across a middle-class hall to a middle-class sitting-room where the colorless domestic comfort stressed her vividness. It was like seeing a bird of paradise in a hen run. I concluded she must still be living at home with Mum and Dad.

She took a bottle and a glass out of a cupboard and poured me a stiff Scotch without so much as asking; I could only assume she recognized the type. As she passed me the drink I noticed how slender her hands were and how her long pointed nails resembled delicate red almonds.

"Sorry to make you come so late in the afternoon," she said. "I've been working all day. Only got back at five."

"It would be a pleasure to see you any time," I said, and meant it. "Aren't you drinking?"

She slapped her waist. "Would never do," she said. "Now, tell me, what do you want to know?"

She curled gracefully up in the armchair opposite while I put her through the stock questionnaire. Her answers were invariably brisk and businesslike. She was twenty-five; started modeling at twenty; had always been a freelance, liked it best that way; enjoyed her work, and specially her occasional jobs abroad; wouldn't be specific about her annual earnings, but admitted she was very nicely paid. Ambition . . . ?

This was the first time she paused before replying. "I think I'd sooner keep that to myself," she said at last, and momentarily a curious look came into her eyes – a look that suggested we were about to share some intimate secret.

I never worked harder to stretch out an interview. I did my best, but of course I couldn't keep it going forever. Presently it began to grow dark, and she turned on a lamp in a way that somehow pronounced the interview at an end. But I still wasn't willing to part with her. I tried another tack.

"Have you any engagement later on tonight?" I asked.

"Why?"

"Because if you haven't, I'd be delighted if you'd come out with me."

It was only one step better than a pick-up. She might have felt bound at that point to have given me a brush-off which there could be no possible question of going back on, and then I should have been loafing around Fleet Street at this moment instead of sitting here in the condemned cell at the Scrubs.

She might or she might not; that I shall never know. For I had hardly uttered the words before I heard a sound outside – the unmistakable, characteristic sound of the key turning in an automatic lock.

Marian heard it too.

"That'll be Jim," she said.

I don't know why it startled me so to discover she was married. Nothing had been said to imply that she was not. She wore no wedding ring, but girls in her line seldom do. And a husband would account for that house as well as a Mum or Dad.

But I had taken it for granted from the outset – so much so I didn't even bother to inquire – that Marian was entirely without strings and unattached. Somehow her personality created that impression, and to clinch it there was that curious look that I had glimpsed – not an invitation, mark, it fell far short of that, and anyway invitations hardly form an acid test – but a look that simply didn't go with a girl who had a husband. I couldn't then have told you why. I could do better now . . .

Jim turned out to be a commonplace bloke, older than Marian by twenty years and shorter by two inches. When my errand was explained to him he fairly glowed with pleasure, poured me a fresh drink, and refused to let me leave. There was so much, he said, he could tell me about Marian which, he knew, she would never tell herself.

Had she told me that when they married, seven years ago, nothing had been further from her thoughts than modeling? No. Had she told me that she had never had a lesson? No. Had she told me that she had reached the top at one bound? No. Had she told me how success had never turned her head, how they still lived in this house he had bought before their wedding, how they were just like any other contented married couple?

I glanced at Marian – and saw that look a second time.

"How, then, did she get the chance of modeling?" I asked.

"Through me." He made a deprecating gesture. "I'm in the gown trade. I had to beg her on my knees, mind. But look where she is now."

It was Jim, not Marian, who made me stay for dinner. It was Jim, not Marian, who did the talking afterwards; half the time, as I recall, she wasn't in the room. It was Jim who walked me to the gate, slapped me on the back, and said he knew for sure I'd write up Marian real good.

I had exchanged barely a word with Marian herself since my interrupted and unfinished pass, and she had given no clue to what she felt about that, if indeed she felt anything at all.

Next morning I wrote about her. Then I thought about her. When I'd thought long and hard enough, I dialed her number.

"So you're not working today?" I said, when eventually she answered.

"Who's that?"

"Bob Holt."

"Oh," she said. "No."

"Good," I said, "because I've got stuck in the draft of my article." I called it an article to make it sound important. "There are one or two points I'm not quite clear about. If you don't mind, I'd like to go through the draft with you in detail."

"All right," she said. "Read it to me."

"No good trying over the phone. I must see you," I said.

"What was that?"

I plunged.

"*I must see you*," I said, and put all my meaning in it.

There was a longish silence, but I could tell she had understood me, and I almost held my breath.

She broke the silence with a laugh – whether of triumph or of amusement or of scorn, I couldn't say.

"I suppose what must be, must be. Come round today at the same time."

"Not till six o'clock?" I said. "But you're at home this afternoon."

She laughed again.

"All right then, make it five."

I was there at half-past four. And I forgot to take the draft.

I was never at any time under any illusion about how and why I wanted Marian. After all, I was thirty-five; I'd knocked about a bit, and even if I didn't know that much about the world, I knew nearly all there was to know about myself. I wasn't inspired by romantic love or by genuine affection; I never even liked Marian very much.

It was a simple case of biological attraction from which all other elements were utterly excluded. I'd had the symptoms far too often not to recognise them — but I also recognised they were exceptionally severe. Marian recognised it too. That was the cause of all the trouble.

Looking back, I can see clearly enough that, even on this plane, Marian didn't really go for me. It was all, I'm certain now, an accident of timing. She had reached an acute stage in a self-suppressed rebellion against her husband and the life he symbolised; the alternative outlet for that rebellion must be a secret lover; I happened to come on the scene and made a play for her; she didn't find me repulsive, and so she took me on. For this inner conflict was positively obsessive.

As we lay in each other's arms, she would intersperse her love talk with bitter attacks on Jim: his stupidity, his unimaginativeness, his lack of elementary social *savoir faire*, and, above all, his stubborn refusal to move from a house and neighborhood which mocked her success and which she had out-grown.

These diatribes had me puzzled; I couldn't see why she didn't walk out on him if she wanted to, and said so. It wasn't as if she need depend on any man to keep her. But she retorted that you couldn't go on for ever modeling; and added that Jim was a very much richer man than I might think, that his will and his insurance policies favored only her, and that she didn't intend to pass them up by being a bloody fool.

This gave me my first inkling of that tough cupidity which I learned later was Marian's ruling passion.

Everything made it an easy affair to manage. Neither of us had any hard-and-fast working hours, and when we were both with a job immediately on hand I would slip up during the daytime to the house. Jim never returned from business until half-past six or so – it turned out he was boss of quite a big concern – and it didn't seem to worry him even when he found me there (as we thought it wiser that he sometimes should). We told him I was working on publicity for Marian, and that satisfied him; he was not the suspicious sort.

Marian fussed much more about her neighbors; they were a nosey lot, she said, always ready to start gossip, and it would soon be noticed and commented on if I regularly ran the gauntlet of the cul-de-sac. So, more often than not, I would use quite a different route, which took me across the railway line on the blind side of the house, over the garden fence which crowned the low embankment, and through the French window of the sitting room – a window normally left unlatched except at night or when nobody was in. This route not only screened me from prying eyes; it also heightened the flavor of forbidden fruit.

Things had been going on that way for the best part of three months – and I was still content they should go on that way forever – when Marian suddenly made the first big move in her campaign.

That afternoon – it was high summer, and I remember the hot sun beating on our bodies – she pulled unexpectedly out of an embrace.

"It can't go on like this, Bob," she said.

"Like what?" I said.

"The three of us," she said.

I wouldn't give her another lead. I just lay quiet and waited.

"I don't sleep any more for thinking," she said presently. "And I know I'm right, Bob. It's either you or Jim."

I was shocked at this transformation in her attitude, which threatened to destroy the nice soft option I had won. I started handing her the arguments she had handed me; think of the money, I urged, the insurance, the will.

"It'll all go by the board," I said, "if Jim divorces you."

"I wasn't thinking about divorce," Marian said.

It would be drawing it mild to call it an unusual experience. Not one person in a million – I should hope – ever in their lives faces a situation where someone they thought they knew as well as they know themselves, someone they'd always credited with normal human instincts, displays the will and purpose to contrive cold-blooded murder. I've had that experience, and I can tell you this: it doesn't work out exactly as you would expect.

Perhaps just because the idea is so shocking, you don't – or, at least, I didn't – get an instantaneous shock. At first you take it for granted that the whole thing is a joke – a grim piece of humor, but humor all the same. Only slowly do you tumble to the fact that it isn't a joke to them – they have a vehemence that doesn't go with jokes; you then decide it's temporary rage, a way of blowing off steam, and that they themselves would be horrified if it ever came to the point.

And when you fail to talk them out of it, and you stand on the brink, you don't draw back as you could and should and meant to, because you can't now without appearing a coward and traitor – and, in my case, without losing what I knew I had to have.

Marian must have thought over her plan to murder Jim for a long time before she ever mentioned it to me; otherwise she couldn't have explained it in such detail. Mind, I wasn't given these details all at once – only bit by bit, spread across a week or more, as, I suppose, she judged I was in proper shape to take them. But I soon grasped the broad lines on which the plan was based; the scheming should be hers, the action should be mine.

Her idea was for me to do it in the house, under conditions which would point to common robbery, which would enable me to come and go entirely unobserved, and which – if, notwithstanding, suspicions turned our way – would provide us *both* with a cast-iron alibi.

How shall we make it look like robbery, I asked, and I laughed, with a peculiar catch in my throat; I was still thinking it a rather ghastly game.

That was the easiest one of all for her to answer; she'd tell him she'd be home in the evening, and she wouldn't be; I'd drop in casually, as he'd quite got used to; after I'd done it, I could turn out his wallet – he always kept a fair amount of money on him – and take away, and lose, one or two valuables from the house. Coming and going unobserved? Didn't I do it already? Wasn't there the railway?

My heart sank as she grew more insistent. I was conscious of nerves around my eyes that I didn't know I had.

"You get hanged for murder," I said.

"If you're caught," she said.

I paced up and down, my thoughts whirling.

"You talk," I said, "as if he would sit quiet and let me do it. And *how* am I supposed to do it anyway? Shoot him and have the bullet traced to my revolver? Strangle him and have the scratches noticed on my hands?"

Marian gave me a rather pitying smile. Then she came up close so that I got the scent of her.

"You'll do it with a mallet."

"You must be raving mad."

"Remember the Rattenbury case? That's how Stoner did it." I remembered something else then – the number of crime books that she'd lately had out of the library. "They'd never have been arrested if she hadn't gabbed. It's the easiest thing coming up behind somebody's chair; if they know you're about the house, they're not going to turn round."

"So it's easy, is it," I said, "for me to come up behind Jim's chair with a mallet?"

"We've a mallet in the tool shed. I'll leave it tucked away in the hall. You have a few drinks with Jim and make an excuse to leave the room. You know both the armchairs have their backs to the door. You come in again. With the mallet."

"And this alibi," I said weakly. "Who's our alibi?"
She pressed her parted lips against my mouth.
"*We shall be each other's alibi*," she said.

We picked the evening with the utmost care; we had to. It
was nearly three months more before all the circumstances
favored us. Meanwhile I'd gone around like a man on whom
the doctors have passed sentence of death, but who can't
believe it simply because he's still alive. Even when we
actually reached the day itself and the preliminaries were
already under way – when I heard Marian make the phone
call we'd rehearsed so often ("Jim, I'm being kept late . . .
Back about 10:30, dear . . . Promise you'll be in . . . You
know I hate coming into an empty house at night") – when I
watched her hide the mallet under the cupboard in the hall –
when I fetched her little traveling-case and she crammed it
with her night things . . .

We registered at the hotel shortly after seven. I purposely
cracked a joke or two with the reception clerk, and Marian
asked him some question which he answered civilly. I signed
us in as Mr and Mrs Robert Holt, and added my address; I
used my natural handwriting.

We were shown up to our room, which we had booked in
advance for its position (we liked the first floor and the
bathroom and the view, I had explained); on the way there I
cracked more jokes with the bellhop. We had dinner upstairs
and we both chatted with the waiter. After dinner we undressed, got into bed, rang for the maid, and gave her
instructions to bring early morning tea.

The moment she went I got up again, drew the bolt across
the door, and took out of my suitcase the only apparel besides
pajamas I had brought – my old reporter's props, my
battered evening clothes . . .

It seemed hours that we stayed taut and silent, listening for
the cue. In the banqueting chamber immediately below, a
well-known anglers' club was holding its annual stag party,
perhaps two hundred strong. We could hear, though greatly
muffled, the shouts of the toastmaster, sudden gusts of

mirth, billows of applause. The speech-making went on and on, and I suppose the fish they were describing got bigger and bigger; certainly the noise grew steadily in volume. I kept looking at my watch, and then across at Marian; in another twenty minutes, fifteen, ten, we'd have to pass it up.

Then, as I started to feel frustration and relief in equal measure – relief at putting it off, frustration at not getting it done with – from the banqueting chamber came a sound of scraping and of shuffling, immediately followed by the strains of Auld Lang Syne.

Without a word or even a glance exchanged between us, I slipped out and gently closed the door behind me.

I met no one in the corridor. Had I done so, I should have turned back; the project would have failed. As it was, the place might have been cleared for my convenience. I walked down the staircase – naturally, I didn't use the elevator – and straightaway got caught up with a seething mass of anglers.

Nobody saw us leave – saw us, that is, as individuals. We were just an amorphous mass; we were The Banquet Breaking Up. The swing doors were swung for us; the porters said "good night"; but not one of us meant any more to them than the faceless silhouettes they use to illustrate statistics.

Immediately outside the door, I made towards a taxi; then deliberately allowed some thrusting chap to win it from me. I moved forward towards another, which I similarly lost. I moved forwards once again, and this time gained the street.

I was out . . .

It was still only September, but quite cold enough at that hour to justify me keeping my coat collar turned well up. I walked as briskly as I could do without drawing attention. I can't remember feeling any emotion, even fear; I was far too busy going over all I had to do, as I might put a story into shape while walking to the office.

Within half an hour I had the back of the house in view, and I could see a light in the sitting room which showed that Jim was home. I crossed the railway line, and as I came over the dark garden I could see him through the partially drawn curtains – a decent, harmless chap patiently waiting for his wife. I noted that impression, without feeling it any concern to me.

I didn't dare go to the front door, with a street lamp opposite. Jim didn't know I ever used the garden route, but I could always say that I'd been ringing and he hadn't heard, and that I'd walked round to see if anyone was in. Jim wouldn't put two and two together – and even if he did it hardly mattered now.

I gave a pretense of a knock at the French window, and walked in.

"Hello, how's tricks?" I said.

I read it myself on the tape in the office shortly after lunch.

The daily woman had called the police as soon as she arrived. They found him lying on the sitting room floor. His skull was broken. A mallet lay nearby. His wallet had been rifled. The pathologist's report would not be available till later, but obviously death had occurred several hours before.

I studied these details with intense concentration but curious detachment. I had no feeling of guilt, no pangs of remorse, no sense of what had happened in terms of life and death. I had one thought only – *Shall we be found out?*

Everything was assessed and measured solely in this context, and, far from flinching at the record of my handiwork, I praised myself afresh for pushing his body to the floor so that it might suggest there had been a struggle with an intruder. It was the sort of precaution that could make all the difference.

Though we were over the biggest hurdles we'd foreseen – like my re-entering the hotel with the cabaret customers, and those breathless seconds on the stairs when I gambled on my luck – there were still the statements we would have to make that afternoon. For we had agreed that, immediately the story reached the papers, Marian should go from the hotel straight to the police and tell them with whom and where she spent the night. And that would naturally bring them round to me.

There was nothing much to worry about so long as we kept our heads, but the more it looked like straight robbery, the less we should be asked.

They came to the office about six – Inspector Gorman and a sergeant. Plainclothes men, of course, but you can never fail to spot them, and I got some ribbing from the chap who told me they were there. Murder will out, he said; murder will out, old boy.

I took them to a little room we used for interviews. The Inspector said who they were, and that they were inquiring into the murder, and that Marian had got in touch with them. Would I be willing to answer a few questions? Certainly.

"She says she stayed last night at the Grand Hotel with you."

"That's right," I said.

"I understand from her this is the first time that it's happened – the first time that she's stayed with you all night, and not gone home."

"That's right," I said.

"We know definitely that death took place after ten o'clock last night." The Inspector looked at me affably. "And not later than two. So it's routine to account for the household in between those hours."

"I understand," I said.

"Then they can be eliminated from the investigation."

"We were in bed before ten," I said. "You can ask the chambermaid."

"We have asked her," the Inspector said. "Did you both stay in bed for the remainder of the night?"

"Until they brought tea at eight."

The Inspector went on looking at me affably. "How long has your affair with this lady been going on?"

"Six months."

"Did the dead man know of it?"

"No."

"What sort of terms were you on with him?"

"Excellent," I said.

"When did you last see him?"

I should have been ready for that one, but it very nearly threw me.

"Oh, earlier this week," I said. "I saw him quite often."

"A terrible end for him," the Inspector said.

"Terrible," I said.

"Well, thank you, Mr Holt."

When they left I got the impression they were satisfied.

I didn't see any more of them for the next two or three days. Marian did, of course, but only on formal matters. We behaved as we supposed they would expect from an erring wife and her paramour. Marian stayed on for the time being at the hotel. I slept at my flat. While there was no point in trying to disguise the fact that we were lovers – that had indeed become our ultimate safeguard – we felt that discretion required we should not flaunt it until we could be certain that the inquiries had been closed.

So I was alone that evening when my bell rang, and I opened the door to Gorman and his sergeant.

"Robert Holt," the Inspector said.

I went, as they say, quietly. They could put me on trial if they liked, but I had a cast-iron alibi.

My counsel decided to call the alibi witnesses first. There was a sporting chance, he said, that the jury might want to hear no more, and then the trial would be over without my having to go into the box.

Certainly the prosecution hadn't been so hot. It was a thin case of identity, depending on an elderly couple who lived in the house next door. It had turned out that my secret visits to Marian hadn't been so secret; this pair could see me cross part of the garden from their window, and, scenting an intrigue, they kept up something like a watch. They knew me as well by sight, they said, as one of their relations; they'd seen me coming and going scores of times these last few months. And they had seen me come and go on the night of the murder too; came about eleven – that was most unusually late – and go less than half an hour afterwards, apparently in a rush.

Wasn't it dark? asked my counsel. Yes, but light shone from the window. Wasn't it past their bedtime? Not at eleven o'clock. But at half-past? Well, they stayed up purposely. To spy? Yes, if he wished to put it so. But on *this* they couldn't be shaken – they were sure that it was me.

Still, as my counsel said in opening my defense, it's the easiest thing in the world to make a mistake of identification. I saw a juryman nod his head in obvious agreement. It seemed as though one good push now would do the trick.

The evidence from the hotel came out nice and smoothly. It fixed me in bed there at ten to ten that night, and in bed there again at eight o'clock next morning. The prosecution hardly challenged that. The only question was: did I go out in between?

My counsel called Marian.

There was a bit of a sensation when she entered the courtroom – a tribute to her loveliness, her mild celebrity.

"I shall be as brief as possible," my counsel said. "You remember the day you learned of your husband's death?"

"Yes."

"Where did you spend the previous night?"

"At the Grand Hotel."

"With anyone?"

"With . . . Mr Holt."

Her hands were trembling, and she didn't look at me.

"What time did you go to bed?"

"Early. Before ten."

"Did you have breakfast in bed together in the morning?"

"Yes."

"Did Mr Holt ever leave you at all during that night?"

Marian shook her head.

"Just give your answer aloud, please, for the purpose of the record. Did he ever leave you that night?"

Marian shook her head again, and finally whispered, "No."

This wasn't at all the Marian I'd been expecting. She had come to see me in prison a few days before the trial, and no one could have overlooked her air of confidence. Now apparently her nerve was failing her. Luckily she hadn't a lot to remember – or forget; so long as she just kept repeating that I'd never left her, there wasn't much that anyone could do.

Prosecuting counsel seemed of the same opinion. He began to cross-examine Marian in a half-hearted style, as if he was resigned to getting absolutely nowhere.

"Are you a heavy sleeper?"

"Not very," Marian said.

"Have you an idea what time you fell asleep that night?"

"Late," Marian said, and a young reporter grinned.

"Before or after two o'clock?"

"After," Marian said.

"So if the prisoner left you before two, you would be bound to know?"

"Yes," Marian said.

It had been drummed into us over and over again that two o'clock was the latest hour at which Jim could have died. The prosecution had arrived at a dead end.

"And you swear he was with you in that hotel bedroom without a break from ten o'clock till two?"

He couldn't think of any other line to take. He was drawing his gown back, ready to sit down. She had only to say one more word to clinch my alibi.

But she didn't say it. Her mouth worked a little, but she didn't speak. Her hands trembled more now. I watched her, helpless, with an uneasy foreboding.

"Do you swear that?"

The prosecutor was on to it too. He'd perked up, and had let his gown fall back again.

"Do you swear that he was with you in that hotel bedroom without a break from ten o'clock till two? *Without a break* – do you swear that on your oath?"

He was pressing without a clear idea of what he was pressing for. He simply recognised the symptoms of a crackup, and went on hammering hard and hopefully.

"You have not answered my question. Do you swear that on your oath?"

Marian's trembling was painful to behold. Nothing had gone wrong, she hadn't been caught out, she'd never even come under any real fire. But here she was bordering on collapse.

Mechanically I gripped the rail before me with both hands, then realised that Marian in the box was doing the same. She had taken off one glove, and irrelevantly I wondered if my knuckles were showing as white as hers.

"*Do you swear that, madam?*"

The whole court waited in an agonizing silence.

"I won't swear," she said in a muffled, strangled voice. "I don't know. I can't remember."

Then she crumpled, and dropped her face into her hands. The judge said something I didn't catch, and they led her out of court.

The vital hours of that night lay unaccounted for. My cast-iron alibi had gone straight down the drain.

It was no longer a question of whether I could hope to escape the witness box. It was a question of whether I could hope to escape the rope.

My solicitor and my counsel had both pointed out to me the dangers inseparable from an alibi defense. If it flops, you can be left much worse off than you were before. For instance, they said, if you *admit* going to the house that night, but maintain that when you left Jim was alive and well, you will stand a reasonable chance of being acquitted; it's just conceivable that somebody came in and killed him later.

But if you call witnesses to prove that you weren't there *at all*, and those witnesses do not convince the jury, they will be disposed to think you are lying when *you* say you weren't there, and, moreover, *to infer you've only one reason to lie*. So you must be very sure, they said, about an alibi.

But I *was* sure of mine, I told them, absolutely sure; and I wanted to be on a cert, not on a reasonable chance.

And the result? I had my back right up against the wall, and the knowledge that in the last resort my only hope was me.

I understand that I gave my evidence well. I felt conscious at the time that I wasn't yielding ground. Maybe prosecuting counsel didn't amount to much; maybe I got a bit of extra lift from desperation. Anyway, I could see his attempts to catch me from a mile off, and I had an answer for every single one.

I did best of all, I think, when he referred to Marian – a reference that he must have saved up for a parting shot. We were engaged in a passionate love affair, were we not, he asked. Spending our very first illicit night together? Could I think of any reason, in those circumstances, why Marian couldn't remember whether I stayed with her or not?

"Of course I can think of a reason." I started pulling out the stops. "It doesn't need an awful lot of imagination, either. We were in love with each other, don't you understand? You can say it was morally wrong if you like, but in fact we weren't hurting anyone; up till then it had been something private and sacred to ourselves."

"I didn't invite you to make a speech," said prosecuting counsel.

"You asked me for a reason why Marian went blank in the box, and I'm giving you a reason. She was the only one who could vouch for me that night, because we were alone together, because we were making love. To prove my innocence she had to reveal that publicly, to turn a part of her intimate life into a public shame. Do you wonder it was more than a woman's nerves could take? If I could stand my trial over again, I'd let it go by default rather than put her to such torture."

That had a good effect. I could tell from the prosecutor's shrug as he sat down, and from my solicitor's expression as I went back to the dock. At least, the latter conveyed, we're in the running again.

But though I may have solved the Marian mystery for others, I was still far short of solving it for myself. Possibly it made sense to them; it didn't make sense to me. Marian wasn't the nervous kind, and she wasn't bashful either; you can't be a Top Model without an exhibitionist streak.

What had destroyed the jaunty self-assurance that she still

possessed when she last visited me in jail? Was it perhaps going back to live in the house she'd shared with Jim, as she told me she had done on the day before that visit? Had it got her down?

I couldn't see any reason for it; and when Marian said something vague about expense I couldn't forget the news with which she'd opened the visit – that her money from Jim totted up to £30,000. She need not, should not, have gone back. But would she let it get her down – and if it did so, would she have stayed?

Whatever it was, I owed to it the fact that even now I'd barely a fifty-fifty chance of getting out . . .

The jury retired in mellow afternoon sunlight. Night had fallen before they reappeared . . .

I dodged everyone. I wouldn't even stop to say more than a single word of thanks to my defenders. I wanted Marian, and when I heard she had gone home I followed.

Automatically I took the route that had become habitual . . .

The light glowed dully through the drawn curtains. The garden stretched out darkly as it had done that other night. I wondered whether the French window would still be left unlocked.

I tiptoed up to it, intent on surprise, and grew aware of an intermittent voice inside.

I couldn't pick out any words, but I knew it to be Marian. She was obviously speaking to someone on the phone, and in tones of such urgency that they stopped me in my tracks.

Very gently I pressed the latch. The French window yielded. I opened it an inch or two, just enough to hear.

". . . doesn't matter how," Marian was saying. "It's not *my* fault, goodness knows . . . All right, all right, but there it is, the fools have let him off . . . Dear darling heart, don't let's argue, there's no time . . . He'll be here before we know where we are, and then what's going to happen? . . . No, listen, honey, bring the car to the usual place . . . I won't have a bag at all, I'm leaving double quick . . . Brighton or somewhere, so long as it's away . . . Yes, dearest boy, in half an hour; my dearest, dearest boy."

She made a noisy, silly, kissing sound – the noisy, silly, kissing sound she used to make to me.

I gave a pretense of a knock at the French window, and walked in, as I had walked in that other night weeks ago.

Her head jerked round and her jaw dropped in the ugliness of horror. She slammed down the phone but kept her hand on it so that the black receiver set off her nails, like delicate red almonds.

"Bob," she said. "Bob."

"Hello," I said, "how's tricks?"

You may call it rough justice. But I don't feel that way. I do feel some remorse now over the man I murdered. But I feel no remorse over the woman who murdered me, and I shall go to the scaffold cursing her lovely, broken corpse.

TO BREAK THE WALL

Evan Hunter

Adapted to:

THE BLACKBOARD JUNGLE

(M.G.M., 1955)

Starring: Glenn Ford,

Sydney Poitier & Vic Morrow

Directed by Richard Brooks

The year 1955 saw the emergence of the juvenile delinquency movie when three pictures were all released within months of each other and became the benchmarks for the future. The films were The Wild One, *a brutal story of rivalry between motor cycle gangs which starred the brooding Marlon Brando;* Rebel Without A Cause *which helped to turn James Dean into an icon of teenage disenchantment; and* The Blackboard Jungle *about violence and juvenile crime in a rundown New York school. Based on a best-selling novel by Evan Hunter, the story of the hostility between* teacher Richard Dadier (Glenn Ford) and his class – in particular Sydney Poitier, a problem pupil who nonetheless shows some signs of sensitivity, and Vic Morrow, a knife-wielding thug – treated the subject honestly with no holds barred. The city outside the classroom windows which had nurtured these alienated young people was shown as little more than an urban jungle. Richard Brooks' powerful directing and a sound track featuring Bill Haley's pioneer rock 'n' roll number, Rock Around The Clock (the first rock record to be used as a theme tune), made the movie as popular with young audiences as it was hated by their parents. Its reputation was not enhanced in the eyes of the older generation when groups of teenagers in cinemas in New York and London rioted and tore up seats during a couple of the early screenings. Just how these incidents started and whether they were carefully staged publicity stunts has never been satisfactorily resolved, but they certainly assured the enduring notoriety of The Blackboard Jungle.

Evan Hunter (1926) was actually a teacher in two vocational schools in New York before he began writing in the early fifties. His first-hand experience of street gangs, drug addiction and racial tension among teenagers inspired his early short stories and novels such as The Jungle Kids (1956) and The Last Spin (1960). Later, he began a series of starkly realistic police procedurals about the cops in the 87th Precinct which he published under the name of Ed McBain. Several of these have been filmed, others adapted for television, and along the way made the author better known under the McBain pseudonym than his own. Hunter has also written scripts for a number of highly regarded crime movies including Daphne du Maurier's story of wild life out of control, The Birds, which Alfred Hitchcock filmed with Tippi Hedren and Rod Taylor in 1963, as well as contributing to a number of TV anthology series. "To Break The Wall" is a rare Evan Hunter short story written in 1953 for Discovery magazine just prior to beginning work on The Blackboard Jungle. It also features Richard Dadier in a confrontation with his pupils and bears all the hallmarks of having been part of the germination process of the best-selling novel and seminal fifties crime movie . . .

*   *   *

The door to Room 206 was locked when Richard Dadier reached it for his fifth period English class. He tried the knob several times, peered in through the glass panel, and motioned for Serubi to open the door. Serubi, sitting in the seat closest the door, shrugged his shoulders innocently and grinned. Richard felt again the mixed revulsion and fear he felt before every class.

Easy, he told himself. Easy does it.

He reached into his pocket and slipped the large key into the keyhole. Swinging the door open, he slapped it fast against the prongs that jutted out from the wall, and then walked briskly to his desk.

A falsetto voice somewhere in the back of the room rapidly squeaked, "Daddy-oh!" Richard busied himself with his Delaney book, not looking up at the class. He still remembered that first day, when he had told them his name.

"Mr Dadier," he had said, and he'd pronounced it carefully. One of the boys had yelled, "Daddy-oh," and the class had roared approval. The name had stuck since then.

Quickly, he glanced around the room, flipping cards over as he took the attendance. Half were absent as usual. He was secretly glad. They were easier to handle in small groups.

He turned over the last card, and waited for them to quiet down. They never would, he knew, never.

Reaching down, he pulled a heavy book from his briefcase and rested it on the palm of his hand. Without warning, he slammed it onto the desk.

"Shut up!" he bellowed.

The class groaned into silence, startled by the outburst.

Now, he thought. Now, I'll press it home. Surprise plus advantage plus seize your advantage. Just like waging war. All day long I wage war. Some fun.

"Assignment for tomorrow," Richard said flatly.

A moan escaped from the group. Gregory Miller, a large boy of seventeen, dark-haired, with a lazy sneer and hard, bright eyes said, "You work too hard, Mr Daddy-oh."

The name twisted deep inside Richard, and he felt the tiny needles of apprehension start at the base of his spine.

"Quiet, Mueller," Richard said, feeling pleasure at mispronouncing the boy's name. "Assignment for tomorrow. In *New Horizons* . . ."

"In what?" Ganigan asked.

I should have known better, Richard reminded himself. We've only been using the book two months now. I can't expect them to remember the title. No.

"In *New Horizons*," he repeated impatiently, "the blue book, the one we've been using all term." He paused, gaining control of himself. "In the blue book," he continued softly, "read the first ten pages of *Army Ants in the Jungle*."

"Here in class?" Hennesy asked.

"No. At home."

"Christ," Hennesy mumbled.

"It's on page two seventy-five," Richard said.

"What page?" Antoro called out.

"Two seventy-five."

"What page?" Levy asked.

"Two seventy-five," Richard said. "My God, what's the matter with you?" He turned rapidly and wrote the figures on the board in a large hand, repeating the numerals slowly. "Two, seven-ty, five." He heard a chuckle spread maliciously behind him, and he whirled quickly. Every boy in the class wore a deadpan.

"There will be a short test on the homework tomorrow," he announced grimly.

"Another one?" Miller asked lazily.

"Yes, Mailler," Richard said, "another one." He glared at the boy heatedly, but Miller only grinned in return.

"And now," Richard said, "the test I promised you yesterday."

A hush fell over the class.

Quick, Richard thought. Press the advantage. Strike again and again. Don't wait for them. Keep one step ahead always. Move fast and they won't know what's going on. Keep them too busy to get into mischief.

Richard began chalking the test on the board. He turned his head and barked over his shoulder, "All books away. Finley, hand out the paper."

This is the way to do it, he realized. I've figured it out. The way to control these monsters is to give them a test every day of the week. Write their fingers off.

"Begin immediately," Richard said in a businesslike voice. "Don't forget your heading."

"What's that, that heading?" Busco asked.

"Name, official class, subject class, subject teacher," Richard said wearily.

Seventy-two, he thought. I've said it seventy-two times since I started teaching here two months ago. Seventy-two times.

"Who's our subject teacher?" Busco asked. His face expressed complete bewilderment.

"Mr Daddy-oh," Vota said quite plainly. Vota was big and rawboned, a muscular, rangy, seventeen-year-old. Stringy blond hair hung over his pimply forehead. There was something mannishly sinister about his eyes, something boyishly innocent about his smile. And he was Miller's friend. Richard never forgot that for a moment.

"Mr Dadier is the subject teacher," Richard said to Busco. "And incidentally, Vito," he glared at Vota, "anyone misspelling my name in the heading will lose ten points."

"What!" Vota complained, outraged.

"You heard me, Vota," Richard snapped.

"Well, how do you spell Daddy-oh?" Vota asked, the innocent smile curling his lips again.

"You figure it out, Vota. I don't need the ten points."

Richard bitterly pressed the chalk into the board. It snapped in two, and he picked up another piece from the runner. With the chalk squeaking wildly, he wrote out the rest of the test.

"No talking," he ordered. He sat down behind the desk and eyed the class suspiciously.

A puzzled frown crossed Miller's face. "I don't understand the first question, teach'," he called out.

Richard leaned back in his chair and looked at the board. "It's very simple, Miltzer," he said. "There are ten words on the board. Some are spelled correctly, and some are wrong.

If they're wrong, you correct them. If they're right, spell them just the way they're written."

"Mmmmm," Miller said thoughtfully, his eyes glowing. "How do you spell the second word?"

Richard leaned back again, looked at the second word and began, "D-I-S . . ." He caught himself and faced Miller squarely. "Just the way you want to. You're taking the test, not me."

Miller grinned widely. "Oh. I didn't know that, teach'."

"You'll know when you see your mark, Miller."

Richard cursed himself for having pronounced the boy's name correctly. He made himself comfortable at the desk and looked out over the class.

Di Pasco will cheat, he thought. He will cheat and I won't catch him. He's uncanny that way. God, how I wish I could catch him. How does he? On his cuff? Where? He probably has it stuffed in his ear. Should I search him? No, what's the use? He'd cheat his own mother. An inborn crook. A louse.

Louse, Richard mused. Even I call them that now. All louses. I must tell Helen that I've succumbed. Or should I wait until after the baby is born? Perhaps it would be best not to disillusion her yet. Perhaps I should let her think I'm still trying to reach them, still trying. What was it Solly Klein had said?

"This is the garbage can of the educational system."

He had stood in the teachers' lunchroom, near the bulletin board, pointing his stubby forefinger at Richard.

"And it's our job to sit on the lid and make sure none of this garbage spills over into the street."

Richard had smiled then. He was new, and he still thought he could teach them something, still felt he could mold the clay.

Lou Savoldi, an electrical wiring teacher, had smiled too and said, "Solly's a great philosopher."

"Yeah, yeah, philosopher." Solly smiled. "All I know is I've been teaching machine shop here for twelve years now, and only once did I find anything valuable in the garbage." He had nodded his head emphatically then. "Nobody knowingly throws anything valuable in with the garbage."

Then why should I bother? Richard wondered now. Why should I teach? Why should I get ulcers?

"Keep your eyes on your own paper, Busco," he cautioned.

Everyone is a cheat, a potential thief. Solly was right. We have to keep them off the streets. They should really hire a policeman. It would be funny, he thought, if it weren't so damned serious. How long can you handle garbage without beginning to stink yourself? Already, I stink.

"All right, Busco, bring your paper up. I'm subtracting five points from it," Richard suddenly said.

"Why? What the hell did I do?"

"Bring me your paper."

Busco reluctantly slouched to the front of the room and tossed his paper onto the desk. He stood with his thumbs looped in the tops of his dungarees as Richard marked a large figure 5 on the paper in bright red.

"What's that for?" Busco asked.

"For having loose eyes."

Busco snatched the paper from the desk and examined it with disgust. He wrinkled his face into a grimace and slowly started back to his seat.

As he passed Miller, Miller looked to the front of the room. His eyes met Richard's, and he sneered, "Chicken!"

"What?" Richard asked.

Miller looked surprised. "You talking to me, teach'?"

"Yes, Miller. What did you just say?"

"I didn't say nothing, teach'." Miller smiled.

"Bring me your paper, Miller."

"What for?"

"Bring it up!"

"What for, I said."

"I heard what you said, Miller. And *I* said bring me your paper. Now. Right this minute."

"I don't see why," Miller persisted, the smile beginning to vanish from his face.

"Because I say so, that's why."

Miller's answer came slowly, pointedly. "And supposing I don't feel like?" A frown was twisting his forehead.

The other boys in the room were suddenly interested. Heads that were bent over papers snapped upright. Richard felt every eye in the class focus on him.

They were rooting for Miller, of course. They wanted Miller to win. They wanted Miller to defy him. He couldn't let that happen.

He walked crisply up the aisle and stood beside Miller. The boy looked up provokingly.

"Get up," Richard said, trying to control the modulation of his voice.

My voice is shaking, he told himself. I can feel it shaking. He knows it, too. He's mocking me with those little, hard eyes of his. I must control my voice. This is really funny. My voice is shaking.

"Get up, Miller."

"I don't see, Mr Daddy-oh, just why I should," Miller answered. He pronounced the name with great care.

"Get up, Miller. Get up and say my name correctly."

"Don't you know your own name, Mr Daddy-oh?"

Richard's hand snapped out and grasped Miller by the collar of his shirt. He pulled him to his feet, almost tearing the collar. Miller stood a scant two inches shorter than Richard, squirming to release himself.

Richard's hand crushed tighter on the collar. He heard the slight rasp of material ripping. He peered into the hateful eyes and spoke quietly. "Pronounce my name correctly, Miller."

The class had grown terribly quiet. There was no sound in the room now. Richard heard only the grate of his own shallow breathing.

I should let him loose, he thought. What can come of this? How far can I go? *Let him loose!*

"You want me to pronounce your name, sir?" Miller asked.

"You heard me."

"Go to hell, Mr Daddy . . ."

Richard's fist lashed out, catching the boy squarely across the mouth. He felt his knuckles scrape against hard teeth, saw the blood leap across the upper lip in a thin crimson slash, saw the eyes widen with surprise and then narrow immediately with deep, dark hatred.

And then the knife snapped into view, sudden and terrifying. Long and shining, it caught the pale sunlight that slanted through the long schoolroom windows. Richard backed away involuntarily, eying the sharp blade with respect.

Now what? he thought. Now the garbage can turns into a coffin. Now the garbage overflows. Now I lie dead and bleeding on a schoolroom floor while a moron slashes me to ribbons. Now.

"What do you intend doing with that, Miller?"

My voice is exceptionally calm, he mused. I think I'm frightened, but my voice is calm. Exceptionally.

"Just come a little closer and you'll see," Miller snarled, the blood in his mouth staining his teeth.

"Give me that knife, Miller."

I'm kidding, a voice persisted in Richard's mind. I must be kidding. This is all a big, hilarious joke. I'll die laughing in the morning. I'll die . . .

"Come and get it, Daddy-oh!"

Richard took a step closer to Miller and watched his arm swing back and forth in a threatening arc. Miller's eyes were hard and unforgiving.

And suddenly, Richard caught a flash of color out of the corner of his eye. Someone was behind him! He whirled instinctively, his fist smashing into a boy's stomach. As the boy fell to the floor Richard realized it was Miller's friend Vota. Vota cramped into a tight little ball that writhed and moaned on the floor, and Richard knew that any danger he might have presented was past. He turned quickly to Miller, a satisfied smile clinging to his lips.

"Give me that knife, Miller, and give it to me now."

He stared into the boy's eyes. Miller looked big and dangerous. Perspiration stood out on his forehead. His breath was coming in hurried gasps.

"Give it to me now, Miller, or I'm going to take it from you and beat you black and blue."

He was advancing slowly on the boy.

"Give it to me, Miller. Hand it over," his voice rolled on hypnotically, charged with an undercurrent of threat.

The class seemed to catch its breath together. No one moved to help Vota who lay in a heap on the floor, his arms hugging his waist. He moaned occasionally, squirming violently. But no one moved to help him.

I've got to keep one eye on Vota, Richard figured. He may be playing possum. I have to be careful.

"Hand it over, Miller. Hand it over."

Miller stopped retreating, realizing that he was the one who held the weapon. He stuck the spring-action knife out in front of him, probing the air with it. His back curved into a large C as he crouched over, head low, the knife always moving in front of him as he advanced. Richard held his ground and waited. Miller advanced cautiously, his eyes fastened on Richard's throat, the knife hand moving constantly, murderously, in a swinging arc. He grinned terribly, a red-stained, white smile on his face.

The chair, Richard suddenly remembered. There's a chair. I'll take the chair and swing. Under the chin. No. Across the chest. Fast though. It'll have to be fast, one movement. Wait. Not yet, wait. Come on, Miller. Come on. *Come on!*

Miller paused and searched Richard's face. He grinned again and began speaking softly as he advanced, almost in a whisper, almost as if he were thinking aloud.

"See the knife, Mr Daddy-oh? See the pretty knife? I'm gonna slash you up real good, Mr Daddy-oh. I'm gonna slash you, and then I'm gonna slash you some more. I'm gonna cut you up real fine. I'm gonna cut you up so nobody'll know you any more, Mr Daddy-oh."

All the while moving closer, closer, swinging the knife.

"Ever get cut; Mr Daddy-oh? Ever get sliced with a sharp knife? This one is sharp, Mr Daddy-oh, and you're gonna get cut with it. I'm gonna cut you now, and you're never gonna bother us no more. No more."

Richard backed away down the aisle.

Thoughts tumbled into his mind with blinding rapidity. I'll make him think I'm retreating. I'll give him confidence. The

empty seat in the third now. Next to Ganigan. I'll lead him there.
I hope it's empty. Empty when I checked the roll. I can't look,
I'll tip my hand. Keep a poker face. Come on, Miller, follow me.
Follow me so I can crack your ugly skull in two. Come on, you
louse. One of us goes, Miller. And it's not going to be me.

"Nossir, Mr Daddy-oh, we ain't gonna bother with you no
more. No more tests, and no more of your noise. Just your
face, Mr Daddy-oh. Just gonna fix your face so nobody'll
wanna look at you no more."

One more row, Richard calculated. Back up one more row.
Reach. Swing. One. More. Row.

The class followed the two figures with fascination. Miller
stalked Richard down the long aisle, stepping forward on the
balls of his feet, pace by pace, waiting for Richard to back
into the blackboard. Vota rolled over on the floor and
groaned again.

And Richard counted the steps. A few more. A . . .
few . . . few . . . more . . .

"Shouldn't have hit me, Mr Daddy-oh," Miller mocked.
"Ain't nice for teachers to hit students like that, Mr Daddy-
oh. Nossir, it ain't nice at . . ."

The chair crashed into Miller's chest, knocking the breath
out of him. It came quickly and forcefully, with the impact of
a striking snake. Richard had turned, as if to run, and then
the chair was gripped in his hands tightly. It sliced the air in a
clean, powerful arc, and Miller covered his face instinctively.
The chair crashed into his chest, knocking him backwards.
He screamed in surprise and pain as Richard leaped over the
chair to land heavily on his chest. Richard pinned Miller's
shoulders to the floor with his knees and slapped him
ruthlessly across the face.

"Here, Miller, here, here, here," he squeezed through
clenched teeth. Miller twisted his head from side to side,
trying to escape the cascade of blows that fell in rapid
onslaught on his cheeks.

The knife, Richard suddenly remembered! Where's the
knife? What did he do with the . . .

Sunlight caught the cold glint of metal, and Richard

glanced up instantly. Vota stood over him, the knife clenched tightly in his fist. He grinned boyishly, his rotten teeth flashing across his blotchy, thin face. He spat vehemently at Richard, and then there was a blur of color: blue steel, and the yellow of Vota's hair, and the blood on Miller's lip, and the brown wooden floor, and the gray tweed of Richard's suit. A shout came up from the class, and a hiss seemed to escape Miller's lips.

Richard kicked at Vota, feeling the heavy leather of his shoes crack against the boy's shins. Miller was up and fumbling for Richard's arms. A sudden slice of pain started at Richard's shoulder, careened down the length of his arm. Cloth gave way with a rasping scratch, and blood flashed bright against the gray tweed.

From the floor, Richard saw the knife flash back again, poised in Vota's hand ready to strike. He saw Miller's fists, doubled and hard, saw the animal look on Vota's face, and again the knife threatening and sharp, drenched now with blood, dripping on the brown, cold, wooden floor.

The noise grew louder and Richard grasped in his mind for a picture of the Roman arena, tried to rise, felt pain sear through his right arm as he put pressure on it.

He's cut me, he thought with panic. Vota has cut me.

And the screaming reached a wild crescendo, hands moved with terrible swiftness, eyes gleamed with molten fury, bodies squirmed, and hate smothered everything in a sweaty, confused, embarrassed embrace.

This is it, Richard thought, this is it.

"Leave him alone, you crazy jerk," Serubi was shouting.

Leave who alone, Richard wondered. Who? I wasn't . . .

"Lousy sneak," Levy shouted. "Lousy, dirty sneak."

Please, Richard thought. Please, quickly. Please.

Levy seized Miller firmly and pushed him backward against a desk. Richard watched him dazedly, his right arm burning with pain. He saw Busco through a maze of moving, struggling bodies, Busco who was caught cheating, saw Busco smash a book against Vota's knife hand. The knife clattered to the floor with a curious sound. Vota's hand reached out and Di Pasco stepped on it with the heel of his foot. The knife disappeared in a shuffle of hands, but Vota no longer had it. Richard stared at the bare, brown spot on the floor where the knife had been.

Whose chance is it now? he wondered. Whose turn to slice the teacher?

Miller tried to struggle off the desk where Levy had him pinned. Brown, a Negro boy, brought his fist down heavily on Miller's nose. He wrenched the larger boy's head back with one hand, and again brought his fist down fiercely.

A slow recognition trickled into Richard's confused thoughts. Through dazzled eyes, he watched.

Vota scrambled to his feet and lunged at him. A solid wall seemed to rise before him as Serubi and Gomez flung themselves against the onrushing form and threw it back. They tumbled onto Vota, holding his arms, lashing out with excited fists.

They're fighting for me! No, Richard reasoned, no. But yes, *they're fighting for me!* Against Miller. Against Vota. For me. For me, oh my God, for me.

His eyes blinked nervously as he struggled to his feet.

"Let's . . . let's take them down to the principal," he said, his voice low.

Antoro moved closer to him, his eyes widening as they took in the livid slash that ran the length of Richard's arm.

"Man, that's some cut," he said.

Richard touched his arm lightly with his left hand. It was soggy and wet, the shirt and jacket stained a dull brownish-red.

"My brother got cut like that once," Ganigan offered.

The boys were still holding Miller and Vota, but they no longer seemed terribly interested in the troublemakers.

For an instant, Richard felt a twinge of panic. For that brief, terrible instant he imagined that the boys hadn't really come to his aid at all, that they had simply seen an opportunity for a good fight and had seized upon it. He shoved the thought aside, began fumbling for words.

"I . . . I think I'd better take them down to Mr Stemplar," he said. He stared at the boys, trying to read their faces, searching for something in their eyes that would tell him he had at last reached them, had at last broken through the wall. He could tell nothing. Their faces were blank, their eyes emotionless.

He wondered if he should thank them. If only he knew. If he could only hit upon the right thing to say, the thing to cement it all.

"I'll . . . I'll take them down. Suppose . . . you . . . you all go to lunch now."

"That sure is a mean cut," Julian said.

"Yeah," Ganigan agreed.

"You can all go to lunch," Richard said. "I want to take Miller and Vota . . . ."

The boys didn't move. They stood there with serious faces, solemnly watching Richard.

". . . to . . . the . . . principal," Richard furnished.

"A hell of a mean cut," Gomez said.

Busco chose his words carefully, and he spoke slowly. "Maybe we better just forget about the principal, huh? Maybe we oughta just go to lunch?"

Richard saw the smile appear on Miller's face, and a new weary sadness lumped into his throat.

He did not pretend to understand. He knew only that they had fought for him and that now, through some unfathomable code of their own, had turned on him again. But he knew what had to be done, and he could only hope that eventually they would understand why he had to do it.

"All right," he said firmly, "let's break it up. I'm taking these two downstairs."

He shoved Miller and Vota ahead of him, fully expecting to meet the resistance of another wall, a wall of unyielding bodies. Instead, the boys parted to let him through, and Richard walked past them with his head high. A few minutes ago, he would have taken this as a sign that the wall had broken. That was a few minutes ago.

Now, he was not at all surprised to hear a high falsetto pipe up behind him, "Oh, Daddy-oh! You're a *hee*-ro!"

DOWN THE LONG NIGHT

William F. Nolan

Adapted for:

NAKED CITY

(ABC, 1958–62)

Starring: John McIntire,

James Franciscus & Leslie Neilsen

Directed by Paul Wendkos

Naked City *has been deservedly described as a milestone in TV production – being the very first crime series to have been filmed on location in the streets of New York where many of its stories were set. Its success with viewers was also very influential, inspiring a number of later cop shows such as the tangled lives of the* 87th Precinct *(1961–62) with Robert Lansing and Norman Fell based on the novels of Ed McBain; the soap opera-like storylines of* Hill Street Blues *(1981–87) starring Daniel J. Travanti and Michael Conrad; and most recently the contro-*

versial **NYPD** Blue *(1994–) featuring David Caruso and Dennis Franz, which was actually banned by some of the smaller US TV stations for alleged excessive violence and "soft core pornography" and, not surprisingly, became the most popular TV cop series in the rest of the nation! All these series had at their heart the theme of a close relationship between two central characters – a concept that had begun in* Naked City *where the veteran Detective Lieutenant Dan Muldoon (John McIntire) and rookie Detective Jim Halloran (James Franciscus) formed a partnership of mutual respect and affection that enabled them to get through any situation and week by week lived up to the show's famous closing line, "There are eight million stories in the Naked City . . . this has been one of them." The episodes all featured different guest stars and among the young hopefuls who earned early breaks working on the crowded streets of the Big Apple were Robert Redford, Martin Sheen, Gene Hackman, Jon Voight, Peter Falk and Dustin Hoffman. For some viewers the city itself was the star of the show, and it certainly added a gritty realism to the stories in which the cops were as likely to have faults as the criminals were to have redeeming features. Spectacular car chases were another feature of the stories which regularly delighted in the oddest titles such as "The Man who Bit a Diamond in Half", "The Well Dressed Termite" and "Make it Fifty Dollars and Add Love to Nona"!*

Naked City *drew the material for many of its episodes from the work of leading Hollywood writers and novelists such as William F. Nolan (1928–), whose novels have included the classic SF story of a future where growing old is a crime,* Logan's Run *(1967) – which has been filmed and made into a TV series – as well as numerous scripts for television specials and series. Recently, Bill has begun an ingenious and entertaining series of novels recreating the days of the hardboiled detectives of the thirties in which the men who wrote those stories – Dashiell Hammett, Raymond Chandler and Erle Stanley Gardner – are themselves the sleuths. The series began with* The Black Mask Murders *in 1994. "Down The Long Night" was adapted from Bill's short story by Charles Beaumont for* Naked City *in November 1960 and starred Nehemiah Persoff,*

Geraldine Brooks and Leslie Neilson, the cult hero of the recent **Naked Gun** *movies. It serves as an ideal reminder of a landmark crime series which deserves to be rerun more often than it is . . .*

The ocean fog closed in, suddenly, like a big gray fist, and Alan Cole stopped remembering. Swearing under his breath, he jabbed the wiper button on the Lincoln's dash, and brought the big car down from fifty to thirty-five. Still dangerous. You couldn't see more than a few yards ahead in this soup. But he said the hell with it and kept the Lincoln at thirty-five because he wanted this mess over in a hurry, because he wanted to hold Jessica in his arms again before the night was done.

Above the damp Santa Monica pavements, looped tubes of neon glowed coldly, like colored seaweed; but there were no other cars. Cole shot through a blinking amber eye.

Actually, he thought, I should have turned him down flat. I should have said, Look, Paul, last week you ripped it. Period. So I don't give a good goddamn *what* kind of trouble you're in.

But then he heard Paul Bowers' anxious voice again, hard and metallic: "*I've got to see you, Alan.*" And he knew that, despite everything – even the way the guy had been acting since Jess had given him the shoulder – he did care. Why?

Nearing Ocean Pier, he thought about the telephone call, attempted to form an attitude. What would he say? For Godsake, how do you talk to a man you've called a loser and a phony and a coddled neurotic?

It had come just after lunch. Cecile couldn't say why she'd put it through against his instructions, except to remark that it sounded important. Of course it had to be Paul. After that screwball telegram from San Francisco, which didn't even start to make sense, Alan had been expecting the call. A big play to get in as a "friend of the family", no doubt. A well thought out pitch on how sorry he was that he'd blown his stack and, needless to say, he wished them both the best of luck, and would they please forgive him – maybe even invite him to the wedding?

Except it didn't turn out that way . . .

Cole punched loose a cigarette, lit it, and went over the conversation for the umpteenth time, searching for clues.

"*I've got to see you, Alan.*"

"*No go. They're shooting this scene tomorrow, and I can't –*"

"*Alan, listen – I'm in trouble. I need your help.*"

"*Like hell. You don't need anybody's help – unquote.*"

"*Wait – Look, I know I said a lot of stupid things last week. But if our friendship ever meant anything to you, for the love of God listen!*"

"*Paul, I said I'm busy. I meant it. Let me give you a ring tomorrow.*"

"*Tomorrow is too late.*" The pleading voice had seemed to crawl from the receiver. A pause. Then: "*The police are after me.*"

"*You're kidding.*"

"*I swear it! Meet me at the pier when you get off work. Crazyville, the funhouse – you know. And don't laugh. It's the only safe place. I'll be waiting for you, Alan. Don't fail me. It may mean my life . . .*"

And then the sharp click as Paul had hung up. Damn him, and damn the day they ever met!

Still, Cole thought, unaware that the Lincoln was wavering on the wrong side of the double white lines, still – it was through Paul that he'd met Jessica. They were engaged then. At least, that's what Paul thought; the poor guy couldn't see how bad he was for the girl. She had been impressed with him, at first. Then, like everyone else, she became disenchanted. And, like everyone else, she had a hell of a time pulling loose.

Was it *my* fault, Cole demanded of himself, that the two of us hit it off so well? I didn't take Jess away from Paul. He'd lost her a long time ago . . .

He spotted a parking place and nosed the car in, cut the engine, sat a moment, quietly, then opened the door.

Chill air went into his throat; it tasted of brine and heavy salt and fathoms. As he locked the automobile, turned and started to walk down the deserted street, Cole remembered how he had always hated this cold, which had nothing of winter in it; and how Bowers had always loved it. As usual, they disagreed. Over the years their likes and dislikes had seldom coincided. Bowers the social lion, the studied Bohemian – to all outward appearances sophisticated and intellectual; and Cole the recluse, the quiet one, the guy over there in the corner. How, Alan wondered, could two such people ever have formed a strong friendship? And was it really that?

Up ahead, the pier stretched, fog-draped and empty. Only the frozen spokes of the ferris wheel and the rotting wooden lacework of the Hi-Boy rose above the pressing blanket of gray.

Alan moved down Marine Street toward the pier, watching his image ripple and flow past streaked shop windows.

What was it with Paul, anyway? What the devil had he done? Robbed someone – no, that was hard to take, not Bowers' long suit. Or –

He passed a window filled with photographs of wild-eyed matted men in silk trunks. Lord Perkins; The Boston Bull; The Strangler.

– murder?

No.

Another window promised salvation to the penitent, damnation to the wicked.

Hotels, shops, missions – all empty and silent. As they had been a million winters ago, when he and Bowers and Jess had walked this street the last time.

Where are the people? he had wondered then. He wondered it now.

Maybe there aren't any people. You never see them moving behind glass. Maybe –

Alan shook his head. Ease off. You're just nervous. Paul's in trouble of some kind, so you're nervous. This place is nothing more than an amusement park, shut down, closed for the season; and that's all. So knock it off, Cole. You're a big boy now.

Yet, Alan felt a slow fear building in him – an uneasiness. With every step, years were peeling away, stripping off in layers. A few moments ago he was Alan Cole, thirty years old, a moderately successful screen writer and not anxious to be anything else. Now . . .

Marine Street flowed into the wide concrete length of Promenade. Alan hurried across, listening to the thin cries of circling gulls and to the lonely night beach.

Taking a final drag on his cigarette, he ground it underheel and turned into the amusement park.

Again the sense of something amiss. Partly Paul and also, this place. As if only a moment before, every stand had been open, every ride spinning and whirling and rolling in colored movements, the walk itself alive with people. And as if magic fingers had been snapped, causing all the people and the movement to vanish instantly.

Passing the roller coaster, Alan could almost hear the chant of the bored, slick-haired ticket seller:

"*The Hi-Boy! The Hi-Boy! Don't miss it, folks! It's safe! It's exciting! The Thrill of a Life-Time!*"

He glanced at the sheeted train of wooden cars, waiting in coiled silence on their tracks, and hurried past.

His stomach felt light. Dizziness had returned with memories. ("Jess, I'd like you to meet an old buddy of mine, Alan Cole. Alan, this is my gal, Jessica Randall. Isn't she a doll?") He quickened his step past the closed concessions, endless rows of shabby canvas curtains; past the rifle range and the Whirlagig and the Caterpillar; past the arcade where you can watch a thirty year old strip-show and then leave, wondering how the dames look today.

A hundred yards ahead, on the tip of the pier, he could see the fog-buried angles of Crazyville.

Paul would be waiting there. And it would all be over soon. He'd see to that, by God.

*   *   *

The ticket booth was a gigantic smiling head. Within its mouth between the plaster teeth, a sign read: CLOSED.

Alan paused at the wicket gate and glanced back along the walkway. It was empty.

He vaulted the gate and peered across the yard. A tiny, twisting path marked LOONEY STREET horseshoed around mad wooden building fronts.

Gravity seemed missing here; it was a force that belonged entirely to the outside world. The houses convoluted above the cobbled walk, gables and roofs and walls leaning at impossible angles, one upon the other.

Alan cupped his hands about his mouth. Softly, he called: "Paul."

No answer.

He swore. He hadn't changed; not a bit. This idiot place was supposed to make you dizzy, so – he was dizzy.

And where the hell was Paul?

He moved toward the bat-wing doors which opened to the black maze of damp tunnels. Beyond this point lay a man-made night so intense and so impenetrable that, once inside, you could no longer imagine day.

"Paul?"

He hesitated, glanced up. A ragged, toothless crone sagged drunkenly from a second-story window. Her throat had been carefully saw-cut; her eyes protruded in dumb disbelief.

Bloodied faces peeped from every window, each with a name and a history. Paul had once claimed that they were his only friends, these plaster nightmares, the only ones who truly understood him.

Standing in the silent yard, Alan felt the familiar horror of the funhouse engulfing him again. The death-figures seemed to writhe just beyond the perimeter of his vision: he could almost *hear* their frozen cries.

He drew a deep breath, pushed open the doors, and hesitated there, divided squarely between the interior shadows and the solid reality of the outside.

"Paul – you in here?"

Like a huge sounding-box, the wooden tunnels bounced the words along, echoing, finally lost.

Then: "Alan?"

"Yeah!" He wiped perspiration from his palms. "Come on out."

A pause. "I can't." The voice was faint.

"What do you mean, you can't?"

"Too dangerous. I might be seen."

"There's nobody around for miles."

"I – can't afford to take the chance."

"All right, all right. God! Where are you?"

"Just follow the tunnel. First room."

"All right, but – this better be *good*."

Alan stepped into the long night of the tunnels; into a colored blackness that danced before his eyes in a million tiny specks of light. The walls, damp and slippery beneath his groping hands, smelled of the sea; the odor of soaked and rotting wood seeped up from the floor. Far below hidden waters sloshed against tired pilings.

The walls began to narrow as he moved forward. The ceiling lowered gradually. He was forced to crouch, turn sideways.

The walls ended.

Alan extended cautious hands, encountered nothingness. "Okay, so I'm out of the first tunnel. What now?"

"You're fine." The voice was much closer. "Keep coming."

"I can't see a damn thing."

Alan remembered his lighter, got it out, thumbed the wheel. It sparked feebly, failed to ignite. Another spin. A tiny guttering flame this time.

He shielded it with his left hand and peered ahead. A cleated platform led upward. He slid his feet over the cleats and reached a wide opening.

"In here, Alan."

The light flickered. "Well, turn on a flashlight or something, will you! I'm going to fall flat on my ass."

Of course, he realized, Paul must know this place as a blind man knows his own bedroom. Always running out here to "think". Or to bang quail. Or – what?

Alan advanced carefully, tapping. A heavy object brushed his shoulder; he hissed, leaping back. The lighter clattered to the plank flooring and winked out.

Total darkness.

"Paul?"

"Over here."

"Over *where*? What am I, a goddamn cat or something?" There was a scrabbling, a fast padding, "Look, buddy, this routine is getting old at a rapid clip. In fact, the hell with the whole thing. I'm getting out of here."

He patted his handkerchief pocket, removed a match-folder. He struck one.

The object that had brushed against him was, he saw, a body – swinging from a thick rope.

No – not a body. By adjusting his eyes to the feeble glow, Alan saw that it was a scarecrow. One of many. The room seemed filled with hanging straw corpses, all revolving in submarine slowness on their corded lengths of hemp. Scarecrows . . . papier mache trees . . . Now he remembered the room. Horse Thief Hall, or something like that.

The flame bit into his finger.

Blackness.

He lit another match, dropped it, tore the last one out savagely. "Okay, kid, you wanted to talk – here I am."

Silence.

He swung the match in a slow arc above his head, knowing, suddenly, that it was useless, knowing that Paul Bowers' entire phone conversation had been another fake. The sincerity and the pleading and the desperation: all fake. Part of a final, elaborate practical joke. Paul didn't need help; what he needed was a long overdue kick in the teeth!

"Fun's over, Cole catches on!" he called.

Silence.

The third match burned out. Alan turned to retrace his steps, thinking about Jessica's probable reaction to a stunt like this. Maybe he oughtn't to tell her. The less said about Paul in her presence, the better.

It takes a certain talent, he thought bitterly; a certain

definite talent to be a perpetual fall-guy. Drop the hook, I'll bite!

He'd almost reached the doorway when four naked green bulbs, one in each corner of the room, bloomed into silent life.

Alan blinked, the pale glow burning into his eyes. He scrubbed at them, realizing, vaguely, that Paul had found the central control box and activated a switch.

The swinging scarecrows came into focus. Alan's fist knotted. His head jerked about the room. "Listen!" he shouted, "I'm going to walk back out of here, Paul. Don't try anything cute. Because if you do I swear I'll break your damn neck. Is that clear?"

He started for the opening. Another scarecrow bumped against his shoulder. He wheeled, buried his fingers in the mouldered straw, and pulled, furiously. The figure tore loose at the neck, collapsed to the floor with a wet, pulpy sound.

Soft laughter from the tunnels.

He was about to push his way through the hanging figures when he paused.

Everything inside him paused.

Sensation became thought: *Scarecrows are made of straw.* And the object that had just touched him was *solid!*

Alan turned, and jammed a fist against his mouth.

Hanging there, swaying amid the rotting scarecrows, was Jessica Randall.

For a long moment, Alan could not move. His body was incapable of movement; every muscle locked tight.

His mind tried to reject what his eyes saw.

She was naked. And cold. Her flesh, once warm and vibrant, carried now an icy chill; and her eyes, though unseeing, were open.

Her sheer silk stockings had been knotted about her throat and about a ceiling beam, and supported her slight weight easily.

"Jess!"

Alan put a trembling hand to the girl's breast, and then he knew she was dead.

Jess was dead. And Paul had killed her. He knew that, too. Because she had fallen in love with someone else. Paul had done this, just as he'd promised in that crazy speech he'd delivered to them. They hadn't believed him, or taken him seriously, because Paul Bowers had always been a lot of talk, a thin red-faced clown full of empty promises and emptier threats. And they'd been wrong.

Alan saw Jess's clothes, her red blouse and white skirt, her undergarments, her black leather ballet-shoes – all folded and placed neatly in a corner on the floor. And he knew a hate and a fear, then, that he had never dreamed of.

Run! he thought. Try to stay calm and get out of this place. He wants you to panic. Don't panic. Just get out, quickly – then wait and get him.

He pulled a shutter in his mind that closed off the reality of Jess and what had happened to her. Out, the same way, he thought; but it wasn't so easy. He'd turned so many times that he had lost all sense of direction. Three separate doorways opened on the room of scarecrows and only one of them led back to the first tunnel: the others were phony. And he couldn't be sure which was which.

He'd taken a single step forward, aware now that the laughter was mechanical, not human, issuing from the cracked lips of a plaster fat man, when the ceiling lights blacked out again. Paul was still at the switch and that meant he had little time. Hurriedly, he knelt on the plank flooring and groped for the fallen lighter. Without luck.

Okay, so you move in the dark – but by God you move!

He touched one wall of the room. He moved along, tapping the rough wood: he would have to try one of the doorways and hope it was the right one.

He thought of Bowers, at home in the darkness, gliding through the looping maze of passageways like a swift fish in green waters, perfectly at ease, perfectly in command.

The funhouse was Paul's world.

Abruptly the wall ended, but not in emptiness. He'd fumbled himself into a corner. A corner – Without knowing exactly why, he reached up and touched a light bulb. It was still warm. He unscrewed it in quick short motions and dropped it into his pocket. Then he followed the next wall and reached one of the doors.

Careful to walk slowly, he entered the tunnel. And walked head-on into a pocket. Wood on all three sides.

Alan groaned softly, his throat went dry. He tried to swallow and couldn't.

All right, you missed. Now turn around and go back to the next one. Move, damn you, move!

He re-entered the still black room and groped numbly along to the second doorway. At least this one would lead somewhere. Alan stepped out onto the cleated platform.

This must be it! It seemed to possess the same dank odor, the same narrow twistings . . .

He pressed forward.

A buzzing, a whirr of turning machinery, and the blackness blazed into light. Far off, the laughter again. Within a niche in the wall directly to Alan's right, a huge gorilla raised its fists, swiveled its savage head back and forth, snarling.

"You son of a bitch, Bowers! I'll kill you."

The apparition faded behind him. He was running now, knowing that this tunnel led deeper into the funhouse. Toward Paul's voice?

Six explosions, deafening, somewhere in the dark. Gunshots. Paul had a gun. But why waste bullets?

To let you know he's armed. To let you know he's waiting . . .

Alan ran on, constantly aware that in order to get Bowers, he would have to get into the open, into *his* world. He stumbled, barking his knuckles on trick partitions, pushed himself forward, his face sweatsoaked, legs weak and trembling.

A dragon sprang into colored life. It lay on painted rocks, a fat reptilean creature, its green-scaled head nodding, forked tongues licking in and out.

Sudden shrill gusts of wind hissed up from the floor.

And the infernal laughter, mocking him, following him wherever he went –

He ran on, crouching, sometimes on hands and knees, blundering forward, knowing, even as he ran, that he was close to death. A bullet or a knife would meet him in the darkness; and he wouldn't have a chance.

Then he saw light – faint, but only moments away. Only a few more steps!

The floor dropped away beneath him. Alan felt himself plunging downward; he thrashed his arms, clutched at shadows and blackness.

The trap-door closed.

The room was full of people. Frightened, angry, staring people, all seated at the bottom of a long slide.

A memory clicked into place for Alan Cole. The Mirror Room – where you spend an hour, alone, trying to find your way out.

He licked his dry lips and wiped the perspiration from his hands.

He listened. Footsteps.

You're unarmed. Move!

Jerkily, he thrust himself into the corridors of glass. He saw his image reflected in a thousand bright distortions as he slammed through the maze, bumping, cursing, moving, moving.

He reached another glass tunnel. A tall, freckled, crewcut man faced him.

Himself. He caught his breath. Everywhere, mirrors. A small skylight above for ventilation. But no exit that he knew of.

"Alan?"

He narrowed his eyes, located the voice, found that he was staring down a dark corridor that could not have existed.

A figure stood there, motionless. Something glinted in the figure's hand.

"Writers should never run," the voice from the darkness said. "It makes their faces turn red. Take a good look at yourself in one of these mirrors, Alan. You've no idea how ridiculous you look!"

"You lousy bastard!"

Alan's perspective had melted; now, suddenly, it reformed. Until this moment he had not been entirely able to connect the man who had murdered Jess with an ineffectual guy he'd bummed around with. Sure, Paul Bowers had been a whiner and a loser and a neurotic; but, God, not a killer. Killers were what he wrote cheap movies about. Yet –

Alan recalled a book he'd once read for research. A study of criminology. It postulated that every human being on Earth was a potential murderer, needing only the right set of circumstances, the right personal motivation, to turn killer. A world full of dynamite sticks, waiting to be sparked. His engagement to Jess had sparked it for Paul, had set the fuse burning. And it had been burning for a week.

Kid-gloves, boy. He's nuts now. You read books on psychology, okay, be psychological. Or, brother, you're dead, too.

"Paul, listen – can't we talk or something?"

The figure did not move. "Clear the air, you mean? Get it all tied up in a neat package?" A small chuckle, like a tapped siphon.

Alan recognized the words, the same words he had used when he gave Paul the straight goods that night. "I didn't mean everything I said. Honest. Is that it?"

"Part of it, Alan."

The blackness stirred. A shape took slow form.

Paul Bowers stepped out of the tunnel, smiling. He was, as always, impeccably dressed. His charcoal gray suit tailored to make him look heavier than his 175 pounds; his shoetips gleaming; his pale, bony face clean-shaven and smelling of lotions. Across his high forehead, the fine blond hair was neatly, perfectly combed. "By the way," he said, "don't try anything dramatic. You're much too clumsy."

He looked white and businesslike and totally unlike a killer, except for his hands. They were powerful and bright red, ending in thick fingers; the hands of a longshoreman or a mechanic – or a strangler. In one of them, held firmly, was a twelve-inch blue-steel hunting knife.

Alan looked at it.

"Ugly monster," Bowers said. "But a hunting knife seemed appropriate for the occasion. Borrowed this one from you quite a while ago, if you'll remember. And I thought, 'Now *there*, by God, would be a touch!' And so it is. At least give me that."

Alan's blood grew hot. "Why did you kill Jess?" he blurted, before he could stop the words.

"The old story, pal. You know: 'If I can't have her, then by the Holies, no one–' Etc. Besides, I wanted to see if I had the nerve. Sort of practice, you might say. For you."

"Paul, listen."

"Of course."

"What do you want me to do? Do you want me to beg for my life, is that it?"

"That would be kind of fun, I must admit. But to tell you the honest to God truth, I'm getting a little tired of the game." Bowers stepped closer, smiling. His eyes were misted over. And the laughter still echoed down the halls.

"You're sick. You know that, I suppose."

"Oh, yes. Mad as a March hare." It was the Party Paul, the bored intellectual who built his words and rolled them out on oiled casters. "I would describe my illness as Acute Reaction to Prolonged Injustice. The prognosis is fair, however; fortunately, I know the cure. Jess was part. You, Brother Rat, will complete the treatment."

Alan's throat moved convulsively. In all his films, a man with a knife was a pushover. You kicked it out of his hand, or rushed him before he could use his arm, or bluffed him. But that was the movies. In real life, it worked out differently. A man with a knife was a man with a formidable weapon. If he knew how to use it – and Paul knew – you might as well be in front of a .45 or a cannon.

"Paul, you'll be caught. The police will investigate sure as hell, find we were all friends and track you down wherever you go."

"You really think so?" Bowers lowered the blade, as if bemused by the thought, and Alan stepped forward; but then the knife was up again, and Bowers was laughing. "Alan, you don't give me any credit. You never did, of course." His voice rose in pitch. The smile had become fixed and deadly. "Exactly how long did you think you could go on kicking me before I kicked back, anyway?"

An auto horn bleated out beyond the pier. A strange sound, part of a different world.

Alan remembered the skylight, was very careful not to look up. Was it possible that he could reach it? No. Too high, too small . . .

"I gave you friendship, Alan, and what did I get in return? Betrayal. Oh, I didn't expect you to break your neck trying to give me a little help, but I thought at least you'd appreciate what I'd done enough to stand by me. Not say, 'Thanks, Paul' – no, not that – but maybe show a little loyalty." He was trembling. The hunting knife jumped in short darting flashes in his hand. "Always take, take, take, and never give. Never a helping hand. No; it's good-bye, Paulie, I'm a big man now. Lots of money. Lots of fame. Too busy to help a two-bit loser like Paul Bowers – after I pushed you to the top with my bare hands. Do you deny it?"

"I –"

"Do you deny that it was I who got you in at the studio, introduced you to Kay, almost forced him to hire you? And who was it that stayed up till four every morning helping you to make that lousy script acceptable?"

"I don't argue that you helped me, Paul. I'm grateful for it."

"Grateful!" The thin man drew his lips back. He breathed heavily. "I guess that's what accounts for your aceing me out, playing along with the rumors about, 'Poor old Bowers, all washed up!' And I guess it was the final expression of your gratitude to turn Jess against me?"

"That's a lie, Paul. I – damn it, Jess just fell in love with me. I couldn't help that."

Bowers' jaw muscles twitched. "I believed that for a while, Alan. Felt that maybe I really *was* the oddball you said I was. But then I started checking around. And I found out a few things. For instance, who it was that talked Kahn into giving me the sack. And who it was that got me blackballed right afterwards." He stepped forward. "I know you pretty well, Alan, enough to know you probably still think of yourself as a noble guy in an embarrassing situation. Those shutters in your mind. They won't let you remember the filthy things you've done."

"It's not true."

"The convenient little shutters won't let you face the fact that you've been scared of me ever since we met. Scared spitless. You know I'd got you in solid at Galactic, so your ego forced you to get rid of me. And it was easy, because I trusted you. I trusted you with Jess, too. All the time you were filling her mind with dirty lies about me, *I trusted you!* And I didn't wake up for a long time. When I did, it was too late. But not too late for me to spoil your little play —"

Bowers raised the knife.

At that instant, Alan grabbed the light-bulb in his pocket and hurled it to the floor with all his strength.

The explosion whipped Bowers' head around. In that split second, Alan leapt for the skylight. His fingers closed over the heavy beam; held. Hidden sacs seemed to burst and flood strength through him. A single surge pulled his body up and over the edge. He could feel hands clutching at his legs, slipping, gathering the cloth of his trousers. He kicked, viciously, at the hands, and swung his ankles against the wood. Bowers' hold loosened. He kicked again. The weight fell away.

Alan drew his legs up swiftly, pivoted, and stood up on the slate roof.

Cold bit into his skin; the fog, a wash of wet mist, billowed and pressed in upon his eyes. He balanced there on the slippery roof a brief moment, breathing.

Take it easy, he thought. Try to run and you'll end up cartwheeling off the edge headfirst.

The roof was an iced pond, impossible to run across. Alan squinted. If he could only see! How far down was the pavement, anyway? Where was the edge? He was on a slat island, surrounded by moving gray tides.

And now Paul Bowers' hands were closing over the beam.

Alan crouched above the opening, braced himself and lashed out with his foot. The blow tipped Paul back, forced one hand off. Alan lifted his right foot, prepared to send it heel-down on the strained white fingers.

Something grabbed his ankle, jerked.

He caught a glimpse of Paul's face, grinning, blazing red, as though every blood vessel had ruptured and tendriled out.

Then Alan fell.

With a grunt, Bowers heaved through the skylight, landed nimbly, and took the knife from its belt position.

Alan struggled up, his eyes on the long blue sweep of steel in Paul's hand.

"Shutters open, Alan? Or do you still think you're a hero?"

Now!

The blow caught the side of Paul's head, sent him reeling back. Alan felt his muscles go cold: bright color fireworked in his mind. He struck out again, blindly, throwing his entire weight into the blow. Soft inner nose cartilage crunched beneath his hand.

He had not fought for a long time, but now hate activated him, put strength into his arms, goaded him. But even as he swung, he knew that he could never win out against Paul and the knife. Perhaps the blade had already entered his body – they say you don't feel a knife thrust right at first – and his life was, even now, ebbing away.

"Go ahead, Alan, fight! You're doing fine!"

He aimed his fist, drove for that grinning red face. Bone and flesh yielded. But the fury of the lunge pulled him forward. He stumbled, slid, his head striking a ledge of plaster at the roof's edge.

More fireworks. He tried desperately to shake them away.

He tried to shake away Paul's burning words, the image of Jess . . . *Was it true?*

Paul Bowers glided toward him, smiling, calm, the knife poised high.

All over now. Done. Finished. He closed his eyes. *In a second now. Another second.* He waited, his breath in a bottle and the bottle sealed. He could smell the honed steel and the rough leather handle; he could taste the metal in his throat.

A strange sound, then. Like the last drops of water draining from a sink – a short bubbling indrawn scream.

Alan opened his eyes.

Paul had slumped to his knees, teetering, making thin dry noises and staring, staring.

Then he toppled, spilled sideway to the roof, and lay there. His fingers spasmed on the wet slats like the overturned legs of two giant spiders.

Then he was quiet.

In his chest was imbedded the long steel of the hunting knife.

Alan rose, shakily. The roof listed, heaved, settled. A sharp wind from the ocean had cleared some of the fog. Without trying to understand, he located the roof edge again and the pavement below. Less than ten feet.

He jumped. The ground was made of needles and electricity. It buckled his knees. He fell against the rusting ribs of an ancient trolley, and leaned there, trying to swallow.

He began to walk. He listened to the sound of the sea washing in on the beach, and the gulls cloaked high in night, and his footsteps.

Is it true? That was all he could think. He knew that Jess was dead and that Paul was dead and this was no nightmare, no bad dream, but something real; yet, he could only think: Is it true? Did I do those things to Paul, actually, turn Jess against him, actually –

The sky revolved: Alan felt that it had suddenly shaken loose. The peppermint striped shroud covering the Caterpillar began to shimmer and twist darkly; the towering wooden immensity of the Hi-Boy swayed and separated into bright pieces and showered soundlessly down upon him.

He staggered on, out of the amusement park, down a street, to an all-night cafe.

He lifted the receiver off its hook. "Give me the police," he said, in a soft, tired voice.

It was 10 a.m. when they knocked on the door. He'd fallen into a pit of black exhaustion, not bothering to wash or change clothes and getting out of the pit was difficult. When he awoke, he didn't question that the night had been real: his hand ached and his head throbbed and he still felt the numbness.

"Just a minute." His mouth was sour. He could barely remember talking to the police, waiting while they checked his story, staggering out of the squad car.

Alan Cole opened the door. A large man in a brown double-breasted suit stood there. He was flanked by two cops in uniform.

"Yes, what is it?"

The large man stepped inside the room. "A good yarn you told us, Cole," he said. "Mighty good yarn. We swallowed it."

Alan shook his head. This was the man he'd spoken to last night. Captain Boylen, Homicide. But now he looked different.

"What do you mean?"

"Cole," the man said, "you can make it easy, or you can make it tough. It doesn't matter much."

"I —" Alan sat down on the bed; his senses began to swim. "I don't know what you're talking about."

"Then I'll tell you," the man said. "Your story washes out. Point one: We found six bullet holes and a 32.20 at the funhouse. Pistol registered under Paul Bowers' name. We examined the knife. It's yours —"

"I know. I admitted that, didn't I?"

"Then I suppose you know that rough leather won't take prints."

"So what?"

The policeman removed a cigar, skinned off its cellophane wrapping, lit it. "Guy was pretty well armed, wouldn't you say? Gun *and* a knife."

Alan sat quietly, trying to understand.

"Point two," Boylen went on. "We got a report from the medical examiner. It's his opinion Bowers didn't commit suicide. Man decides to kill himself with a knife, Cole, he stabs within an area of a couple inches, like this —" The policeman made stabbing motions against his chest. "There were *four* wounds in Bowers. One here, in the ribs; and here — and here — and finally the one that got him. All spread out. Suicides don't do that, Mister. Care to say anything?"

Alan remembered Paul's telling him of the criminal medicine course he'd taken in Zurich — a course for student lawyers and insurance investigators, the purpose to show the difference between a murder victim and a suicide . . .

"Keep talking, Captain."

"Point three." The policeman removed an envelope from his breast pocket and tossed it over to Alan. "It's been photostated," he said. "Read it."

Alan removed the letter. Flawlessly typewritten, with thick margins. From Paul, addressed to the police.

"Mailed sometime yesterday afternoon, late," Boylen said. "Downtown got it. Sent it over to me early this morning. Go on, read it."

But even before he began, Alan knew. Everything fell instantly into place. The screwy telegram from San Francisco, (*'Sorry it turned out this way. The best man lost. Paul.'*); the shots in the dark and the pistol (to make it appear that they had struggled); the borrowed hunting knife.

He forced himself to read, knowing what the letter would say, knowing fully.

Homicide Div.
LA Police Department
Los Angeles, California
To Whom It May Concern:

    I hope that this letter will end up in your crank files and that I'll wake up tomorrow feeling pretty ridiculous about the whole thing. But record – just in case.

I have reason to believe that Alan Cole, an employee of Galactic Pictures, Galactic City, Calif., is preparing to do harm to my fiancée, Jessica Randall. Cole and I have been friends for years, and I know him well. He was engaged to Miss Randall up until two weeks ago, at which time Miss Randall confessed that it was I whom she loved and wished to marry. Cole pretended to take it well. But this morning he called Jessica, asking her to have one last drink with him at a little bar they used to frequent, across from Ocean Pier, Santa Monica – Bisco's. I tried to dissuade her from going, but she likes Alan and doesn't feel there's anything to it.

Maybe there isn't. But, as I say, I know Cole. Somewhere inside him, there is definitely a strange and vicious streak. He is a man capable of almost anything.

It's likely nothing will happen. In that case, I'll phone tomorrow. If not, and if this fear of mine turns out to have any justification – contact Alan Cole. But make sure you're armed.

Sincerely,

Paul A. Bowers

Alan folded the letter and put it back in the envelope and handed it to the large man.

"You want to tell us about it, Mister Cole?"

Alan thought of Paul's words, of shutters that would not close inside his mind; of Jess and the clever lies he had told her, unconsciously. The lies he had told everyone, including Alan Cole . . .

Hell of a script, he told himself. Who's the hero? Who's the villain?

"Sure," he said, thinking this was *one* job he wasn't going to ruin for Paul. "I'll tell you about it."

Then he started laughing, and it sounded like the mechanical man at the funhouse. Only he couldn't turn it off.

THE CASE OF
THE HOWLING DOG

Erle Stanley Gardner

Adapted for:

PERRY MASON

(CBS, 1957–67; 1985–93)

Starring: Raymond Burr,

Barbara Hale & William Hopper

Directed by Sam White

From a real-life lawyer like Edgar Lustgarten introducing a television series, it was only a small step to a programme in which a lawyer was the star – and the overwhelming success of Perry Mason, *based on the novels of Erle Stanley Gardner about a brilliant defence counsel, which CBS first screened in September 1957 and ran for the next decade, has had a profound effect on TV crime drama. In its stead have followed*

several other series about men of the law including CBS' The
Defenders *(1961–4), featuring a father and son team played
by E.G. Marshall and Robert Reid (in the pilot episode, the
stars were actually Ralph Bellamy and William Shatner – later
of* Star Trek *– with Steve McQueen as their client!), and*
Thames TV's Rumpole of the Bailey *(1978–), with Leo
McKern in the continuing cases of John Mortimer's droll
barrister. Most recently there has been* Kavanagh QC
*(1994–) with John Thaw, fresh from his role as Inspector
Morse, playing a barrister who is notorious for his rapier-like
cross examinations, and the pudgy, balding Theodore "Teddy"
Hoffman (Daniel Benzali) the top LA defence lawyer in*
Murder One *(1996–97). Perry Mason, of course, originated
from the pages of the novels which Erle Stanley Gardner started
writing about him in 1933 with* The Case of the Velvet Claws,
*and he had already been featured in movies in the thirties played
by Warren William, and a decade later on radio by John
Larkin, before being taken up by TV. But it was the television
series which made Perry an icon and the man who played him,
Raymond Burr, into a household name. Burr's death from
cancer in 1993 was mourned by fans all over the world. The
actor had, in fact, only just completed work on a new Perry
Mason TV film,* The Case of the Killer Kiss, *the last of two
dozen television specials in a second series which had commenced
in 1985. However, but for a twist of fate, Raymond Burr might
never have played Perry Mason at all: for when the series was
first auditioning actors in 1956, he read for the part of District
Attorney Ham Burger, but on an impulse also asked to play a
scene as Mason. The rest is history.*

*Erle Stanley Gardner (1889–1970) had himself been a
lawyer in California where he specialized in championing hope-
less cases in which penniless defendants were at the mercy of
authority or big business. Later, to augment his funds, he decided
to make use of these experiences in fictional form and began
contributing to the crime pulp magazines such as* Black Mask
and Detective Story Weekly. *But it was with his first Perry
Mason novel,* The Case of the Velvet Claws *– which was
actually rejected by several publishers before being taken on by*

William Morrow – that he created a hero who was to feature in over 80 more novels as well as being adapted for all the entertainment mediums. Today, quite a number of the novels are still in print, while the movies are regularly rerun on television as are the two series of made-for-TV productions. "The Case of the Howling Dog" which Gardner wrote in 1934 and filmed that same year, was also adapted for the small screen in the third season of Perry Mason *in 1960, and is here presented in an adapted version prepared by the author for* TV Guide.

Perry Mason was admitted to be the cleverest criminal lawyer in the city, but he was more than that. He was a great counsel, either for the prosecution or the defence, though Perry himself always preferred to save a man than to get him sentenced. A fine, handsome man in the early thirties, he was as big a success in Society as he was in the courts. He entertained lavishly, and in other ways spent money as fast as he made it.

Della Street, his pretty confidential secretary, who was also his fiancée, reminded him of this one morning.

"A cheque for three figures would send the old bank balance on the wrong side," she said, showing him his pass-book.

"So bad as that," said Perry, pushing the pass-book back. "Well, we'll have to put the brake on, I guess. Thank goodness the business is good."

A little while later Della announced Arthur Cartwright. It was Perry's invariable custom to look his clients over carefully while they were doing the talking. From this observation he often got more information from them than they gave him by their words.

The first thing Perry noticed about Arthur Cartwright was that he was in a terribly nervous state, and he knew the cause was neither drink nor drugs.

"It's about a dog that howls all through the night," began Cartwright.

"I'm sorry," said Perry. "But I can't be bothered with such a paltry case."

"But there's a will as well," said Cartwright. "A will involving quite a lot of money."

"Let's hear about that first," said Perry.

"Is a will valid no matter how a man dies?" asked Cartwright. "I mean if he died by hanging or anything like that."

"If the will was all right in other respects it would stand," Perry assured him.

Cartwright seemed greatly relieved.

"All right, then," he said. "I want to leave all my property to Mrs Clinton Foley, of Milpas Drive."

Perry glanced at Cartwright's visiting card.

"A neighbour of yours?"

"Next door. Just one other thing. Supposing that Mrs Foley isn't married to Foley but is living with him as his wife?"

"That could be made clear and legal," said Perry. "You simply state in your will that you leave your money to the woman now living at the address you name and who is known as Mrs Clinton Foley."

"Thanks. I'll send you the will some time to-day. Now about this howling dog."

Perry waved a protesting hand.

"I have already told you I cannot take such a case."

Cartwright threw down a bundle of notes.

"There's a sum to recompense you, and more if need be," he said. "I'm quite sane, and there's more in this howling dog than you think. However, the will is the first matter to consider. I'll send it to you."

Cartwright picked up his hat and walked out.

Perry Mason sent for Della and told her what had happened.

"He's in a shocking nervous state," he said. "He may be eccentric, but I'm sure he's quite sane."

The next morning the will arrived, and Perry got a shock.

Instead of leaving his money to the woman "known" as Mrs Clinton Foley, Cartwright had left it to "the real Mrs Foley, the legally wedded wife of Clinton Foley".

"The will is perfectly drawn up," said Perry to Della. "Cartwright is sane enough, as I told you. But I'm curious to know why he changed his mind overnight. It's not a question of old age and doddering. The fellow can't be over forty."

That, so far as Perry Mason was concerned, was the beginning of what he afterwards set down in his records as "The Case of the Howling Dog."

The next move was made by Clinton Foley, who came to the district attorney with a statement that Arthur Cartwright was insane, and that he wanted a warrant issued to that effect.

Foley's complaint was that Cartwright had made himself objectionable by continuous observation of his house.

"He looks at my place through a pair of field-glasses," said Foley. "The nuisance has become so great that my servants have left me, and I am getting into a state of nerves myself."

Perry, who had been sent for by the district attorney, smiled.

"And Cartwright complains you are driving him frantic by keeping a dog that howls all through the day and night."

"Nonsense!" exclaimed Foley. "My dog never howls."

"Suppose we all go over and see your dog," suggested Perry.

He said nothing of a mysterious message he had received from Cartwright, which read: "I know now why the dog howls. I appoint you to represent the beneficiary under my will and fight for her interests."

Perry had already told the district attorney this. That was why he was at the conference.

Perry had quickly decided that he did not like Foley.

The man was good-looking enough, about forty, and well mannered, when he was not angry, but he had a blustering way which irritated the lawyer.

When they arrived at Foley's house they were met by Lucy Benton, whom Foley introduced as his housekeeper. She showed a note to Foley, and when he had read it he passed it to the others. The note read:

> "A few days ago I found out who was living next door. I know now that I have always loved him and not you. We are going away together, and I know we shall be happy again. – EVELYN."

"Then the so-called Mrs Foley must be Cartwright's wife," thought Perry. But he said nothing.

Foley was tearing up and down like a madman, threatening what he would do to Cartwright.

"He must have forced her to go away with him," he shouted. "She would never have gone willingly. She hated him. That's why she left him."

Perry focused his attention on Lucy Benton. There was something strange about the woman.

She was young, and would have been pretty had she cared to make the most of her looks, but she had not done so. Her hair was arranged in a most unattractive way, and her dress was old-fashioned. It was strange to find a woman who did not want to look her best. Perry noticed her right arm was bandaged, and he asked her about it. She told him the dog had bitten her, but hastily added that it was not his fault because he was ill at the time.

Perry's attention was next called to a building that was being erected.

He asked Foley what it was.

"I'm extending my garage," replied Foley sharply.

Perry went back to his office and started his staff on making inquiries.

Information came through about the Foleys and the Cartwrights.

Two years before the two families had been living in Ventura on very friendly terms. Then Foley had run away with Evelyn Cartwright. Mrs Foley had not taken any steps to get a divorce, nor had Cartwright. Mrs Foley still lived in

Ventura, though she travelled a lot, and Cartwright had gone from place to place until for some reason he had taken the house next to Foley.

Perry ordered Dobbs, one of his best men, to watch Foley's house and put the others on to trace Cartwright and his wife. But all inquiries drew a blank. Neither could be found. Baffled in this direction, Perry decided to have another go at Foley. He rang him up and asked for an appointment. Rather grudgingly, Foley made an appointment for eight o'clock that night. As he approached the house, Perry saw Dobbs watching it from a vantage-point across the street, but he did not speak to him.

He rang the bell, but there was no reply.

Perry tried the door and found it open.

Calling Foley by name he entered.

An uncanny stillness pervaded the house, and Perry felt a sense of disaster as he walked through the hall into the library on the right.

His fears were confirmed. Clinton Foley was lying on his back, dead, and a short distance away was a police dog, also dead.

Both had been shot.

Perry telephoned the police, and then rushed across the street to Dobbs.

"Better make yourself scarce," he said, when he had told him the facts. "The police will want to question you if they see you."

The lawyer went back to the house, and presently a number of police cars came along.

In the first were Claude Drumm, the district attorney, and Detective-sergeant Holcomb. Perry told them of his appointment with Foley and of his discovery.

"Cartwright must have done it," said the D.A. To this the lawyer made no reply.

Perry rushed back to his office where Dobbs was waiting for him.

He had plenty to report.

Shortly after seven o'clock Lucy Benton had left Foley's

house in a motor-car, accompanied by a man. A few minutes later the real Mrs Foley had arrived at the house in a taxi.

She sent the driver to the Cartwright house, and while he was knocking at the door Mrs Foley entered the Foley house. A minute later there had come from the Foley house a blare of radio.

"I guess it was the radio and the driver's pounding at the Cartwrights' door that prevented me from hearing the shots that must have been fired," said Dobbs. "Anyway, Mrs Foley drove away, and soon after that you came along."

Dobbs had taken the number of the taxicab, and it was an easy matter to trace it.

And from the information given by the taxi-driver they traced Mrs Foley, who was living under an assumed name at a quiet hotel.

The taxi-driver had told Perry's assistant that he could certainly recognise his fare again. He described her appearance and the fur coat she was wearing. Moreover, he had noticed a very fragrant perfume that had come from a handkerchief she had left in the car.

Della Street was with Perry when the report came in.

"We've got to see Mrs Foley at once," he said to Della. "That woman has left a trail that even the dumbest cop could follow. Come on. We've not a second to lose."

Della did not ask any questions. She knew that when Perry Mason was working at high pressure he wanted quick action – not talk.

As they drove to the hotel a glimmer of an idea began to focus in Perry's brain.

He knew nothing of the real Mrs Foley, and had only the photographs his staff had collected of her to imagine what kind of a woman she might be.

But he had decided that he liked her face just as strongly as he had disliked the face of her husband.

On the drive he kept looking closely at Della.

"Might be done," he said to himself.

On arriving at the hotel, he pushed his way past all who

asked his business and made his way to the room occupied by Mrs Foley.

"There's no time for talk," he said to Mrs Foley. "I'm Perry Mason, and I've got an order to look after your interests. I want that fur coat you wore to-night and a lot of your scent."

"Perry Mason," said Mrs Foley. "I'm so glad you've come."

"Get the coat," said Perry, "and the scent."

But Della had already got the fur coat and the scent-bottle.

"Miss Della Street, my secretary, and the smartest girl in the city," explained Perry. "She's going to get back the handkerchief you left in the taxicab. Big mistake leaving things in taxis."

He turned to Della.

"You know where to find the driver of the taxi. Dobbs told you. You've got to be the woman who drove to the Foley house in Sam Kerr's taxi. You've come back for the hand-kerchief you left in the cab. Got me?"

"I got you a good two minutes ago, great chief," said Della. "It will be easy. Mrs Foley and I are both very pretty and resemble each other quite a lot."

She waved a hand and disappeared.

"Now tell me all that happened," said Perry to Mrs Foley. "I know when you arrived at the house, and I got there a bit later to find Foley dead – shot. There was also a police dog, also shot dead. I may tell you that the police also know this."

Mrs Foley shivered.

"Hurry," warned Perry. "There's not a second to lose."

"I did go there," said Mrs Foley. "I went there to see my husband. But instead of listening to me he set a dog at me. As the animal leapt at me shots were fired. I saw the dog drop, and then my husband. I was horrified, and rushed from the house. The taxi was waiting. I came here. That's all."

Perry looked at her closely.

"You're in a bad jam, Mrs Foley. You can't afford to lie. Why don't you trust me. I'm your lawyer."

"I've told you the truth," said Mrs Foley in a weak voice.

"All right," said Perry. "But don't tell that truth to the police. It's not convincing."

"The police! Do you mean they're going to arrest me?" cried Mrs Foley.

"They'll be here any minute," said Perry. "But don't get frightened. I'll be here as well. All you've got to remember is you don't answer any questions."

Perry was about to add some more instructions when there came a heavy pounding at the door.

"The cops," said Perry laconically, as he smiled at Mrs Foley. "Leave everything to me. Don't answer a single question."

He opened the door and let in the police. They were not pleased to see him there, but they respected him as much as they feared him when he was against them in a case. Perry could not prevent the police arresting Mrs Foley for the murder of her husband, but he did prevent them from questioning her by warning them that any attempt at the now notorious third degree would result in something that would make the police of the city an object of public derision.

The big thing that worried Perry after the police had taken Mrs Foley away was where were Arthur Cartwright and his wife. They must know something about the shooting of Clinton Foley. But all the efforts of his staff failed to discover the Cartwrights.

As for the real Mrs Foley, Perry had failed to convince her that if she wanted him to save her life she must tell him the whole truth.

She stuck to her original story as she had told it to him on the night he had first seen her.

Perry knew she was not telling him everything. He wanted to save her because he felt sure that she was just as good a woman as Clinton Foley had been a bad man. But he was helpless in the face of her determination not to confide in him. The case worried him so much that he began to show signs of a nervous breakdown, and that sent Della Street into a state of great anxiety.

"You've done all you can," she said to him one morning, after he had been down to the court and once more succeeded in getting the trial postponed.

"No," cried Perry, "I've not done all. There's something I've missed. And that something is the link I want."

Three days later Della came down to the office to find Perry his old self.

"I'm ready for the trial now," he told her.

"What has happened?" she asked.

"Don't ask questions," said Perry, pinching her cheek. "You know I am a bit theatrical. I like to keep my big surprise till the last act – even from the one I love so much."

"That's all right with me," said Della. "I feel in my bones you're going to do something great, but my big joy is that you're better yourself."

"Never fitter, never fitter," said Perry, arranging his tie with that exactitude that showed his mind was at rest. "I've fixed it up with the D.A. that the trial shall open to-morrow. Here's your piece, little sweetheart, and don't forget it."

In the opinion of the public Mrs Foley was as good as convicted when she stood before the judge charged with the murder of her husband. But that was not the opinion of some of the reporters who had become wise from experience of Perry Mason.

"He's sure going to drop a bomb," said the "Herald" man to his rival on the "Recorder". "When Perry smiles like he's smiling now there's going to be wailing from the other side."

The district attorney put his case with a clearness that not only carried conviction to the people in the court, but was also sufficiently strong to carry a conviction of sentence of death from the mouths of the jury.

But Perry Mason was in no way perturbed. He scarcely seemed to listen when Sam Kerr, the taxi-driver, swore that Mrs Foley was the woman he had driven to the Foley house on the night of the murder. He identified her positively.

"Your witness, Mr Mason," said the district attorney, resuming his seat with a quiet smile of triumph.

"Della Street," said Perry, in a voice that was quiet in tone but which thrilled the court. "Stand up in court, Della Street."

Della stood up.

Perry turned to the taxi-man.

"Look closely at this lady and tell the court if you have ever seen her before."

The taxi-driver's face was a study in surprise.

"Did you return a handkerchief to this lady – a hand-kerchief she had left in your cab?" thundered Perry.

"Well, it certainly looks like the lady. Yet the other one –"

Sam, the taxi-driver, broke down and looked helplessly at the judge.

"Go on," said Perry. "Tell the court the truth. That's what you're here for."

"I don't know. I can't say which was the lady I drove," admitted Sam.

"That will be all," said Perry, as he sat down.

The next witness for the prosecution was Lucy Benton.

She swore she had seen Evelyn Cartwright, who had lived with Clinton Foley as his wife, leave the house on the morning of the day when Foley was murdered.

Perry did not attempt to cross-examine her. Instead he put an amazing proposition before the court. He asked that the proceedings be transferred to the Foley house.

"It is essential in the interests of justice," he pleaded with the judge.

The amazing fact of a court moving from the recognised seat of justice to the scene of a crime was then carried out.

The court was reconstructed.

The judge took a chair, and Lucy Benton took another chair in lieu of the witness stand.

From outside came the noise of hammering, so insistent, that the judge complained.

"If I am to hear evidence," he said to Perry testily, "you must see that that noise is stopped."

"In a moment, your Honour," said Perry.

He faced Lucy Benton.

"You have sworn that you saw Evelyn Cartwright leave

the Foley house on the morning Foley was murdered," he said.

Lucy Benton paid no heed to him.

"Stop that hammering!" she screamed.

Perry smiled.

He turned to the door of the library.

As though at a signal from his eyes Dobbs rushed in.

"It's right, sir," he said, breathing heavily. "We've just found the bodies of Mr and Mrs Cartwright under the cement in the new garage. Both have been shot – murdered!"

Perry turned to the judge.

"I shall bring medical evidence to prove that the unfortunate Evelyn Cartwright was murdered some days before this witness says she saw her leave the house. And she was murdered by Clinton Foley. This woman here, Lucy Benton, has sworn false testimony. That is for another court to deal with. In regard to my client, I can say this. The prosecution have admitted that whoever shot Clinton Foley, also shot the dog. That dog was an Alsatian, or a police dog, as we call them. He was my client's dog, her servant. He was one of the best of his breed and could not possibly have attacked his mistress. Some hand shot down Clinton Foley and the dog, but it was not the hand of Mrs Foley."

Perry sat down, and the jury did not even move from their chairs before returning a verdict of "Not guilty".

In his office the next morning Perry saw a thankful Mrs Foley.

"I don't know how to thank you, Mr Mason," she said.

"You don't have to thank me, Mrs Foley," said Perry, placing his arm round her. "I just did my best."

Later, Della said to Perry:

"What is the real inside story?"

"I know this much," replied Perry. "Cartwright was right about the howling dog. He did howl. He howled on the night Foley murdered Mrs Cartwright. Cartwright found out the truth, challenged Foley – after altering his will to give the real Mrs Foley his money – and Foley murdered him. You see, dear, knowing his wife was dead, he had nobody else to leave his money to except the real Mrs Foley, who had suffered from Foley's brutality and double-crossing as much as he had. Lucy Benton lied because she wanted Foley to marry her, and doubtless was an accessory to the murder of Evelyn Cartwright. But that is for the D.A. to deal with."

"But the howling dog?" persisted Della. "Why didn't he howl afterwards, when you went that morning?"

"Because he wasn't there. Foley took him to a dealer and changed him. These Alsatians are pretty much alike."

"Then you lied when you said Mrs Foley couldn't have killed her husband and the dog. You said it was her dog."

"Sure I did," said Perry, taking a cigarette and lighting it with a smile.

"Well, what about Mrs Foley's story, about somebody shooting both Foley and the dog?" said Della.

Perry smiled once more.

"Mrs Foley's story is her own. I don't want to hear it now I've got her acquitted. After all, if she did kill Foley, he deserved it, and I could have brought it in as self-defence. But I don't *know* exactly what happened. Now, what about a little dinner? I've been working terribly hard lately – and so have you."

EQUAL STATUS

Elwyn Jones

Adapted for:

SOFTLY, SOFTLY

(BBC TV, 1966–76)

Starring: Stratford Johns,

Frank Windsor & Norman Bowler

Directed by Leonard Lewis

In Britain, the sixties opened with another ground-breaking television crime series that remains famous more than thirty years later: Z Cars. At one fell swoop, the series changed for ever the image of the British policeman as he had become epitomized in Dixon of Dock Green *and let viewers into the much tougher world of policing a fictional patch called Newtown, which was clearly modelled on an area of Liverpool. The officers of all ranks were seen warts and all – and from the young PCs like Bert Lynch (James Ellis), Jock Weir (Joseph*

Brady), "Fancy" Smith (Brian Blessed), and Bob Steele (Jeremy Kemp), via the Desk Sergeants Blackitt (Robert Keegan) and Twentyman (Leonard Williams), right up to Detective Inspector Charlie Barlow (Stratford Johns) and his assistant Detective Sergeant John Watt (Frank Windsor), these were quite clearly policemen drawn from life and their cases soon became essential viewing in British homes every Saturday night. The realism of the series in terms of bad language and the occasional rough treatment of suspects, brought complaints from some members of the public and a number of senior police officers – but with its penny whistle signature tune and excellent scripts, Z Cars ran for 667 episodes until 1966. Thereupon Barlow, Watt and Blackitt were all promoted to their own series, Softly, Softly, concerning a regional crime squad based at Wyvern which was said to be near Bristol. The irascible Barlow (now a Detective Chief Superintendent) and long-suffering Watt (a Detective Chief Inspector) proved as popular as ever and the new series ran for the next ten years with a total of 264 episodes. Some viewers believed it to be a superior programme to Z Cars – and certainly more memorable than its successors, Barlow at Large (1971–73) and Barlow (1974–75), in which Charlie was promoted yet again to work for the Home Office.

The mastermind behind the success of Softly, Softly was Elwyn Jones (1923–82), a television scriptwriter who had joined the team working on Z Cars and proved very influential in the development of the series and its characters. He was then instrumental, and perhaps even more crucial, in devising its sequel. A Welshman, Jones had been a staff writer for Odhams Press in London in the years immediately after the Second World War before working on Radio Times from 1950 to 1957 which gave him an entrée into the world of television. Here he joined the BBC Drama Department and, thanks to a lifetime interest in crime and mystery stories, slipped easily into script-writing for Z Cars. Later he became producer of Softly, Softly and pioneered the introduction of police politics into a crime series – previously a taboo subject – as well as writing some of the programme's most memorable scripts. "Equal Status" was *written for the 1973 season and co-starred Clive Merrison as David James and Clive Roberts as Daniel Owen.*

One of the Wyvern files had pasted inside the back cover a copy of the front page of a morning paper. John Watt recalled how he'd been sitting at his desk in the Wyvern office reading that paper, when a small explosion reached his ear from the far end of the corridor. A few moments earlier, Barlow had galumphed along there in the direction of the washroom. The explosion which followed was the raising of his voice in angry protest. John Watt allowed himself the shadow of a smile. He knew what had angered his boss; he knew too that he had the answers to a number of questions that Barlow had not as yet asked. He quietly folded over the front page of the newspaper and sat back in his chair as Barlow stormed into the office.

"John, d'you know what! I just went into the washroom to freshen up . . . turned on the tap . . . and all it did was spit at me."

"Good morning, sir." Watt politely reproached his boss for the unceremonious entry.

"You what? Oh . . . good morning." But Barlow continued to glare at him, as though the insolence of the plumbing were his fault. "So what's happened to the water?" he demanded.

"I'm not the caretaker," said Watt, "but I do read the papers." He unfolded the one in his hand for Barlow to see the headline. "BOMB OUTRAGE" it read, in thick black type.

Barlow took the paper and quickly scanned through the paragraphs below. It told him of an act of sabotage the previous night upon the main pipe line bringing the water supply for the Wyvern area down from the Welsh hills. The details were sparse, but imagination filled in the picture: the dark-clothed figures treading soft-footed through the sleeping darkness towards the gleaming curve of the newly installed water main; the deft hands taping the explosive charge to a riveted joint where it would do the greatest damage; the hastily retreating figures leaving a length of trailing fuse behind them; the sudden flare of the match, and the line of fire running thinly across the gorse towards the packed joint, where it suddenly erupted in a sheet of flame; the belly-rumbling explosion that made the distant cottagers turn in their beds several miles away; and then the waste of waters pouring from the jagged hole in the pipe over the hillside.

"Why, John? Why?" Barlow demanded.

"They don't want us to have their water."

"Us? . . . Them?"

"The Welsh over there, and us over here," Watt patiently explained, though he knew that Barlow was fully alive to the protests that had been voiced, in English and in Welsh, over the flooding of some of the most tranquil valleys in Wales to provide water-supplies for the increasing thirst of the industrial Midlands and West of England. But protests being of no avail, action had followed, violent action, explosive action, of which the sabotage of the previous night had been the eighth incident in rapid succession. And Watt had heard a whisper, passed on to him by Jim Cook, the Squad's Intelligence Officer, that the Wyvern Regional Crime Squad was going to be asked to assist in finding the terrorists.

Barlow stared when Watt told him this. "Thanks," he said. "I'll bone up on the background." On his way to the door he hesitated.

"John . . ." Barlow's heavy early-morning look had already lightened, and a blandly ingratiating smile was beginning to lift the corners of his mouth. John Watt knew what was coming, but he didn't look up. Barlow cleared his throat. "Er . . . John . . . er . . . what's your analysis of this little explosion?"

Crafty old fox, thought Watt. He's not done his own homework, so he's hoping that I have. But his response to Barlow was an innocent, "Me, sir?"

"You're our political expert now," Barlow was laying it on

thick, ". . . since you sorted out our local red revolutionary at the aircraft works."

"Who turned out to be a very confused little night watchman," Watt reminded him, ". . . so afraid of being alone in the dark that he set off those security alarms just so's he could get someone to come running along and keep him company."

"Ay . . . well . . ." Barlow wasn't giving up, ". . . but our Mr Gilbert was impressed with your political grasp . . . told me so himself."

John Watt relented. "All right, sir. What do you want to know?"

"This Welsh Nationalism . . . what's it all about?" Barlow pulled up a chair and sat down. "It's not just about water, is it."

"It's about patriotism, sir. Local patriotism. Like you and I feel about Lancashire. Finest place in the world."

"Widnes is," Barlow said, confining this Lancastrian patriotism to his own home town.

"Widnes . . ." and there was just a hint of questioning in Watt's voice as he went on to murmur, ". . . where no birds sing."

"That's right. But so what?" Barlow demanded.

"So why shouldn't the Scots be local patriotic as well," Watt reasoned. "Or the Welsh."

"They can be as local patriotic as I am. But I don't go blowing things up to prove it."

"You don't need to," Watt told him, "since nobody's stopping you talking the way you want."

"You mean the way I've always spoken?" Barlow's usually subdued Lancastrian tones became unusually prominent. "Why should anyone object? I've not heard objections to the Welsh accent either, though this part of England is busting with it."

"It's not busting with the Welsh language, though," Watt pointed out.

"I should hope not," said Barlow. And went on to ask slyly, "How much Welsh do they speak in Wales?"

Watt contrived to make his answer sound casual as he trotted out the hard facts. "About a third of the population of Wales speaks Welsh. Only half of that number thinks Welsh."

Barlow was impressed. "Expert," he murmured.

"Not really . . ." Watt's modesty was genuine. A very modest man, John Watt thought himself, which was still no reason for hiding lights under bushels. "As a detective, I try to understand motives."

Barlow was incredulous. "You think you know what makes these bomb fellows tick?"

"I understand a bit of their attitude . . . what they're on about. I've got it written down somewhere." Watt's neat little pocket book fell open naturally at the last page written on, which was taken up with only two words printed in large block capitals; strange words to Barlow's eye, being made up of double ds and ys and odd combinations of consonants unpronounceably lacking in vowels. 'DDILYSRWYDD CYFARTAL' was what it spelled out, though Watt's careful pronunciation of it was more like 'Thilisrooth cavartal.'

"And that," said Barlow, "doesn't sound anything like what you've got written down."

"Easy really." Watt explained. "Double d is like th as in 'thick'. F is always v as in 'vanity'."

"And then what the hell does it mean?"

Watt translated: " 'Equal validity'. They want the Welsh language to be equal to the English language."

Barlow was magnanimous. "They can have that, as far as I'm concerned."

"And as far as Whitehall's concerned, in theory." Watt's voice hardened. "But only in theory. I'll give you an example. The birth of a child can be registered in Welsh; but only if the local Registrar understands it. Otherwise your ardent Welshman has to journey umpteen miles to find a Registrar who does understand Welsh, and then gets fined for registering outside his own district."

Barlow tut-tutted at this bureaucratic injustice.

"So they protest." Watt reached the inevitable conclusion.

"By blowing up water mains?" There was little doubt of Barlow's abhorrence of such a form of protest.

"That's the violent fringe." Watt shot a hard look at Barlow. "And whether we accept it or not, the fact is that there haven't been many political successes without violence."

Barlow's voice was as caustic as the effluent of the Mersey. "You sound like a public relations man for a bunch of crooks."

Watt explained himself. "It helps to know what we're up against."

"You are against, are you? I was beginning to wonder."

Watt angrily exploded, "Don't be so . . . !" And then hastily caught himself up. The boss was always the boss, and police discipline had to be observed. "I'm sorry, sir." Barlow nodded his acceptance of the apology. And having both cooled down after their brief spat, their faces were sombre as Watt went on to say, "Of course, I'm against violence. I'm against the destruction of property, public or private. And we both know that it doesn't stop there. Because this lot will kill somebody one of these days, whether they intend to or not."

They were both silent, aware that beyond the abstractions of politics were the harsh realities of death and destruction which they as police officers were pledged to prevent.

Detective Sergeant Hawkins had already gone to the site of the previous night's explosion where he noted, almost with admiration, the skilful way that the amount of explosive and the placing of it had been so exactly judged as to cut a large enough hole for the purpose, without raising so big a bang that every copper in the valley would come racing to the scene to find out what was amiss; noting as well that one unexploded stick of gelignite bore the printed lettering which would enable its source to be traced, and that several detonators, which were also traceable, even after they'd been fired, had been found among the debris.

But what might have been a couple of helpful leads turned

out to be more of a confusion, for the gelignite had come from a quarry in North Wales, while the detonators were traceable to a colliery in the South.

The Special Branch Officer who confirmed this came back with Hawkins to meet Detective Chief Superintendent Barlow and Detective Chief Inspector Watt, who had now been officially requested to assist in tracing the terrorists. Hawkins went in to prepare his bosses for the arrival of the Special Branch man. "I've brought Superintendent Evans with me, from the scene," he told them, discreetly lowering his voice.

Barlow looked up sharply. "Evans?" he queried. Hawkins nodded. "You mean . . . a Welshman?" Barlow asked, in total disbelief.

Superintendent Evans, waiting in the corridor, clearly heard this last, though it had been spoken in Barlow's softest tones, for he slipped past Hawkins to say breezily, "That's right . . . set a Taffy to catch a Taffy." Then, not a whit abashed by Barlow's fish-eyed look, he forced the introductions with a cheerful, "Good morning gentlemen! You'll be Mr Barlow." And when John Watt introduced himself, Evans responded with the same plump-fisted and over-sweaty handshake that Barlow had just been treated to, accompanied with a knowing, "Heard of you too, Johnnie-Boy!"

God help us, thought John Watt. Johnnie-Boy! We've got a right one here. And he exchanged a glance of sympathetic wariness with Barlow.

But despite his outward flabbiness, Superintendent Evans of Special Branch was brisk enough and hard enough when it came down to discussing terrorist suspects. "I've got a list, see," said Evans, making no attempt whatsoever to produce it for Barlow's information. "I've got a list of extremists, activists, and belligerents. It's not a long list."

"Is it accurate?" Barlow slipped in with a malicious twist to his lips.

Evans chose to ignore the malice and answer the question. "As far as we know, it's accurate, Mr Barlow. As far as we know. Can't say it's complete, of course. But every name on it is active, fighting, even extreme."

"So what do you do about them . . ." asked John Watt, not forgetting to say "sir" to his senior in rank, who had so far failed to give this entitlement to Mr Barlow, who was senior to both of them.

"We watch them, boy," said Evans. "We watch our suspects . . ." and a far-away and somewhat pained look came into his eyes as he added, ". . . as far as we can."

Barlow quickly seized on this. "Which is not very far?"

"How can it be?" Evans's voice was plaintive. "It's not like watching a bunch of crooks. I've got names written down here"; he tantalizingly tapped his breast pocket where his list of terrorists was presumably kept. "I've got names of professors, librarians, even lecturers at Theological colleges as well as other Reverend gentlemen. These are not criminals. These are not thieves. These are respectable people; people of *status*."

If Barlow's eyes could have bored through the cloth to read that list they would have done so. As it was, he had to content himself with asking: "Were any on that list away from their homes last night?"

Evans hesitated before he answered, and Hawkins quickly came in with, "Those who live near either the colliery or the quarry where the explosive materials came from have supposedly been cleared."

"Five of them," explained Evans, "none of whom were away from their homes."

"How do you know?" demanded Barlow.

"I've checked," Evans told him.

"Did you ask them? Did you interview them?"

"Not all of them," Evans was as cautious in his answers as he clearly was in his investigations. He went on to defend this caution, "We've got to watch our step. There's one gentleman, very learned he is. I only have to be wrong about questioning him once more, and he'll have my head on the block."

Watt was thoughtful. "They can't all be so highly educated."

"Indeed no," Evans agreed. "Some of them are only students."

Barlow had picked up John Watt's line of thought. "Students . . . whose status is not so great."

"That is so."

Barlow threw a significant glance at Evans's breast pocket. "How many?"

"About seven."

"And have *they* been interviewed in connection with last night's explosion?"

Evans's reply was guardedly non-committal. "I can't guarantee that they all have."

Barlow and Watt were both sitting upright now, thinking together, working together; and though it was Barlow who kept throwing the questions, it was as though the two of them were speaking with one voice.

"Could you find us two youngish suspects who haven't yet been questioned over last night? Preferably linked in some way to either of the two places where the explosives came from, the quarry or the mine."

"Does it matter which?"

"No. I just need an excuse to call on them. A 'reason to believe' if you like."

Evans's hand crept to his breast pocket and slowly brought forth several closely spaced pages of typescript. Watt's eyebrows lifted as he exchanged a look with Barlow. Were there really so many Welshmen suspected of terrorism? But Evans had little difficulty in picking out of that number the one who fitted the bill for Barlow's devious purpose. "If you have in mind, sir, what I think you have in mind, sir, I'd suggest young Daniel Owen."

John Watt wondered at the sudden sly rash of "sirs", and whether it had anything to do with Evans's astonishing alacrity in producing this one name. He'd hardly looked at his list to find it. Hawkins, who was more fully briefed on the morning's investigations, knew the reason why. "Daniel Owen is the one real lead, sir."

Evans explained, "Daniel Owen has a car. And whoever

did last night's little job would need a car since the place is miles from nowhere."

"And a car was seen . . . ?"

"By a sergeant who noted a grey Morris 1100 in the early hours of the morning, about three miles from the scene of the explosion. He had no reason to pay it special attention, there was no road check on at the time; and if he did hear the bang, well it was just another noise. But he's a careful type, so any traffic he sees tootling around at four thirty AM he takes a note of. And the number he noted is this."

Evans placed on the desk a slip of paper with a car number written on it in thick black pencil. Watt stared at it; it was too good to be true. "That number can be traced to Daniel Owen?"

"Not quite," said Evans. "Daniel Owen does have a grey Morris 1100. But its number is this."

He produced another slip of paper with a typewritten number which he placed above the pencilled one. There was a one figure difference between the two numbers.

"The Sergeant could have made a mistake," said Barlow, jabbing at the pencilled registration. Evans did not disagree with this possibility.

"Has the Sergeant's report been checked?" Watt demanded. "Not with Daniel Owen," Evans told him. And then added, choosing his words slowly and carefully, "I was saving him for you."

Barlow looked up in surprise. "Why?"

"He's young, tough, and a bit wild," Evans told him.

"Are you frightened of him?" Barlow nearly said. But though he bit the words off half way, Evans caught at his meaning. "No, Mr Barlow, sir," he answered, with no apparent rancour at the imputation. "I'm not frightened of him. But neither is he frightened of me. He knows me too well. He's seen me too often."

Barlow looked at Watt thoughtfully. "But he's not seen either of us."

Evans ignored the inclusion of Watt, and said straight out to Barlow, "He's certainly never seen *you*."

Barlow sat back heavily in his chair. "And you want me to frighten him?"

"Certainly not," Evans said hastily. And then with a bland deviousness that was near the equal of Barlow's he carefully explained, "It's just that . . . well, I'd feel there were better hopes of a satisfactory outcome if someone of your status saw him."

Watt nodded his head in understanding. "Sefyllfa," he said slowly. Only it sounded like "sevulva". Barlow raised an astonished eyebrow. "Means 'status'," Watt explained to him. And Evans nodded admiringly. "They told me you were conscientious, Johnnie. You've been learning Welsh."

"Just a word or two," said Watt modestly.

"That's one of the important words," said Evans.

And Sergeant Hawkins, whose own lack of status pressed heavily upon him, uttered his sombre agreement.

Barlow, impatient of this mood of solemnity, broke their triple reverie. "Aye. Where does this Daniel Owen live?"

Evans wrote the address on the slip of paper with the typewritten car number upon it, and handed it to Barlow. "You remember the colliery where the detonators came from . . . it's quite near there."

The Crime Squad trio drove to the Welsh mining valley which was the home of Daniel Owen. When they came in sight of the pit-head that stood tall sentinel above the village they went separate ways, Watt going off alone to follow up a lead that Evans had provided on one of Owen's close acquaintances, while Barlow and Hawkins went straight to the terraced street where the young man lived. They parked the car away from the house and walked the last few hundred yards, but for all their efforts to obscure their arrival their brisk and confident march along the street was the tread of strangers in a place where men walked slowly to pass the time of day. Barlow slowed his pace to let Hawkins go ahead and beat a rat-tat on the gleaming knocker of number twenty-seven. For a long moment there was neither sound nor movement from inside the house. Barlow patiently shifted his weight from one foot to another; all his life he was used to waiting on doorsteps.

At last, the door opened slowly, reluctantly. The woman who stood with her hand upon the latch was all stillness, but it was the stillness of resignation rather than repose. In answer to Hawkins' enquiries she admitted nothing more than that she was the mother of Daniel Owen, that her son was in, and – after having closed the door on Barlow and Hawkins for a further few minutes – that her son did not wish to speak to them. Hawkins put his foot in the door before she could close it again. "We don't want a fuss, Mrs Owen, do we?"

"Why not then?" she answered, with spirit. "Our neighbours are used to the police coming here. Don't even bother to look out of the windows any more. Used to it, they are."

Barlow, who saw through this show of unconcern, asked her directly, "Are *you*? . . . used to it?" And Mrs Owen's bravado blew away like thistledown. "No," she admitted, and there was more sorrow in the single word than in a valley of tears. Barlow was gentle with her: "Don't make it harder for yourself. Let us in, or send Daniel out. We need a word with him – for his own good." And in a harder voice, pitched up for the benefit of the listener within, he said to Hawkins, "Imagine . . . a man of twenty-two sheltering behind his mother's apron."

This clearly upset Mrs Owen's pride, maternal and domestic, and the flash of spirit shone through again as she answered, "Why not then? Though I'm sorry about the apron." She removed it with neat dignity, already folding and smoothing it as she looked up at Barlow and told him, "There's no welcome for you in this house. I am *not* asking you in."

She went back into the house leaving the front door open. Hawkins would have slipped in after, but Barlow was not content with this minor victory. "Easy now," he said, holding back Hawkins's impatience. He was playing a bigger fish.

The young man who did come to the door, after keeping

them waiting a while longer, had his mother's composure . . . but there was no resignation in it. He answered Hawkins' questions politely enough, except that the answers were in Welsh; it was only the nod of the head that indicated his acknowledgement of being the Daniel Owen they were seeking, and the gesture of invitation that showed his consent to their entering the house.

Barlow and Hawkins followed him down the passage and into the parlour, the neat domestic appearance of which was overlaid by the litter of books stacked in heaps everywhere. Barlow picked one up; the title on the cover was in that same strange consonantal mixture of ds and ws and ls that Watt had lectured him on the same morning; and when he placed it back upon the pile that stood shoulder high, he saw that they too were all Welsh. Barlow regarded them with astonishment; he'd no idea that there were so many different Welsh-language books. Well, if the lad wanted to do all his reading in that strange lingo, it was his look-out, but he had no right to go on answering Hawkins's questions in Welsh. At best, it was lack of courtesy; at worst, it was deliberate obstruction of the police in the execution of their duty. He warned the young man of this, making the statement quietly and in reasonable tones. If there was going to be any hot blood raised by this breakdown in communication, it would come from the young man's side, not from his.

Daniel Owen responded to Barlow's warning with the belligerent utterance of two Welsh words which Barlow immediately recognized from his discussion with Watt the same morning . . . Dilis-something-or-other. "You mean Equal Validity," Barlow snapped back at him. And Owen was so surprised at the Englishman's recognition of the slogan that he unconsciously answered in English, "That's right."

Barlow's lips twitched in a half smile; first round to him. Owen still insisted, though, "I don't do myself justice in English. I prefer to answer your questions in my own language."

Barlow shrugged at this. "Go ahead." And added with a hint of sarcasm that diminished the young man's heroic stance, "After which, you can translate your own reply. Take a little longer, but I'm in no rush."

Owen's response was an angry sputter of Welsh, the tone of which made the meaning clear without any need for translation. Barlow turned an amused look to Hawkins. "Funny how frightened men always get nasty."

Owen's need to deny the accusation of cowardice was strong enough to make him lapse into English for a second time. But in reply to the questions that Barlow then put to him, concerning his whereabouts the previous night, and the present location of his car, Owen once again retreated into Welsh. Barlow had had enough. With a word of warning to the young man first, he and Hawkins closed on him, ready to take him into custody, by force if necessary.

The parlour door opened quietly, so quietly that Barlow knew that Mrs Owen must have been standing outside clutching the handle, waiting for the necessary moment to intervene.

"You've asked the boy where he was last night," she said to Barlow. "He's told you, if you had the wit to understand. He was in his bed upstairs."

"How d'you know?" Hawkins demanded.

"I heard him go to bed," Mrs Owen told him. "I didn't hear him get up again until the morning."

Hawkins dismissed this as an alibi; Daniel Owen might have slipped out while Mrs Owen was asleep. She denied the possibility. "Mr Detective," she addressed him with firm dignity, "I would have heard. I barely sleep you see. Not at night. Not any more."

Barlow's head came up. He had the whiff of a trail that he knew he could pursue with success. And he would be gentle, ever so gentle in pursuing it. "Why don't you sleep, Mrs Owen?" he asked.

"Because I'm worried sick . . . !" Daniel tried to dam the overflowing of his mother's anxieties, but there was no holding them back. "I'm afraid for him. In and out at all hours. People coming and going at all hours. The police coming at all hours . . ."

"And last night?" Barlow gently led her on.

"Nothing last night. He was in his bed."

Barlow knew that she was speaking the truth, and he meant it when he said to her, "I'm glad." Turning to Daniel with studied politeness he asked him to write down the Welsh equivalent phrase for "I was in my bed" in the notebook which Hawkins held open for him. "I've a feeling I'll be hearing that phrase again," he explained. "And I'd like to be able to recognize it." Daniel smiled as he wrote it down. They certainly would be hearing it again . . . and again and again . . . He scarcely noticed what Barlow was saying to his mother, quietly and with great sympathy.

"I had a sergeant once, Mrs Owen. One of the old school. Tough but very human. He used to say that he was really sorry for only one thing. 'I'm sorry,' he used to say, 'for all the thieves' mothers in the world'." Barlow's voice was equally sorrowful as he went on, "I'm beginning to be sorry for the mothers of agitators. You bring them into the world, look after them, educate them . . . and that's a struggle for some folk – widows, for instance, as I understand you are Mrs Owen . . ."

Daniel rudely interrupted Barlow's sob story. "You'll bring tears to my eyes."

"Look at your mother's . . ." Barlow grated at him. Mrs Owen was sobbing quietly, making no attempt to wipe away the tears.

Hawkins took the opportunity of hammering at the agonized young man. "Where's your car, Mr Owen?" Before Daniel could half utter his expectedly incomprehensible Welsh reply, Mrs Owen had answered for him, "He gave permission to some friends to borrow it."

"I was afraid of that," said Barlow.

"Which friends?" Hawkins asked.

Daniel's terse outburst in Welsh was as good as a refusal to answer. Barlow guessed that Mrs Owen knew who had borrowed the car. Well, she was a sensible woman. It should be possible to persuade her to cough up for her son's own good. "Mrs Owen . . ." his tone was reasonable, ". . . last night a water main was damaged by explosives. You tell me that Daniel was in his bed at the time and I believe you. But a car was seen not far from where the explosion took place, of exactly the same colour and make as your son's, and with nearly the same licence number."

She seized upon this loophole in the case against Daniel. "Only *nearly* the same . . . ?"

Barlow nodded. "You see, I'm being straight with you, Mrs Owen. I'm admitting the possibility that it was another car altogether." Mrs Owen breathed her relief which Barlow gave her no time to enjoy. "It's also possible," he pointed out, "that it *was* your son's car, and the officer who saw it simply made a mistake, a very slight mistake, in noting the number. So we'd like to check on wherever Daniel's car is now."

Still Mrs Owen hesitated to tell him; Barlow drove home the final warning that would play upon her fears, and though his voice was gentle, his words conjured up a picture of bloody violence. "Last night, Mrs Owen, four and a half ounces of gelignite were used to blow that main. Nearly enough to blow up this house and half the street with it." Mrs Owen uttered a gasp of horror; Barlow pressed on, "There's more to it than that, and I'll be frank in telling you. Last night's job was an expert one. Is your son an expert in explosives?"

Mrs Owen's reply was in Welsh, but her face agonizingly said "no".

"I was afraid of that, too," said Barlow. "You see, these amateurs get hold of explosives, they don't know how to look after them, they keep them for months, maybe long after they've become dangerous to handle, and what's the result? I'll tell you, Mrs Owen. One of these days, or one of these nights, these bright boys are going to blow *themselves* up." And as he saw the shocked look come upon her Barlow quickly slipped in, "Who borrowed Daniel's car?"

"David James . . ." Mrs Owen's reply was that of an

automaton, ". . . lives over in Ebenezer Street. Number thirty-one." Daniel's reproachful, "Oh mam!" was near to despair.

Barlow and Hawkins exchanged a quick look. Chief Inspector Watt, acting on information from Evans, Special Branch, was even then making enquiries about the man James, over in the vicinity of Ebenezer Street. "I'll get the message to Mr Watt, sir," said Hawkins. "He'll need to know about the car when he talks to James."

John Watt could see that David James was pleased with the way the interview was shaping. He'd been nervous at first, frightened of the contained man in the grey overcoat who didn't smile very much, though he didn't shout or bluster either. In fact, for a police officer, and an English one at that, Detective Chief Inspector Watt seemed to be very sympathetic – very understanding, and even approving of the different forms of civil action taken by the Welsh Nationalists to further their cause. John Watt had even expressed his willingness to sign any petition in support of maintaining the Welsh culture, the Welsh institutions, or the Welsh language, as long as it stopped short of approval of any kind of violent protest. But when John Watt tackled the young man on his own attitude towards violence, there was a hesitation in the lad's reply which Watt pigeon-holed for future reference.

In the meantime, and having persuaded the lad that no one was going to subject him to third degree questioning, Watt sought some answers on questions of fact. "Where were you last night?" he asked.

"In bed," David told him.

"Where?"

"Here, of course."

"Why 'of course'?" Watt didn't even try to conceal his astonishment. "At your age I quite often slept away from home."

David James nodded, "So do I." But he said it so solemnly that Watt wondered if the lad had caught his meaning. "So you slept at home last night." Watt pressed the point, "Can you prove it?"

"How?"

"How the hell should I know!" Watt was beginning to get irritated with David James. Wet, that's what he was. Couldn't even provide his own alibi. Did he want Detective Chief Inspector Watt to provide one for him? "You didn't sneak some little Welsh sweetheart into your bedroom?" he suggested.

David was shocked at the idea, which Watt didn't think so very implausible. The lad wasn't at all bad looking, and he'd already said that his parents were away on holiday, which would have made it possible, even easy, to sneak in a girl friend. But if he said he hadn't, well he hadn't. In which case, nobody could possibly have seen him in bed, which made it difficult – as Watt explained to the lad – for anyone to believe his story; managing to convey that he, John Watt, would like to believe it, if only young David could produce a scrap of substantiation. "What time did you go to bed?" he asked, with an underlying air of saying "let's try to tackle your alibi that way".

David had a ready answer. "About eleven," he said promptly. "Just after the Welsh telly news."

Watt shook his head at this, and his tone was that of regret rather than disbelief. "That reply of yours, David . . . it was just a bit too pat. Do you follow me?" And he leaned forward as though to share a confidence. "It's like the too clever thief who says: 'I was watching Panorama at the time, which was about the American Presidential Election'."

"It would be," said David.

Watt nodded his agreement, "Just so." And while the lad was still smirking at this shared insight, Watt shot the next question at him. "Where is Daniel Owen's car? Now, think before you answer, since you were the one who borrowed it."

David's jaw dropped open; and it wasn't all that firm when it was closed, thought Watt. He was glad that he had been given the information about the borrowed car before he came in to talk to David James; it was going to be the clincher in cracking the lad who was, God knew, close enough to cracking already. "It is true, isn't it, that you borrowed the car," demanded Watt. "Or are you going to call your friend, Daniel Owen, a liar?"

David stared in disbelief. "Did he tell you?"

John Watt himself never told a lie when he could avoid it. "Let's say he didn't deny that you've got the car," was his careful reply. "Which Daniel could have done. Except that he's got his own skin to save."

There was a fierceness about David's refusal to believe this imputation of his friend's disloyalty which Watt shoved in the same mental pigeon-hole as his earlier thoughts about the lad. But there was the matter of the borrowed car to clear up first. "Where is it?" he demanded. And went on to threaten the lad with arrest if he refused to answer, a threat which he had every intention and every right of carrying out.

David clearly had no stomach for taking his resistance that far. "The car's in the garage," he told Watt. "Our garage. My dad's garage."

"What's it doing there?"

David shrugged. "Better than out in the street."

"It's going to be looked at," said Watt. "A touch of the old forensics. Did you use it last night? Or anybody else?"

"I didn't. Nor did anyone else . . . to the best of my knowledge."

Watt shook his head . . . "That's another tricky answer. Never mind. When did you borrow it?"

"Two days ago."

"Why did you borrow it?"

"To go for a run."

"Did you go?"

"No."

Watt's ear had picked out a note of envy in the lad's last replies. "You've no car of your own?" he asked casually.

"No."

"Do you want one?"

"Of course."

Watt held the lad's gaze, like a snake fixing a rabbit. "You could get a car of your own, you know." He kept talking, spelling it out slowly, "By keeping your eyes open . . . And opening your mouth a bit . . . In a good cause."

David's gaping mouth snapped shut. "I would never betray . . ." he began, without saying just what it was that he held so sacred.

"Just consider who you'd be helping," Watt pointed out. "You lot are doing all right now. Every time you make a legal protest, you're winning. But if you mean to go beyond that, then watch it."

"We're not afraid," said David James. But his voice was not as firm as he intended it to be.

Watt's face was sombre as he told the lad, "I am afraid, David. Not *of* you, but *for* you. Somebody's already been hurt by these bomb protests, you know that. One of these days, someone might even be killed." Watt caught the shade of a tremor across the lad's face, and he pressed home the point. "You're like me, David. You get frightened. When you see a stick of gelignite, you want to run. I know that I do. I'm against gelignite."

"So am I," David said.

"Then make your own protest," Watt told him, ". . . against explosives." Watt took a pencil from his pocket, and while the lad watched him, he wrote a number in the margin of a newspaper that lay on the table. It was the number of the private telephone line at the Wyvern Crime Squad office, the line reserved for police informants. "I'm glad to have met you, Dafydd," he said, giving the name its Welsh pronunciation. "Any time you want to talk to me, just call that number. You could be doing everybody a favour. Your cause, your country . . ." hat in hand, Watt was already at the doorway; he turned to say as an afterthought, "And you'd be doing a favour for yourself."

"David James didn't do it."

"And Daniel Owen didn't do it."

The three Crime Squad officers had met up again with Superintendent Evans of Special Branch to compare notes on their investigations of the two young men. Barlow was convinced that Mrs Owen was telling the truth in claiming that her son was in bed at the time of the blowing up of the water main; while Watt's instinct told him that the other lad hadn't the guts to tell a straight-out lie about it. Moreover, the car seen on the road nearby . . . the car that looked like Daniel Owen's, was the same colour as Daniel Owen's, and had nearly the same registration number as Daniel Owen's, turned out to be a different car entirely, owned by someone else in the locality with a perfectly good reason for being out and about at four-thirty in the morning.

Barlow had a feeling though, that there was some purpose behind one of the lads loaning his car to the other.

"They were going to do something," John Watt agreed. "But I don't think that David James will now."

Superintendent Evans looked at the quiet self-contained man with a new respect. "Scared him off, did you?" he suggested.

"A bit." Watt's face was expressionless as he added, "I said we'd be interested in buying him off too."

Barlow and Evans responded with equal casualness to the possibility, sorting out in a moment that neither of them were likely to make a suitably soft impression on the young man, which left it to Detective Sergeant Hawkins to follow up John Watt's first sounding out. Watt noticed that Harry Hawkins' usually prognathous jaw jutted out even further as his senior officers discussed the method of approach. What's biting our Harry? John Watt wondered. It wouldn't be the first time he'd done a deal with an informant.

"How much are we going to offer?" John Watt raised the question as a practical issue; which Barlow followed up with an even more loaded question, directed straight at Superintendent Evans of Special Branch: "Whose funds will it come from?"

"There'd be no trouble about who paid, sir," Evans assured him. "We would." And then added hastily, lest Crime Squad should let their generosity run away with

Special Branch's funds, "Keep it around fifty quid . . . for the first time anyway."

While Barlow and Evans went off to continue their higher level deliberations – over a shared bottle of whisky, Watt suspected – Hawkins stayed to splutter up his bubbling dissatisfaction to John Watt. "What a job you've landed me this time, sir! . . . Trapping a kid into betraying his mates."

"It's distasteful," John Watt agreed. But to Hawkins's impertinent "You can say that again!" he snapped back "And you can keep a civil tongue in your head." Cheeky young devil. And him only a Detective Sergeant, speaking like that to a Detective Chief Inspector. Still, the young 'uns had to learn, and some of the lessons weren't easy. Like this one of betrayal. It was distasteful, even creepy. But as he explained patiently, if somewhat wearily, to Harry Hawkins, "We shall never crack this bombing set-up without an informant. Not in a month of Sundays. But over in Ebenezer Street there is a potential informant. So go and recruit him. And discover there's more to police work than shouting."

Harry Hawkins needed a reason for calling at Ebenezer Street. You don't knock at a man's door and offer to buy his conscience straight out. So he presented himself to David James as a forensics expert, come to inspect the car borrowed from Daniel Owen, and confirm that it had not been driven about in the vicinity of the sabotaged water main within the previous twenty-four hours. James opened up the garage and stood looking on while Hawkins scraped bits of earth from various parts of the car's chassis and put them into labelled envelopes in what he trusted was a suitably scientific sort of way. And while he worked, he talked, letting the conversation hover, like a butterfly around a buddleia bush, round and about the subject of selling information. Soon Hawkins forgot his scruples and lost himself in the enjoyment of playing his "snout" like a fish on the end of a line; baiting the hook with talk of sports cars and the kind that young David James wished he could afford to buy; casting it on the

water with practical advice on how David could explain a
sudden rush of wealth as a win on a Premium Bond; making a
strike with a precise demand for information on where and
when the next sabotage incident was likely to take place;
giving the lad his head on a loose line while his conscience
kept him dashing to and fro; then slowly reeling him in . . .
closer . . . closer . . . ready to fall into the net. It wasn't so
much different from playing a criminal snout, except that the
cost of ideological betrayal seemed to be higher. "Fifty
pounds . . ." Hawkins dropped into the conversation, going
to the limit that he'd been authorized to offer; to which
David James responded with a phrase in Welsh and a wry
twist of his mouth.

"What are you on about?" asked Hawkins. And wasn't
surprised when James translated the phrase as: Thirty pieces
of silver. It was just the sort of melodramatic attitudinizing
that had got these crackpots up to whatever antics they'd
been dallying with.

"You were going to do something, weren't you?" Hawkins
put to him.

"He was."

"Daniel Owen?"

"Yes."

"But not you?"

James shook his head. Hawkins casually asked, "What
were you going to do?" When James tried to hedge by
pleading uncertainty of the plans, Hawkins brutally told
him, "You're no good to us then."

David James's sallow face took on an even more waxen
tinge. It was the crunch; he either had to talk to Hawkins
now, tell all he knew; or forget about whatever hungers were
driving him on to betraying his friends. He still seemed to be
dithering as he stated obscurely, "His mother thinks I've got
the car."

"She was right."

"He wasn't really keeping it a secret then," James pointed
out. "Even you know I've got it."

Hawkins was puzzled. What was this leading to? James

babbled on, "Daniel Owen . . . he's not stupid. He wants me to drive the car about . . . tonight."

Hawkins's back went rigid. Tonight! Christ, was it going to be as soon as that? Outwardly though, he was as casual as ever, as he prompted the lad, "Just drive it about?"

James explained, "He reckons you'll follow the car. Keep an eye on it anyway. And you'll see nothing. For I shan't be doing anything."

"But somebody else will?"

"Yes."

"Daniel Owen?"

James nodded.

"What will he be doing?"

"I'm not sure."

Hawkins was already translating promises into hard cash, counting out five one-pound notes from his wallet as he told the lad, "We could test your idea. If there's anything in it, we'd pay . . . just for the idea. Meantime, this is on account." He held out the cash; before James could even crook his fingers to take it, Hawkins drew it back, slowly, just enough to leave the fluttering notes within reach of a longer grasp, if David James would only stretch out his hand. "There's more for you, now," Hawkins promised, ". . . if you tell more now."

James was really caught. The plan, of which he clearly knew every detail, spilled forth from his lips. "Daniel's coming here at seven. We drive around a bit. Perhaps have a drink or a bit of supper somewhere. I drop him back home by nine."

"And then we follow you?"

James nodded. "He reckons you'll do that as long as I'm driving his car."

"While he slips out on foot?"

"Out of the back of his house. He's counting on your not watching it back *and* front . . ." He faltered in the telling of the plan. Hawkins added five more one-pound notes to the five already in his hand. "Keep on talking."

James drew a deep breath. "He'll be meeting two others

. . . going by bus to the rendezvous . . . 9.23 from the bus station."

"Where to?" Hawkins demanded.

"Hir Deitho."

He could just as well have said Llanfair . . . whatever it was, for all that meant to Harry Hawkins. "What's at this place . . . ?"

"Hir Deitho? It's where there's a water main."

Another one, thought Hawkins, like last night's. These jokers are not kidding. "Does the bus go all the way there?" he questioned. And when James retreated into a sideways glance, he demanded, "Come on! Come on!"

"He'll be getting off two stops before the Hir Deitho terminal . . ." the words were tumbling out now in his eagerness to void the last bitter-tasting residue, ". . . there'll be a car waiting to pick him up. From then on I don't know . . . I don't know . . . I don't know."

Hawkins was already adding another five to the ten one-pound notes in his hand, having satisfied himself that he'd got from the lad all that he had to tell, when a sudden creak of the garage door made him turn and brought a gasp of alarm from David James. It was Watt, with a word of caution for James. "Your voice pitches up, you know. I heard some of that. Not that I'm saying it to frighten you. Just speaking the truth . . . as I hope you were."

"I was," James assured him.

Watt nodded. "In which case . . . you'll be driving Daniel Owen about for two hours this evening before you go your separate ways. Two hours of just you and your friend together, with him not knowing about this chat, and you not letting on. Do you think you can keep it up?"

"Oh yes." There was a half smile on David James's face, and all the half hints that Watt had previously pigeon-holed suddenly fell into place as he said, "You see, I don't very much like Daniel Owen."

The trailing operation that evening was carefully set up, even to the extent of laying on a rather too conspicuous car-full of plain clothes men to continue following David James when he drove away, alone, from Daniel Owen's front door. A more discreet observer checked Daniel into his own house and out of it again – after a brief but far from reassuring word with Mrs Owen – by the back door.

Meanwhile John Watt was making his way to the bus station to catch the 9.23 bus to Hir Deitho. A quiet man in a grey overcoat who looked as though he might be an insurance collector out on an evening round as he boarded the bus a few seconds after Daniel Owen and settled himself a couple of seats in front of the lad. The bus whined its way along the quiet roads, up and down the sides of the valley, through the villages already half slumbering, climbing towards the crouching hill top; and in its wake a small car meandered gently, sometimes close enough for the driver to read the destination board "HIR DEITHO", but more often so far back that the bus was no more than a faint glow around a bend of the valley road. Hawkins's hands on the wheel of the car were relaxed, now that his earlier qualms were submerged in the need for action. This was something he understood; the hard-grinding, patient, solitary existence that was so much a part of Crime Squad life; watching, waiting for the crime to take place or at least be attempted; being almost disappointed when it didn't happen, which was more often than not; but getting that adrenalin kick of satisfaction on the rare occasions when one of the "big ones" was caught and put inside for a stretch that would confound his knavish tricks for a long while to come. These bombers now; true enough, they weren't criminals, but a quantity of "gelly" going off was a nasty business, no matter who it was that was doing it or for what reason. Bombing was dangerous; people got killed.

Daniel Owen didn't look like a killer as he got off the bus at a deserted wayside stop and turned about to head back the way he'd just come. John Watt saw him go, watching the lad's reflection in the side window as the bus started up again to carry him on to the next stop. A pleasant young man who looked as though he cared; if he'd only channel his caring in a more sensible direction . . . and the others mixed up with him in the whole silly business.

The two young men in the car that picked up Daniel Owen a few moments after he got off the bus were very much like him, young, alert, eager-looking. Hawkins saw the pick-up take place and nodded his satisfaction; so far the James boy's information had proved accurate; if they stopped the car now they'd likely find the gelly on board and be able to take the three lads on a charge of unlawful possession of explosives. But they needed more, they needed evidence of intention, which meant letting them get a bit closer to the water main before dropping on them. Anyway, picking the right moment was something for Mr Watt to decide.

Watt got off the bus at the stop after the one where Daniel Owen had alighted and walked briskly along the road like a man with somewhere to get to and no time to be lost in getting there. The car with the three young men in it passed him, and if Daniel Owen did feel a flash of alarm at once again seeing his fellow passenger on the bus, his fears must have been allayed by the rear view sighting of the grey-coated man being rapidly left behind as their car turned the corner. A moment after their tail lights disappeared, Hawkins's car stopped to pick up Watt and swiftly followed at their heels.

The two cars were now approaching the village at the HIR DEITHO bus terminal, above which was the water main now under threat from the saboteurs. Two side roads led up towards the water main. The car containing the three young Welsh lads and perhaps the sticks of gelignite slowed down as it neared the first of these side roads. Hawkins automatically speeded up and passed it; follow-the-leader was a dead give-away in the trailing game; better to go past and then turn round and come back again. No fear of losing the quarry with other police cars lying tucked away in the vicinity, waiting for the radio call that would bring them roaring up to their rendezvous with the bombers.

Nervous and edgy were these three bombers as their car stopped within sniffing distance of the water pipe-line.

Daniel Owen got out and took from the back seat a bundle that looked like a number of dirty greasy candles bound round with black insulating tape. Sweaty they were in his hands, and sweaty was he himself, feeling the trickles soak his skin and then turn icy cool in the night air. The car howled and moaned as it made a three point turn on the rough lane, manoeuvring to face the way it came from for a quick get-away. The wheels spun on a patch of loose earth as the driver wrenched at the steering wheel in the darkness that was suddenly, blazingly lit up by the headlight flare of two cars approaching at speed, two police cars, the one a patrol car with two uniformed men, the other the small saloon with Hawkins and Watt; all four police officers already out and running across to where the two young men still sat in their car, held there by the paralysing headlight glare. But the third man, Daniel Owen, already out of the car and on his feet, with desperation to drive his heels, sprang for the covering darkness and fled like a fox across the hillside. Over the gorse he sped, with Watt and Hawkins close behind him. But it was his country not theirs, and gradually the distance between them lengthened until he was only a remote figure sharply outlined on the hill crest, with what looked like a bundle of sticks clutched in his hand; a figure that stumbled and nearly fell, pitching the bundle sharply to the ground at his feet.

John Watt saw it go, and automatically shielded his face with his arm; Hawkins was caught by the searing flash that blinded him for a moment and made his heart start a sudden thumping. When he'd blinked his vision back again, he saw that on the hill crest nothing stirred. Next to him, John Watt shuffled his feet and coughed. There was no need of going to look for a body; with that much of an explosion there'd only be bits left. The night air was cold and there was a bitter taste in it; of exploded gelignite and drifting dust; of an investigation successfully carried out and a file closed; of a mother's heart broken and a young man's life thrown away.

INSPECTOR MAIGRET HESITATES

Georges Simenon

📺

Adapted for:

MAIGRET

(BBC TV, 1960–63)

Starring: Rupert Davies,

Ewen Solon & Helen Shingler

Directed by Andrew Osborn

---

*Another television crime series that also became essential view-
ing on Monday nights in the sixties was* Maigret, *based on the
best-selling novels by Georges Simenon. The methodical, pipe-
smoking Parisian Commissioner of Police who had first appeared in the novel,* The Strange Case of Peter the Lett *in
1931, came to the small screen in October 1960, having already
been broadcast on the radio in France and been adapted for*

several European and American films starring Albert Préjean, Harry Baur, Jean Gabin and Charles Laughton. But it was undoubtedly the performance by Rupert Davies, a stolid, heavy-set English character actor who also enjoyed smoking a pipe, that established the French detective as a top favourite with television audiences. Even Georges Simenon, who had not been very impressed with any of the earlier impersonations of Maigret, congratulated Davies and gave his blessing to several years of adaptations. Sadly for the star, however, Rupert Davies became so typecast by Maigret *that he found it virtually impossible to get any further acting roles after the end of the programme on Christmas Eve, 1963. The popularity of the character has remained undiminished, nonetheless: many of the Maigret novels are still in print, and in 1992 he was brought back to British television screens in a new series featuring the distinguished Shakespearean actor, Michael Gambon, which ran for two seasons until the star, probably fearing a repeat of what had happened to his predecessor, refused to make any more.*

Georges Simenon (1903–89) is one of the phenomenons of twentieth-century literature. Born in Belgium, he began his working life as a police court reporter in Liège, but in 1932 moved to Paris where he launched what was to prove an amazingly prolific writing career, producing crime stories under a variety of pen-names for various magazines. It was with the creation of Maigret in 1931, however, that Simenon found fame – and within a year his first three novels about the unique detective had been translated into a dozen languages and the detective was well on his way to challenging the worldwide popularity of those other two icons of the genre, Sherlock Holmes and Hercule Poirot. (Holmes has, of course, also been the subject of a hugely successful Granada TV series which ran from 1984 to 1994 starring Jeremy Brett, and Poirot has been equally well portrayed by David Suchet for LWT between 1989 and 1996.) Today, the majority of the Maigret novels have been adapted for TV in either the Rupert Davies or Michael Gambon eras, although a number of short stories still await adaptation for British audiences. One such is "Inspector Mai-

*gret Hesitates", written in 1944, which was used in a German
TV series, Maigret, starring Heinz Ruhmann (1965–68).
Described as "a case so puzzling that Maigret could not make
up his mind to take action" it is surely ideal for when – not if –
the next series of this classic crime-fighter reaches the small
screen . . .*

Inspector Maigret stood still for a moment in front of the
black-iron railings separating him from the garden. The
enamel plate bore the number 47B.

It was five o'clock in the evening, and totally dark. Behind
him a branch of the Seine flowed sullenly round the long
unfrequented island of Puteaux, with its waste ground,
coppices, and tall poplars.

In front of him, by way of contrast, on the other side of the
railings was a small modern property of Neuilly, the Bois de
Boulogne district, all comfort and elegance, and, just now,
carpeted with autumn leaves.

Number 47B stood at the corner of the Boulevard de la
Seine and the Rue Maxime-Baes. Lights were on in the
second-floor rooms, and Maigret, standing with hunched
shoulders under the rain, decided to press the electric bell set
in the garden gate.

It is always embarrassing to disturb a quiet house, particularly on a winter's evening, when it is snugly self-contained and full of intimate warmth, and especially when the
intruder has come from Police Headquarters with his pockets full of unpleasant documents.

A light appeared on the ground floor, the front door
opened, and a manservant peered out, trying to see the
visitor before crossing the garden in the rain.

"What is it?" he asked through the railings.

"Dr Barion, please?"

Maigret could see that the hall of the house was elegant, so
he automatically stuffed his pipe into his pocket.

"Who shall I say?"

"You must be Martin Vignolet, the chauffeur?" asked the Inspector, to the great surprise of his questioner.

At the same time Maigret slipped his visiting card into an envelope, which he sealed.

Vignolet was a rawboned, thick-haired fellow of between forty-five and fifty, quite clearly a countryman.

He went up to the first floor and came back a few minutes later.

Maigret followed him up, past a child's stroller.

"Come in, won't you?" said Dr Armand Barion, opening the door of his consulting room.

He had the pale face and dark-ringed eyes of a man who has not slept for several nights.

As Maigret was about to speak he caught the sound of children's voices at play, coming from the ground floor . . .

Even before he went into the house the Inspector had already known what the household consisted of.

Dr Barion, a specialist in tuberculosis, and a former student of Laennec Hospital, had been living at Neuilly only three years, and, while taking private patients, he still carried on his laboratory research.

He was married, with three children – a boy of seven, a girl of five, and a baby of a few months, whose stroller Maigret had noticed.

The domestic staff consisted of Martin Vignolet, who was both chauffeur and manservant, his wife Eugenie the cook, and finally – until three weeks ago – an eighteen-year-old Breton girl, Olga Boulanger . . .

"I suppose you know what I have come about, Doctor? As a result of the post-mortem, Miss Boulanger's parents, on their lawyer's advice, have decided to bring an action, and it is my duty . . ."

His whole attitude seemed to express apology and, in fact, Maigret felt a certain reluctance at tackling this case.

Three weeks before, Olga Boulanger had died in a rather mysterious way, but the doctor who was called in had, nevertheless, signed the death certificate.

The girl's parents had come up from Brittany for the funeral, a pair of typical hard, wary countryfolk, and they had discovered, heaven knows how, that their daughter was four months pregnant.

Somehow they had got in touch with Barthet, one of the most ruthless of lawyers. And on his advice, a week later, they had demanded the exhumation and an autopsy of the body.

"I've got the report with me," Maigret sighed, with a gesture toward his pocket.

"You needn't bother! I know all about it, particularly as I got permission to assist the police surgeon."

The doctor was calm, although he looked weary and even feverish. Dressed in his lab coat, he stood with his face under the light, looking Maigret in the eyes without trying to avert his own.

"Of course I was expecting you, Inspector."

A photograph of his wife stood on his desk in a silver frame, a pretty young woman of barely thirty, with a delicate appearance.

"Since you've got Dr Paul's report with you, you must be aware that we found the poor girl's intestine riddled with minute perforations which must have induced rapid blood poisoning. You know, too, that after intensive research we succeeded in determining the cause of these perforations, which had puzzled my learned colleague and myself.

"It had puzzled us so much that we felt bound to appeal for help to a colonial doctor to whom we owe the answer to the riddle."

Maigret was nodding restlessly and Barion seemed to guess what he wanted, for he broke off to say, "Please smoke, by all means. I don't smoke myself, for my patients are mostly children. A cigar? No? Then I'll go on.

"The method used to kill my maid – for there's no question that she was killed – is current, so it seems, in Malaya and the New Hebrides. The victim is induced to swallow a certain quantity of those fine bristles, as sharp as needles, that are found on some ears of grain, such as rye.

"These bristles remain in the intestine, the walls of which they gradually pierce, which inevitably causes –"

"Excuse me." Maigret sighed. "The post-mortem also confirmed that Olga Boulanger was four months pregnant. Is she known to have associated with anyone?"

"No. She seldom if ever went out. She was a rather awkward little thing with a freckled face . . ."

And the doctor hurriedly went back to his story.

"I must confess, Inspector, that since that post-mortem ten days ago I've been entirely taken up by this business. I've no ill-feeling toward the girl's parents, who are simple people and who obviously consider me responsible.

"But it would be an absolute tragedy for me if I did not succeed in finding out the truth. Fortunately, I've already done so to some extent."

Maigret found it hard to conceal his surprise. He had come to investigate a problem, only to find himself confronted, so to speak, with a ready-made investigation and faced by a calm, clear-headed man making a full statement.

"What day is it today?" said the doctor. "Thursday? Well, since last Monday, Inspector, I've had material proof that poor Olga was not the intended victim.

"How did I find out? In the simplest possible way. I had to discover in what article of food she could have swallowed the rye bristles. As she would never have thought of killing herself, particularly in such an unusual and extremely painful way, clearly some outside cause was indicated."

"Do you think perhaps your chauffeur Martin was involved with her?"

"He was. I know it for a fact," agreed Dr Barion. "I questioned him on the subject and he eventually admitted it."

"Has he ever lived in the colonies?"

"Only in Algeria. But I can assure you right away that you're on the wrong track.

"Patiently, with the help of my wife and the cook, I drew up a list of all the foodstuffs we have had in the house lately and I even analyzed some of them.

"On Monday, when I had almost given up hope of getting any results, as I was sitting here in the consulting room my attention was caught by the sound of footsteps on the gravel and I saw an old man making his way toward the kitchen, as if he were a familiar visitor.

"It was old Mr Monday, as we call him, whom I'd quite forgotten about."

"Mr Monday?" echoed Maigret with a smile of amusement.

"It's the children's name for him because he comes every Monday. He's a beggar of the old-fashioned sort, clean and respectable, who goes on a different round every day.

"Here, it's on Monday. And it has gradually become a tradition with us to keep a whole meal ready for him, and it's always the same meal, for on Monday we have chicken with rice, and he sits quietly in the kitchen eating his share.

"He amuses the children who go and chat to him.

"I had already noticed some time ago that he used to give each of them one of those cream cakes they call eclairs, and I rather objected . . ."

Maigret, who had been sitting still for too long, got up, and the doctor went on, "You know the way tradesmen have of giving presents out of their stock to the poor rather than money. I suspected that these eclairs came from a local pastry cook's and were probably stale. I said nothing to the old man for fear of hurting his feelings, but I told my boy and girl not to touch the eclairs."

"And the maid ate them instead."

"Most probably."

"And it was in these eclairs . . . ?"

The doctor said, "This week Mr Monday came as usual with his two eclairs wrapped up in white paper. After he had gone I examined the cakes, which I shall show you presently, and I found there enough rye bristles to have caused the damage that brought about Olga's death.

"Do you understand now? The intended victim was not that poor girl, but my children."

The children's voices could still be heard on the floor

below. It was quiet and warm in the room; from time to time the swish of motor tires sounded on the asphalt of the embankment.

"I've not spoken to anyone yet. I was waiting for you."

"Do you suspect that old beggar?"

"Mr Monday? Certainly not! In any case I've not told you the whole story and the rest of it will certainly clear the poor old fellow.

"Yesterday I went to the hospital and then I visited some of my colleagues. I wanted to know whether they had recently had to certify any cases similar to that of Olga Boulanger."

His voice was unemotional, but he passed his hand across his forehead.

"Now I have found out conclusively that at least two people have died in the same way – one nearly two months ago, the other only three weeks ago."

"Had they eaten any eclairs?"

"I couldn't find that out, for the doctors had unfortunately mistaken the cause of death and hadn't thought it necessary to demand an inquest.

"Well, there you are, Inspector. I know nothing more, but I've learned enough, as you see, to be terrified. Somewhere in Neuilly there's a lunatic who, I cannot think how, manages to put death into pastries . . ."

"You said just now that you thought your children were the intended victims?"

"Yes – I'm convinced of it. I know what your question implies. How can the murderer have contrived things so that it's only Mr Monday's eclairs that –"

"Particularly as there have been at least two other cases!"

"I know. I can't understand it . . ."

The doctor seemed sincere and yet Maigret could not help watching him surreptitiously.

"May I ask you a personal question?"

"By all means."

"Forgive me if it offends you. The Boulangers accuse you of having had an affair with their daughter."

The doctor hung his head and muttered, "I knew that would come out! I don't want to lie to you, Inspector. It's true, stupidly true. It all happened one Sunday when I was alone here with the girl . . .

"I'd give everything in the world for my wife not to know, for it would distress her too much. On the other hand I can give you my word as a doctor that Olga had already become my chauffeur's mistress . . ."

"So that the child –"

"Was not mine, I assure you. Anyhow, Olga was a good girl who'd never have dreamed of blackmailing me. You see –"

Maigret was anxious not to allow him time to collect himself.

"And you know nobody who . . . Wait a minute. You spoke just now of some lunatic –"

"Of course! Only it's impossible – physically impossible! Mr Monday never goes to *her* place before coming here! When he goes there afterward, she leaves him standing in the street and throws him a few coppers out of the window."

"Who are you talking about?"

"Miss Wilfur. You'll see that there's a certain justice in things! I adore my wife and yet there are two things I keep secret from her.

"You know the first already. The other is even more absurd. If it were still daylight you could see through this window a house where an Englishwoman of thirty-eight, Laura Wilfur, lives with her invalid mother.

"They are the daughter and widow of the late Colonel Wilfur of the colonial army.

"Over a year ago, when the two women came back from a long stay in the South of France, I was sent for one evening by the young woman, who was complaining of some pain or another.

"I was rather surprised, for one thing because I'm not in general practice, and for another, because I could find nothing wrong with the young woman. I was even more astonished to learn, in conversation with her, that she knew all about my movements, even my most trivial habits, and I only understood when I got back here and saw her window.

"To cut the story short, Inspector . . . Absurd as it may seem, Miss Wilfur is in love with me – hysterically in love as only a woman of her age is liable to be when she lives alone with an old invalid in a huge gloomy house.

"On two further occasions I let myself in for it. I went to see her and while I was examining her she suddenly seized my head and pressed her lips against mine.

"Next day I got a letter beginning: *My darling* . . . And the worst of it is that Miss Wilfur seems convinced that we are lovers!

"I can assure you of the contrary. Since then I've avoided her. I have had to turn her out of this consulting room, where she came to badger me, and if I've never mentioned it to my wife it's been out of professional discretion and also to avoid arousing unfounded jealousy.

"I know nothing more. I've told you everything, as I had made up my mind to. I'm not accusing anyone! But I'd give ten years of my life to prevent my wife . . ."

By now Maigret understood that the doctor's previous self-possession had been deliberate, prepared in advance, achieved by a great effort of will, and that the man was now almost on the verge of tears.

"Carry on with your inquiry, Inspector. I don't want to influence you."

As Maigret crossed the hall a door opened and two children, a small boy and an even smaller girl, ran past him laughing.

Martin the chauffeur followed behind Maigret and closed the garden gate.

That week, Maigret got to know the district until he was sick of it. With laborious obstinacy he spent hours at a time walking up and down the embankment in spite of the persistently rainy weather and in spite of the astonishment of some servants who had wondered if this suspicious-looking stranger wasn't up to some mischief.

Seen from the outside, Dr Barion's house seemed an oasis of peace, professional activity, and quiet.

Several times Maigret caught sight of Mme. Barion pushing her youngest child in the stroller along the embankment. And during an interval between showers one morning he watched the two older children at play in the garden, where a swing had been put up.

As for Miss Wilfur, he saw her only once. She was tall and solidly built, quite devoid of grace, with large feet and a mannish walk.

Maigret followed her on the off-chance, but she merely went to change her books at the lending library in a nearby English bookshop.

Then Maigret gradually widened the circle of his wanderings and went as far as the Avenue de Neuilly, where he noticed two pastry shops. The first, narrow and gloomy, with its facade painted an ugly yellow, would have fitted in quite well with the sinister story of the lethal eclairs.

But the Inspector scanned the window display in vain and inquired within. They never made eclairs.

The other was the smart *patisserie* of the neighborhood, with two or three small marble tables at which tea was served: *Patisserie Bigoreau*. Here everything was bright and fragrant and delicious.

A rosy-cheeked girl tripped gaily to and fro, while a distinguished-looking lady presided over the cashier's desk.

Was it possible? . . . Maigret could not make up his mind to take action.

As time passed and his conversation with the doctor grew more remote, the doctor's accusations, re-examined as it were through a magnifying glass, became more and more insubstantial.

So much so that sometimes the Inspector really had the impression of some ridiculous nightmare, some story invented lock, stock, and barrel by a megalomaniac or a desperate man.

And yet the police doctor's report confirmed Barion's statement: poor freckle-faced Olga had really died as a result of swallowing bristles of rye!

And the following Monday's eclairs, brought by that mysterious figure, Mr Monday, had also contained a considerable number of these bristles, inserted between the layers of pastry.

But couldn't they have been put in later?

To crown everything, although Olga's father had gone home to the village inn he kept in Finisterre, his wife, wearing deepest mourning, had stayed in Paris and hung about police headquarters for days, waiting in the anteroom to waylay Maigret and get news from him. Another believer in the almighty power of the police!

Once she got angry with him and he could almost hear her say with grim features and pinched lips, "When are you going to arrest him?"

Meaning the doctor obviously! Who knew if she wouldn't eventually accuse Maigret himself of some sinister complicity?

Maigret decided to wait until Monday, although he felt almost remorseful about this, particularly as he saw, every morning, a vast tray of eclairs covered with coffee icing in the window of the Bigoreau *patisserie*.

Could he be certain that these were not lethal, too, and that the girl who was carrying three of them away with such tender care, the boy devouring one on his way home from school, were not doomed to suffer Olga's fate?

By one o'clock on Monday he was at his post not far from the cake shop, but it was two o'clock before he caught sight of an old man whom he recognised without ever having seen him.

This was surely Mr Monday, shuffling along with a calm philosophical air, smiling at life, tasting its minutes, treasuring every crumb of them. With a gesture he was obviously used to making, he pushed open the door of the cake shop, and Maigret, from outside, could see Mme. Bigoreau and her daughter good-humoredly exchanging jokes with the old man.

They were pleased to see him, no doubt of that! His poverty was not of the depressing sort.

He was telling them something that made them laugh, till the plump girl at last remembered Monday's ritual. Leaning forward over the window display she chose two eclairs which with a professional gesture she wrapped in a twist of white paper.

Mr Monday, without hurrying, went into the shoe-repair shop next door where he got nothing but a small coin, and then into the corner tobacconist's where he was given a pinch of snuff.

There was nothing unpredictable about his days – that was quite obvious. Monday's people here, Tuesday's people in another district, and Wednesday's people somewhere else – they could all set their watches by his visits. He soon reached the Boulevard de la Seine and his step grew livelier as he drew near the doctor's house.

That was the house he liked, the house where they gave him a real meal – the same meal the family had eaten a little while before; the house where he'd sit down at a table in a clean warm kitchen.

He went in through the back door, like someone who was used to the place, and Maigret rang at the front.

"I should like to see the doctor at once." Maigret told Martin, the chauffeur-houseservant.

He was taken upstairs.

"Would you have the two eclairs brought up at once? The old man's down below."

Old Monday ate his meal without suspecting that in the doctor's consulting room two men were examining the gift he had brought the children.

"Nothing!" Dr Barion concluded after a close scrutiny.

So there were some weeks when the eclairs were filled with death, and others when they were harmless.

"Thank you," Maigret murmured.

"Where are you going?"

He was too late: Maigret was already halfway downstairs . . .

"This way, monsieur."

Poor Mme. Bigoreau was panic-stricken at the thought

that one of her customers might discover that a policeman was visiting her. She took Maigret into a little parlor with leaded-glass windows, adjoining the shop. Tarts were laid out to cool on every available piece of furniture, even on the arms of the chairs.

"I'd like to ask you, why you always give two eclairs rather than any other cakes, to the old man who comes on Monday."

"That's simple enough, monsieur. To begin with, we used to give him anything we had – damaged pastries or stale cakes. Once or twice it happened to be eclairs. Then we gave him something different and I remember how on that occasion he insisted on buying two eclairs as well.

" 'They bring me luck,' he said. So as he's a good old fellow, we fell into the habit –"

"One other question. Have you a customer by the name of Miss Wilfur?"

"Yes. Why do you ask?"

"Oh, nothing. She's a nice person, isn't she?"

"Do you think so?"

And the tone of that "Do you think so?" encouraged Maigret to go on.

"Of course, she's a bit of an eccentric –"

"You're right there! An eccentric, as you said, who never knows what she wants! If there were many customers of her sort we'd need twice the staff!"

"Does she come here often?"

"Never! I don't believe I've ever seen her. But she telephones, half in French and half in English so that we're always making mistakes. Do sit down, monsieur. Forgive me for having left you standing."

"I've finished. And please forgive me, madame, for having troubled you."

Three little remarks – enough to explain everything – echoed in Maigret's head.

Hadn't the woman in the shop said about Miss Wilfur: "An eccentric who never knows what she wants."

And then: "If there were many customers of her sort we'd need twice the staff."

And a moment later she admitted that this woman whom she had never seen "telephones half in French and half in English."

Maigret had not wanted to make a point of it. It would be time enough for that when the official examination took place, elsewhere than in the rather sickly atmosphere of the pastry shop.

Apart from the fact that Mme. Bigoreau might quite likely recover her business woman's pride and refuse to speak, rather than admit that she allowed people to send pastries back . . .

For that must be it! The three little remarks she had made couldn't mean anything else!

Maigret walked to Dr Barion's house, his hands thrust deep in his pockets, and as he reached the gate he almost collided with Mr Monday coming out of it.

"Well, did you bring your two eclairs?" Maigret remarked gaily. And as the old man stood dumfounded: "I'm a friend of the Barions. I know that you bring the children some cakes every Monday. But I can't help wondering something: why are they always eclairs."

"Didn't you know? It's a very simple story! Once when I had been given some eclairs, I had them with me and the children saw them. They told me those were their favorite pastry. So, as they're the kindest people on earth who give me the same sort of meal they have themselves, with coffee and all, you understand . . ."

Next day, when Maigret presented himself with a warrant in his pocket to arrest Miss Laura Wilfur, she got on her high horse and threatened to appeal to her ambassador; then she defended herself inch by inch with remarkable coolness.

"Which is just another proof of her insanity!" said the psychiatrist who examined her.

As were her lies – for she insisted she had been the doctor's mistress for a long time. And when the house was closely inspected, a large number of beards of rye were discovered hidden in a desk.

And finally it was learned through her mother that Colonel Wilfur had died in the New Hebrides from multiple perforation of the intestine brought about by a native plot . . .

Maigret saw Martin, the chauffeur, again at the last examination.

"What would you have done about the child?" he asked.

"I'd have gone off with Olga and we'd have opened a country inn somewhere."

"And your wife?"

He merely shrugged . . .

Miss Laura Wilfur, who was so much in love with Dr Barion that she had wanted to kill his children out of spite, had spied on all his movements, had poisoned the eclairs in her ferocious determination to attain her end – she had inserted the lethal beards of rye before telephoning Mme. Bigoreau, pretending there had been a mistake in her pastry order, and asking that the eclairs be picked up . . . Miss Laura Wilfur, who had the inspired notion of using innocent Mr Monday as her unsuspecting instrument, was confined for life in a mental institution.

And there for the past few years she has been telling her companions that she's about to become the mother of a son!

KICK IT OR KILL

Mickey Spillane

Adapted to:

THE GIRL HUNTERS

(Colorama, 1963)

Starring: Mickey Spillane,

Shirley Eaton & Lloyd Nolan

Directed by Roy Rowland

Mike Hammer, the hard-boiled sleuth introduced by Mickey Spillane in I, The Jury published in 1947, has been described as probably the toughest private detective in fiction — and there have been few tougher investigators on the screen, either. A rough fighter when cornered, he is quick with a gun and never slow in making a play for any beautiful woman who comes into his orbit. As a result of the success of the early Hammer titles, he was soon transferred to the screen and featured in a series of movies played by such different stars as Biff Elliot, Ralph

*Meeker, Robert Bray and even the author himself! (Mike
Hammer has also appeared on television, portrayed by Darren
McGavin and Stacy Keach.) Among the biggest selling of the
titles about him have been* Vengeance is Mine! *(1950),* The
Big Kill *(1951), and* Kiss Me, Deadly *(1952). A number of
Spillane's other violent crime novels have also been filmed
including* The Long Wait *(1954) which starred Anthony
Quinn;* The Delta Factor *(1970) with Christopher George;
and* Ring of Fear *(1954) starring Clyde Beatty and Pat
O'Brien. Mickey also made an appearance in this picture.*

*Mickey Spillane (1918–) is as much of a character as any of
those to be found in his books. Born in a tough area of New
York, he was a comic book writer until the outbreak of the
Second World War when he distinguished himself as a combat
pilot. Back in the US he worked as a federal agent for a number
of years during which time he helped to break up a narcotics ring
and was several times in danger of his life. Deciding to quit and
try the less violent occupation of writer, his creation of Mike
Hammer soon made him a rich man. Although there have been
breaks in his writing career in the intervening years, he still
remains one of the best-known authors of crime fiction. In 1963
he made a little piece of history in the genre by becoming the first
author to play his own character in the film of* The Girl
Hunters. *Though actually shot in England, the picture is set
in New York where Hammer relentlessly tracks down the
instigator of a criminal conspiracy. "Kick it or Kill" is one
of Spillane's few short stories and was written for* Cavalier
magazine shortly before he came to England to make The Girl
Hunters.

An old switcher engine pulled the two-car train from the
junction at Richfield over the 12-mile spur into Lake
Rappaho. At the right time the ride could have been
fun because the cars were leftovers from another era,
but now it was a damn nuisance. Coal dust had powdered
everything, settling into the mohair seats like sand and
hanging in the air so you could taste it. Summer was two
months gone and the mountains and valleys outside were

funnelling down cold Canadian air. There was no heat in the car.

Ordinarily, I wouldn't have minded, but now the chill made my whole side ache again under the bandage and I was calling myself an idiot for listening to that doctor and his wild ideas about me having to take a complete rest. I could have holed up just as well in New York, but instead I fell for the fresh air routine and took his advice about this place.

Lake Rappaho was the end of the line. A single limp sack of mail and a half dozen packages came off the baggage car as I stepped down from the last one.

On the other side of the platform, a black '58 Chevy with a hand painted *TAXI* on its door stood empty. I saw the driver, all right. He and a wizened old stationmaster were in the office peering at me like I was a stray moose in church. But that's mountain country for you. When you're out of season and not expected, everybody goes into a G.I. hemorrhage.

I waved my thumb at the taxi, picked up my old B-4 bag and the mailing tube I kept my split bamboo rod in, walked across the station to the car, threw my gear in the back seat, then got in front for the drive into Pinewood. It was another five minutes before the driver came out.

He opened the door on the other side. "Afternoon. You going to Pinewood?"

"Anyplace else to go?"

He shook his head. "Not for fifty miles, I guess."

"Then let's go there."

He slid under the wheel and kicked the motor over. In backing around the corner of the station he made a pretense of seeing my duffel in the back. "You going fishing?"

"That's the general idea."

"No fishing now, you know. Wrong season."

"It's still open, isn't it?"

He nodded. "For the rest of the month. But there's no fish."

"Shut up," I said.

It was a four-mile trip into the fading sun to Pinewood and

he didn't say anything again, but every foot of the way his hands were white around the wheel.

Pinewood had a permanent population of 2,500. It lay where the valley widened on one end of Lake Rappaho, a mile and a half long and four blocks wide. The summer cabins and homes on the outskirts were long closed and what activity there was centered around the main crossroads.

The Pines Hotel stood on the corner, a three-story white frame building whose second-story porch overhung the entire width of the sidewalk.

I paid the cabby, grabbed my luggage and went inside.

The two big guys bordering the door waited until I had crossed the lobby and was at the desk. Then they came up and watched while I signed the register. The heavy one took my card from the clip and looked at it.

"Mister Kelly Smith, New York City," he said. "That's a big place for a whole address."

"Sure is." The clerk edged up from his desk with a small, fixed smile divided between the other two and me.

"I'll be here two weeks," I told him. "I want a room upstairs away from the sun and take it out in advance." I pushed a hundred dollar bill across the desk and waited.

"Like if somebody wanted to find you in New York . . ." the big guy started to say.

I snatched the card from his fingers. "Then you look in the phone book. I'm listed," I said. I was feeling the old edge come back.

"Smith is a common name . . ."

"I'm the only Kelly Smith."

He tried to stare me down, but I wasn't playing any games. So instead he reached out and picked up my C note and looked at it carefully. "Haven't seen one of these in a long time."

I took that away from him too. "The way you're going you'll never see one," I said.

The clerk smiled, his eyes frightened, took the bill, and gave me $16 back. He handed me a room key. "Two-nine-teen, on the corner."

The big guy touched me on the shoulder. "You're pretty fresh."

I grinned at him. "And you're a lousy cop. Now just get off my back or start conducting a decent investigation. If it'll make you happy, I'll be glad to drop by your office, give you a full B.G., let you take my prints, and play Dragnet all you want. But first I want to get cleaned up and get something to eat."

He suddenly developed a nervous mouth. "Supposing you do that. You do just that, huh?"

"Yeah," I said. "Later maybe," and watched him go out.

When the door closed the clerk said, "That was Captain Cox and his sergeant, Hal Vance."

"They always pull that act on tourists?"

"Well, no . . . no, of course not."

"How many are in the department here?"

"The police? Oh . . . six, I think."

"That's two too many. They pull that stunt on me again while I'm here and I'll burn somebody's tail for them."

Behind me, a voice with a cold, throaty quality said, "I don't know whether I want you here or not."

I glanced at the clerk. "Nice place you run here. Who is she?"

"The owner." He nodded to a hand-carved plaque on his desk. It read, Miss Dari Dahl, Prop.

She was a big one, all right, full breasted and lovely with loose sun-bleached hair touching wide shoulders and smooth, tanned skin.

"You haven't any choice, honey. I got a receipt for two weeks. Now smile. A lovely mouse like you ought to be smiling all the time."

She smiled. Very prettily. Her mouth was lush like I knew it would be and she hip-tilted toward me deliberately. Only her eyes weren't smiling. She said, "Drop dead, you creep," and brushed by me.

There was something familiar about her name. The clerk gave me the answer. "It was her sister who killed herself in New York last year. Flori Dahl. She went out a window of the New Century Building."

I remembered it then. It made headlines when she landed on a parked U.N. car and almost killed a European delegate about to drive off with a notorious call girl. The tabloids spilled the bit before the hush needles went in.

"Tough," I said, "only she oughtn't to let it bug her like that."

I had supper in White's restaurant. I had a table in the corner where I could see the locals filter in to the bar up front. The few who ate were older couples and when they were done I was alone. But everybody knew where I was. They looked at me often enough. Not direct, friendly glances, but scared things that were touched with some hidden anger.

My waitress came over with a bill. I said softly, "Sugar . . . what the hell's the matter with this town?"

She was scared, too. "Sir?" was all she could manage.

I walked up to the bar.

At 8 o'clock, Captain Cox and Sergeant Vance came in and tried to make like they weren't watching me. Fifteen minutes later, Dari Dahl came in. When she finally saw me her eyes became veiled with contempt, then she turned away and that was that.

I was ready to go when the door opened again. You could feel the freeze. Talk suddenly quieted down. The two guys in tweedy coats closed the door behind them and walked up to the bar with studied casualness. Their clothes were just the right kind, but on the wrong people because they weren't Madison Avenuers at all. One was Nat Paley and the bigger guy you called Lennie Weaver when you wanted to stay friends, but, if you had a yen for dying quick, you gave him the Pigface tab Margie Provetsky hung on him years ago.

I felt that crazy feeling come all over me and I wanted to grin, but for now I kept it in. I pushed my stool back and that's as far as I got. The little guy who stormed in was no more than 20, but he had an empty milk bottle in one hand and he mouthed a string of curses as he came at Paley and Weaver.

Trouble was, he talked too much. He tried to spill it out

before he cut loose. Lenny laced him with a sudden backhand as Nat grabbed him, took the bottle away, and slammed him to the floor.

He wasn't hurt, but he was too emotionally gone to do anything more than cry. His face was contorted with hate.

Lenny grunted and picked up his drink. "You crazy, kid?"

"You dirty bastard!" The words were softly muffled. "You talked her into working for him."

"Get outa here, kid."

"She didn't have to work up there. She had a job. You showed her all that money, didn't you? That's why she worked. She always talked about having that kind of money. You bastards! You dirty bastards!"

When Nat kicked him, the blood splashed all over his shoes and the kid just lay there. He twitched, vomited, and started to choke. The only one who moved was Dari. She managed to get him face down and held him like that until he moaned softly and opened his eyes.

She glanced up with those wild eyes of hers and said, "Sonny was right. You're dirty bastards."

"Would you like a kick in the face too, lady?" Lennie asked her.

For a second it was real quiet, then I said, "Try it, Pigface."

He spun around and my shoe ripped his sex machine apart and while he was in the middle of a soundless scream I grabbed Nat's hair and slammed his face against the bar. He yelled, swung at me, and one hand tore into the bandage over my ribs and I felt the punk draining right out of me. But that was his last chance. I almost brained him the next time and let him fall in a heap on the floor with his buddy.

I faked a grin at Dari, walked past the two cops at the table, and said so everybody could hear me, "Nice clean town you got here, friend," and went outside to get sick.

The window was open and I could see my breath in the air, but just the same I was soaked with sweat. When the knock came on the door I automatically said to come on in, not caring who it was. My side was one gigantic ball of fire and it was going to be another hour before the pills I had taken helped.

There was no sympathy in her voice. The disdain was still there, only now it was touched by curiosity. She stood there, her stomach flat under her dress, her breasts swelling out, and I remembered pictures of the Amazons and thought that she would have made a good one. Especially naked.

"Sonny asked me to thank you."

Trying to make my voice sound real wasn't easy. "No trouble."

"Do you . . . know what you're doing?"

She paused.

"What do you want in Pinewood?"

"A vacation, kitten. Two weeks. I have to do it. Now, will you do me a favor?" I closed my eyes. The fire in my side was building up again.

"Yes?"

"In my B-4 bag over there . . . in the side pocket is a bottle of a capsules. Please . . ."

I heard the zipper run back, then the sharp intake of her breath. The gun she found in the wrong side pocket suddenly fell to the floor with a thump and then she was standing over me again. She had the bottle in her hand.

"You're a damned drug addict, aren't you? That's the way they get without their dosage. They get sick, they sweat, they shake." She poured the caps back in the bottle and capped it. "Your act in the restaurant stunk. Now act this one out." With a quick flip of her wrist she threw the bottle out the window and I heard it smash in the street.

"You filth," she said and walked out.

It was three in the afternoon when I woke up. I lay there panting and, when the sudden sickness in my stomach subsided, I got to my feet and undressed. Outside, a steady light rain tapped against the windows.

A hot shower was like a rebirth.

The .45 was still on the floor where Dari Dahl had let it

drop and I hooked it with my foot, picked it up, and zippered it inside my leather shaving kit.

Every time I thought of that crazy broad throwing that bottle out the window I felt like laying her out. That wasn't getting those capsules back, though. I had maybe another two hours to go and I was going to need them bad, bad, bad. I stuffed 50 bucks in my pocket and went downstairs.

Outside my window, I found the remains of the bottle. The capsules inside had long since dissolved and been washed away by the rain.

I shrugged it off, found the drugstore and passed my spare prescription over to the clerk. He glanced at it, looked at me sharply, and said, "This will take an hour."

"Yeah, I know. I'll be back."

I headed for the restaurant. Although lights were on in store fronts and the corner traffic blinker winked steadily, there wasn't a car or a person on the street. It was like a ghost town.

The restaurant was empty. The waitress recognized me with a peculiar smile, took my order, and half-ran to the kitchen. The bartender walked across the room to me.

He was a graying man in his late 40s, a little too thin with deep tired eyes. "Look, mister," he said, "I don't want trouble in here."

I leaned back in my chair. "You know who those jokers were?"

He nodded. "We'll handle things our own way."

"Then start by keeping out of my hair, friend," I told him. "I don't know how or why those punks are here, but they're the kind of trouble people like you just don't handle at all, so be grateful for the little things, understand?"

He didn't understand at all and his face showed it. He glanced outside toward the distant slope of the mountain. "You aren't . . . on the hill?"

"Mac, I don't know what the hell you're talking about. I think you people are nuts, that's all. I pull those punks off the kid's back last night while you, the cops, and everybody else just watch and I catch the hard time. I don't get it."

The door slammed open and Sergeant Vance came in. He came sidling over and tossed a sheet of paper down on the table. It was my prescription.

"This calls for narcotics, mister. You better come up with a damn good explanation."

Real slowly I stood up. Vance was a big guy, but he wasn't looking down on me at all. Not at all. His face was all mean but scared too like the rest and his hand jumped to the butt of his service revolver.

I said, "Okay, you clown, I'll give you one explanation and if you ask again I'll shove that gun of yours up your pipe. That's a legitimate prescription you got there and, if you do any checking, you check the doctor who issued it first. Then, if it's bad, you come back to me. Meanwhile, you have a certain procedure to take that's down in black and white in the statute books. Now you take that prescription back and see that it gets filled or you'll be chewing on a warrant for your own arrest."

He got it, all right. For a minute, I thought I was going to have to take the rod away from him, but the message got through in time. He went out as fast as he came in.

What a hell of a vacation this was. Brother!

Willie Elkins, who owned a garage, was willing to rent me his pickup truck for 15 bucks a week. It was a dilapidated thing, but all I needed. He told me how to find old Mort Steiger, who rented boats. The old guy let me have my pick, then shook his head at me and grinned through his broken plate. "You ain't no fisherman, are you?"

"Nope," I shook back. "I try once in a while, but I'm no fisherman."

He paused, watching me warily. "You on the hill?"

"What is this 'hill' business? Who's up on what hill?"

He waited a moment, sucking on his lips. "You kiddin'? No, guess you ain't." He pointed a gnarled finger over my shoulder. "Big place up there just around that ridge. Can't see it from here, but she has a private road that comes right down to the lake, all fenced in. Whole place like that. You can't get in or out unless they let you."

"Who let's you?"

"City people. That's Mister Simpson's place. Big manufacturer of something or other. Never met him myself. He likes it private."

I let out a grunt. "He sure does. He has a real goon squad working for him. I met a couple last night. They needed straightening out."

This time his grin got broader and he chuckled. "So you're the one. Willie told me about that. Could be you'll make trouble for yourself, you don't watch out."

"It won't come from two-bit punks, pop. Trouble is, if Simpson's such a big one, what's he doing with guys like that on his place?"

"Maybe I could tell you."

I waited.

"This Simpson feller was a big one long time ago. Bootlegging or something, then he went straight. He had all this money so he went into business. Few times a year he comes up here, does some business, and leaves."

"Everybody in town is scared, pop. That's not good business."

His eyes seemed to scratch the ground. "Ain't the business he does."

"What then?"

"The girls. He sends down to Pinewood for girls."

"The place looks big enough to support a few hookers."

"Mister, you just don't know country towns. Comes end of summer and *those* girls pack up and leave. It's the others he gets."

"Listen, a guy that big wouldn't try . . ."

He interrupted with a wave of his hand. "You got me wrong. He . . . employs them."

"Well, what's wrong with that?"

"They go up there, all right, but they don't come back . . . well, the same . . . Rita Moffet and the oldest Spencer girl moved over to Sunbar. Bob Rayburn's only girl, she never would speak to anybody and last year they had to send her to the State Hospital. She still won't speak to anybody at all.

Flori Dahl and Ruth Gleason went off to New York. Flori died there and nobody has heard from Ruth in months."

"Nice picture."

"Others, too. That's not all. Some are still here and every time Simpson and the bunch comes in they go up there to work. Like they enjoy it. He pays them plenty, oh, you can bet that. What stuff they buy, and all from New York."

"Any complaints?"

The old man frowned. "That's the funny part. None of 'em say nothing."

I stood up and stretched. "You know what I think? This Simpson guy pays them mighty generously and for the first time they get a look at how the other half lives and want to give it a try. So they leave town. It's an old story. The others won't leave, but let the gravy come to them. How about that?"

"He got funny people working for him. They bring trouble to town, mister."

"Okay, so he hires hoods. I know reputable businessmen who have done the same."

Steiger thought it over. "Maybe, but did you ever see such a scared town in your life, mister?"

The drizzle had stopped. I zippered up my jacket and shoved my hat on. Mort Steiger watched me carefully.

Finally he said, "You're a funny one, too, mister."

"Oh?"

"You got a real mean look. You're big and you look mean. You tell me something true?"

I opened the door of the pickup and said over my shoulder, "Sure I'll tell you true, pop."

"You ever kill anybody?"

I slammed the door shut and looked at him. He was completely serious.

Finally I nodded. "Yes. Six people."

"I don't mean in the war, son."

"I wasn't talking about the war."

"How'd you do it?"

"I shot them," I said and let the clutch out.

                    *   *   *

The druggist had my prescription ready and handed it over without a word. I knew he had checked on the doctor who issued it and had another check going through different channels. I ordered a Coke, took two of the capsules, and pocketed the rest.

A fresh rain slick was showing on the street and the weather forecast was that it would continue for a few days. So I'd fish in the rain. I'd take a six-pack of Blue Ribbon and a couple sandwiches along and anchor in the middle of the lake under an umbrella.

I went outside, flipped a mental coin to see where I'd eat. The coffee shop in the hotel won and I hopped in the truck. At the corner the blinker was red on my side and I rolled to a stop. As I did, a new black Caddy with Kings County (New York) plates made the turn and I had a fast look at the driver.

His name was Benny Quick, he had done two turns in Sing Sing on felony counts and was supposedly running a dry-cleaning place in Miami. There was somebody beside him and somebody in the back, but I couldn't make them out.

I made a U turn, passed the sedan, turned right two blocks farther on, and let the Caddy pass behind me. That's all I needed to pick up the license number. A friend back in New York would do the rest.

I couldn't figure what Benny Quick was doing up this way, but I made a living being nosy and I had been too long at it to let a vacation take me out of the habit.

Back at the Pines Hotel, I shared the coffee shop with a half dozen teen-agers sipping coffee and feeding the juke box. None of them paid any attention to me. The waitress snapped the menu down in front of me.

When I looked up I said, "You ought to smile more, Miss Dahl."

"Not for you, Mr Smith."

"Call me Kelly."

She ignored me completely and waited. I told her what I wanted, and while I waited scanned a newspaper. The headlines were still all about Cuba.

Dari Dahl came back, fired my cheeseburgers at me, and

put the coffee down so hard it spilled. I said, "Go back and get me another cup."

"What?"

"Damn it, you heard me. I've had about all the crap from you I can take. You be as sore as you please, but baby, treat me like a customer or for kicks I'll throw these dishes through your front window. This town is giving me the business and from now on the business stops. Now shake your but and get me another coffee and do it right."

The next time the coffee came slow and easy. I said, "Sit down."

She paused. "Mr Smith . . ."

When I looked up and she saw my face, she grew chalky and pulled out a chair.

Dari Dahl was a magnificent woman, even scared. The tight nylon uniform outlined the daring cut of her under-things. The word bra was disputable for all that it was, and below it, far below, was a bikini-like thing beautifully discernible.

"I heard about your sister," I said.

"Let's not discuss it."

"Dari baby, it won't be too hard to find out someplace else. I remember the rough details. Any old newspaper account could fill me in. Anybody around town ought to be glad to talk about the bit."

The hardness came back again, her mouth pulling tight at the corners. "You should be able to understand it. My sister was a drug addict, when she could no longer supply her need, she killed herself. Eventually, you'll do the same."

"I will?"

"Your supposed legitimate source of supply through our druggist won't last very long. My sister used stolen and forged prescriptions, too, for a while. It was when they ran out that she killed herself." She stopped, her eyes glinting. "Tell me, Mr Smith, are you here now because there are no other pharmacists who will honor your prescriptions? Is that it?"

Slowly, I finished my coffee. "You really are bugged, kid. You really are."

She walked away, tall, cool, a lovely, curvy animal, as beautiful as any woman ever was, but going completely to waste.

I left a buck and a half by my plate, went upstairs where I showered and changed into a city suit. I decided to try the air again. There should be a movie or a decent bar someplace.

I reached for the phone, but remembered the clerk downstairs and hung up. In the lobby, I called from a house phone where I could watch the desk, gave a New York number, and waited.

When my number answered, I said, "Artie?"

"Yeah, hi ya, Kelly, how's it going?"

For a full five minutes we made idle conversation about nothing, throwing in enough dirty words so any prudish operator bugging in would knock it off in disgust. Then I said, "Run a number through for me, kid, then get me all the information on its owner. Next, find out what you can about Benny Quick. He's supposed to be in Miami." I fed him the license number, talked a little more about nothing, and hung up.

Outside, the rain had started again, harder this time. I looked each way, saw a couple of recognizable lights, grinned, and walked toward them.

Like a whore's is red, police lights have to be green, old-fashioned, and fly-specked. You know from the sight of them what it's going to smell like inside. There's a man smell of wet wool, cigars, and sweat. There's a smell of wood, oiled-down dust; of stale coffee, and musty things long stored. On top of that, there's another smell a little more quiet, one of fear and shame that comes from the other people who aren't cops and who go down forever in the desk book.

I walked in and let Sergeant Vance stare at me like a snake and then said, "Where's your captain?"

"What do you want him for?"

The pair of young beat cops who had been standing in the corner moved in on the balls of their feet. They were all set to take me when the office door opened and Cox said, "Knock it off, Woodie." He ran his eyes up and down me. "What do you want?"

I grinned at him, but it wasn't friendly at all. "You wanted my prints, remember? You said to stop by."

He flushed, then his jaw went hard. He came out of the doorway and faced me from three feet away. "You're a rough character, buddy. You think we don't know what to do with rough guys?"

And I gave it to him all the way. I said, "No, I don't think you know what to do with rough guys, Captain. I think you're all yak and nothing else."

Across his forehead, a small pulse beat steadily. But he held it in better than I thought he could. His voice was hard but restrained when he told the beat cop behind me, "Take his prints, Woody."

I gave him my name and address and stopped right there. If he wanted anything on me he could get it only after he booked me. I grinned at everybody again, left a bunch of stinking mad cops behind me, and went out into the fresh air.

It was 9 o'clock, too late for a show but not for a bar. I found one called JIMMIE'S with Jimmie himself at the bar and ordered a beer. Jimmie was a nice old guy and gassed with me.

When I finally got around to the Simpson place, he made a wry face and said, "Nobody ever saw the guy I know of. Not down here in town."

"How about the girls?"

He nodded. "You don't get much out of them. Simpson turns out to be either big or little, skinny or fat and you get the point. They don't talk it up any."

"So they don't talk about their boss. They get paid plenty, I hear."

"Hell, yes. Bonnie Ann and Grace Shaefer both sport minks and throw plenty of bucks around. Every once in a while I see Helen Allen in a new car. She comes through about once a month to see her folks. Used to be a nice kid. All of them were."

"Making money changed that?"

Jimmie shook his head, squinting. "No, but used to be they were plain hustlers and not high on anybody's list."

I asked, "You mean that's their job up there?"

His shrug was noncommittal. "They won't say. Some of them do secretarial work, answering phones and all that, because the switchboard operators here have talked to them often enough."

"If they're that interested, why doesn't somebody just ring Simpson's bell and ask?"

Jimmie gave a short laugh. "Besides the brush-off at the gate, who wants to spoil a good thing? Before that bunch leaves there'll be a bunch of money in this town, and off season you don't kick out found loot. Then there's another angle. That boy's a big taxpayer. He's got connections where they count, as some busybodies found out. A few local do-gooders tried some snooping and wound up holding their behinds. Nobody goes to the cops, though I can't see them doing much about it. Cox is like a cat who's afraid of a mouse yet getting hungry enough so he knows he has to eat one or die. I think he figures if he eats one it'll be poisoned and he'll die, too."

He opened me another bottle and moved on down the bar to take care of a new customer. It was the nervous taxi driver who tried to steer me away from Pinewood in the first place. I was beginning to wish I had let him talk me into it.

He ordered a beer, too, said something about the weather, then confidentially told Jimmie, "Saw somebody tonight. Didn't recognize her at first, but it was Ruth Gleason."

I poured my glass full, making like I was concentrating on it. Ruth Gleason was the girl Mort Steiger told me ran off to New York the same time Flori Dahl did.

"You sure?" Jimmie asked him.

"Oughta know her, I guess. She's changed though. She's got on fancy clothes and all that, but her face is sure old looking. Wouldn't look at me. She kind of turned away when she saw me."

"Well what's she doing back here?"

"Who knows? She got in that blue ranchwagon from the hill place and drove off." He waved off another beer and went out.

Jimmie came back wiping his hands on his apron.

Bluntly, I said, "Mort told me about the Gleason kid, too."

He didn't question my tone. "Nice girl. She was up there a whole month. Hardly ever came down and when she did she wouldn't speak to anybody. Flori and she went in at the same time. Flori used to come to town occasionally and the way she changed was hard to believe."

"How?"

He waved his hands expressively. "Like you can't pin it down. Just changed. They wouldn't look at you or hardly speak. It was real queer."

"Didn't any of those kids have parents?"

"Flori's old man was dying and they had no mother. I think Flori took the job up there to help get her old man into the Humboldt Hospital. They got him there, but he died soon after. Cancer."

"That's only one," I pointed out.

"Ah, who can tell kids anyhow? They do what they please anyway. Sure, some of them had folks, but there's big money up there."

He popped the top from another bottle and passed it over. "On the house." He took a short one himself, and we gave a silent toast and threw them down.

Then he said, "Better not do too much talking around town. This is a spooky place."

I grinned, paid off my tab, and waved him good night.

For a few minutes I stood under the awning watching the rain, then started back toward the center of town. I had crossed the street and almost reached the corner when the big Imperial came from my left, turned left, and stopped half a block up ahead of me. Unconsciously, I stepped into the darker shadows and walked faster.

Someone stepped out of the car, turned and pulled at

another. They stood there together a moment and then I heard the unmistakable spasm of a sob.

I ran then, holding one hand tight against my ribs to muffle the fire that had started there. I was too late. They heard my feet pounding and the one by the car turned sharply, ducked inside, and slammed the door. The car pulled away silently and slowly as if nothing had happened.

But they left a beautiful young girl behind them. She was sobbing hysterically and started to collapse as I reached her.

She was a lovely brunette wrapped tightly in a white trench-coat, her hair spilling wetly over her shoulders. She tried to shove me away while she hung on desperately to an oversize handbag and kept saying over and over, "No . . . please, no!"

I said, "Easy, kid," and pulled her to the porch steps of the nearest house. When I got her seated I tried to take her hand. She stopped sobbing then, jerked her hand, and held her pocketbook on the opposite side.

For a second the hysteria passed and she said, "Get out of here. Let me alone!"

"Relax, I'm . . ."

"There's nothing the matter with me," she nearly shouted. "Get out of here. *Let me alone!*"

She clenched her teeth on the last word with a crazy grimace and tried to stand up. But I was sitting on one edge of her coat and when she did the thing yanked open and half-pulled off her shoulder.

She was naked from the waist up and I didn't need any light to see the welts and stripes across her body and the small bleeding spots where something with a sharp tip had dug in.

I stood up, pulled the trench coat closed. When she realized I had seen her, she closed her eyes, let out a soft, mewing sound, and let herself fold up in my arms. I put her down on the steps again and as I did, her pocketbook fell open. There was a sheaf of brand new bills inside, held by a bank wrapper. On it was printed the number *1,000*.

Suddenly the porch light snapped on, the door opened,

and a man stood there clutching his bathrobe at his middle. His wife peered over his shoulder, her face worried.

"You," he called out. "What are you doing there?" His voice didn't have too much snap to it.

I motioned to the girl. "There's a sick woman here. Look, call a doctor for me and hurry it, will you?"

"A doctor? What's . . ."

"Never mind what's the matter. You call. And turn out that light."

They were glad to get back inside. The porch light went out and inside one turned on. I propped the kid up, put her bag under her arm, and walked away from the house.

I didn't get very far. The car hissed up behind me and a voice said, "It's him again. The one who jumped Lennie and me in the restaurant."

There wasn't any sense running. A dozen fast steps would tear my side anyway. I just stood there and because I did the action that was all set to explode went sour. Nat Paley and the new guy who hopped out and came at me from different sides slowed, not able to figure me out.

Nat's hand came out of his pocket with a gun. The gun came up and Nat's face said it was the right time and the right place. Except somebody else thought differently and a strangely cold voice from inside the car said, "No noise."

They moved before I could yell. The other guy came in fast from the side, but I ducked in time to get the load in his fist off the top of my head. I kicked out, jabbed at his eyes, and made the touch. He couldn't yell with the sudden pain, ducked into my right and his face seemed to come apart under my knuckles.

And that was the end of it. Nat got me just right, one stunning blow behind the ear, and, as I sunk to my knees, went over me expertly with a clubbed gun and ruthless feet. As one terrible kick exploded into my side, I thought I screamed and knew with absolute certainty that Nat had one more blow to deliver. It would come with bone-crunching force in that deadly spot at the base of the brain. I knew it was coming and I hoped it would, anything that would erase the awful thing that was happening to me inside.

It came all right, but a sudden convulsion that wracked my side made it miss and my shoulder took it all. Nat didn't realize that, though. A tiny part of my mind that could still discern things heard him laugh and drag the other guy into the car.

In the middle of a wild dream of sound and light I coughed, tried to turn my head away from the jarring, acrid fumes of ammonia, and then swam back into a consciousness I didn't want.

Somebody had carried me to the steps and a face peered anxiously into mine. The old guy watching me said, "It's all right. I'm Doctor McKeever."

"The girl . . ." I started.

"She's all right. She's inside. We'd better get you in there, too."

"I'm fine."

"What happened? Was there an accident?"

I shook my head, clearing it. "No . . . not actually."

When I moved my arm my shoulder muscles screamed. At least nothing was broken. I'd taken some bad ones before, but this took the cake. Under the bandages I could feel the warmth of blood and knew what was happening.

I said, "You saw the girl?"

"Yes."

"You got an idea of what happened?"

He chewed his lips a moment and nodded. "I know."

"You've seen it before, haven't you?"

At first he wasn't going to say anything, then he looked at me again. His voice had an edge to it. "Yes."

"Then you do like you did before, doc. You keep this under your hat, too. Let it get out and that kid is ruined here in town. She can be ruined no matter where she goes and it isn't worth a public announcement."

"Somebody has got to stop it," he said.

I said, "It'll be stopped, doc. It'll be stopped."

A small frown furrowed his forehead. His smile was crooked. "Toxin-anti-toxin," he said.

"What?"

"Poison against poison."

I nodded, spit, and said, "You go take care of that kid, then ride me back to the hotel."

When he had left I got sick again. I had to get those capsules I had left in my room. In just a few minutes now it was going to be worse than it ever had been and I'd be a raving maniac without a big jolt from the small bottle.

I couldn't tell how long he had been gone, but finally he came out leading the girl. A car pulled around from the side and the doctor bundled her into it, telling the driver to take her to his office and deliver her to his wife.

As soon as the car left, he had me on my feet, got me in his Ford, and started up. At the hotel he got out, opened my door, and took the arm on my good side to lead me in.

Dari Dahl was behind the desk, in white nylon no longer. She was wearing a black sweater and skirt combination that dramatized every curve of her body and making the yellow of her hair look like a pool of light.

The brief flicker of concern that hit her face turned to a peculiar look of satisfaction. She came around the desk, tiny lines playing at the corner of her mouth and said, "Trouble?"

"What else. Now get my key, please."

She smiled, went back, picked the key out, and came over and handed it to me. "Are you hurting, Mr Smith?"

Both of us shot her funny looks.

"Is it true that when a narcotic addict tries to lay off he fights it until he's almost tortured to death before he takes a dose?"

McKeever said, "What are you talking about, Dari?"

"Ask him." She smiled too sweetly.

"She's bugged, doc, let's go."

We walked to the stairs, started up them, when Dari called, "Mr Smith . . ."

I stopped, knowing somehow what was coming.

"Quite accidentally I dropped a bottle of capsules while cleaning your room. They fell down the toilet." She stopped, letting it sink in, then added, "And so did several prescriptions that were with the bottle. I hope you don't mind too much."

She could see the sweat that beaded my face and laughed. I could hear it all the way up the steps.

I flopped on the bed and it was then, when my coat came open, that McKeever saw the blood. He opened my shirt, saw the red seeping through the bandages, took one look at the color of my face, and rushed out.

Lying there, my ribs wouldn't flex to my breathing and the air seemed to whistle in my throat. It was like being branded; only the iron never left.

The door opened and I thought it was McKeever back, then I smelled the fragrance of her across the room. My eyes slitted open. She wasn't wearing that funny smile she had before.

"What the hell do you want?" I managed to get out.

"Doctor McKeever told me . . ." she paused and moistened her lips, "about Gloria Evans. You tried to help her."

"So what?" I said nastily.

"You tried to help Sonny Holmes the other night, too."

"Sure, I'm everybody's buddy."

I closed my eyes, trying to control my breathing. She said softly, a still determined tone in her voice, "About the other thing . . . drugs. I'm not sorry about that at all."

McKeever came in then, panting from the run up the stairs. He uncovered me, got his fingers under the bandage and worked it off. He said, "A doctor took care of you, didn't he?"

All I could do was nod.

I smelled the flower smell of her as she came closer and heard the sharp intake of her breath as she saw me. "What . . . happened?"

"This man has been shot. He's recuperating from an operation." I heard Dr McKeever open the bag and the clink of bottles. "Didn't you have anything to take periodically to kill the pain?"

I nodded again, my face a pool of sweat. I felt the needle go in my arm and knew it would be all right soon. I said through teeth held so tight they felt like they'd snap off, "Capsules. Morphine sulphate."

"*Oh, no!*" Her voice sounded stunned.

McKeever said, "What?"

"I thought he was a drug addict. I destroyed them."

The doctor said nothing.

Slowly the pain was lifting like a fog. Another second and I'd sleep.

Tonelessly, Dari said, "How he must hate me!"

Then I was past answering her.

It stopped raining on Wednesday. For two days I had lain there listening to my bedside radio. The hourly news broadcasts gave the latest U.N. machinations, then into the Cuban affair. Now the finger was pointing at Cuba as being the new jumping off place for narcotic shipments to the States. Under suspected Soviet sponsorship, the stuff came in easily and cheaply from China – a cleverly different kind of time bomb a country can use to soften an enemy.

But two days were enough. I found my clothes, shaved, dressed, and tried to work the stiffness out of my muscles. Even then, the stairs almost got me. I took it easy going down, trying to look more unconcerned than I felt.

McKeever wasn't glad to see me. He told me I had no business being up yet and told me to sit down while he checked the bandage. When he finished he said, "I never asked about that gunshot wound."

"Go on."

"I assume it has been reported."

"You assume right."

"However. I'm going to report it again."

"Be my guest, doc. To save time I suggest you get the doctor's name from the prescription I had filled here."

"I will." He got up and reached for the phone.

The druggist gave him the doctor's name, then he called New York. When the phone stopped cackling, McKeever nodded, "It was reported, all right. Those prescriptions were good. Then you really are here on . . . a vacation."

"Nobody seems to believe it."

"You've been causing talk since you came."

"What about the girl?" I said. "Gloria Evans."

He slumped back in his chair. "She's all right. I have her at my wife's sister's place."

"She talk?"

The doctor shook his head. "No, they never talk." He took a deep breath, tapped his fingers against the desk and said, "She was badly beaten, but there was a marked peculiarity about it. She was *carefully* beaten. Two instruments were used. One appears to be a long, thin belt; the other a fine braided whip-like thing with a small metal tip."

I leaned forward. "Punishment?"

McKeever shook his head. "No. The instruments used were too light. The application had too deliberate a pattern to it."

"There were others like that?"

"I took care of two of them. It wasn't very pretty, but they wouldn't talk. What happened to them would never leave permanent scars . . . but there are other ways of scarring people."

"One thing more, doc. Were they under any narcotic influence at all?"

McKeever sighed deeply. "Yes. The Evans girl had two syringe marks in her forearm. The others had them too, but I didn't consider them for what they were then."

I stood up. "Picture coming through, doc?"

He looked like he didn't want to believe it. "It doesn't seem reasonable."

"It never does," I told him.

I stopped at the hotel and took the .45 from my shaving kit. I checked the load, jacked one in the chamber and let the hammer down easy, then shoved it under my belt on my good side. I dropped a handful of shells in my coat pocket just in case. In the bathroom I washed down two of my capsules, locked my door, and went downstairs.

The clerk waved me over. "New York call for you, Mr Smith. Want me to get the number back? It was paid."

I told him to go ahead. It was Artie on the other end and after helloing me he said, "I have your items for you Kelly."

"Go ahead."

"One, the car belongs to Don Casales. He's a moderate-sized hood from the L.A. area and clean. Casales works for Carter Lansing who used to have big mob connections in the old days. Now he's going straight and owns most of So-Flo Airways with headquarters in Miami. Two, Benny Quick has left the Miami area for parts unknown. Benny has been showing lots of green lately. Anything else?"

"Yeah. Name Simpson in connection with Nat Paley or Lennie Weaver mean anything?"

"Sure, remember Red Dog Wally? He's got a bookie stall on Forty-ninth . . . other day he mentioned old Pigface Weaver. Some broad was around looking him up with tears in her eyes. A real looker, he said, but nobody knew a thing about Lennie. Red Dog said he'd ask around, found out that Lenny and Nat had something big going for them with an out of town customer and were playing it cozy. No squeal out on them either. So Red Dog told the broad and she almost broke down."

"Then their client could be Simpson."

"Who knows. Hell, they've strong-armed for big guys from politicians to ladies' underwear manufacturers."

"Okay, Artie, thanks a bunch."

I hung up and stood there a minute, trying to think. I went over the picture twice and picked up an angle. I grinned at the thought and turned around.

She was waiting for me, tall, beautiful, her hair so shiny you wanted to bathe in it. The gentle rise and fall of her breasts said this was a moment she had thought about and planned. She tried a tiny smile and said, "Kelly?"

"Let's keep it Mr Smith. I don't want to be friendly with the help."

She tried to hold her head up and keep the smile on, but I saw her eyes go wet.

I tipped her chin up. "Now that we've exchanged nasties, everybody's even. Think you can smile again?"

It came back, crookedly at first, but there it was and she was something so damn crazy special I could hardly believe it.

"Mr Smith . . ."

I took her hand. "Kelly. Let's make it Kelly, sugar."

Before I knew what she was going to do it was over, a kiss, barely touching, but for one fraction of an instant a fierce, restrained moment. We both felt it and under the sheer midnight of her blouse a ripple seemed to touch her shoulder and her breasts went hard.

She went with me, out to the truck, waiting while I went into police headquarters. I asked for Captain Cox and when he came said, "I want to lodge a complaint against two of Mr Simpson's employees. One is Nat Paley, the other a stranger."

Cox's face drew tight. "About your brawl, I suppose."

"That's right. They attacked me on the street. I recognized Paley and can identify the other by sight."

Nodding, Cox said, "We checked that one through already. The housekeeper whose place you used called us. Another party down the street thought he recognized one of Simpson's cars. However, Mr Simpson himself said none of his cars was out and all his employees were on the premises. A dozen others can vouch for it."

"I see."

"Anybody else to back up your side?"

I grinned at him. "I think it can be arranged."

"You're causing a lot of trouble, Mister," he told me.

My grin got big enough so he could see all the teeth. "Hell, I haven't even started yet."

Dari and I drove through town and picked up a macadam road leading into the hills. Below us to the right Lake Rappaho was a huge silver puddle. Two lesser roads intersected and joined the one we were on.

At the next bend we came upon the outer defenses of Simpson's place. A sign read Hillside Manor Private. It was set in a fieldstone wall a good 10 feet high and on top were shards of broken glass set in concrete. That wasn't all. Five feet out there was a heavy wire fence with a three-strand barbed wire overhang.

"Nice," I said. "He's really in there. How long has it been like this?"

"Since the war. About '47."

"This guy Simpson . . . he's always had the place?"

"No. There was another. It changed hands about ten years ago. That is, at least the owners changed. But the visitors; they're always the same. You never see them in town at all. They come and go at night or come in by the North Fork Road or by Otter Pass. Sometimes there are a hundred people up there a week or two at a time."

"It can accommodate that many?"

"At least. There are twenty-some rooms in the big house and six outbuildings with full accommodations. It's almost like a huge private club."

"Nobody's ever been nosy enough to look inside?"

After a moment she said, "They caught Jake Adler in there once and beat him up terribly. Captain Cox has been in a couple of times, but said he saw nothing going on. Several years ago two hunters were reported missing in this area. They were found dead a week later . . . fifty miles away. Their car went over a cliff. The police said they had changed their plans and decided to hunt elsewhere."

"Could have been."

"Possibly. Only one of them made a phone call from the hotel the day they were supposed to have disappeared."

I looked at her incredulously. "You report that?"

"They said I wasn't positive enough. I only had a photograph to go on and in brush clothes all hunters tend to look alike."

"Nice. Real nice. How can we get a look in there then?"

"You can see the house from the road a little way up. I don't know how you can get inside though. The wall goes all the way around and down to the lake."

"There's an approach on the water?"

Her forehead creased in thought. "There's a landing there with a path leading through the woods. It's well hidden in a finger cove. Are you . . ."

"Let's see the house first."

We found the spot. I parked the car and stood there at the lip, looking across a quarter-mile gulf of densely wooded valley at the white house that looked like a vacation hotel.

A few figures moved on the lawn and a few more clustered on the porch, their dark clothes marking them against the stark white of the building.

Behind me, Dari said, "A car is coming."

It was a blue sedan, an expensive job, the two in front indiscernible in the shadows. But the New York City plate wasn't. I wrote the number down and didn't bother putting the pencil back. Another plume of dust was showing around the Otter Pass intersection and I waited it out. We were back to black Caddies again and this one had four men in it and upstate New York plates. Fifteen minutes later a white Buick station wagon rolled past and the guy beside the driver was looking my way.

Harry Adrano hadn't changed much in the five years he had been up the river. His face was still set in a perpetual scowl, still blue-black with beard, his mouth a hard slash. And Harry was another number in a crazy combination because wherever Harry went one of the poppy derivatives was sure to follow.

Very softly I said, "Like Apalachin . . . I got to get inside there."

"You can't. The main gate is guarded."

"There's the lake . . ."

"Somebody will be there, too. Why do you have to go inside?"

"Because I want to get the numbers on any cars that are up there."

"You'll get killed in there."

"You know a better way?"

The smile she gave me matched her eyes. "Yes. Grace Shaefer was in town yesterday. She'll be making herself available for the . . . festivities there."

"Do you think she'll go along with that?"

"Dari's smile changed. "I figure you'll be able to coax her into it."

"Thanks," I said.

I took her arm and headed for the car. Before we reached it I heard tires digging into the road up ahead and tried to duck back into the brush. It wasn't any good. The black Cad swept by going back toward town and both the guys in it had plenty of time to spot the two of us, if they had bothered to look. It didn't seem that they had, but Benny Quick was driving and that little punk could see all around him without moving his head.

We waited, heard the car fade off downhill, then got in the truck. At the Otter Pass turn-off, fresh tire tracks scarred the dirt and a broken whiskey bottle glinted at the side of the road.

Just beyond the North Fork Road, the road turned sharply, and that's where they were waiting. The Cad was broadside to us and Benny was standing beside it. If we were just casual tourists, it would look like a minor accident, but anything else and it was a neat trap.

I braked to a stop 20 feet short of the Caddy and stuck my head half out the window so the corner post covered most of my face. Benny Quick tried to adjust a pleasant smile to fit his squirrely expression, but did a lousy job of it.

But Benny wasn't the one I was worried about. Someplace nearby the other guy was staked out and there was a good chance he had a rod in his fist. I tugged the .45 out and thumbed the hammer back. Beside me Dari froze.

I put on the neighborly act, too. "Trouble, friend?"

Benny started toward me. I opened the door of the cab and swung it out as if I were trying to get a better look. I saw Benny take in the Willie Elkins' Garage, Repairs and Towing Call Pinewood 101 sign printed there, make a snap decision, figure us for locals in the woods, and decide to write us off as coincidence.

His smile stretched a little. "No . . . no trouble. Pulled a little hard on the turn and skidded around. Just didn't want anybody ramming me while I turned around."

He got in the Cad, gunned the engine, and made a big production of jockeying around in the small area. He wound up pointing back toward the mountain and waved as he went by. I waved too and at that moment our eyes met and something seemed to go sour with Benny Quick's grin.

Either he was turning it off as a bad fit a little too fast or he recognized me from a time not so long ago.

Around the bend ahead I stopped suddenly, cut the engine, and listened. Then I heard a door slam and knew Benny had picked up his passenger. Dari was watching me and I didn't have to tell her what had just happened.

Silently, her eyes dropped to the .45 on the seat, then came back to mine. She said, "You would have killed him, wouldn't you?"

"It would have been a pleasure," I said.

"It's terrible," she whispered.

"Well, don't let it snow you, kid. I may have to do it yet."

It was dark when we reached the hotel. The clerk waved Dari over and said, "Right after you left a call came in. Girl said she was Ruth Gleason. She sounded almost hysterical. I couldn't make much out of it. She was crying and talking about needing somebody."

Dari's face turned ashen. She turned to me, waiting. "You said you could reach Grace Shaefer," I reminded her.

Dari nodded.

"See if she can meet us at Jimmie's bar in an hour."

Ten minutes went by before the operator got my call through to Artie. As usual, we made idle talk before I gave him the plate numbers I had picked up on the mountain road. He grunted disgustedly when I told him I wanted it right away. This would take a little time, so I left the number of the hotel and said I'd stand by.

I looked at my watch and told the clerk to put any calls through to me in Dari's room.

Dari's room was on the ground floor at the end of the corridor. I knocked and heard her call for me to come in. I stood there a moment in the semidarkness of the small foyer and then, unlike her, turned the key in the lock. Inside I could hear her talking over the phone.

She was curled up on the end of a studio couch, wrapped in a black and red mandarin robe that had a huge golden dragon embroidered on it. The fanged mouth was at her throat.

She had a Mrs Finney on the wire. Trying to conceal her annoyance, Dari said, "Well, when Grace does call, can you have her meet me at Jimmie's in an hour? Tell her it's very important. All right. Thanks, Mrs Finney."

She hung up and grimaced. "She knows where Grace is, damn it."

"Why is it a secret?"

"Because . . ." she gave me an impish grin, "Mrs Finney's rooming house is . . . a little more than a rooming house. During the summer, that is."

"Oh," I said. "And she's still loyal to her . . . clients?"

"Something like that."

"The national pastime. No place is too big or too little for it. Any town, anyplace, and there's always a Mrs Finney. Do you think she'll speak to Grace?"

"She'll be there." She stood up, the satiny folds of the robe whipping around her until the golden dragon seemed almost alive.

There is some crazy fascination about a big woman. And when I looked at her I knew that her love was my kind, greedy, wanting to have everything; violent, wanting to give everything. Her eyes seemed to slant up and the front of the robe followed the concavity of her belly as she sucked in her breath. Her breasts were high and firm, their movement making the dragon's head move toward her throat hungrily.

I held out my hand and without hesitation she took it. When I pulled her toward me she came effortlessly, sliding down beside me, leaning back against the cushions with eyes half-slitted to match those of the guardian golden dragon.

My hands slid around her, feeling the heat of her body through the sheen of the satin. There was nothing soft about her. She was hard and vibrant, quivering under my touch and, although she was waiting, she was tensing to spring, too, and I could sense the flexing and rolling of the muscles at her stomach and across her back.

Her fingertips were on me, touching with wary gentleness and having the knowledge of possession, but first exploring the fullness of something she now owned. One hand went behind my head, kneaded my neck, and the other guided my face to hers. No word was spoken. There was need for none. This was the now when everything was known and everything that was to be would be.

She held me away an instant, searching my face, then, realizing how we both desperately hated the silent restraint, did as a woman might and licked my lips with her tongue until they were as wet as her own and with a startled cry let herself explode into a kiss with me that was a wild maelstrom of a minute that seemed to go on endlessly.

My fingers bit into her wrists. "Now you know."

"Now I know," she answered. "It never happened to me before, Kelly."

Dari raised my hands to her mouth, kissed the backs of my hands and smiled.

"What do we do now?" she asked me.

"We don't throw this away, kid. It's ours. We'll take it right and keep it forever."

Slowly she uncoiled, stood in front of me and let all the love in her face tell me I had said what she wanted to hear but didn't expect.

She let me watch her, then laughed deep in her throat and said, "What are you thinking?"

"I'm thinking that you're not wearing anything at all under that . . . geisha thing."

"You're right," she said.

She let me look and hunger another moment, then fingered the clasp of the robe. She held each edge in her hand and threw her arms back slowly, unfolding the robe like immense, startlingly crimson wings, and stood outlined against them in sheer sun-tanned beauty highlighted by the mouth so red and hair so blonde.

With another smile my Valkyrie turned and moved away slowly into the bedroom opposite, and behind me the phone rang so suddenly I jumped.

The desk clerk said, "Mr Smith, I have your New York call."

My tone stopped Artie's usual kidding around.

"Okay, buddy," he said, "but you got yourself a mixed-up package. Two of those cars, a station wagon and a sedan, belong to businessmen who show clean all the way."

"Maybe, Art, but Harry Adrano was riding in the wagon and that boy's been working with the happy dust."

"That one Cadillac is a rented car. The guy who signed out for it is a Walter Cramer nobody knows anything about, but the guy who paid the tab *is* something. He's Sergei Rudinoff, a Soviet attaché who's been in this country three months."

I thanked Art, hung up, and stared at the phone. The picture was coming through loud and clear.

Dari took me out back to her car and handed me the keys.

It was 8:30. Jimmie spotted us when we walked in and came down.

"Grace Shaefer's in the back. Said she's waiting for you."

I grinned back and we headed for the back room.

Grace Shaefer sat there nursing a highball. She was a wide-eyed brunette with a voluptuously full body in no way disguised by the black, low-cut dress. The white swell of her breasts was deliberately flaunted, the outline of her crossed legs purposely apparent. One time she had been beautiful, but now her beauty had gone down the channels of whoredom.

"Hello, Dari. Who's your big friend?"

"This is Kelly Smith. How have you been, Grace?"

Her smile was to me, a plain invitation, though she spoke to Dari. "I've been fine. Let's say, I have everything I've ever wanted."

"Grace . . . are you going up on the hill this time?"

"Yes, I am," she said, almost defiantly. "Why?"

Before Dari could answer I said, "How thick are you involved, Grace?"

"Say, look . . ."

"You're hooked, baby. You can get out of it if you want to."

There was genuine fear in her eyes. "I got the feeling you're looking to get yourself killed," she told me.

"It's been tried. Now . . . how about you? If you want, you can do me a favor up there."

When she answered I knew she had made up her mind. She said, "Smithy boy, like you know my kind, I know yours. Let's not turn our backs on ourselves. The day I want to commit suicide I'll do you a favor, otherwise from now on stay clear of me. That plain?"

I nodded. But Grace wasn't finished yet. With that subtle intuition some people have, she knew what was between us and said to Dari, "I could do you a favor though, Dari. Mr Simpson is having a party tonight. He could do with more girls. One thing a pretty bitch like you can be sure of, you'll always be welcome up there. Just come willingly. Remember?"

I grabbed Dari's arm before she could hit her and with a deliberate smirk Grace tossed her furs over her shoulders and walked out.

The outside door slammed open. The kid who came in was scared and out of breath. He gasped and said, "Mr Smith . . ."

Then I recognized him. Sonny Holmes, the one who braced Paley and Weaver in the bar over the Evans girl.

"Mr Smith . . . they're looking for you. I'm telling you, they're after you bad."

I grabbed his shoulder. "Who?"

"Those two you fought with because of me. They were over at your hotel asking for you and the desk clerk said you'd be here."

"Those two don't bother me."

"Maybe not them, but they went outside and talked to some others in a car. A Cadillac from the hill."

"Benny Quick spotted me. That little bastard finally got his memory back. Well, the next time I tag him he won't have any memory left." My voice came through my teeth.

"Mr Smith, you better get out of here."

Without knowing it, I had the .45 in my hand.

"Look, kid, you take Miss Dahl out of here. Get in her car and make sure you're not followed. Try to get to the police. You tell Cox his town is about to explode."

"No, Kelly . . ."

"Don't start bugging me now, Dari. Do what you're told. This is my kind of business and I'll take care of it my way."

She glanced at the gun. "That's what I'm afraid of. Kelly . . . don't let's spoil it so quickly, please, Kelly." She paused, her eyes wet. "You've been one of them. I think everybody knew it. You carry a gun . . . you've been shot . . . you're here in the middle of all this. Run, darling . . . please. I don't care what you were, don't stay part of this or they'll kill you!"

"Not while I have a rod, kitten."

Her words sounded flat. "That's just as bad, isn't it?" she asked. "You kill them . . . and the law kills you."

I could feel the amazement in the short laugh I let out. I cut it off, grinned, and handed her the .45. "Okay, kitten, have it your way."

She dropped the gun in her pocket, went to kiss me, and then everything out in the bar went quiet. Before she could move, I shoved her in Sonny's arms and whispered harshly, "Take her, damn it!"

When the door closed behind them I turned, ran to the bank of windows at the side of the room, and felt for the catch. Slowly, a drop of sweat trickled down my back. The windows were the steel casement awning type and somebody had moved the crank handles. Another second and they'd be back here and there wasn't time to break out.

At the end of the room were the johns and on a sudden thought I turned into the one marked WOMEN. If they searched the place they'd go to the other one first instinctively. There was no lock on the outside door, but a waste basket fitted under the knob. Another couple of seconds maybe. The window there was the same as the others, steel casement with the handle gone. It was shoulder high and the opaque, wire-impregnated glass was practically unbreakable.

Outside, I heard muffled voices. I cursed softly, fighting the stem of the window handle. It wouldn't budge. I reached back, grabbed a handful of paper, and wrapped a section around the toothed edges. This time when I twisted, the stem gave a little. With exasperating slowness the window began to swing out. On the other side of the wall a heavy foot kicked the door open and somebody said, "Come on out of there!"

If the men's room was the same as this, they could see the shut window and know I didn't go out it, but they couldn't see into the closed toilet booth and would figure I was holed up there. I grinned, thinking that it was a hell of a place to be trapped.

The window was out far enough then. I hauled myself up, squirmed through the opening as a hand tried the door.

Under me was a driveway. One end was blocked by a building, the other was open into the lighted street. I ran toward the light and was a second too late because somebody cut the corner sharply and I could see the gun in his fist.

But the edge was still mine. He had not yet adjusted to the deep black of the alley, and for me he was a lovely silhouette. He could hear my feet and raised the gun. Before he could pull the trigger I crossed one into his jaw that took bone and teeth with it and he hit the ground as if he were dead and I spilled on my face across him.

The other guy was on top of me before I could get up. I dove for the gun the first guy had dropped, fumbled it, and the other one had me.

He should have shot me and been done with it. Instead he cut loose with a running kick that seemed to splinter into my bad side like I had lain on a grenade. It was the amazing agony of the kick that saved me. I arched away from the next one with a tremendous burst of energy and my spasmodic kick spilled the guy on top of me.

I had the other gun then. Grabbing it was instinctive. Slamming it against his ear was instinctive.

Never before had the bulging fire in my side been like this, not even when it happened. I tried to wish myself unconscious . . . anything to get away from it. And instinctively I realized that the only thing that would stop it was up in my room at the hotel.

Then it's over and you don't know how it happened. You don't remember the route, the obstacles, the staircase. You can almost forget instinct as you open the door, then it's there again, because the door should have been locked and you throw yourself on the floor as a little bright flash of light winks in the darkness. Getting the gun up is instinctive and as something tugs into the flesh of your upper arm you put out the light that has been trying to kill you.

A few feet away something crumples to the floor and you get up, flip the switch, and see Benny Quick lying face up with a hole between his eyes.

I didn't waste time. I shook out six capsules and washed them down. For a minute I stood there, waiting for the relief to come. And gently it came, like a wave of soft warm water, so that once more I could think and act like a person instead of an instinct-led animal.

They were looking for me on the street. They'd come here next to check with Benny. They'd find Benny dead and the big hunt would be on. My mind was fuzzy now. I shoved the gun under my belt, stuck Benny's in my pocket, and got my hands under his arms. Benny had died quickly. A scatter rug covered the signs of his final exit and I dragged him outside, closing the door after me.

I could think of only one place to put him. I got him down the back stairs and around the corner to the door of Dari's room. I dragged the body in and dumped it on the floor because it was as far as I could go with it.

Across the room a girl was trying to scream. She watched me with eyes so black they seemed unreal and when she got done trying to scream she collapsed on the floor.

The girl began to sob. I knew who she was. Tentatively, I said, "Ruth? Ruth Gleason?"

She seemed to realize that I wouldn't hurt her. The glazed look left her eyes and she got her feet under her. "Y-yes."

"Dari . . . have you seen Dari?"

"No . . . I tried to . . . I waited . . ."

Think, I thought, *damn it, THINK!*

The Holmes kid would have taken her somewhere. Dr McKeever had the Evans girl at his wife's sister's place. The kid would go there.

"Would you know Dr McKeever's wife . . . or her sister?" I asked.

For a second Ruth Gleason stopped being scared and bobbed her head, puzzled. "Her sister is Emma Cox . . . Captain Cox's wife. They . . . don't live together anymore."

"Can you drive?"

She nodded again. I reached in my pocket and threw her the truck keys. "Willie Elkin's truck. It's out back. You call Doctor McKeever and tell him to meet us at his sister's. You'll have to drive."

I could hear her voice but couldn't concentrate on it. I felt her hand on my arm and knew I was in the truck. I could smell the night air and sometimes think and cursed myself mentally for having gone overboard with those damned capsules.

Time had no meaning at all. I heard Dr McKeever and Dari and felt hands in the hole in my side and knew pieces of flesh were being cut away from the hole in my arm. There was Dari crying and the Gleason girl screaming.

All she could say was, "You're a doctor, give it to me, please. You have to! Oh, please . . . I'll do anything . . . please!"

Dari said, "Can you . . . ?"

There were other voices and McKeever finally said, "It'll help. Not much, but it will quiet her."

"And Kelly?" she asked.

"He'll be all right. I'll have to report this gunshot wound."

"No." There was a soft final note in her voice. "He has to get away."

Ruth Gleason was crying out for Lennie to please come get her.

The pain-killing fog I was wrapped in detached me from the scene then.

"You've been withdrawing, haven't you, Ruth?" Dr McKeever asked.

Her voice was resigned. "I didn't want to. Lennie . . . took it away. He wanted to . . . get rid of me."

After a moment McKeever continued, "When did it start, Ruth?"

Her voice sounded real distant. "On the hill. Flori and I . . . went there. Flori needed the money . . . her father . . ."

"Yes, I know about that. What about you?"

"A man . . . before Lennie. We met downtown and he . . . invited me. It sounded like fun. He gave me some pot."

Dari said, "What?"

"Marihuana," the doctor told her. "Then what, Ruth?"

"Later we popped one. For kicks. Week later."

"Flori, too?"

Ruth giggled. "Sure," she said, "everybody. It was fun. We danced. Nude, you know? No clothes. Mr Simpson came in and watched. He gave me five hundred dollars, can you imagine? Flori too. And that was only the first time. Oh, we did lots of dances. We wore costumes for Mr Simpson and we made his friends laugh and we . . ."

You could barely hear her voice. "Mr Simpson wanted . . . something special. On different nights . . . he'd take one of us. He made us undress . . . and he had whips. He said . . . it wouldn't hurt." She almost choked, remembering. "I screamed and tried to get away, but I couldn't!" She buried her face in her hands.

"You went back, Ruth?"

"I . . . had to. The money. It was always there. Then there was Lennie. Then I had to because . . . my supply was gone . . . I needed a shot bad. I . . . what's going to happen to me?"

"You'll be taken care of, Ruth. Tell me something . . . are any girls up there now?"

"Yes . . . yes. The ones who are usually there. But there will be more. Mr Simpson likes . . . new ones. Please . . . you'll have to let me go back."

The voices were miles away now. Sleep was pressing down on me and I couldn't fight it off.

It was daylight. I cursed and yelled for somebody and the door opened and McKeever was trying to push me back on the cot. Behind him was Sonny Holmes.

I managed to sit up against the pressure of McKeever's hand. My mouth was dry and cottony, my head pounding. A tight band of wide tape was wound around my torso and the pain in my side was a dull throbbing, but it was worse than the hole in the fleshy part of my arm.

"I haven't seen anything like you since the war," McKeever said.

From the door Cox said, "Can he talk?"

Before McKeever could stop me I said, "I can talk, Captain. Come on in."

Cox's arrogant smile was gone now. Like everybody else in Pinewood, he had a nervous mouth.

I said, "I made you big trouble, boy, didn't I?"

"You had no right . . ."

"Tough. You checked my prints through, didn't you?"

He couldn't hide the fear in his eyes. McKeever was watching me too now. "I'm a federal agent, laddie, and you know it. At any time my department has authority to operate anywhere and by now you know with what cooperation, don't you?"

Cox didn't answer. He was watching his whole little world come tumbling down around him.

"You let a town run dirty, Cox. You let a worm get in a long time ago and eat itself into a monster. The worm got too big, so you tried to ignore it and you played a mutual game of Let Alone. It outgrew you, buddy. I bet you've known that for a long, long time. Me happening along was just an accident, but it would have caught up to you before long anyway."

Cox still wouldn't put his head down. "What should I do," he asked.

I got up on the edge of the bed, reached for my pants, and pulled them on. Somebody had washed my shirt. Luckily, I could slide my feet into my moccasins without bending down.

I looked hard at the big cop. "You'll do nothing," I said. "You'll go back to your office and wait there until I call and tell you what to do. Now get out of here."

We both watched Cox shuffle out. His head was down a little now. McKeever said, "Can you tell me?"

I nodded. "I have to. If anything happens to me, you'll have to pass it on. Now I'm going to guess, but it won't be wild. That big house on the hill is a front, a meeting place for the grand brotherhood of the poppy.

"It isn't the only one they have . . . it's probably just a local chapter. It's existed, operated, and been successful for . . . is it ten years now? Down here, the people maybe even suspected. But who wants to play with mob boys? It wouldn't take much to shut mouths up down here. To make it even better, that bunch spread the loot around. Even the dolls could be hooked into the action and nobody would really beef. Fear and money were a powerful deterrent. Besides, who could they beef to? A cop scared to lose his job? And other cops scared of him?

"But one day the situation changed. Overseas imports of narcotics had been belted by our agencies and the brotherhood was hurting. But timed just right was the Cuban deal and those slobs on the hill got taken in by the Reds who saw a way of injecting a poison into this country while they built up their own machine. So Cuba became a collection point for China-grown narcotics. There's a supposedly clean businessman up there on the hill who owns an airline in Florida. The connection clear?"

I grinned, my teeth tight. "There's an even bigger one there, a Russian attaché. He'll be the one who knows where and when the big delivery will be made. There's a rallying of key personnel who have to come out of hiding in order to attend a conclave of big wheels and determine short-range policy.

"It's a chance they have to take. You can't be in the business they're in without expecting to take a chance sooner or later. Lack of coincidence can eliminate chance. Coincidence can provide it. I was the coincidence. Only there was another element involved . . . a Mr Simpson and his peculiar pleasures. If he had forgone those, chance never would have occurred."

It was a lot of talk. It took too damn much out of me. I said, "Where's Dari?"

The doctor was hesitant until I grabbed his arm. When he looked up his face was drained of color. "She went after Ruth."

My fingers tightened and he winced. "I put Ruth . . . to bed. What I gave her didn't hold. She got up and left. The next morning, Dari left too."

"What are you talking about . . . *the next morning?*"

"You took a big dosage, son. That was yesterday. You've been out all this time."

It was like being hit in the stomach.

I stood up and pulled on my jacket.

The doctor said, "They're all over town. They're waiting for you."

"Good," I said. "Where's Sonny Holmes?"

"In the kitchen."

From Sonny's face, I knew he had heard everything we had said. I asked him, "You know how to get to the lake without going through town?"

Sonny had changed. He seemed older. "There's a way. We can take the old icecart trail to the lake."

I grinned at the doctor and handed him a card, "Call that number and ask for Artie. You tell him the whole thing, but tell him to get his tail up here in a hurry. I'm going to cut Dari out of this deal, doc." The look on his face stopped me.

"She's gone," he said. "She went up there as guest . . . She said something about Ruth Gleason saying they wanted girls. She had a gun in her pocketbook. She said it was yours. Kelly . . . she went up there to kill Simpson! She went alone. She said she knew how she could do it . . ."

And that was a whole day ago.

Sonny was waiting. We used his car. My rented truck was gone. Ruth Gleason had taken it and the silenced gun I had used was in it.

Mort Steiger said, "I was waiting for you."

"No fishing, pop," I told him.

"I know what you're going to do. I knew it all along. Somebody had to. You looked like the only one who could and who wanted to."

I turned to Sonny. "Call the doc, kid. See if he got through to my friend."

Mort held out his hand and stopped him. "No use trying. The phones are all out. The jeep from the hill run into a pole down by the station and it'll be two days before a repair crew gets here."

"Sonny," I said, "you get back to Captain Cox. You tell him I'm going inside and to get there with all he has. Tell him they're my orders."

Mort spit out the stub of a cigar. "I figured you right, I did. You're a cop, ain't you?"

I looked at him and grinned. My boat was still there where I had left it. The sun was sinking.

The guy on the dock died easily and quietly. He tried to go for his gun when he saw me and I took him with one sudden stroke. The one at the end in the neat gray suit who looked so incongruous holding a shotgun went just as easily.

An eighth of a mile ahead, the roof of the house showed above the trees. When I reached the main building I went in through the back. It was dark enough now so that I could take advantage of shadows. Above me the house was brilliantly lit. There was noise and laughter and the sound of music and women's voices and the heavier voices of men.

There could only be a single direct line to the target. I nailed a girl in toreador pants trying to get ice out of the freezer. She had been around a long time, maybe not in years, but in time you can't measure on a calendar. She knew she was standing an inch from dying and when I said, "Where is Simpson?" she didn't try to cry out or lie or anything else.

She simply said, "The top floor," and waited for what she knew I'd do to her. I sat her in a chair, her feet tucked under her. For an hour she'd be that way, passed out to any who noticed her.

It was another 20 minutes before I had the complete layout of the downstairs.

What got me was the atmosphere of the place. It was too damn gay. It took a while, but I finally got it. The work had been done, the decisions made, and now it was time to relax.

My stomach went cold and I was afraid of what I was going to find.

It didn't take any time to reach the top floor. Up here you couldn't hear the voices nor get the heavy smell of cigar smoke. I stood on the landing looking toward the far end where the corridor opened on to two doors. To the left could be only small rooms because the corridor was so near the side of the building. To the right, I thought, must be almost a duplicate of the big room downstairs.

And there I was. What could I do about it? Nothing.

The gun in my back said nothing.

Lennie Weaver said, "Hello, jerk."

Behind Lennie somebody said, "Who is he, Len?"

"A small-time punk who's been trying to get ahead in the business for quite a while now. He didn't know what he was bucking." The gun nudged me again. "Keep going, punk. Last door on your left. You open it, you go in, you move easy, or that's it."

The guy said, "What's he doing here?"

I heard Lennie laugh. "He's nuts. Remember what he

pulled on Nat and me? They'll try anything to get big time. He's the fink who ran with Benny Quick and turned him in to the fuzz."

We came to the door and went inside and stood there until the tremendously fat man at the desk finished writing. When he looked up, Lennie said, "Mr Simpson, here's the guy who was causing all the trouble in town."

And there was Mr Simpson. Mr Simpson who only went as far as his middle name in this operation. Mr Simpson by his right name, everybody would know. They would remember the recent election conventions or recall the five percenters and the political scandals a regime ago. Hell, everybody would know Mr Simpson by his whole name.

The fleshy moon face was blank. The eyes blinked and the mouth said, "You know who he is?"

"Sure." Lennie's laugh was grating. "Al Braddock. Like Benny Quick said, he picked up something some place and tried to build into it. He wouldn't have sounded off, Mr Simpson. He'd want any in with us for himself. Besides, who'd play along? They know what happens.

"What shall we do with him, Mr Simpson?" Lennie asked.

Simpson almost smiled. "Why just kill him, Lennie," he said and went back to the account book.

It was to be a quiet affair, my death. My hands were tied behind me and I was walked to the yard behind the building.

"Why does a punk like you want in for?" Lennie asked. "How come you treat life the way you do?"

"The dame, pal," I said. "I got a yen for a dame."

"Who?" His voice was unbelieving.

"Dari Dahl. She inside?"

"You are crazy, buddy," he told me. "Real nuts. In ten minutes that beautiful broad of yours goes into her act and when she's done she'll never be the same. She'll make a cool grand up there, but man, she's had it. I know the kind it makes and the kind it breaks. That mouse of yours won't have enough spunk left to puke when she walks out of there." He laughed again. "If she walks. She may get a ride back to the lights, if she wants to avoid her friends. A guy up there is willing to take second smacks on her anytime."

"Too bad," I said. "If it's over, it's over. Like your two friends down at the lake."

Lennie said, "What?"

"I knocked off two guys by the lake."

The little guy got the point quickly. "Hell, he didn't come in over the wall, Len. He came by the path. Jeeze, if the boss knows about that, he'll fry. The whole end is open, if he's right."

But Lennie wasn't going to be taken. "Knock it off, Moe. We'll find out. We'll go down that way. If he's right or wrong, we'll still fix him. Hell, it could even be fun. We'll drown the bastard."

"You watch it, Len; this guy's smart."

"Not with two guns in his back and his hands tied, he's not." His mouth twisted. "Walk, punk."

Time, time. Any time, every time. Time was life. Time was Dari. If you had time, you could think and plan and move.

Then time was bought for me.

From somewhere in the darkness Ruth Gleason came running, saying, "Lennie, Lennie . . . don't do this to me, please!" and threw herself at the guy.

He mouthed a curse and I heard him hit her, an open-handed smash that knocked her into the grass. "Damn these whores, you can't get them off your back!"

Ruth sobbed, tried to get up, her words nearly inaudible. "Please Lennie . . . they won't give me . . . anything. They laughed and . . . threw me out."

I just stood there. Any move I made would get me a bullet so I just stood there. I could see Ruth get to her feet and stagger, her body shaking. She held on to a stick she had picked up. I could see the tears on her cheeks.

"Lennie . . . I'll do anything. Anything. Please . . . you said you loved me. Tell them to get me a fix."

Lennie said two words.

They were his last.

With unexpected suddenness she ran at him, that stick in her hands, and I saw her lunge forward with it and the thing sink into Lennie's middle like a broken sword and heard his horrible rattle. It snapped in her hands with a foot of it inside him and he fell, dying, while she clawed at him with maniacal frenzy.

The other guy ran for her, tried to pull her off, and forgot about me. My hands were tied. My feet weren't. It took only three kicks to kill him.

Ruth still beat at the body, not realizing Lennie was dead.

"Ruth . . . I can get you a fix!" I said.

The words stopped her. She looked at me, not quite seeing me. "You can?"

"Untie me. Hurry."

I turned around and felt her fingers fumble with the knots at my wrists until they fell free.

"Now . . . you'll get me a fix? Please?"

I nodded and hit her. Later she could get her fix. Maybe she'd made it so she'd never need one again. Later was lots of things, but she'd bought my time for me and I wouldn't forget her.

The little guy's gun was a .32 and I didn't want it. I liked Lennie's .45 better, and it fitted my hand like a glove. My forefinger found the familiar notch in the butt and I knew I had my own gun back and knew the full implication of Lennie's words about Dari.

She had tried for her kill and missed. Somebody else got the gun and Dari was to get the payoff.

This time I thought it out. I knew how I had to work it. I walked another 100 yards to the body of the gray-suited guard I had left earlier, took his shotgun from the ground and four extra shells from his pocket, and started back to the house.

Nothing had changed. Downstairs they were still drinking and laughing, still secure.

I found the 1,500-gallon fuel tank above ground as I expected, broke the half-inch copper tubing, and let the oil run into the whiskey bottles I culled from the refuse dump. It didn't take too many trips to wet down the bushes around the house. They were already season-dried, the leaves crisp. A huge puddle had run out from the line, following the contour of the hill and running down the drive to the front of the house.

It was all I needed. I took two bottles, filled them, and tore off a hunk of my shirt tail for a wick. Those bottles would make a high flash-point Molotov cocktail, if I could keep them lit. The secret lay in a long wick so the fuel oil, spilling out, wouldn't douse the flame. Not as good as gasoline, but it would do.

Then I was ready.

Nothing fast. The normal things are reassuring. I coughed, sniffed, and reached the landing at the first floor. When the man there saw me he tried to call out and died before he could. The other one was just as unsuspecting. He died just as easily. Soft neck.

Mr Simpson's office was empty. I opened his window, lit my wick on the whiskey bottle, and threw it down. Below me there was a small breaking of glass, a tiny flame that grew. I drew back from the window.

I had three more quarts of fuel oil under my arm. I let it run out at the two big doors opposite Simpson's office and soak into the carpet. This one caught quickly, a sheet of flame coming off the floor. Nobody was coming out that door.

Some place below there was a yell, then a scream. I opened the window and got out on the top of the second floor porch roof. From there the top floor was blanked out completely. Heavy drapes covered the windows and, though several were open for ventilation, not a streak of light shone through.

I stepped between the window and the draperies, entirely concealed, then held the folds of the heavy velvet back. It was a small theatre in the round. There was a person shrouded in black tapping drums and that was all the music they had. Two more in black tights with masked faces were circling about a table. They each held long thin whips, and whenever the drummer raised the tempo they snapped them, and sometimes simply brought them against the floor so that the metal tips made a sharp popping sound.

She was there in the middle, tied to the table. She was robed in a great swath of silk.

From where I stood I could see the town and the long line of lights winding with tantalizing slowness toward the hill.

Down below they were yelling now, their voices frantic, but here in this room nobody was listening. They were watching the performance, in each one's hand a slim length of belt that could bring joy to minds who had tried everything else and now needed this.

She was conscious. Tied and gagged, but she could know what was happening. She faced the ring of them and saw the curtain move where I was. I took the big chance and moved it enough so she alone could see me standing there and when she jerked her head to keep anyone from seeing the hope in her eyes I knew it was the time.

There was only one other door in the room, a single door on the other side. It was against all fire regulations and now they'd know why. I lit the wick on the last bottle, let it catch hold all the way, stepped inside, and threw it across the room.

Everything seemed to come at once . . . the screams, the yelling from outside. Somebody shouted and opened the big doors at the head of the room and a sheet of flame leaped in on the draft.

There was Harry Adrano. I shot him.

There was Calvin Bock. I shot him.

There was Sergei Rudinoff. I shot him and took the briefcase off his body and knew that what I had done would upset the Soviet world.

There was the man who owned the airlines and I shot him.

Only Nat Paley saw me and tried to go for his gun. All the rest were screaming and trying to go through the maze of flame at the door. But it was like Nat to go for his gun so I shot him, too, but not as cleanly as the rest. He could burn the rest of the way.

I got Dari out of the straps that held her down, carried her to the one window that offered escape, and shoved her out. In the room the bongo drummer went screaming through the wall of flame. From far off came staccato bursts of gunfire and now no matter what happened, it was won.

I shoved her on the roof and, although everything else was flame, this one place was still empty and cool.

And while she waited for me there, I stepped back inside the room, the shrivelling heat beating at my face, and saw the gross Mr Simpson still alive, trapped by his own obesity, a foul thing on a ridiculous throne, still in his robes, still clutching his belt . . .

And I did him a favor. I said, "So long, Senator."

I brought the shotgun up and let him look all the way into that great black eye and then blew his head off.

It was an easy jump to the ground. I caught her. We walked away.

Tomorrow there would be strange events, strange people, and a new national policy.

But now Dari was looking at me, her eyes loving, her mouth wanting, her mind a turbulence of fear because she thought I was part of it all and didn't know I was a cop, and I had all the time in the world to tell her the truth . . .

LARGER THAN LIFE

Anthony Shaffer

Adapted to:

SLEUTH

(Twentieth-Century-Fox, 1972)

Starring: Laurence Olivier,

Michael Caine & Margo Channing

Directed by Joseph L. Mankiewicz

Sleuth *which first opened as a play on Broadway in 1970 has been called one of the best mystery dramas ever written, while the film version made the following years is undeniably a classic among crime movies. The account of a celebrated crime novelist, Andrew Wyke (Laurence Olivier), who entices his wife's lover, Milo Tindle (Michael Caine), into his country mansion with plans to murder him, the drama is a combination of mind-games and deception which holds audiences enthralled right up to the moment of the remarkable denouement. The contrasting acting styles of Olivier and Caine were superbly melded together by the American director, Joseph L. Mankiewicz, to create a movie that was stylish and atmospheric and earned universal praise from the critics as "the most fascinating mystery seen for years". It also has the distinction of being the only picture for which the director and entire cast (Alec Cawthrone was the fourth member) were nominated for Oscars! The success of* Sleuth *led to the filming of a number of other literary psychological thrillers during the Seventies as well as establishing the reputation of Anthony Shaffer, who went on to write the screenplays of such box-office hits as* Frenzy *(1973),* Death on the Nile *(1980), and* Evil Under The Sun *(1982).*

Anthony Shaffer (1926–) was a barrister, advertising executive and television producer before earning international acclaim with Sleuth. *Earlier, in the fifties, however, he had written a trio of detective novels in collaboration with his brother, Peter, all about a bulky, cigar-smoking, rather shady private detective called Mr Verity: namely* The Woman in the Wardrobe *(1951),* How Doth the Little Crocodile? *(1952), and* Withered Murder *(1953). These three volumes are now very rare and much sought after by collectors of detective stories. (Peter Shaffer, of course, has also become famous as a playwright with his dramas including* The Royal Hunt of the Sun *staged in 1964,* Equus *produced in 1974 and* Amadeus *five years later.) Anthony admits to having been a reader of crime fiction since his youth, and says that it was the works of Agatha Christie which gave him the idea for* Sleuth. *In 1983 he created another unique stage drama,* Whodunnit, *which is also a clever exercise in character study and mystery. "Larger than Life" was written in 1953 after Anthony had finished collaborating on the last of the three Verity novels and appeared in the December issue of the* London Mystery Magazine. *Unlike his other work, it features a traditional policeman, Inspector Grayson – but in the officer's clever unravelling of the clues surrounding a suspected murder are clear signs of the author's mastery of word-play which would later become such a stunning element in* Sleuth . . .

*   *   *

Inspector Grayson stretched out his long legs in the back of the police car, sighed and scratched the top of his nearly bald head. He reflected silently, and finally said:

"You know, it's a funny thing this man Morrison living at Willow House. I used to live there myself."

"Did you, sir?" Sergeant Sanders replied with a creditable show of interest. "When was this?"

"Oh, years ago when I was a kid. I left when I was eight. The family moved to Wales for some quite unplausible reason, and I have never been back. It's a nice old house with big airy rooms, high ceilings, huge fireplaces and long corridors set in an unkempt garden which we used to explore as if it were the most impenetrable jungle in the world, and surrounded by a high stone wall which we used to scale as if it were Everest itself."

Inspector Grayson sighed again. "It's amazing what you remember about your childhood."

Sergeant Sanders seemed unimpressed by his superior's nostalgia. He said quietly, "And now this fellow Morrison has gone and killed his wife there."

"We don't know that," Grayson replied severely. "All we've got to work on is a lot of wild rumour and a couple of letters from curious neighbours."

"There's no smoke without fire, sir, if you ask me. Women always know what's going on in the house next door, and if they say Mrs Morrison has disappeared mysteriously, you can bet there's something to it."

"Well, we'll soon know," Grayson said as the police car swung in through the gates and up to the house. As it moved up the drive, Grayson looked about him with an air of wistfulness on his face. "It's very curious," he said at last. "Very curious, indeed."

"What, sir?"

"Childhood memories, Sergeant. They are at once accurate and distorted."

Sanders nodded his head slowly and rang the bell.

After a full minute the door was opened by a large, florid man who was wearing startling brown-and-orange check plusfours and a golfing wind-breaker. The small close-set grey eyes staring out of the fleshy face were troubled and suspicious.

"Mr James Morrison?"

"Yes."

"We are police officers. Sorry to bother you like this, but we think you might be able to help us."

Morrison took a step backwards.

"Police officers . . . Good Lord! I can't think what you want with me. You'd better come in."

He stood aside for them to pass, and then, having closed the door, led them through a fair-sized hallway furnished with a large brick fireplace, a magazine-strewn table and three ill-assorted high-backed chairs, down a short corridor festooned with school photographs into a rather dingy, fussy drawing-room. Grayson, who had been looking about him like an excited schoolboy, gave the room a disgruntled stare.

"It's just as I remembered it, but so much smaller. Not in the least palatial."

"I beg your pardon," said Morrison uneasily.

"I used to live in this house as a kid . . . These windows and doors . . . and everything . . . seem so much smaller than I had remembered them."

Morrison laughed affably. "Well, there's a coincidence. I've been here over ten years now."

"Do you live alone?"

"There's just my wife and myself."

"Ah. It was about your wife that we wanted to see you."

Morrison's genial manner vanished in a flash, to be replaced by an unconvincing aggressiveness.

"Well, you can't see her. She's not here."

"We know she's not here. If she were, there would be no reason for our presence."

"I'm afraid I don't understand you."

"Mr Morrison, where is your wife?"

"She's on holiday."

"Where?"

"In the Isle of Wight."

"Have you got her address?"

"Of course I've got her address . . ." Morrison nervously wiped his large mottle hands on a not too clean crêpe-de-Chine handkerchief. "Here, what is all this. I can't see it's got anything to do with you where my wife is taking her holiday . . . She hasn't committed a crime, has she?"

Inspector Grayson regarded his quarry narrowly.

"*She* hasn't. Let me explain, Mr Morrison. We received a couple of letters from your neighbours. They appear to think that all is not as it should be between yourself and your good wife. To put it bluntly, they suspect something sinister."

While he was speaking, Grayson pulled two envelopes out of his pocket. Morrison's eyes fastened on them as if hypnotically drawn.

"This is preposterous, Inspector."

"Perhaps so. Let me read you one. If it does nothing else, it presents a fascinating study in how our neighbours' minds work."

Very slowly he extracted a letter and smoothed it on his knee. Morrison watched every move with apprehension.

"Dear Sir,
"I think there has been a murder done at Willow House, Rickmansworth. About a fortnight ago I heard a scream in the middle of the night, about 2 a.m. I think it was. I only live next door, and I heard it plain as anything. The following day was a Thursday, and regular as clockwork Mrs Morrison and I play bridge at the club. But she didn't turn up. I was surprised at this because we always had this definite arrangement, and so I went round to her house to see if anything was the matter. Mr Morrison opened the door and said his wife was not feeling very well. I have never seen her since then, nor has anyone else I know. I have called a few times but each time Mr Morrison is more unpleasant, as if he had a guilty conscience. Yesterday he told me his wife had gone away for a long holiday in Ireland, and would not be back for many months. This seems very strange to

me, and that is why I report it to you. I have also asked my friend, Mrs Garnett, to write to you, as she can confirm what I say. I hope I have not done wrong in this.

"Your faithfully,

"Ethel Bridgers."

Inspector Grayson paused and stroked his chin thoughtfully.

"The other letter is in much the same terms, except that you said Scotland, and not Ireland, as the place of your wife's holiday. Of course, Mrs Garnett could have been mistaken."

"And now you say the Isle of Wight," Sanders put in.

"So you can see why we're curious, can't you, Mr Morrison?"

James Morrison passed his tongue over his dry lips. He tried a laugh, but it emerged as a groan.

"There's been a horrible mistake, Inspector. I admit I told lies about my wife's holiday place, but it was only because I was so upset. You see, the truth is I don't know where my wife is . . . We had a terrible row, and – er – well, I hate to admit it, but she said she couldn't stand life with me any longer and just walked out. Naturally I couldn't tell the truth to those old cats in the village. That is why I invented the holiday."

"Invention would appear to be the key to the whole thing, wouldn't it, Mr Morrison?"

James Morrison said nothing.

In the ensuing silence Sergeant Sanders suddenly spoke up.

"Have you a car, sir?"

"No, why?"

"Just a thought, sir."

Inspector Grayson beamed appreciatively at his subordinate.

"If I understand the sergeant aright, he is thinking that if you have murdered your wife you would need to get rid of the body. If you had a car, it would be easy. If not, she might very well be concealed about the premises."

"It's a lie," Morrison roared. "I told you. She left me."

"For a better place, doubtless," Grayson pursued smoothly.

He moved absently to the window and stood looking out at the neat garden.

"You know, it's a funny thing. For thirty years I have carried round with me a picture of this garden as being a jungle, fearsome and savage. The lawn was much bigger, the trees higher, the drive longer. And inside, as I remarked before, everything was similarly on a palatial scale. The ceilings were high and the corridors long, and to a child it was a hide-and-seek paradise. You see, children being so small get their proportions wrong. Everything seems much bigger to them than it actually is. That is why when we return to places we haven't visited since childhood, everything seems much smaller. Don't you agree, Mr Morrison?"

"Yes, I suppose I do," Morrison replied, puzzled.

"Exactly. You see, in a way it's rather a good thing. Supposing, in fact, these grounds had been an endless jungle, and inside the house here a hide-and-seeker's paradise, and supposing you had wanted to hide the body of your wife, it would have been easy, wouldn't it?"

"Er – quite . . . But I don't see –"

"Oh, it's really very simple. I believe there is a body on these premises concealed hereabouts. I believe you murdered your wife. And what leads me to that conclusion?"

Morrison remained silent.

"I look out on this garden, and I don't see the large lawn I remembered, or the never-ending drive, or the high wall I scraped my knees on as a boy, or the thick and mysterious forests of privet."

Very deliberately, his every step watched by the terrified eyes of James Morrison, Inspector Grayson crossed the room and opened the door which led to the hall.

"Nor do I see," he continued, "the vast expanse of rooms and corridors. These things were never here. They existed only in a small boy's imagination. But the thing that I see which is strange is a large brick fireplace into whose disused and bricked-up flue I used to squeeze myself as a small boy in many a game of hide-and-seek. Now I see it once again. But it hasn't dwindled like the lawn and the drive, the corridors and the wall. I expected to see a broad brick fireplace, and that in fact is what I do see. But that is all wrong, yes, I know. It should be a narrow fireplace fronting a narrow flue into which a tiny boy of eight could barely squeeze himself. It should be in proportion to everything else here. And what do I conclude from that, Mr Morrison?"

Morrison had gone white. The hands which lit his cigarette trembled convulsively.

"I haven't the faintest idea," he said hoarsely.

"Haven't you, Mr Morrison . . . ? I conclude that this brick fireplace has been recently enlarged to mask extensions made to that small bricked-up flue in which I used to hide. Closer examination will doubtless reveal just how recently. I will take a sporting bet that poor Mrs Morrison is entombed behind that fireplace I know and love so well, right at this moment. And not a bad hiding-place either, when you come to think of it. You wouldn't happen to have a sledge-hammer in the house, Mr Morrison?"

James Morrison's answer was incomprehensible.

THERE ARE SOME DAYS . . .

Frederick Forsyth

Adapted to:

THE DAY OF THE JACKAL

(Universal Pictures, 1973)

Starring: Edward Fox,

Cyril Cusack & Delphine Seyrig

Directed by Fred Zinnemann

The seventies also saw the debut of Frederick Forsyth who, with his very first novel, The Day of the Jackal *(1971), demonstrated that he was going to be a major figure in the crime genre. The book almost at once captured a huge international audience and two years later was adapted for the screen to the even greater enhancement of Forsyth's reputation. Now regarded as one of the most celebrated thrillers ever written,* The Day of the Jackal *tells the story of an anonymous Englishman who is hired by the Operations Chief of the O.A.S. to assassinate General de*

Gaulle. What made this book, and the others which Forsyth has subsequently written, so outstanding was their atmosphere of authenticity and realistic depiction of criminality. The movie version was highlighted by Fred Zinnemann's purposeful direction and Edward Fox's coldly efficient playing of the professional killer. In later books such as The Odessa File *(1972) – which won an Edgar Award from the Mystery Writers of America –* The Fourth Protocol *(1985), and* The Fist of God *(1994), Forsyth has continued to demonstrate his remarkable ability at utilizing contemporary facts and inside information to tell stories that have earned him the accolade of being today's foremost "documentary" thriller writer.*

Frederick Forsyth (1938–), a former RAF pilot, local newspaper reporter, Reuters correspondent and BBC staff member, has drawn on his inside knowledge of politics, technology, and especially the workings of the criminal mind, to create the series of novels which have put him near the top of the world's best-selling authors – almost 50 million copies to date. Each of his seven books have been a media event, and although Forsyth has more than once talked of retiring from writing thrillers to enjoy the sedate life on his farm in the heart of the English countryside, that final work has not yet materialized. He does, though, always enjoy writing the odd newspaper article and the occasional short story inspired by ideas he gets while researching his novels. "There are Some Days . . ." is one of the best of these. Set in Ireland (where he lived for several years), it is ostensibly the story of an attempt to hijack a lorry load of French brandy. But as with everything that Frederick Forsyth writes, the tension and the surprises come thick and fast . . .

The *St Kilian* roll-on roll-off ferry from Le Havre buried her nose in another oncoming sea and pushed her blunt bulk a few yards nearer to Ireland. From somewhere on A deck driver Liam Clarke leaned over the rail and stared forward to make out the low hills of County Wexford coming closer.

In another twenty minutes the Irish Continental Line ferry would dock in the small port of Rosslare and another European run would be completed. Clarke glanced at his watch; it was twenty to two in the afternoon and he was looking forward to being with his family in Dublin in time for supper.

She was on time again. Clarke left the rail, returned to the passenger lounge and collected his grip. He saw no reason to wait any longer and descended to the car deck three levels down where his juggernaut transport waited with the others. Car passengers would not be called for another ten minutes, but he thought he might as well get settled in his cab. The novelty of watching the ferry dock had long worn off; the racing page of the Irish newspaper he had bought on board, though twenty-four hours old, was more interesting.

He hauled himself up into the warm comfort of his cab and settled down to wait until the big doors in the bow opened to let him out onto the quay of Rosslare. Above the sun visor in front of him his sheaf of customs documents was safely stacked, ready to be produced in the shed.

The *St Kilian* passed the tip of the harbour mole at five minutes before the hour and the doors opened on the dot of two. Already the lower car deck was a-roar with noise as impatient tourists started up their engines well before necessary. They always did. Fumes belched from a hundred exhausts, but the heavy trucks were up front and they came off first. Time, after all, was money.

Clarke pressed the starter button and the engine of his big Volvo artic throbbed into life. He was third in line when the marshal waved them forward. The other two trucks breasted the clanking steel ramp to the quayside with a boom of exhausts and Clarke followed them. In the muted calm of his cab he heard the hiss of the hydraulic brakes being released, and then the steel planking was under him.

With the echoing thunder of the other engines and the clang of the steel plates beneath his wheels he failed to hear the sharp crack that came from his own truck, somewhere beneath and behind him. Up from the hold of the *St Kilian* he came, down the 200 yards of cobbled quay and into the gloom again, this time of the great vaulted customs shed. Through the windscreen he made out one of the officers waving him into a bay beside the preceding trucks and he followed the gestures. When he was in position he shut down the engine, took his sheaf of papers from the sun visor and descended to the concrete floor. He knew most of the customs officers, being a regular, but not this one. The man nodded and held out his hand for the documents. He began to riffle through them.

It only took the officer ten minutes to satisfy himself that all was in order – licence, insurance, cargo manifest, duty paid, permits and so forth   the whole gamut of controls apparently required to move merchandise from one country to another even within the Common Market. He was about to hand them all back to Clarke when something caught his eye.

"Hello, what the hell's that?" he asked.

Clarke followed the line of his gaze and saw beneath the cab section of the truck a steadily spreading pool of oil. It was dripping from somewhere close to the rear axle of the section.

"Oh Jaysus," he said in despair, "it looks like the differential nose-piece."

The customs man beckoned over a senior colleague whom Clarke knew, and the two men bent down to see where the flow of oil was coming from. Over two pints were already on the shed floor and there would be another three to come. The senior customs man stood up.

"You'll not shift that far," he said, and to his junior colleague added, "We'll have to move the others round it."

Clarke crawled under the cab section to have a closer look. From the engine up front a thick strong drive shaft ran down to a huge boss of cast steel, the differential. Inside this casing the power of the turning drive shaft was transmitted sideways to the rear axle, thus propelling the cab forward. This was effected by a complex assembly of cogwheels inside the casing, and these wheels turned permanently in a bath of lubricating oil. Without this oil the cogs would seize solid in a very short distance, and the oil was pouring out. The steel nose-piece casing had cracked.

Above this axle was the articulated plate on which rested the trailer section of the artic which carried the cargo. Clarke came out from under.

"It's completely gone," he said. "I'll have to call the office. Can I use your phone?"

The senior customs man jerked his head at the glass-walled office and went on with his examination of the other trucks. A few drivers leaned from their cabs and called ribald remarks to Clarke as he went to phone.

Then there was no one in the office in Dublin. They were all out at lunch. Clarke hung around the customs shed morosely as the last of the tourist cars left the shed to head inland. At three he managed to contact the managing director of Tara Transportation and explained his problem. The man swore.

"I won't be carrying that in stock," he told Clarke. "I'll have to get on to the Volvo Trucks main agent for one. Call me back in an hour."

At four there was still no news and at five the customs men wanted to close down, the last ferry of the day having arrived from Fishguard. Clarke made a further call, to say he would spend the night in Rosslare and check back in yet another hour. One of the customs men kindly ran him into town and showed him a bed-and-breakfast lodging house. Clarke checked in for the night.

At six head office told him they would be picking up another differential nose-piece at nine the following morning and would send it down with a company engineer in a van. The man would be with him by twelve noon. Clarke called his wife to tell her he would be twenty-four hours late, ate his tea and went out to a pub. In the customs shed three miles away Tara's distinctive green and white artic stood silent and alone above its pool of oil.

Clarke allowed himself a lie-in the next day and rose at
nine. He called head office at ten and they told him the van
had got the replacement part and was leaving in five minutes.
At eleven he hitch-hiked back to the harbour. The company
was as good as its word and the little van, driven by the
mechanic, rattled down the quay and into the customs shed
at twelve. Clarke was waiting for it.

The chirpy engineer went under the truck like a ferret and
Clarke could hear him tut-tutting. When he came out he was
already smeared with oil.

"Nose-piece casing," he said unnecessarily. "Cracked
right across."

"How long?" asked Clarke.

"If you give me a hand, I'll have you out of here in an hour
and a half."

It took a little longer than that. First they had to mop up
the pool of oil, and five pints goes a long way. Then the
mechanic took a heavy wrench and carefully undid the ring
of great bolts holding the nose-piece to the main casing. This
done, he withdrew the two half-shafts and began to loosen
the propeller shaft. Clarke sat on the floor and watched him,
occasionally passing a tool as he was bidden. The customs
men watched them both. Not much happens in a customs
shed between berthings.

The broken casing came away in bits just before one.
Clarke was getting hungry and would have liked to go up
the road to the café and get some lunch, but the mechanic
wanted to press on. Out at sea the *St Patrick*, smaller sister
ship of the *St Kilian*, was moving over the horizon on her
way home to Rosslare.

The mechanic started to perform the whole process in
reverse. The new casing went on, the propeller shaft was
fixed and the half-shafts slotted in. At half past one the *St
Patrick* was clearly visible out at sea to anyone who was
watching.

Murphy was. He lay on his stomach in the sere grass atop
the low line of rising ground behind the port, invisible to
anyone a hundred yards away, and there was no such person.

He held his field glasses to his eyes and monitored the approaching ship.

"Here she is," he said, "right on time."

Brendan, the strong man, lying in the long grass beside him, grunted.

"Do you think it'll work, Murphy?" he asked.

"Sure, I've planned it like a military operation," said Murphy. "It cannot fail."

A more professional criminal might have told Murphy, who traded as a scrap metal merchant with a sideline in "bent" cars, that he was a bit out of his league with such a caper, but Murphy had spent several thousand pounds of his own money setting it up and he was not to be discouraged. He kept watching the approaching ferry.

In the shed the mechanic tightened the last of the nuts around the new nose-piece, crawled out from under, stood up and stretched.

"Right," he said, "now, we'll put five pints of oil in and away you go."

He unscrewed a small flange nut in the side of the differential casing while Clarke fetched a gallon can of oil and a funnel from the van. Outside, the *St Patrick*, with gentle care, slotted her nose into the mooring bay and the clamps went on. Her bow doors opened and the ramp came down.

Murphy held the glasses steady and stared at the dark hole in the bows of the *St Patrick*. The first truck out was a dun brown, with French markings. The second to emerge into the afternoon sunlight gleamed in white and emerald green. On the side of her trailer the word TARA was written in large green letters. Murphy exhaled slowly.

"There it is," he breathed, "that's our baby."

"Will we go now?" asked Brendan, who could see very little without binoculars and was getting bored.

"No hurry," said Murphy. "We'll see her come out of the shed first."

The mechanic screwed the nut of the oil inlet tight and turned to Clarke.

"She's all yours," he said, "she's ready to go. As for me,

I'm going to wash up. I'll probably pass you on the road to Dublin."

He replaced the can of oil and the rest of his tools in his van, selected a flask of detergent liquid and headed for the washroom. The Tara Transportation juggernaut rumbled through the entrance from the quay into the shed. A customs officer waved it to a bay next to its mate and the driver climbed down.

"What the hell happened to you, Liam?" he asked.

Clarke explained to him. A customs officer approached to examine the new man's papers.

"Am I okay to roll?" asked Clarke.

"Away with you," said the officer. "You've been making the place untidy for too long."

For the second time in twenty-four hours Clarke pulled himself into his cab, punched the engine into life and let in the clutch. With a wave at his company colleague he moved into gear and the artic rolled out of the shed into the sunlight.

Murphy adjusted his grip on the binoculars as the juggernaut emerged on the landward side of the shed.

"He's through already," he told Brendan. "No complications. Do you see that?"

He passed the glasses to Brendan who wriggled to the top of the rise and stared down. Five hundred yards away the juggernaut was negotiating the bends leading away from the harbour to the road to Rosslare town.

"I do," he said.

"Seven hundred and fifty cases of finest French brandy in there," said Murphy. "That's nine thousand bottles. It markets at over ten pounds a bottle retail and I'll get four. What do you think of that?"

"It's a lot of drink," said Brendan wistfully.

"It's a lot of money, you fool," said Murphy. "Right, let's get going."

The two men wriggled off the skyline and ran at a crouch to where their car was parked on a sandy track below.

When they drove back to where the track joined the road from the docks to the town they had only a few seconds to wait and driver Clarke thundered by them. Murphy brought his black Ford Granada saloon, stolen two days earlier and now wearing false plates, in behind the artic and began to trail it.

It made no stops; Clarke was trying to get home. When he rolled over the bridge across the Slaney and headed north out of Wexford on the Dublin road Murphy decided he could make his phone call.

He had noted the phone booth earlier and removed the diaphragm from the earpiece to ensure that no one else would be using it when he came by. They were not. But someone, infuriated by the useless implement, had torn the flex from its base. Murphy swore and drove on. He found another booth beside a post office just north of Enniscorthy. As he braked, the juggernaut ahead of him roared out of sight.

The call he made was to another phone booth by the roadside north of Gorey where the other two members of his gang waited.

"Where the hell have you been?" asked Brady. "I've been waiting here with Keogh for over an hour."

"Don't worry," said Murphy. "He's on his way and he's on time. Just take up your positions behind the bushes in the lay-by and wait till he pulls up and jumps down."

He hung up and drove on. With his superior speed he caught up with the juggernaut before the village of Ferns and trailed the truck out onto the open road again. Before Camolin he turned to Brendan.

"Time to become guardians of law and order," he said and pulled off the road again, this time into a narrow country road he had examined on his earlier reconnaissance. It was deserted.

The two men jumped out and pulled a grip from the rear seat. They doffed their zip-fronted windbreakers and pulled two jackets from the grip. Both men already wore black shoes, socks and trousers. When the windbreakers were off they were wearing regulation police-style blue shirts and black ties. The jackets they pulled on completed the deception. Murphy's bore the three stripes of a sergeant,

Brendan's was plain. Both carried the insignia of the Garda, the Irish police force. Two peaked caps from the same grip went onto their heads.

The last of the contents of the grip were two rolls of black, adhesive-backed sheet plastic. Murphy unrolled them, tore off the cloth backing and spread them carefully with his hands, one onto each of the Granada's front doors. The black plastic blended with the black paintwork. Each panel had the word GARDA in white letters. When he stole his car, Murphy had chosen a black Granada deliberately because that was the most common police patrol car.

From the locked boot Brendan took the final accoutrement, a block two feet long and triangular in cross-section. The base of the triangle was fitted with strong magnets which held the block firmly to the roof of the car. The other two sides, facing forwards and backwards, also had the word GARDA printed on the glass panels. There was no bulb inside to light it up, but who would notice that in daytime?

When the two men climbed back into the car and reversed out of the lane, they were to any casual observer a pair of highway patrolmen in every way. Brendan was driving now, with "Sergeant" Murphy beside him. They found the juggernaut waiting at a traffic light in the town of Gorey.

There is a new section of dual carriageway north of Gorey, between that ancient market town and Arklow. Halfway along it, on the northbound lane, is a lay-by, and this was the spot Murphy had chosen for his ambush. The moment the column of traffic blocked behind the artic entered the dual carriageway section, the other car drivers joyfully sped past the lorry and Murphy had it all to himself. He wound down his window and said "Now" to Brendan.

The Granada moved smoothly up beside the cab of the truck, and held station. Clarke looked down to see the police car beside him and a sergeant waving out of the passenger seat. He wound down his window.

"You're losing a rear tyre," roared Murphy above the wind. "Pull in to the lay-by."

Clarke looked ahead, saw the big P on a notice by the

roadside indicating a lay-by, nodded and began to slow. The police car moved ahead, swerved into the lay-by at the appointed spot and stopped. The juggernaut followed and drew up behind the Granada. Clarke climbed down.

"It's down here at the back," said Murphy. "Follow me."

Clarke obediently followed him round the nose of his own truck and down its green and white length to the rear. He could see no flat tyre, but he hardly had a chance to look. The bushes parted and Brady and Keogh came bounding out in overalls and balaclavas. A gloved hand went over Clarke's mouth, a strong arm round his chest and another pair of arms round his legs. Like a sack he was swept off his feet and disappeared into the bushes.

Within a minute he had been divested of his company overalls with the Tara logo on the breast pocket, his wrists, mouth and eyes were sticky-taped and, shielded from the gaze of passing motorists by the bulk of his own lorry, he was bundled into the rear seat of the "police" car. Here a gruff voice told him to lie on the floor and keep still. He did.

Two minutes later Keogh emerged from the bushes in the Tara overalls and joined Murphy by the door of the cab where the gang leader was examining the driving licence of the unfortunate Clarke.

"It's all in order," Murphy said. "Your name's Liam Clarke, and this load of documents must be in order. Did they not pass it all at Rosslare not two hours back?"

Keogh, who had been a truck driver before he served time as a guest of the Republic in Mountjoy, grunted and climbed into the truck. He surveyed the controls.

"No problem," he said, and replaced the sheaf of papers above the sun visor.

"See you at the farm in an hour," said Murphy.

He watched the hijacked juggernaut pull out of the lay-by and rejoin the northward stream on the Dublin road.

Murphy went back to the police car. Brady was in the back with his feet on the recumbent and blindfolded Clarke. He had lost his overalls and balaclava and was in a tweed jacket. Clarke might have seen Murphy's face, but only for a few seconds, and then with a police cap on top of it. He would not see the faces of the other three. That way, if he ever accused Murphy, the other three would give Murphy an unbreakable alibi.

Murphy glanced up and down the road. It was empty for the moment. He looked at Brendan and nodded. Both men tore the Garda signs from the doors, screwed them up and tossed them in the back. Another glance. A car sped by unheeding. Murphy yanked the illuminated sign off the roof and threw it to Brady. A further glance. Again, no traffic. Both uniform jackets came off and went to Brady in the back. The windbreakers went back on. When the Granada pulled out of the lay-by it was just another saloon car with three civilians visible in it.

They passed the juggernaut just north of Arklow. Murphy, driving again, gave a discreet toot of the horn. Keogh raised one hand as the Granada passed, thumb upward in the okay sign.

Murphy kept driving north as far as Kilmacanogue then pulled up the lane known as Rocky Valley towards Calary Bog. Not much happens up there, but he had located a deserted farm high on the moor which had the advantage of a great barn inside it, large enough to take the juggernaut unseen for a few hours. That was all that would be needed. The farm was reached by a muddy track and screened by a clump of conifers.

They arrived just before dusk, fifty minutes before the juggernaut and two hours before the rendezvous with the men from the North and their four vans.

Murphy reckoned he could be justifiably proud of the deal he had clinched. It would have been no easy task to dispose of those 9000 bottles of brandy in the South. They were bonded, each case and bottle numbered and sooner or later bound to be spotted. But up in Ulster, the war-torn North, it was different. The place was rife with shebeens, illegal drinking clubs that were unlicensed and outside the law anyway.

The shebeens were strictly segregated, Protestant and

Catholic, with control of them firmly in the hands of the underworld, which itself had long been taken over by all those fine patriots they had up there. Murphy knew as well as any man that a fair proportion of the sectarian killings performed for the glory of Ireland had more to do with protection racketeering than patriotism.

So he had done his deal with one of the more powerful heroes, a main supplier to a whole string of shebeens into which the brandy could be filtered with no questions asked. The man, with his drivers, was due to meet him at the farm, unload the brandy into four vans, pay cash on the spot and have the stuff into the North by dawn through the maze of country lanes crossing the border between the lakes along the Fermanagh – Monaghan line.

He told Brendan and Brady to carry the hapless driver into the farm where Clarke was thrown on a pile of sacks in the corner of the derelict kitchen. The three hijackers settled down to wait. At seven the green and white juggernaut grunted up the track in the near darkness, lights out, and the three ran outside. By muffled flashlights they heaved open the old barn doors; Keogh ran the truck inside and the doors were closed. Keogh climbed down.

"I reckon I've earned my cut," he said, "and a drink."

"You've done well," said Murphy. "You'll not need to drive the truck again. It'll be unloaded by midnight and I'll drive it myself to a point ten miles away and abandon it. What will you drink?"

"How about a nip of brandy?" suggested Brady, and they all laughed. It was a good joke.

"I'll not break a case for a few cups," said Murphy, "and I'm a whiskey man myself. Will this do?"

He produced a flask from his pocket and they all agreed it would do nicely. At a quarter to eight it was completely dark and Murphy went to the end of the track with a flashlight to guide the men from the North. He had given them precise instructions, but they could still miss the track. At ten past eight he came back, guiding a convoy of four panel vans. When they stopped in the yard a big man in a camel overcoat descended from the passenger seat of the first. He carried an attaché case but no visible sense of humour.

"Murphy?" he said. Murphy nodded. "Have you got the stuff?"

"Fresh off the boat from France," said Murphy. "It's in the truck still, in the barn."

"If you've broken the truck open I'll want to examine every case," threatened the man. Murphy swallowed. He was glad he had resisted the temptation to look at his loot.

"The French customs seals are intact," he said. "You can examine them yourself."

The man from the North grunted and nodded to his acolytes who began to haul open the barn doors. Their torches shone on the twin locks that kept the rear doors closed upon the cargo, the customs seals still covering the locks unbroken. The Ulsterman grunted again and nodded his satisfaction. One of his men took a jemmy and approached the locks. The man from the North jerked his head.

"Let's go inside," he said. Murphy led the way, torch in hand, into what had been the sitting room of the old farm. The Northerner unclipped his attaché case, laid it on the table and opened the lid. Rows of bundles of sterling notes greeted Murphy's gaze. He had never seen so much money.

"Nine thousand bottles at four pounds each," he said. "Now that would make thirty-six thousand pounds, would it not?"

"Thirty-five," grunted the Northerner. "I like round numbers."

Murphy did not argue. He got the impression from this man that it would not be wise. Anyway, he was satisfied. With £3000 for each of his men and his outlay recouped, he would be well over £20,000 clear. "Agreed," he said.

One of the other Northerners appeared at the broken window. He spoke to his boss.

"You'd better come and have a look," was all he said.

Then he was gone. The big man snapped the case closed, gripped the handle and stalked outside. The four Ulstermen, along with Keogh, Brady and Brendan, were grouped round the open doors of the truck in the barn. Six torches illuminated the interior. Instead of neatly stacked columns of cases bearing the world-renowned name of the brandy producer, they were looking at something else.

There were rows of piled plastic sacks, each bearing the name of a famous manufacturer of flower-garden aids, and beneath the name the words "Rose Fertilizer". The man from the North stared at the cargo without change of expression.

"What the hell's this?" he grated.

Murphy had to pull his lower jaw back from somewhere near his throat. "I don't know," he croaked. "I swear I don't know."

He was telling the truth. His information had been impeccable – and costly. He had got the right ship, the right transporter. He knew there was only one such truck on that afternoon's arrival of the *St Patrick*.

"Where's the driver?" snarled the big man.

"Inside," said Murphy.

"Let's go," said the big man. Murphy led the way. The unfortunate Liam Clarke was still trussed like a chicken upon his sacks.

"What the hell's this cargo of yours?" the big man asked without ceremony.

Clarke mumbled furiously behind his gag. The big man nodded to one of his accomplices who stepped forward and tore the medical plaster unceremoniously from Clarke's mouth. The driver still had another band across his eyes.

"I said what the hell's this cargo of yours," the big man repeated. Clarke swallowed.

"Rose fertilizer," he said. "Sure, it's in the cargo manifest."

The big man flashed his torch over the sheaf of papers he had taken from Murphy. He stopped at the cargo manifest and thrust it under Murphy's nose.

"Did you not look at this, you fool?" he asked.

Murphy took out his growing panic on the driver. "Why didn't you tell me this?" he demanded.

Sheer outrage gave Clarke boldness in the face of his unseen persecutors. "Because I had a fecking gag over my mouth, that's why," he shouted back.

"That's true, Murphy," said Brendan, who was rather literal.

"Shut up," said Murphy, who was becoming desperate. He leaned closer to Clarke. "Is there not any brandy underneath it?" he asked.

Clarke's face gave away his utter ignorance. "Brandy?" he echoed. "Why should there be any brandy? They don't make brandy in Belgium."

"Belgium?" howled Murphy. "You drove into Le Havre from Cognac in France."

"I've never been to Cognac in my life," yelled Clarke. "I was driving a cargo of rose fertilizer. It's made of peat moss and dessicated cow manure. We export it from Ireland to Belgium. I took this cargo over last week. They opened it in Antwerp, examined it, said it was substandard and they wouldn't accept it. My bosses in Dublin told me to bring it back. It cost me three days in Antwerp sorting out the paperwork. Sure, it's all there in the papers."

The man from the North had been running his torch over the documents he held. They confirmed Clarke's story. He threw them to the floor with a grunt of disgust.

"Come with me," he said to Murphy and led the way outside. Murphy followed, protesting his innocence.

In the darkness of the yard the big man cut short Murphy's protestations. He dropped his attaché case, turned, gripped Murphy by the front of his windcheater, lifted him off his feet and slammed him into the barn door.

"Listen to me, you little Catholic bastard," said the big man.

Murphy had wondered which side of the Ulster racketeers he had been dealing with. Now he knew.

"You," said the big man in a whisper that froze Murphy's blood, "have hijacked a load of bullshit – literally. You have also wasted a lot of my time and my men's time and my money . . ."

"I swear to you . . ." croaked Murphy, who was having trouble with his air supply, "on my mother's grave . . . it must be on the next ship, arriving at two p.m. tomorrow. I can start again . . ."

"Not for me," whispered the big man, "'cos the deal's off. And one last thing; if you ever try and pull a stroke like this on me again I'll have two of my lads come down here and redistribute your kneecaps. Do you understand me?"

Sweet Jesus, thought Murphy, they're animals these Northerners. The British are welcome to them. He knew it was more than his life was worth to voice the thought. He nodded. Five minutes later the man from the North and his four empty trucks were gone.

In the farmhouse by the light of a torch Murphy and his disconsolate gang finished the flask of whiskey.

"What do we do now?" asked Brady.

"Well," said Murphy, "we clear up the evidence. We have gained nothing but we have lost nothing, except me."

"What about our three thousand quid?" asked Keogh.

Murphy thought. He did not want another round of threats from his own people after the scare the Ulsterman had thrown into him.

"Lads, it will have to be fifteen hundred apiece," he said. "And you'll have to wait a while until I make it. I cleaned myself out setting up this stroke."

They appeared mollified if not happy.

"Brendan, you, Brady and Keogh should clear up here. Every scrap of evidence, every footprint and tyre track in the mud, wipe it out. When you're done, take his car and drop the driver somewhere south of here by the roadside in his stockings. With tape on his mouth, eyes and wrists, he'll be a while getting the alarm up. Then turn north and drive home.

"I'll stick by my word to you, Keogh. I'll take the truck and abandon it way up in the hills towards Kippure. I'll walk back down and maybe get a lift on the main road back to Dublin. Agreed?"

They agreed. They had no choice. The men from the North had done a good job of smashing the locks on the rear of the artic's trailer, so the gang hunted round for wooden pegs to secure the two hasps. Then they closed the doors on its disappointing cargo and pegged them shut. With Murphy at the wheel the juggernaut growled back down the track from the farm and turned left towards the Djouce Forest and the hills of Wicklow.

It was just after 9.30 and Murphy was past the forest on the Roundwood road when he met the tractor. One would think farmers would not be out on tractors with one faulty headlight, the other smeared with mud, and ten tons of straw bales on a trailer at that hour. But this one was.

Murphy was bombing along between two stone walls when he discerned the looming mass of the tractor and trailer coming the other way. He hit the brakes rather sharply

One thing about articulated vehicles is that although they can manoeuvre round corners that a rigid-frame lorry of similar length could not get near, they are the very devil when it comes to braking. If the cab section which does the towing and the trailer section which carries the cargo are not almost in line, they tend to jackknife. The heavy trailer tries to overtake the cab section, shoving it sideways into a skid as it does so. This is what happened to Murphy.

It was the stone walls, so common in those Wicklow hills, that stopped him rolling clean over. The farmer gunned his tractor clean through a handy farm gate, leaving the straw bales on the trailer to take any impact. Murphy's cab section began to slither as the trailer caught up with it. The load of fertilizer pushed him, brakes locked in panic, into the side of the bales, which fell happily all over his cab, almost burying it. The rear of the trailer behind him slammed into a stone wall and was thrown back onto the road, where it then hit the opposite stone wall as well.

When the screech of metal on stone stopped, the farm trailer was still upright, but had been moved ten feet, shearing its coupling to the tractor. The shock had thrown the farmer off his seat and into a pile of silage. He was having a noisy personal conversation with his creator.

Murphy was sitting in the dim half-light of a cab covered in bales of straw.

The shock of hitting the stone walls had sheared the pegs holding the rear of the artic shut and both doors had flown open. Part of the rose fertilizer cargo was strewn on the road behind the truck. Murphy opened his cab door and fought his way through the bales of straw to the road. He had but one instinct, to get as far away from there as possible as fast as he could. The farmer would never recognize him in the darkness. Even as he climbed down, he recalled he had not had time to wipe the interior of the cab of all his fingerprints.

The farmer had squelched his way out of the silage and was standing on the road beside Murphy's cab reeking of an odour that will never really catch on with the aftershave industry. It was evident he wished for a few moments of Murphy's time. Murphy thought fast. He would appease the farmer and offer to help him reload his trailer. At the first opportunity he would wipe his prints off the inside of the cab, and at the second vanish into the darkness.

It was at this moment that the police patrol car arrived. It is a strange thing about police cars; when you need one they are like strawberries in Greenland. Scrape a few inches of paint off someone else's body work and they come out of the gratings. This one had escorted a minister from Dublin to his country home near Annamoe and was returning to the capital. When Murphy saw the headlights he thought it was just another motorist; as the lights doused he saw it was the real thing. It had a Garda sign on the roof, and this one *did* light up.

The sergeant and the constable walked slowly past the immobilized tractor-trailer and surveyed the tumbled bales. Murphy realized there was nothing for it but to bluff the whole thing out. In the darkness he could still get away with it.

"Yours?" asked the sergeant, nodding at the artic.

"Yes," said Murphy.

"A long way from the main roads," said the sergeant.

"Aye, and late too," said Murphy. "The ferry was late at

Rosslare this afternoon and I wanted to deliver this lot and get home to my wee bed."

"Papers," said the sergeant.

Murphy reached into the cab and handed him Liam Clarke's sheaf of documents.

"Liam Clarke?" asked the sergeant.

Murphy nodded. The documents were in perfect order. The constable had been examining the tractor and came back to his sergeant.

"One of your man's headlights doesn't work," he said, nodding at the farmer, "and the other's covered with clay. You would not see this rig at ten yards."

The sergeant handed Murphy the documents back and transferred his attention to the farmer. The latter, all self-justification a few moments ago, began to look defensive. Murphy's spirits rose.

"I wouldn't want to make an issue of it," he said, "but the garda's right. The tractor and trailer were completely invisible."

"You have your licence?" the sergeant asked the farmer.

"It's at home," said the farmer.

"And the insurance with it, no doubt," said the sergeant. "I hope they're both in order. We'll see in a minute. Meanwhile you can't drive on with faulty headlights. Move the trailer onto the field and clear the bales off the road. You can collect them all at first light. We'll run you home and look at the documents at the same time."

Murphy's spirits rose higher. They would be gone in a few minutes. The constable began to examine the lights of the artic. They were in perfect order. He moved to look at the rear lights.

"What's your cargo?" asked the sergeant.

"Fertilizer," said Murphy. "Part peat moss, part cow manure. Good for roses."

The sergeant burst out laughing. He turned to the farmer who had towed the trailer off the road into the field and was throwing the bales after it. The road was almost clear.

"This one's carrying a load of manure," he said, "but

you're the one up to your neck in it." He was amused by his wit.

The constable came back from the rear of the artic's trailer section. "The doors have sprung open," he said. "Some of the sacks have fallen in the road and burst. I think you'd better have a look, sarge."

The three of them walked back down the side of the artic to the rear.

A dozen sacks had fallen out of the back of the open doors and four had split open. The moonlight shone on the heaps of brown fertilizer between the torn plastic. The constable had his torch out and played it over the mess. As Murphy told his cellmate later, there are some days when nothing, but absolutely nothing, goes right.

By moon and torchlight there was no mistaking the great maw of the bazooka jutting upwards, nor the shapes of the machine guns protruding from the torn sacks. Murphy's stomach turned.

The Irish police do not normally carry hand-guns, but when on escort duty for a minister, they do. The sergeant's automatic was pointing at Murphy's stomach.

Murphy sighed. It was just one of those days. He had not only failed signally to hijack 9000 bottles of brandy, but had managed to intercept someone's clandestine arms shipment and he had little doubt who that "someone" might be. He could think of several places he would like to be for the next two years, but the streets of Dublin were not the safest places on that list.

He raised his hands slowly.

"I have a little confession to make," he said.

THE EMBASSY INCIDENT

Brian Clemens

📺

Adapted for:

THE PROFESSIONALS

(LWT, 1977–83)

Starring: Martin Shaw,

Lewis Collins & Gordon Jackson

Directed by Tom Clegg

Another development of the seventies was the violent crime television series in which agents of the law fought criminals with their own weapons: fists, guns and the uncompromising language of the backstreets. The first of these, The Sweeney *(1975–78) was about the Metropolitan Police's Flying Squad, which derived its name in cockney rhyming slang from the notorious Fleet Street mass murderer, Sweeney Todd, and featured the exploits of Detective Inspector Jack Regan (John Thaw) and Detective Sergeant George Carter (Dennis Water-*

man), who were almost as bloodthirsty and earned their fair share of condemnation from viewers and sections of the press. The BBC's answer to the undeniable success of the series was Target *(1977–78)* with Patrick Mower as the unscrupulous Detective Superintendent Steve Hacket who used tough and often unpleasant methods to combat the smugglers, murderers and bombers who "targeted" his patch. The Professionals *took the formula a step further in 1977 with stories about CI5 (Criminal Intelligence 5), an élite undercover crime-fighting squad whose most visible officers were Ray Doyle (Martin Shaw) and William Bodie (Lewis Collins) reporting to their ruthless taskmaster, George Cowley, played by Gordon Jackson. (Originally, the roles of Doyle and Bodie had been intended for Jon Finch and Anthony Andrews, but both opted out.) The all action series was an immediate hit although, as a result of complaints about the level of violence, LWT ordered that there should be a maximum of two explosions per episode – and made media celebrities of its stars.*

The creator of the series, Brian Clemens (1931–) had been a freelance writer of plays for the theatre and TV before coming to widespread public attention in 1960 by devising the influential comedy suspense series, The Avengers, *which started its life as* Police Surgeon *with Ian Hendry, but became a cult show once Patrick Macnee had become the dandified central character partnered in his crime-busting exploits by, alternately, three beautiful girls: Honor Blackman, Diana Rigg and Linda Thorson. Brian followed this in 1971 with another success,* The Persuaders, *about two wealthy adventurers, Roger Moore and Tony Curtis, fighting corruption all over the world, before working on* The Professionals *with Albert Fennell who had been an associate on the Patrick Macnee series. Clemens and his production team took full advantage of real-life events while making the series – but this rebounded on them on one notorious occasion. After the tragic shooting of policewoman Yvonne Fletcher during the seige of the Libyan Embassy in St James's Square, London in April 1984, demonstrators in Libya apparently believing C15 to be a real organization staged their own demonstration around the British Embassy in Tripoli with cries*

of, "Down with CI5!" "The Embassy Incident", written in
1982, is also interesting because of the similarity it bears to
another famous incident in May 1980 when members of the
SAS stormed the terrorist-occupied Iranian Embassy in
Knightsbridge to rescue nineteen hostages. This time, though,
there was no suggestion that Doyle and Bodie might have been
involved . . . (A new series, CI5 – The Professionals, also
largely written by Brian Clemens, is due to return to television
screens in the autumn of 1998 with a group of completely new
nineties characters: Sam Curtis (Colin Wells), Chris Keel
(Kal Webber), a girl agent named Tina Backus (Lexa Doig)
and Edward Woodward as Declan Malone, a former CIA agent
who has risked his life in all four corners of the world, as their
controller.)

Cowley's car turned into Pickwick Street and slowed to a halt
a discreet distance from the Embassy. He gestured vaguely
with his right hand as his left opened the suitcase on the seat
beside him and began searching for some documents.

"Take a good look," said Cowley over his shoulder, "I'll
give you plans of the inside later."

Bodie and Doyle studied the tall building with the large
green and red flag over the door. On the first floor balcony a
huge poster of a man in a uniform covered with medals
drooped in the afternoon rain. A banner hung from the
balustrade proclaiming FAISAK: SAVIOUR OF THE PEOPLE in
both English and Arabic.

"Seems a popular sort of fellow," observed Bodie.

"He has a simple method of staying that way."

"What's that?"

"He has anyone who disagrees with him killed."

"It's one way to run a country, I suppose," said Doyle.

"It's why so many of his people have fled the country. But
even then, his critics aren't safe. Faisak's secret police are
sent after them." Cowley brought a folder from his suitcase.

"It seems our General is a sensitive wee chappie – critics seem to bring the worst out of him, even from long distances. Listen to this . . ." Cowley began reading aloud from the folder.

"New York, September: Two outspoken exiles shot dead on a Bronx subway. Paris, November: Attempted poisoning of an exiled family. London, November: Former leader's son falls from penthouse window. Rome, December: Exiled couple disappear." Cowley put the folder down . . . "There's plenty more."

"They're either bumped off or taken back home to stand trial for treason. When they're found guilty, they get shot. Quite a card is Faisak," said Doyle.

"But why should this concern CI5?" asked Bodie.

Cowley opened another folder and handed them a photograph.

"This is Professor Haroud Rashid," he said. "A scientist. He fled to England five years ago after Faisak's men killed his wife and children. He was granted asylum and given protection. He began working for the Nuclear Fuels Advisory Commission, and did very well for himself. Had access to some extremely sensitive information."

"Like where to find the makings of a nuclear bomb?"

"Among other things. Faisak is openly hostile to our country. If he could find out the weak spots in our nuclear power stations he could cause us a lot of aggravation."

"But Rashid wouldn't tell him anything, would he?" asked Doyle.

"Not voluntarily. The trouble is . . . Haroud Rashid disappeared three days ago."

"You reckon they've snatched him?"

"Looks like it. He told a colleague that two of Faisak's men had been following him the day before he disappeared."

"We're too late then," said Bodie, "they'll have him back home by now."

"Or dead," said Doyle.

"We don't think so," said Cowley. "We think they've got him stashed away in the Embassy there."

"Then it's stalemate," said Bodie. "They can't get him out of the country with us watching and we can't get inside because of international law."

Bodie studied Cowley's humourless smile and realised the danger of the forthcoming assignment.

"The Embassy may be out of bounds to CI5," said Cowley, "but since when did two fanatical terrorists pay attention to international law?"

Cowley started up the car and began the drive back to his office. On the way, he explained his plans.

"You get inside the building," said the Scot, "take the entire staff hostage then issue your demands. When these are refused you negotiate. Then you release some prisoners in exchange for concessions."

"What are our demands?"

"It doesn't matter. Just make sure you release Rashid. As soon as you've done that, you can surrender."

"Too simple," said Bodie.

"It can work," argued Cowley as they pulled up in the car park. He led them to the sliding doors of the basement weapons room. "Keep the hostages away from the window and I'll get the press to leave it alone. No-one will be any the wiser."

Inside the weapons room, the noise was deafening. On the practice ranges other CI5 agents fired at moving shadow targets and Cowley had to shout to make himself heard over the staccato explosions of their weapons. They approached a bench where a technician was working on a row of grenades. Cowley indicated a large green shoulder bag.

"Twenty-eight sticks of dynamite, fuses, detonators and eight grenades," he explained.

"What's he doing with the grenades?" asked Doyle, nodding toward the technician.

"He's making them safe. Taking the detonators out. The dynamite's already safe – it's made out of plasticine."

"Safe for whom?" asked Bodie.

"Safe for everyone. The people in the Embassy will never know the explosives aren't real."

"Maybe we should tell them," said Doyle with a grim smile. "After all, we don't want an unfair advantage."

That night Bodie and Doyle set out. Their first inkling that something was wrong came when they found no guard on the Embassy door. He was inside the darkened hallway with a big red hole where his left eye should have been. Bodie bent over the body, and was about to speak when a blinding flash of pain exploded at the base of his skull and fireworks started going off all over his brain.

When he came to, Bodie was still in the hallway. The lights were on and he was staring down the barrel of a Kalashnikov. A hooded figure held the rifle in shaking hands. Against the opposite wall, Doyle stood with his hands held high above his head.

"You're not going to believe this, mate," said Doyle, ignoring the second hooded figure, who was prodding him in the ribs with another Kalashnikov, "but these jokers have beaten us to the punch. The Cow's got a real siege on his hands."

The second man gave Doyle another prod. His voice was on the verge of hysteria.

"Do not speak! Do not move! You are the prisoners of the People's Liberation Army. Understand that we wish you no harm personally, but if you no obey – we kill you!"

Bodie groaned as he climbed to his feet and he and Doyle were hustled up the stairs to a first floor room. The curtains were closed and a third gunman stood over a line of hostages seated against a wall. Bodie and Doyle were pushed to the ground.

"English?" asked the hostage next to Bodie after some minutes.

Bodie nodded.

"You must understand the position. We are all prisoners of these extremists. They hope to engineer the downfall of General Faisak and the destruction of our country."

"What are their demands?"

"The release of all prisoners and the resignation of the government. Of course, General Faisak will not accept these demands."

"And what happens when he refuses?"

"Then we shall be killed," said the man in the same matter of fact tone. "But it will be an honour to die for Faisak, saviour of our people."

"Listen," said Bodie in a low, fierce whisper, "I don't intend dying for anyone just yet; not for Faisak, not for you, not even for your fat uncle Freddie. So tell us how many terrorists there are and just how they intend to blow the place up."

The man looked sullen and averted his gaze. Bodie grasped the man's arm and twisted until he began to talk. "There are three terrorists here. They brought that suitcase you see on the table, the one with the key in it. Inside is a bomb big enough to destroy the building. All it needs to detonate it is for someone to turn the key."

Bodie fingered the fake grenade he had taped to the small of his back. The terrorists had missed it. "Maybe we could bluff them with our grenades," he whispered.

Doyle shook his head. "These guys are too desperate, they don't care if they die. And I wouldn't count on any help from any of our fellow hostages either. They're under the impression that getting blown to bits for the great and glorious Faisak will make them heroes and martyrs."

"Someone should tell them about dead heroes," muttered Bodie.

Suddenly and eerily the sound of Cowley's voice, amplified and distorted by a loudhailer, drifted up to the curtained window from somewhere in the street below. He was asking the terrorists to negotiate.

One of the two hooded men crossed to the window, peered round the curtains and smashed one of the windowpanes with the Kalashnikov's barrel. "Our demands are already known. None of them are negotiable."

"Then release some of your hostages. Give us some assurance that you do not intend people to die needlessly."

"No hostages can be released until our demands are met."

"Then we shall talk again in an hour," said Cowley's voice.

Bodie turned worriedly to Doyle. "He doesn't know it's for real. He thinks that we're still calling the shots."

"I know. And these guys are working on a short fuse."

"We've got to make our move soon. There are only three of them and one is permanently downstairs in the hall. Now when Cowley calls from the street one of the remaining two is going to go over to the window to talk to him. That leaves just the one guarding us. We won't get a better opportunity. If we can get hold of one of those rifles then at least we stand a chance."

A tense hour passed in which the three gunmen argued fiercely with one another in Arabic and spat insults at their hostages. Then once more Cowley's voice came up from the street. "Can you hear me? Release some hostages and we can begin negotiations."

Once again one of the gunmen crossed to the window and replied. However this time it was with an angry, incomprehensible shout and a burst of fire. Bodie and Doyle heard sudden, startled screaming from outside the window and knew it was time to act. Doyle dived head first at the man standing before them while Bodie endeavoured to knock the rifle barrel aside. He did so just as the guard fired, the bullets spattering into the plaster above the hostages' heads and leaving a scar across the wall and through a portrait of General Faisak. "The window, Bodie," yelled Doyle as his partner grabbed the Kalashnikov from the prostrate gunman. Bodie squeezed the trigger as he fell and the second gunman was spun round with the impact of the bullets, shattering what remained of the glass as he fell through the window onto the balcony. Bodie turned to see Doyle knocking the prone gunman unconscious with a rabbit punch. Behind him the third gunman appeared in the doorway. Bodie fired once more and the man crumpled up against the wall, the unfired Kalashnikov cradled in his lap. Doyle was already dragging the hostages to their feet. "All right. Down the stairs and out of the front door as quickly as you can," he yelled.

Outside Cowley had guessed that something was wrong

after the first burst of automatic fire. Consequently, as soon as the hostages emerged into the daylight he was prepared and he and his men rushed them across the street to the safety of a protective cordon of cars. Bodie and Doyle were the last to leave the building, both grinning with obvious relief at how lucky they had been. "Are you all right?" Cowley called from across the street.

"Sure," called back Bodie. "There are three gunmen in there. Two of them are dead and the other's unconscious." But even as he spoke there was a tremendous explosion and the two men were lifted bodily into the air and then flung to the ground in a blizzard of flying glass and bricks. Behind them, in a roaring chaos of smoke and flame, melting metal and fragmenting stone, the Embassy had ceased to exist.

When Bodie awoke he was in a hospital bed. At its foot stood Doyle and Cowley. His head ached and reaching up he found it wrapped in bandages.

"What happened?" he asked.

"Just concussion. You should be out in a couple of days."

"But they blew up the Embassy?"

"Either the guy I hit wasn't unconscious or the other guy wasn't quite dead. One of them got to the suitcase and turned the key. Then Boom. Up goes the Embassy."

"Rashid?"

Doyle looked at Cowley and Cowley looked at his feet.

"Rashid's dead," said Doyle.

"He was still in the Embassy when it went up?" asked Bodie.

"He was dead before that," said Cowley. "You shot him."

Bodie's head began to ache. He rubbed his brow with his fingertips as Cowley explained.

"Intelligence got it wrong. Rashid had disappeared to set up a raid on the Embassy. He'd been in touch with other exiles and they'd asked him to do something to draw the world's attention to Faisak's regime."

"So he set up a siege," said Doyle. "Not very original for a professor."

"But I thought –" began Bodie.

"Don't worry," Cowley cut in, "it's not your fault these people chose London to settle their differences."

But the pain in Bodie's head wouldn't go away.

"We're sent to rescue someone and I killed him," he said quietly. "Faisak couldn't have planned it better himself."

"Rashid got what he wanted," said Cowley, "the story's all over the papers. You saved innocent people from getting killed. As for Faisak . . ." Cowley's cheeks twitched as he gazed out of the hospital window. ". . . We'll just have to wait . . ."

THE GLORY HUNTER

Brian Garfield

Adapted to:

DEATH WISH

(Paramount, 1975)

Starring: Charles Bronson,

Hope Lange & Vincent Gardenia

Directed by Michael Winner

Among the most notorious series of crime movies of the seventies and eighties were the Death Wish *pictures, starring Charles Bronson, and produced and directed by Michael Winner. Inspired by Brian Garfield's 1972 novel and its sequel,* Death Sentence *(1975), the films feature Paul Benjamin (Bronson), an accountant who returns one night to his New York apartment on the upper West Side to find his wife murdered and his daughter beaten into catatonia. Despite having always lived on the right side of the law, Paul is so shattered by this crime that he decides to get a gun, learn to use it, and become a vigilante murderer, fighting back against the criminals who plague his city. The first book had been greeted as a "convulsive* tour de force" *and the movie went even further, becoming a box-office sensation and reviewed as "one of the best crime stories of the decade". The popularity of the film led to a wave of unashamed imitations, but Michael Winner's ability to stay one step ahead of the competition has kept the sequels as exciting – not to say as violent – as the original, turning the whole* Death Wish *concept into a cult with a worldwide following.*

Brian Garfield (1939–) is himself a New Yorker; he was educated at the University of Arizona in Tucson, and served in the United States Army in the late fifties and early sixties before becoming a writer. A number of his early books were Westerns, but it was with his stories of power-greedy organizations such as the Mafia, FBI, CIA, KGB and even the police that he came to public notice. Among Brian's most popular books in the genre have been The Hit *(1970),* The Threepersons Hunt *(1974), and* Death Wish, *which he has described as the only modern urban crime thriller he has written. The fame of this book has tended to overshadow some of his other excellent characters such as Sam Watchman, an Arizona State Trooper, and Charlie Dark, a fat, conceited but resourceful counter-espionage agent. His contributions to thriller fiction won him an Edgar Award from the Mystery Writers of America in 1976. Garfield is also a brilliant short story writer and has regularly appeared in* Alfred Hitchcock's Mystery Magazine *and* Ellery Queen's Mystery Magazine *from which "The Glory Hunter" (September 1977 issue) is reprinted. It is a mixture of the kind of Western yarn which he first practised and the crime story of a lone killer that has made his name. It is certainly one of the most unusual stories in this collection.*

On the evening when the kid came to kill me, the man returned from the day's labor at his usual time.

The man and the woman went out each morning from the ruined fort to the cliff. It was about a half-mile walk. They worked side by side inside the mountain.

In the course of four years of work they had tunneled deep into the quartz. Hardrocking was not easy work, especially for a man and woman both in their fifties and neither of them very large in size; but they accepted the arduous work because it had a goal and the goal was in sight.

Inside the tunnel they would crush the rock together and shovel it into the wooden dumpcart. They would wheel the cart out of the tunnel and dump it into the sluice that the man had designed in the second year to replace the rocker-box they'd begun with. The sluice carried water at high speed. This was water that came down through a wooden flume from a creek 70 yards above them, above the top of the low cliff. The floor of the sluice was rippled with wooden barriers; these were designed to separate the particles and retain the heaviest ones – the gold flakes – while everything else washed away downstream.

It was a good lode and during the four years they had washed a great deal of gold out of the mountain, flake by flake. Most of it was hidden in various caches. When they made the forty-mile muleback ride to Florence Junction for stocking up, they would take only enough gold dust to pay for their purchases; the town knew they had a claim back in the Superstitions but from the amount they spent it appeared they were barely making ends meet. They had never been invaded by gold-rush crowds.

They'd started working the claim when the man was 51 and the woman 48 and he figured to quit when he was 56, at which time they should have enough money to live hand-somely in one of those big new gabled houses over in San José or Palo Alto or San Francisco. They'd be able to afford all the genteel things. In the meantime they worked hard to pay for it, pitting their muscles and pickaxes against the hard skeleton of the mountain.

The mountain was called Longshot Bluff because it was topped by a needle-shaped pinnacle like the spike on a

Prussian helmet; from up there you could command everything in sight with an unobstructed circle of fire and because
of the altitude you could make a bullet travel an extremely
long distance.

The cavalry, back in 1879, had chased a small band of
warriors onto the mountain and the Apaches had taken up
positions on top of the spire. There were only five Apaches;
there were 40 soldiers in the troop but the Indians barricaded
themselves and there was no way the army could get at them.
A siege had ensued and finally the Apaches were starved out.
After that the army built the little outpost on a hilltop about a
mile out from the base of Longshot Bluff. Troops had
occupied the post for five years; then the Indian wars came
to an end and the camp was abandoned. It was the ruins of
this fort that the man and the woman used as their home.

The abandoned camp had no stockade around it; the
simple outpost consisted merely of a handful of squat adobes
built around a flat parade ground. There had been a post-
and-rail corral, but travelers had consumed the rails for
firewood over the twelve years since the camp had been
decommissioned by the army. The man and the woman had
kept their four mules loose-hobbled for the first few weeks of
their residence; after that they let the animals graze at will
because this had become home and the mules had nowhere
else to go.

When you sat on the veranda after supper, as the man and
the woman often did, you faced the east. You looked down a
long easy hardpan slope dotted with a spindle tracery of
desert growth – catclaw and ocotillo, manzanita and cholla
and sage. The foot of the slope was nearly a half-mile away.
At that point you saw the low cliff where the man and the
woman had drilled their mining tunnel. Beyond it lofted the
abrupt mass of Longshot Bluff. The pinnacle was perhaps
800 feet higher than the fort. From this angle the spire
appeared as slender as a lance, sharp enough to pierce the
clouds. It stood, as the crow flies, perhaps three miles from
the veranda.

They came in from work in the late afternoon and the man

packed his pipe on the veranda while he waited for supper. Over on the southern slope of Longshot Bluff he saw briefly the movement of an approaching horseman. From the window the woman must have seen it as well; she appeared on the veranda. "He'll be too late for supper unless we wait on him."

"Then we'll wait on him," the man said.

It would take the rider at least an hour to get here and it would be about 45 minutes short of sunset by then. But the man went inside immediately and opened the threadbare carpetbag that he kept under the bed.

The woman said, "I hope he's not another glory hunter." She said it without heat; when the man glanced at her she cracked her brief gentle smile.

He unwrapped his revolver from the oiled rags that protected it. The revolver was a single-action Bisley model with a 7½-inch barrel, caliber .45 Long Colt. It had been designed for match target competition and the Colt people had named it after the shooting range at Bisley in England where marksmen met every year to decide the championship.

The man put the revolver in his waistband and snugged it around until it didn't abrade his hipbone.

On his way to the door he glanced at the woman. She was, he thought, a woman of rare quality. When he'd met her she'd been working in a brothel in Leadville. After they'd known each other a few years the man had said, "We're both getting kind of long in the tooth," and they'd both left their previous occupations and gone out together looking for gold.

At the door he said, "I'll be back directly," and walked down toward the cliff.

He covered the distance briskly; it took some 15 minutes and when he reached the mouth of the tunnel he ran the empty ore cart out past the sluice and pushed it up onto a little hump of rocky ground. In the debris of the tailings dump he found two cracked half-gallon jugs they'd discarded. He set the jugs on two corners of the ore cart; they balanced sturdily and nothing short of a direct blow would knock them off.

Then he walked back up toward the fort, but he moved more slowly now, keeping to cover because it wasn't certain just when the approaching horseman would come into sight down along the far end of the base of the mountain.

The man laid up in a clump of manzanita about 30 feet from the veranda and kept his eye on the little stand of cottonwoods a mile away. That was where the creek flowed off the mountain. The creek went underground there but you could trace the line of its passage out onto the desert plain by the deep green row of mesquite and scrub sycamore. The rider would appear somewhere along there; he'd have to cross the creek.

After a little while the visitor came across the creek and rode along the slope toward the ruined fort. *Coming in straight up*, the man observed; but still he didn't show himself.

Halfway up to the house the horseman drew his rifle out of the saddle scabbard and laid it across his pommel, holding it that way with one hand as he approached without hurry.

The man lay in the brush and watched.

He saw that the rider was just a kid. Maybe 18, maybe 20. A leaned-down kid with no meat on him and a hungry narrow face under the brim of a pretentious black hat.

The horse went by not ten feet from the man's hiding place. Just beyond, the kid drew rein, not riding any closer to the fort.

"Hello the house. Anybody home?"

The man stood up behind him. "Right back here. Drop the rifle first. Then we'll talk."

The man was braced for anything; the kid might be a wild one. The man had the Bisley Colt cocked in his fist. The kid's head turned slowly until he picked up the man in the corner of his vision; evidently he saw and recognized the revolver because he let the rifle slide to the ground.

"Now the belt gun," the man said, and the kid stripped off his gunbelt and let it drop alongside the rifle. The kid eased his horse off to one side away from the weapons and the man said, "All right, you can speak your piece."

"Ain't rightly fair coming up from behind me like that," the kid said. He had a surprisingly deep voice.

"Well you came calling on me with a rifle across your bow."

"Place like this, how do I know what to expect? Could be rattlers in there. Place could be crawling with road agents for all I know."

"Well, that's all right, son. You won't need your weapons. You want to come inside and share a bit of supper?"

The kid looked uncertainly at the man's Bisley revolver. The man walked over to the discarded weapons and picked them up. Then he uncocked the revolver and put it back in his waistband. He went up to the house and the woman came out onto the veranda and shaded her eyes to look at the visitor. She smiled a welcome, but when she glanced at the man he saw the knowledge in her face.

The kid had come to kill the man, right enough. All three of them knew it, but nobody said anything.

The kid ate politely; somebody had taught him manners. The woman said, to make conversation, "You hail from Tucson?"

"No, ma'am. Laramie, Wyoming."

"Long way off," the man said.

"I reckon."

After supper the three of them sat on the veranda. The sun was behind the house and they were in shadow; another ten minutes to sundown. The hard slanting light struck the face of Longshot Bluff and made the spire look like a fiery signal against the dark sky beyond it. The man got his pipe going to his satisfaction, broke the match, and contemplated the kid who had come to kill him. "How much they paying you for my scalp, son?"

"What?"

"The last one they sent, it was two thousand dollars they offered him."

"Mister, I ain't quite sure what you're talking about."

"That's a powerful grudge they're carrying, two thousand dollars' worth. It happened a long while back, you know."

The woman said, "But I suppose two thousand dollars looks like the world of money to a young man like you."

The man said, "It's not legal any more, you know, son. No matter what they told you. There was a fugitive warrant out on me from the state of Wyoming, but that was some years back. The statute of limitations expired three years ago."

"I'm sorry, mister, I just ain't tracking what you mean."

"The cattlemen up there were hiring range detectives like me to discourage homesteaders," the man explained. "This one cattleman had an eager kind of streak in him. I told him to keep out of the way but he had to mess in things. Got in the way of a bullet. My bullet, I expect, although I've never been whole certain about that.

"Anyhow, that cattleman's been in a wheelchair ever since. Accused me of backshooting him, said I'd sold out to the homestead crowd. It wasn't true, of course, but it's what he believes. All he does is sit in that wheelchair and brood over it. He's sent seven bounty men after me, one time or another. He just keeps sending them. Reckon he won't give it up till one of us dies of old age. You're number eight now. Maybe you want to think on that – think about the other seven that came after me, pretty good professionals some of them. I'm still here, son."

The kid just watched him, not blinking, no longer protesting innocence.

The man said, "That fellow in the wheelchair, how much did he offer you?"

The kid didn't answer that. After a moment the woman said, "You probably want the money for some good purpose, don't you, young fellow?"

"Ma'am, I expect anybody could find his own good purpose to turn money to if he had it."

"You got a girl back in Laramie, Wyoming?" she asked.

"Yes, ma'am."

"Fixing to marry her?"

"That's right, ma'am."

"On two thousand dollars you'd have a right good start," she said.

"That would be true, ma'am," the kid said with great courtesy.

"Well, I hope you make your way proper in the world," she said, "but you ain't likely to do that here. You do a sight of hunting, I imagine, from the look of that rifle you carry. You must have seen buck antelope square off a time or two. The young buck tries to get the better of the old buck, tries to displace him in the herd. Rarely happens. I expect you know that. The old buck knows all the tricks that the young buck still needs to learn. That's why you're setting on this porch now without a gun."

The man's pipe had gone out. He struck another match and indulged himself in the ritual of spreading the flame around the bowl. Then he said, "If you ain't ready to give it up, son, I'll take your weapons out there on the desert in the morning and then let you go out and get them and we'll finish this thing between us. If that's the way you want it."

The kid looked at him and uncertainty crept into his young face.

The man said, "The only weapon I own is this Bisley revolver here. Of course you may think you can outrange me with that forty-four-forty rifle of yours. You may think that, but I reckon as how you'd be mistaken."

The light was beginning to fade, but he still had another 15 or 20 minutes of light good enough for shooting. The wind had died; that was what he had waited for. He went inside the house and got the kid's rifle and brought it out onto the veranda. The kid watched him while the man worked the lever-action, jacking out the cartridges one by one until the rifle was empty.

Then the man picked up one of the cartridges off the floor and wiped it clean with his hand and chambered it into the rifle. He locked the breech shut and looked at the kid.

"Now I've put one load into this rifle of yours. I'm going to let you shoot it, if you like, but not at me. You can aim it down there toward the cliff. If I see that rifle start to swing toward me I'll just have to shoot you."

The kid, baffled, just stared at him.

The man pointed off toward the cliff. You could see the little ore cart down there; you could, if you had good eyesight, make out the two jugs perched on it.

"You see those jugs on the ore cart, son?"

"Yes, sir, if that's what they are."

"Half-gallon clay jugs. You think you can hit those with that rifle?"

The kid stood up and went to the rail of the veranda. He peered down the slope. "That's an awful long way off," he said, half to himself.

"Pret' near half a mile," the man agreed. "Six, seven hundred yards anyhow."

The kid said, "I don't know as how even Wild Bill Hickok could have made a shot like that, sir."

"Well, you can try it if you like."

"I don't see the point."

The man handed the rifle to the woman. Then he drew out his Bisley revolver and stepped over to the pillar that supported the veranda roof.

"I'll show you why," he said, and lifted his left arm straight out from the shoulder and braced his palm against the pillar. Then he twisted his body a little and set his feet firm, and holding the Bisley revolver in his right fist he lowered it until his two wrists were crossed, the left one supporting the right one – the shooter's-rest position. He cocked the revolver and fired it once, almost with careless speed.

Down below at the cliff all three of them plainly saw one of the clay jugs hurtle off its perch on the corner of the ore cart. The jug struck the rocky ground and shattered.

The kid's eyes, big and round, came around slowly to rest on the man. "Lordy. Seven hundred yards – with a *handgun*?"

The man cocked his Bisley revolver again and held it in his right hand pointed more or less at the kid. The woman walked behind the kid and held the rifle out over the railing, pointing it toward the cliff. She was proffering it to the kid. "Go ahead," she said. "You try."

Slowly the kid took the rifle from her. He was careful to make no sudden motions. He got down on one knee and braced his left forearm against the porch railing to steady his aim. He took his time. The man saw him look up toward the sky, trying to judge the elevation and the windage and the range. The kid adjusted the rear sight of the rifle twice before he snugged down to take serious aim.

Finally he was ready and the man saw the kid's finger begin to whiten on the trigger as he squeezed. The kid was all right, the man thought. Knew what he was doing. But then that had been clear from the start – when the kid hadn't tried something foolish at the moment when the man had taken him by surprise back there on the horse. The kid was wise enough to know you didn't fight when the other man had the drop.

The kid squeezed the trigger with professionally unhurried skill and the rifle thundered. The man was watching the cliff and saw the white streak appear on the rocks where the bullet struck.

"Not bad," the man said. "You only missed by about ten feet."

"Lordy," the kid said. He handed the empty rifle back to the woman.

Then the man took his position again and fired a single shot from his Bisley revolver.

They saw the remaining jug shatter.

The light began to fade. The man said, "I did that to show you the first one wasn't a fluke."

The kid swallowed. "I expect I'm kind of over-matched." He wiped his mouth. "I take it right kindly you did it this way. I mean you could've proved the same thing by using me instead of those jugs." He sat down slowly. "You was right. But that old man in the wheelchair, he showed me a warrant. He said it was all fair and legal. He even showed me where it said dead-or-alive."

The woman said, "Likely he didn't show you the date on that warrant, though, did he?"

"I don't recollect that he did, no, Ma'am."

The man said, "If you ask at the courthouse when you get home you'll find out those charges expired three years ago."

In the morning they watched the kid ride away to the

north. The man packed his Bisley revolver away after he
cleaned it. Then he took the woman's hand and they went
down to the cliff to start the day's work.

The man picked up the shards of the broken jugs and tossed
them on the tailings pile. "It's a good thing he's that young. If
he'd been older he'd have known for a fact that you just can't
make a shot that far with a handgun. But a fellow that young,
you can trick him because he believes what he sees."

The woman smiled. "Well, it wasn't exactly a trick. You
still had to aim rock-steady. And figure the wind."

"I waited until there wasn't no wind. If the air's moving
you can't do a trick like that."

He'd set up for it four years ago because he'd known they'd
keep coming after him. He'd been counting on the statute of
limitations; he hadn't reckoned, at the time, on that old man
being so obsessed that he'd keep sending bounty men forever. But the trick still worked.

He'd done it by figuring the shot in reverse. He'd made a
little notch on the pillar of the veranda and that was where he
aimed the revolver from. He'd taken aim at the left side of the
spire on top of Longshot Bluff. Then he'd taken aim at the
right side of it. Then he'd gone down the hill and marked the
spots where the two bullets had struck. After that, all he had to
do was set up his two targets on exactly those spots. If there
wasn't any wind, all you had to do was aim at one side of the
spire or the other. You'd hit the same spots every time.

It had fooled the kid, of course, because it hadn't occurred
to the kid that there was a fixed aiming point. The kid had
had to guess the drop of his bullet over a seven-hundred-
yard range. He'd guessed pretty close, matter of fact, but it
hadn't been close enough.

The man was pleased with it. Because all the time he'd
been a gun-handler by profession he'd managed to do it
without ever killing a man. He'd arrested a lot of them and
he'd shot a few, but none of them fatally. He wasn't about to
let a bitter old fool in a wheelchair make a killer out of him at
this time of his life.

SAINT NICK ALAS

Tony Hoare

Adapted for:

MINDER

(ITV, 1980–)

Starring: George Cole,

Dennis Waterman & Gary Webster

Directed by Johnny Goodman

Comedy crime series are a comparatively new phenomenon on TV. Although earlier police and detective shows had quite often been unintentionally funny, the first to set out deliberately to get laughs from crime was Porridge *(BBC, 1974–77) with comedian Ronnie Barker playing an old lag in prison, along with Richard Beckinsale as his young cellmate and Fulton McKay as a constantly frustrated prison officer. The series with its insight into life in jail, as seen through the day-to-day activities of a group of characters ranging from unregenerate villains to senti-*

mental guards, was for years one of the top sitcoms on television and its popularity has resulted in frequent reshowings. Recently, Porridge *has been in the same schedules as another very popular comedy series,* The Detectives *(1992–), which co-stars stand-up comedian Jasper Carrott and actor Robert Powell as two inept and accident-prone sleuths, forever bungling cases and infuriating their boss, George Sewell. ITV's contribution to comic crime,* Minder, *enjoys a similar cult status to both of these series. Created by Leon Griffiths in 1980, the stories about a shady secondhand car dealer, Arthur Daley (George Cole), constantly embroiled in dodgy deals from which he needs extricating by the muscle or nous of his "minder", Terry McCann (Dennis Waterman) – superseded by Arthur's nephew, Ray (Gary Webster) – the series not only became a huge hit in Britain, but has also been shown in seventy other countries. Described once as "the Richard Nixon of the forecourt", Daley's name has become both an insulting and complimentary catchword, while his malapropisms are legendary. Interestingly, in the first series, the emphasis of the stories was on the minder (hence the title) while Denholm Elliott was originally intended to play the Arthur Daley role. Since Dennis Waterman left the series, there have been fewer episodes, but the possibility of the occasional two-hour special still remains according to ITV.*

Leon Griffiths (1928–) has stated that Arthur Daley is "an amalgam of lots of people" and the reason for his success is probably because of the public affection for "slightly dodgy, anti-authority characters". Prior to creating Minder, *Griffiths was best known for his critically acclaimed TV dramas such as* Dinner at the Sporting Club *(1978) (which Kenneth Trodd produced), with John Thaw as the gritty manager of a young boxer just turned professional. For his contributions to television crime and mystery series, he won the Writers' Guild Award in 1964 and a BAFTA award in 1984. Although Leon Griffiths has frequently written scripts for* Minder, *the writer who has actually contributed more than any other and been responsible for some of the most amusing episodes and hilarious lines is Tony Hoare (1952–) who wrote the following short story for* TV Times *in December 1991. It is a superb reminder of Arthur*

Daley, the man known to millions as Thatcherism's funniest by-product . . .

Said Arthur Daley: "The thing about Christmas, it's a time for giving."

"Or in your case, receiving," Terry said, dismally watching the windscreen wipers push the lightly falling snow aside as they headed for Arthur's lock-up.

Arthur changed gear, deliberately ignoring this, wanting to keep Terry sweet, trying to ease into the proposition without making it sound like a nice little earner. "A time for goodwill to all men . . . especially kids," he offered, glancing at Terry, searching for agreement. A way in. Terry cast him a suspicious look, sensing a move. Arthur smiled with a face that he hoped radiated sincerity and continued: "Nothing quite like watching their beamin' faces as they open up all the pressies Santa's brought them, right?"

Terry responded with a wary: "I guess so."

"You don't sound too sure," said Arthur. "What are you tellin' me, you don't like kids? You've got something about not making children happy?"

Terry sighed. All the signs were there. Arthur slipping whatever it was in sideways. Never direct. Which didn't stop him answering: "I like kids to be happy, okay?"

Fatal. He knew by the way Arthur smiled. It was confirmed when Arthur said: "I knew you were the right man for the job."

The car skidded slightly to a halt in the settling snow outside the lock-up. Terry didn't want to ask what job? In fact, he was thoroughly dispirited by the thought he had allowed Arthur to corner him yet again.

Detective-Constable Jones, sitting at a desk in the squad room, also felt dispirited. Here it was, Christmas Eve and here he was on duty. A mood guaranteed not to be enhanced

by the fact that his superior officer, Sgt Rycott, was also on
duty at the sparsely-manned station. He tried to cheer
himself up by thinking of the three valleys and the Welsh
Orpheus Choir singing *We'll Keep a Welcome in the Hillside*.
He gave up. It made him homesick. But homesickness
degenerated into a moment of despair when Rycott, pretending to be busy at *his* desk, said: "Don't just sit there
daydreaming, Jones, *do* something." DC Jones realised in
that moment that his father had given him bad advice when
he told him *not* to follow his footsteps down the mines.

"I am doing something, guv," he said.

"Really? I'm amazed. I'm agog," in a voice that exuded
sarcasm. "Blinking vacantly into space constitutes serious
activity, does it?"

DC Jones glanced at the pathetic Christmas trimmings
some desperate optimist had seen fit to drape around the
room, and thought maybe it was time to consider a change of
career – funeral director, something like that.

Terry didn't like the idea but Arthur kept laying the guilt
trip on him about how he would be letting the kids down.
Toddlers is what Terry was calling them by now. He also felt
a right wally standing there in the lock-up dressed in the
Father Christmas costume. It didn't help that the beard had
a grey tinge and smelt distinctly unsavoury.

"I'm supposed to be meeting Arnie and a few of the chaps
down the Winchester for a drink-up," he tried again as
Arthur thrust what appeared to be a school bell in his hand
– his voice overlapping: "Cop this . . . give it some stick and
a few 'Ho, ho, ho's. Merry Christmas, children'."

Terry rang the bell, heard himself saying: "Ho! Ho! Ho!
Merry Christmas, children," and experiencing a sense of
unreality. "Forget the bell," he said, handing it back to
Arthur, whose face dropped while his brain told him not to
push it when Terry had that look in his eyes.

"You're right," Arthur said, setting the bell aside, "you're
going to need both hands anyway." Then he quickly realised
now was not the time to go into that particular detail and

added, ". . . for the sack of pressies." Like it was all one sentence.

"Sack?"

The snow was falling more heavily now. It was dark and visibility was poor as they headed in the car towards Mr Jackson's house. Mr Jackson was the man with the kids. A dear friend of mine, Arthur had said. "If he's such a 'dear friend' how come I've never heard of him?" Terry asked. Arthur muttered something about keeping his social life separated from his business life. Terry didn't believe a word of it. "So how much is my wack for doin' this job?" he enquired.

"Payment? Please, Terry, do not insult me an' demean yourself. This is an act of goodwill, suffer little children to come unto me, and all that. D'you think the geezers who shlepped across the desert humping gold, frankincense an' myrrh to Bethlehem were lookin' to be on an earner?" And before Terry could protest, Arthur slammed on the brakes, skidding and smashing into the curb. Whiplash caused the Santa hat to drop over Terry's eyes. Arthur, "oh my gawding" it, stumbled from the car to examine the damage.

"What the hell happened?" asked Terry. A cat had run out into the road. "Was it a black one?" asked Terry, trying to remember if it meant good or bad luck. "Can't be good," groaned Arthur, pointing at the nearside front wheel sticking out from the wing at an unnatural angle.

"So what do we do now?" Terry asked.

"We'll have to walk it . . . it's only round the corner. Get the sack of pressies from the boot."

Around the corner turned out to be about half a mile away.

And so there they were, eventually, outside Mr Jackson's huge Gothic house, snow-capped and looking like Christopher Lee's castle in Transylvania against the black sky. Terry's feet were wet and icy cold in the synthetic boots with the white nylon fur trim. So what was he supposed to do, just knock on the door, or what, he asked Arthur –

snuggled up in his Crombie overcoat and hand-made brogues.

"Nothing so mundane, my son," said Arthur, heading up the driveway. "D'you think Prancer, Dancer, Vixen an' Rudolf tug Santa from the North Pole across the rooftops of the world just to knock on doors? No, it has to be done proper, in keeping with tradition. You nip down the chimney."

"*What?*"

"Don't worry. Mr Jackson's had it swept 'specially'." As if *that* made a difference! "The kids'll be gathered waiting at the bottom. Think how surprised an' delighted they'll be when you drop, uh, show up in the inglenooky."

"Forget it, no way am I climbing *inside* a chimney! Are you crazy?"

"If being sentimental and filled with the yuletide spirit is crazy, then I cop a plea, Terence," Arthur said in tones that suggested great sacrifice and even greater humility.

"Arthur, I'm *twelve* stone!" Terry protested. "I couldn't get down the chimney even if I wanted, which I most definitely *don't!*"

"Not a problem, my son," smiled Arthur with breathtaking confidence, giving Terry a reassuring pat and guiding him towards the back of the house. "This gaff was built in the days when they shovelled kids up the flue to give 'em a dusting."

"Right, *not* grown men in Santa suits humpin' sacks of toys!"

"Sack, Terence. Singular."

"What difference, I ain't doing it!"

So Arthur explained how he and Mr Jackson had discussed the practicalities, how Mr Jackson even had a builder check out the measurements and remove the chimney pots to make room for access. Of course it might be a little *confined*, but nothing someone with Terry's suppleness and physical prowess couldn't overcome.

The two of them were at the rear of the house now, with Arthur pointing at the ladder reaching up to the roof, saying:

"See, you don't even have to climb a drainpipe. Anticipation an' preparation is the hallmark of my continuing success, as you should well know, Terence."

"Oh really. I thought it was telling porkies and conning people," was the best defence Terry could muster against Arthur's onslaught of perverse logic.

"Uncalled for, Terry, not to add un-Christian," said Arthur, pointing a digit heavenward. "Shall we try and have some respect for His birthday?" Then glancing at his watch he indicated the ladder again and handed Terry a torch. "Up you go then . . . we're running late as it is."

DC Jones still felt confused about his future. He thought about therapy as a solution to his disenchantment with the job – then decided against it on the grounds it would undermine his career prospects. A promotion board, if they found out, would view it as some sort of mental instability – a condition of the mind that immediately brought Sgt Rycott to the forefront of his thoughts.

Now there was a *real* nutter. Why else would the scourge of his professional life decide it would be a good idea for them to leave the relative warmth and comfort of the squad room and 'patrol the manor' in search of criminal activity. Real villains took a break at Christmas to be with their families and *spend* their ill-gotten gains.

Suddenly Rycott was shouting: "Pull over, pull over!" Jones did as bid as Rycott twisted in his seat to peer and point dramatically through the rear window. "D'you see it?"

All DC Jones could see was a badly parked Jaguar. "See what, guv?"

"Arthur bloody Daley," is what Rycott said.

Fortunately, the immediate area around the base of the chimney stack was flat and Terry was able to stand with relative safety, carefully wedging the sack of presents between his numbed feet, while he flashed the pencil torch down into the blackness of the flue. It appeared clear of soot. There was even a series of small iron lugs sticking out at regular intervals where he could get a toehold. That at least

was reassuring. The actual width of the flue wasn't. Maybe
he could just about squeeze down it. He could hold the torch
in his mouth and sort of balance the sack on his head. "It gets
wider as you descend," Arthur had assured him. But then he
would.

"It's Daley's car, all right," Rycott said. "And those are his
footprints. I'd recognise them anywhere!" The sergeant's
obsessive preoccupation with the activities of Arthur were
legendary on the manor, but to claim he could recognise the
man's *footprints* . . . in the snow? Jones was incredulous.
They were stood by Arthur's damaged car observing the two
sets of footprints leading off into the distance.

"Remarkable observation, guv," DC Jones said dryly.
"And it's my guess there's someone with him."

"McCann!" Rycott exclaimed – then realising. "Is that
supposed to be some form of Celtic wit, Jones?"

It took them about five minutes in the police car to follow
the footprints to the entrance of Mr Jackson's residence. And
a feeling of euphoria swept over Rycott as he peered around
the corner of the house and saw Arthur standing near the foot
of a *ladder* . . . staring up at the roof! Got the slippery sod at
last. Bang to rights! Capturing Arthur Daley for burglary
and in all likelihood his colleague in crime, Terry McCann,
was the best Christmas present he could ever wish for! And
he leaped from the shadows, calling: "Get the cuffs on him,
Jones!" Startled out of his wits, Arthur tripped and fell over.

Mr Jackson was somewhat bemused. He had opened the
door to reveal Arthur handcuffed to one police officer while
the other one said: "Do you know this man, sir?"

Having first got his wife to usher the children upstairs so
they wouldn't be upset, Mr Jackson led the trio into the
living room, where he proceeded to confirm he knew Arthur
and had hired his services to supply one Santa Claus.

Rycott's disappointment and frustration was immeasur-
able. DC Jones could've sworn he saw tears forming in his
superior's eyes as he released Arthur from the handcuffs, and

squirming as Arthur demanded an apology for the unwarranted assault on his person.

It was during this exchange that a brick fell into the inglenook fireplace, and the muffled, distressed voice of Terry was heard calling for help.

It took the firemen three hours to release him.

Long before this, Arthur had felt it prudent to use Mr Jackson's phone to call for a taxi. Terry could be very unreasonable about this sort of thing. Sitting at home now, snuggled into his favourite armchair, sipping a glass of port, puffing on a cigar and warming his feet at the open fireplace while 'er-in-doors prepared his dinner, he mused about the evening's events.

Mr Jackson had been very understanding, apologetic even. He insisted on paying Arthur the hundred sovs fee that had been agreed upon a week earlier. Naturally Arthur had accepted it, feeling it was only fair considering the ordeal *he'd* been through. And, as an afterthought, Terry, too. Perhaps he should bung the boy, say, twenty quid. Tell him it was out of his own pocket.

After all, it was Christmas.

THE DRIPPING

David Morrell

Adapted to:

RAMBO: FIRST BLOOD

(Orion, 1982–)

Starring: Sylvester Stallone,

Brian Dennehy & Richard Crenna

Directed by Ted Kotcheff

Another recent phenomenon in crime movies has been the "avenger" film in which the "heroes" dispense their own justice because the law has failed them. The genre, for such it has become, began in the early eighties with David Morrell's novel, First Blood, *which was adapted for the screen in 1982 by actor Sylvester Stallone and scriptwriters Michael Kozoll and William Sackheim. When the picture was released, it quickly broke box-office records and generated an interest in the theme which has continued for the last fifteen years. The story of John Rambo (Stallone), a former Green Beret in Vietnam, who returns to the US, a lonely and unsettled man, and soon gets involved in violent outbursts with the police – in particular a wicked sheriff (Brian Dennehy) – captured the imagination of public and critics alike.* David Robinson in The Times *wrote with commendable perception, "The reason for the success of* First Blood *is not far to seek: this story of a man pushed around like the rest of us, but with the strength to wreck single-handed vengeance on the world, is a universal daydream." Although there were those members of the public who found Stallone's inarticulate performance on behalf of the inarticulate difficult if not impossible to like, the picture went on to inspire several sequels, generate an industry of souvenirs (including a man who set himself up as a "Rambogram" and caused panic when he appeared in a New York Court House) as well as several imitators. The second picture in the series, released in 1985, was also a huge success; it was banned in Zimbabwe and even caused a riot in the UK when some youths gatecrashed a late night showing.*

The success of the Rambo pictures also made novelist David Morrell (1943–) a household name, and his subsequent books and short stories have established him as one of the finest and most ingenious writers in the crime genre. Although born in Canada, David studied in the US at Pennsylvania State University and became assistant professor of American litera-ture at the University of Iowa. It was while he was in his late twenties that he became fascinated with crime fiction and submitted his first short story, "The Dripping" to Ellery Queen's Mystery Magazine *where it was immediately greeted as an impressive debut by a new voice in mystery writing. In the tale, David began to explore the theme of a lonely man drawn inexorably into murder, a theme which would flower so trium-phantly in* First Blood *published in 1972. Producer Stanley Kramer was one of the first men in the film industry to spot the potential of the book, but it was the intervention of Sylvester Stallone that really got the project off the ground. Now Rambo stands as a landmark in the contemporary history of crime movies and the story which follows shows how the phenomenon it*

*has become first began to stir in David Morrell's
imagination . . .*

That autumn we lived in a house in the country, my mother's
house, the house I was raised in. I have been to the village,
struck more by how nothing in it has changed, yet everything
has, because I am older now, seeing it differently. It is as
though I am both here now and back then, at once with the
mind of a boy and a man. It is so strange a doubling, so
intense, so unsettling, that I am moved to work again, to try
to paint it.

So I study the hardware store, the grain barrels in front,
the twin square pillars holding up the drooping balcony onto
which seared wax-faced men and women from the old
people's hotel above come to sit and rock and watch. They
look the same aging people I saw as a boy, the wood of the
pillars and balcony looks as splintered.

Forgetful of time while I work, I do not begin the long
walk home until late, at dusk. The day has been warm, but
now in my shirt I am cold, and a half mile along I am caught
in a sudden shower and forced to leave the gravel road for the
shelter of a tree, its leaves already brown and yellow. The
rain becomes a storm, streaking at me sideways, drenching
me; I cinch the neck of my canvas bag to protect my painting
and equipment, and decide to run, socks spongy in my shoes,
when at last I reach the lane down to the house and barn.

The house and barn. They and my mother, they alone
have changed, as if as one, warping, weathering, joints
twisted and strained, their gray so unlike the white I recall
as a boy. The place is weakening her. She is in tune with it,
matches its decay. That is why we have come here to live. To
revive. Once I thought to convince her to move away. But of
her sixty-five years she has spent forty here, and she insists
she will spend the rest, what is left to her.

The rain falls stronger as I hurry past the side of the house, the light on in the kitchen, suppertime and I am late. The house is connected with the barn the way the small base of an L is connected to its stem. The entrance I always use is directly at the joining, and when I enter out of breath, clothes clinging to me cold and wet, the door to the barn to my left, the door to the kitchen straight ahead, I hear the dripping in the basement down the stairs to my right.

"Meg. Sorry I'm late," I call to my wife, setting down the water-beaded canvas sack, opening the kitchen door. There is no one. No settings on the table. Nothing on the stove. Only the yellow light from the sixty-watt bulb in the ceiling. The kind my mother prefers to the white of one hundred. It reminds her of candlelight, she says.

"Meg," I call again, and still no one answers. Asleep, I think. Dusk coming on, the dark clouds of the storm have lulled them, and they have lain down for a nap, expecting to wake before I return.

Still the dripping. Although the house is very old, the barn long disused, roofs crumbling, I have not thought it all so ill-maintained, the storm so strong that water can be seeping past the cellar windows, trickling, pattering on the old stone floor. I switch on the light to the basement, descend the wood stairs to the right, worn and squeaking, reach where the stairs turn to the left the rest of the way down to the floor, and see not water dripping. Milk. Milk everywhere. On the rafters, on the walls, dripping on the film of milk on the stones, gathering speckled with dirt in the channels between them. From side to side and everywhere.

Sarah, my child, has done this, I think. She has been fascinated by the big wood dollhouse that my father made for me when I was quite young, its blue paint chipped and peeling now. She has pulled it from the far corner to the middle of the basement. There are games and toy soldiers and blocks that have been taken from the wicker storage chest and played with on the floor, all covered with milk, the dollhouse, the chest, the scattered toys, milk dripping on them from the rafters, milk trickling on them.

Why has she done this, I think. Where can she have gotten so much milk? What was in her mind to do this thing?

"Sarah," I call. "Meg." Angry now, I mount the stairs into the quiet kitchen. "Sarah," I shout. She will clean the mess and stay indoors the remainder of the week.

I cross the kitchen, turn through the sitting room past the padded flower-patterned chairs and sofa that have faded since I knew them as a boy, past several of my paintings that my mother has hung up on the wall, bright-colored old ones of pastures and woods from when I was in grade school, brown-shaded new ones of the town, tinted as if old photographs. Two stairs at a time up to the bedrooms, wet shoes on the soft worn carpet on the stairs, hand streaking on the smooth polished maple bannister.

At the top I swing down the hall. The door to Sarah's room is open, it is dark in there. I switch on the light. She is not on the bed, nor has been; the satin spread is unrumpled, the rain pelting in through the open window, the wind fresh and cool. I have the feeling then and go uneasy into our bedroom; it is dark as well, empty too. My stomach has become hollow. Where are they? All in mother's room?

No. As I stand at the open door to mother's room I see from the yellow light I have turned on in the hall that only she is in there, her small torso stretched across the bed.

"Mother," I say, intending to add, "Where are Meg and Sarah?" But I stop before I do. One of my mother's shoes is off, the other askew on her foot. There is mud on the shoes. There is blood on her cotton dress. It is torn, her brittle hair disrupted, blood on her face, her bruised lips are swollen.

For several moments I am silent with shock. "My God, Mother," I finally manage to say, and as if the words are a spring releasing me to action I touch her to wake her. But I see that her eyes are open, staring ceilingward, unseeing though alive, and each breath is a sudden full gasp, then slow exhalation.

"Mother, what has happened? Who did this to you? Meg? Sarah?"

But she does not look at me, only constant toward the ceiling.

"For God's sake, Mother, answer me! Look at me! What has happened?"

Nothing. Eyes sightless. Between gasps she is like a statue.

What I think is hysterical. Disjointed, contradictory. I must find Meg and Sarah. They must be somewhere, beaten like my mother. Or worse. Find them. Where? But I cannot leave my mother. When she comes to consciousness, she too will be hysterical, frightened, in great pain. How did she end up on the bed?

In her room there is no sign of the struggle she must have put up against her attacker. It must have happened somewhere else. She crawled from there to here. Then I see the blood on the floor, the swath of blood down the hall from the stairs. Who did this? Where is he? Who would beat a gray, wrinkled, arthritic old woman? Why in God's name would he do it? I shudder. The pain of the arthritis as she struggled with him.

Perhaps he is still in the house, waiting for me.

To the hollow sickness in my stomach now comes fear, hot, pulsing, and I am frantic before I realize what I am doing – grabbing the spare cane my mother always keeps by her bed, flicking on the light in her room, throwing open the closet door and striking in with the cane. Viciously, sounds coming from my throat, the cane flailing among the faded dresses.

No one. Under the bed. No one. Behind the door. No one.

I search all the upstairs rooms that way, terrified, constantly checking behind me, clutching the cane and whacking into closets, under beds, behind doors, with a force that would certainly crack a skull. No one.

"Meg! Sarah!"

No answer, not even an echo in this sound-absorbing house.

There is no attic, just an overhead entry to a crawl space under the eaves, and that opening has long been sealed. No sign of tampering. No one has gone up.

I rush down the stairs, seeing the trail of blood my mother

has left on the carpet, imagining her pain as she crawled, and search the rooms downstairs with the same desperate thoroughness. In the front closet. Behind the sofa and chairs. Behind the drapes.

No one.

I lock the front door, lest he be outside in the storm waiting to come in behind me. I remember to draw every blind, close every drape, lest he be out there peering at me. The rain pelts insistently against the windowpanes.

I cry out again and again for Meg and Sarah. The police. My mother. A doctor. I grab for the phone on the wall by the front stairs, fearful to listen to it, afraid he has cut the line outside. But it is droning. Droning. I ring for the police, working the handle at the side around and around and around.

They are coming, they say. A doctor with them. Stay where I am, they say. But I cannot. Meg and Sarah, I must find them. I know they are not in the basement where the milk is dripping – all the basement is open to view. Except for my childhood things, we have cleared out all the boxes and barrels and the shelves of jars the Saturday before.

But under the stairs. I have forgotten about under the stairs and now I race down and stand dreading in the milk; but there are only cobwebs there, already reformed from Saturday when we cleared them. I look up at the side door I first came through, and as if I am seeing through a telescope I focus largely on the handle. It seems to fidget. I have a panicked vision of the intruder bursting through, and I charge up to lock the door, and the door to the barn.

And then I think: if Meg and Sarah are not in the house they are likely in the barn. But I cannot bring myself to unlock the barn door and go through. *He* must be there as well. Not in the rain outside but in the shelter of the barn, and there are no lights to turn on there.

And why the milk? Did he do it and where did he get it? And why? Or did Sarah do it before? No, the milk is too freshly dripping. It has been put there too recently. By him.

But why? And who is he? A tramp? An escapee from some prison? Or asylum? No, the nearest institution is far away, hundreds of miles. From the town then. Or a nearby farm.

I know my questions are for delay, to keep me from entering the barn. But I must. I take the flashlight from the kitchen drawer and unlock the door to the barn, force myself to go in quickly, cane ready, flashing my light. The stalls are still there, listing; and some of the equipment, churners, separators, dull and rusted, webbed and dirty. The must of decaying wood and crumbled hay, the fresh wet smell of the rain gusting through cracks in the walls. Once this was a dairy, as the other farms around still are.

Flicking my light toward the corners, edging toward the stalls, boards creaking, echoing, I try to control my fright, try to remember as a boy how the cows waited in the stalls for my father to milk them, how the barn was once board tight and solid, warm to be in, how there was no connecting door from the barn to the house because my father did not want my mother to smell the animals in her kitchen.

I run my light down the walls, sweep it in arcs through the darkness before me as I draw nearer to the stalls, and in spite of myself I recall that other autumn when the snow came early, four feet deep by morning and still storming thickly, how my father went out to the barn to milk and never returned for lunch, nor supper. There was no phone then, no way to get help, and my mother and I waited all night, unable to make our way through the storm, listening to the slowly dying wind; and the next morning was clear and bright and blinding as we shoveled out to find the cows in agony in their stalls from not having been milked and my father dead, frozen rock-solid in the snow in the middle of the next field where he must have wandered when he lost his bearings in the storm.

There was a fox, risen earlier than us, nosing at him under the snow, and my father had to be sealed in his coffin before he could lie in state. Days after, the snow was melted, gone, the barnyard a sea of mud, and it was autumn again and my mother had the connecting door put in. My father should have tied a rope from the house to his waist to guide him back in case he lost his way. Certainly he knew enough. But then he was like that always in a rush. When I was ten.

Thus I think as I light the shadows near the stalls, terrified of what I may find in any one of them, Meg and Sarah, or him, thinking of how my mother and I searched for my father and how I now search for my wife and child, trying to think of how it was once warm in here and pleasant, chatting with my father, helping him to milk, the sweet smell of new hay and grain, the different sweet smell of fresh droppings, something I always liked and neither my father nor my mother could understand. I know that if I do not think of these good times I will surely go mad in awful anticipation of what I may find. Pray God they have not died!

What can he have done to them? To assault a five-year-old girl? Split her. The hemorrhaging alone can have killed her.

And then, even in the barn, I hear my mother cry out for me. The relief I feel to leave and go to her unnerves me. I do want to find Meg and Sarah, to try to save them. Yet I am relieved to go. I think my mother will tell me what has happened, tell me where to find them. That is how I justify my leaving as I wave the light in circles around me, guarding my back, retreating through the door and locking it.

Upstairs she sits stiffly on her bed. I want to make her answer my questions, to shake her, to force her to help, but I know it will only frighten her more, maybe push her mind down to where I can never reach.

"Mother," I say to her softly, touching her gently. "What has happened?" My impatience can barely be contained. "Who did this? Where are Meg and Sarah?"

She smiles at me, reassured by the safety of my presence. Still she cannot answer.

"Mother. Please," I say. "I know how bad it must have been. But you must try to help. I must know where they are so I can help them."

She says, "Dolls."

It chills me. "What dolls, Mother? Did a man come here

with dolls? What did he want? You mean he looked like a doll? Wearing a mask like one?"

Too many questions. All she can do is blink.

"Please, Mother. You must try your best to tell me. Where are Meg and Sarah?"

"Dolls," she says.

As I first had the foreboding of disaster at the sight of Sarah's unrumpled satin bedspread, now I am beginning to understand, rejecting it, fighting it.

"Yes, Mother, the dolls," I say, refusing to admit what I know. "Please, Mother. Where are Meg and Sarah?"

"You are a grown boy now. You must stop playing as a child. Your father. Without him you will have to be the man in the house. You must be brave."

"No, Mother." I can feel it swelling in my chest.

"There will be a great deal of work now, more than any child should know. But we have no choice. You must accept that God has chosen to take him from us, that you are all the man I have left to help me."

"No, Mother."

"Now you are a man and you must put away the things of a child."

Eyes streaming, I am barely able to straighten, leaning wearily against the doorjamb, tears rippling from my face down to my shirt, wetting it cold where it had just begun to dry. I wipe my eyes and see her reaching for me, smiling, and I recoil down the hall, stumbling down the stairs, down, through the sitting room, the kitchen, down, down to the milk, splashing through it to the dollhouse, and in there, crammed and doubled, Sarah. And in the wicker chest, Meg. The toys not on the floor for Sarah to play with, but taken out so Meg could be put in. And both of them, their stomachs slashed, stuffed with sawdust, their eyes rolled up like dolls' eyes.

The police are knocking at the side door, pounding, calling out who they are, but I am powerless to let them in. They crash through the door, their rubber raincoats dripping as they stare down at me.

"The milk," I say.

They do not understand. Even as I wait, standing in the milk, listening to the rain pelting on the windows while they come over to see what is in the dollhouse and in the wicker chest, while they go upstairs to my mother and then return so I can tell them again, "The milk." But they still do not understand.

"She killed them of course," one man says. "But I don't see why the milk."

Only when they speak to the neighbors down the road and learn how she came to them, needing the cans of milk, insisting she carry them herself to the car, the agony she was in as she carried them, only when they find the empty cans and the knife in a stall in the barn, can I say, "The milk. The blood. There was so much blood, you know. She needed to deny it, so she washed it away with milk, purified it, started the dairy again. You see, there was so much blood."

That autumn we live in a house in the country, my mother's house, the house I was raised in. I have been to the village, struck even more by how nothing in it has changed, yet everything has, because I am older now, seeing it differently. It is as though I am both here now and back then, at once with the mind of a boy and a man . . .

YOUR APPOINTMENT IS CANCELLED

Antonia Fraser

Adapted for:

JEMIMA SHORE INVESTIGATES

(Thames TV, 1983–)

Starring: Patricia Hodge,

Yasmin Pettigrew & Don Henderson

Directed by Tim Aspinall

If the seventies was the era of the violent cop series, then the eighties can claim to have seen the arrival of the female crime fighter. In April 1980, LWT launched The Gentle Touch *(1980–84), which introduced Detective Inspector Maggie Forbes, played by Jill Gascoine, who is now acknowledged to have been Britain's first starring female detective. The hour-long episodes featured Maggie at work on her Seven Dials patch*

in the heart of London, battling with the Soho criminal fra-
ternity and the male chauvinism of some of her colleagues. Less
than five months later, in August 1980, she had a rival on BBC
in Juliet Bravo *(1980–85), with Inspector Jean Darblay*
(Stephanie Turner), combining the roles of a senior police
officer and housewife in a small Lancashire town called Hart-
ley. After three seasons of the series, Inspector Darblay was
"promoted" and Anna Carteret replaced her as Inspector Kate
Longton and carried out the same duties without any decline in
the show's popularity. While both these ladies were still on the
small screen, the BBC launched Agatha Christie's classic
amateur detective Jane Marple played by Joan Hickson, in
Miss Marple, *in which she gave a wonderfully authentic*
portrayal which continued in adaptations of the novels until
the nineties when age finally precluded her from playing the role
any longer. Into this bevy of female crime fighters came perhaps
the most unusual of all, Jemima Shore, an investigating TV
reporter for Megalith Television, who was forever stumbling
into mysteries of one kind or another and solving them with a
mixture of intuition and painstaking research. Based on the
novels and short stories by Antonia Fraser, Jemima Shore
Investigates, *starred the beautiful and versatile Patricia Hodge*
who took on her first case, "A Splash of Red" in August 1983 in
which the authoress herself also made a brief cameo appearance.

Antonia Fraser (1932–) is acknowledged as one of our
foremost contemporary biographers. Apart from her critically
acclaimed books such as Mary Queen of Scots *(1969) which*
won the James Tait Black Memorial Prize, Antonia has a
strong affection for crime and mystery stories and created
Jemima Shore as an outlet for this interest. A sophisticated,
intelligent and music-loving woman, Jemima has a passion for
driving fast cars and lying in hot baths where, she says, she does
her best thinking when trying to solve mysteries. Two of the
great supports in her life are Mrs Bancroft, her possessive
landlady, and the resourceful Detective Inspector J.H. Ports-
mouth – nicknamed "Pompey of the Yard" – who has more than
once come to her aid in a tight corner. "Your Appointment is
Cancelled" is a typical Jemima Shore story which begins

innocently enough with the cancellation of a hair appointment,
but soon leads her into a case of mystery and brutal murder . . .

"This is Arcangelo's Salon, Epiphany speaking. I am very
sorry to inform you that your appointment is cancelled . . ."
In sheer surprise, Jemima Shore looked at the receiver in her
hand. But still the charming voice went on. After a brief
click, the message started all over again. "This is Arcangelo's
Salon, Epiphany speaking. I am very sorry to inform you
that your appointment is cancelled . . ."

In spite of the recording, Jemima imagined Epiphany
herself at the other end of the telephone – the elegant black
receptionist with her long neck and high cheekbones. Was
she perhaps Ethiopian, Somali, or from somewhere else in
Africa, which produced such beauties? Wherever she came
from, Epiphany looked, and probably was, a princess. She
was also, on the evidence of her voice and manner, highly
educated; there was some rumour at the salon that Epiphany
had been to university.

As the message continued on its level way, Jemima
thought urgently: What about my hair? She touched the
thick reddish-gold mass whose colour and various styles had
been made famous by television. Jemima thought it was
professional to take as much trouble about her hair as she
did about the rest of the details concerning her celebrated
programme looking into the social issues of the day, *Jemima
Shore Investigates.* She had just returned from filming in
Morocco (working title: New Women of the Kasbah) and her
hair was in great need of the attentions of Mr Leo, the Italian
proprietor of Arcangelo's – or, failing that, those of his
handsome English son-in-law, Mr Clark.

But her appointment was cancelled and Jemima wondered
what had happened at Arcangelo's.

A few hours later, the *London Evening Post* ran a brief
front-page bulletin: a male hair-stylist at a certain fashion-

able salon had been found when the salon opened that morning with his head battered in by some form of blunt instrument. The police, led by Jemima's old friend, Detective Chief Inspector J.H. Portsmouth – more familiarly known as Pompey of the Yard – were investigating.

As Jemima was mulling this over, she received a phone call from Mr Leo who told her in a flood of Italianate English that the dead stylist was none other than his son-in-law, and that it was he, Leo, who had discovered the body when he unlocked the salon this morning. Epiphany, who normally did the unlocking, having been delayed on the Underground.

"Miss Shore," he ended brokenly, "they are thinking it is I, Leo, who am doing this dreadful thing, I who am killing Clark. Because of her, *mia cara, mia figlia, Domonica mia*. And yes, it is true, he was not a good husband, in spite of all I did for him, all she has been doing for him. In spite of the *bambino!*"

He paused and went on as though reluctantly. "A good stylist yes, it is I who have taught him. Yes, he is good. Not as good as me, no, who would say that? But good. But he was a terrible husband. *Un marito abominabile*. I knew, of course. How could I not know? Everyone, even the juniors knew, working in the salon all day together. *My* salon! The salon *I* have created, I, Leo Vecchetti. They thought they were so clever. Clever! Bah!

"But for that I would not have killed him. She still loved him, my daughter, my only child. For her I built up everything, I did it all. My child, Domenica, and the little one, Leonella, who will come after her. Now he is dead and the police think I did it. Because I'm Italian and he's English. You Sicilians, they say. But I'm not Sicilian. I'm from the North, *sono Veneziano* – " Mr Leo gave an angry cry and the flood poured on:

"What about *her* then?" he almost shouted. "Maybe *she* killed him because he would not leave Domenica and marry her!" He now sounded bitter as well as enraged. "No, Clark would not leave my fine business – the business he would one day inherit. Not for one of those *savages*, not he. Maybe *she* kill him – kill him with a *spear* like in the *films!*"

From this, Jemima wondered if Leo was saying that Epiphany had been Mr Clark's mistress.

"Mr Leo," she said. "When the salon reopens, I want an immediate appointment."

A few days later, Jemima drew up at Arcangelo's in her white Mercedes sports car. The golden figure of an angel blowing a trumpet over the entrance made the salon impossible to miss. Jemima was put in a benign mood by being able to grab a meter directly outside the salon from under the nose of a rather flashy-looking Jaguar being propelled at a rather more dignified pace by its male driver. She glimpsed purple-faced anger, rewarded it with a ravishing smile, and was rewarded in turn by the driver's startled recognition of the famous television face.

Well, I've certainly lost a fan there, thought Jemima cheerfully. She looked through the huge plate-glass window and saw Epiphany, on the telephone, austerely beautiful in a high-necked black jersey. One of the other stylists – Mr Roderick, she thought his name was – was bending over her. Epiphany was indeed alluring enough to make a man lose his head.

Pompey of the Yard, being a good friend of Jemima's from several previous co-operations beneficial to both sides, had filled in a few more details of the murder for Jemima. The blunt instrument had turned out to be a heavy metal hairdryer. Mr Clark's body had been found – a macabre touch – sitting under one of the grey-and-gold automatic dryers. The medical examiner estimated the time of death as between ten and eleven the previous evening, more likely later than earlier because of the body temperature. The salon closed officially at about six, but the staff sometimes lingered until six-thirty or thereabouts, tending to each other's hair – cutting, restyling, putting in highlights, unofficial activities they had no time for during the day.

The night of the murder, Mr Clark had offered to lock up the salon. (Being one of the senior stylists and, of course, Mr

Leo's son-in-law, he possessed his own set of keys.) At five o'clock, he had telephoned Domenica at home and told her he had a last-minute appointment: he had to streak the hair of a very important client and he might be home very late because this client was then going to take him to some film gala in aid of charity, to which she needed an escort – he couldn't offend her by refusing. Domenica, brought up in the hairdressing business and used to such last-minute arrangements, had a late supper with Clark's sister Janice, who had come to admire the baby, and went to bed alone. When she woke up in the morning and found Mr Clark still absent, she simply assumed, said Pompey of the Yard with a discreet cough, that the party had gone on until morning.

"Some client!" said Jemima indignantly. "I suppose you've questioned her. The client, I mean."

"I'm doing so now," Pompey had told her, with another discreet cough. "You see, the name of the famous client whose offer Mr Clark simply could not refuse, according to his wife, was *yours*. It was you who was supposed to have come in at the last minute, needing streaks in a hurry before beginning the new series."

"Needing streaks *and* an escort, to say nothing of what else I was supposed to need," commented Jemima grimly. "Well, of all the cheek –"

"*We* think," Pompey had interposed gently into Jemima's wrath, "he had a date with the black girl there at the salon after everybody had gone. There is a beautician's room which is quite spacious and comfortable, couch and all. And very private after hours."

"All very nice and convenient," Jemima said, still smarting from the late Mr Clark's impudence. "So that's where they were in the habit of meeting."

"We think so. And we think Mr Leo knew that – and, being Sicilian and full of vengeance –"

"He's Venetian actually."

"Being *Venetian* and full of vengeance. There's plenty of vengeance in Venice, Jemima. Have you ever been to the place? Mrs Portsmouth and I went once and when you encounter those gondoliers –" He broke off and resumed a more official tone. "Whatever his genesis, we believe he decided to tackle his son-in-law. That is to say, we think he killed him with several blows with a hair-dryer.

"Mr Leo has no alibi after nine o'clock. After a quick supper at home, he went out – he says – to the local pub, returning after it closed. But nobody saw him in the pub and he is, as you know, a striking-looking man. He had plenty of time to get to the salon, kill his son-in-law, and get back home."

"What about Epiphany? Mr Leo blames her."

"She admits to having been the deceased's mistress – she could hardly deny it when everybody at the salon knew. She even admits to having an occasional liaison with him at the salon in the evening. But on this particular evening, she says very firmly that she went to the cinema – alone. She's given us the name of the film. *Gandhi*. All very pat. What's more, the commissionaire remembers her in the queue – she is, after all, a very beautiful woman – and so does the girl at the box office. The only thing is, she had plenty of time once the film was over to get back to the salon and kill her lover."

"She has no alibi for her activities after the movie?" put in Jemima.

"Not really. She lives with a girl friend off the Edgware Road. But the friend's away – a very convenient fact if there was anything sinister going on – so according to Epiphany she just went home after the cinema, had a bit of supper, got into her lonely bed, and slept. Saw no one. Talked to no one. Telephoned no one. As for being late the next morning, that, too, was a piece of luck – stoppage on the Underground. We've checked that, of course, and it's true enough. But she could have come by a slower route, or even just left home later than usual so as to avoid opening up the shop and seeing the grisly consequences of her deed. As it was, we were there before she arrived."

With this information in her head, Jemima now entered the salon. Epiphany gave her usual calm welcome, asking the nearest junior – Jason, who had a remarkable coxcomb of

multi-coloured hair – to take Miss Shore's coat and lead her
to the basin. But Jemima didn't think it was her imagination
that made her suppose Epiphany was frightened under her
placid exterior. Of course, she could well be mourning her
lover (presuming she had not killed him, and possibly even if
she had) but Jemima's instinct told her there was something
beyond that – something that was agitating, even terrifying
Epiphany.

In the cloakroom, Pearl, another junior with a multi-
coloured mop, took Jemima's fleecy white fur.

"Ooh, Miss Shore, how do you keep it so clean? It's white
fox, is it?"

"I dump it in the bath," replied Jemima with perfect
truth. "Not white fox – white nylon."

At the basin, Jason washed her hair with his usual scatty
energy and later Mr Leo set it. Mr Leo was not scatty in any
sense of the word. He did the set, as ever, perfectly, handling
the thick rollers handed to him by Jason so fast and yet so
deftly that Jemima, with much experience in having her hair
done all over the world, doubted whether anyone could beat
Mr Leo for speed or expertise.

Nevertheless, she sensed beneath his politeness, as in
Epiphany, all the tension of the situation. The natural
self-discipline of the professional hairdresser able to make
gentle, interested conversation with the client whatever his
own personal problems: in this case, a son-in-law brutally
murdered, a daughter and grandchild bereft, himself the
chief suspect, to say nothing of the need to keep the salon
going smoothly if the whole family business was not to
collapse.

At which point Mr Leo suddenly confounded all Jemima's
theories about this unassailable professionalism by thrusting
a roller abruptly back into Jason's hand.

"You finish this," he commanded. And with a very brief,
muttered excuse in Jemima's general direction, he darted off
toward the reception desk. In the mirror before her, Jemima
was transfixed to see Mr Leo grab a dark-haired young
woman by the shoulder and shake her while Epiphany, like

a carved goddess, stared enigmatically down at the appointments book on her desk as though the visitor and Mr Leo did not exist. But it was interesting to note that the ringing telephone, which she normally answered at once, clamoured for at least half a minute before it claimed her attention.

The young woman and Mr Leo were speaking intensely in rapid Italian. Jemima spoke some Italian but this was far too quick and idiomatic for her to understand even the gist of it. Then Jemima recognized the distraught woman – Domenica, Mr Leo's daughter. And at the same moment she remembered that Domenica had worked as receptionist at the salon before Epiphany. Had she met Mr Clark there? Probably. And probably left the salon to look after the baby, Leonella. It was ironic that it was Epiphany who had turned up to fill the gap. But why had Domenica come to the salon today? To attack Epiphany? Was that why Mr Leo was hustling her away to the back of the salon with something that looked very much like force?

Jason had put in the last roller and fastened some small clips on the tendrils Jemima sometimes liked to wear at her neck. Now he fastened the special silky Arcangelo's net like a golden filigree over her red hair and led Jemima to the dryers with his usual energetic enthusiasm. Jason was a great chatterer and in the absence of Mr Leo he really let himself go.

"I love doing your hair, Miss Shore – it's such great hair. Great styles you wear it in on the box, too. I always look for your hair-style, no matter what you're talking about. I mean, even if it's abandoned wives or something heavy like that, I can still enjoy your hair-style, can't I?"

Jemima flashed him one of her famously sweet smiles and sank back under the hood of the dryer.

A while later, she watched, unable to hear with the noise of the dryer, as Mr Leo led Domenica back toward the entrance. As they passed the reception desk, Jemima saw Epiphany mouth something, possibly some words of condolence. In dumb show, Jemima saw Domenica break from her father's grip and shout in the direction of Epiphany.

"*Putana*." In an Italian opera, that would have been the word, *putana* – prostitute – or something similarly insulting concerning Epiphany's moral character. Whatever the word was, Epiphany did not answer. She dropped her eyes and continued to concentrate on the appointments book in front of her as Mr Leo led his daughter toward the front door.

"I am very sorry to inform you that your appointment is cancelled . . ." The memory of Epiphany's voice came back to Jemima. Could she really have recorded that message so levelly and impersonally after killing her lover?

Yet why had Mr Clark lingered in the salon if not to meet Epiphany? He had certainly taken the trouble to give a false alibi to Domenica, who was expecting her sister-in-law for a later supper. Someone had known he would still be there after hours. Someone had killed him between ten and eleven, when Mr Leo – unnoticed was still allegedly at the pub and Epiphany was at home – alone.

Jemima closed her eyes. The dryer was getting too hot. Jason, through general enthusiasm no doubt, had a tendency to set the temperature too high. She fiddled with the dial – and in so doing, it occurred to her to wonder under which dryer Mr Clark's corpse had been found sitting. She began, in spite of herself, to imagine the scene. Having been struck – several times, the police said – from behind by the massive metal hair-dryer, Mr Clark had fallen onto the long grey plush seat. The murderer had then propped him up under the plastic hood of one of the dryers to be found when the shop opened in the morning. The killer had left no fingerprints, having – another macabre touch – worn a pair of rubber gloves throughout, no doubt a pair that was missing from the tinting room. The killer had then locked the salon, presumably with Mr Clark's own keys since these too had now vanished.

"At the bottom of the Thames now, no doubt," Pompey had said dolefully, "and the gloves along with them."

Jemima shifted restlessly, sorting images and thoughts in her head. Epiphany's solitary visit to a particularly long-drawn-out film followed by a lonely supper and bed, Mr

Leo's alibi. Domenica entertaining her sister-in-law in Clark's absence, Jason's dismissal of abandoned wives – it all began to flow together, to form and re-form in a teasing kaleidoscope.

Where was Jason? She really was getting very hot.

Suddenly Jemima sat upright, hitting her head, rollers and all, on the edge of the hood as she did so. To the surprise of the clients watching (for she still attracted a few curious stares even after several years at Arcangelo's), she lifted the hood, pulled herself to her feet, and strode across the salon to where Epiphany was sitting at the reception desk. Both telephones were for once silent.

"It was true," said Jemima. "You *did* go to the cinema and then straight home. Were you angry with him? Had you quarrelled? He waited here for you. But you never came."

"I told the police that, Miss Shore." It was anguish, not fear, she had sensed in Epiphany, Jemima realized. "I told them about the film. Not about the rendezvous. What was the point of telling them about that when I didn't keep it?"

"His appointment was cancelled," murmured Jemima.

"If only I *had* cancelled it," Epiphany said. "Instead, he waited. I pretended I was coming. I wanted him to wait. To suffer as I suffered, waiting for him when he was with her – with her and the baby." Epiphany's composure broke. "I could have had any job, but I stayed here like his *slave*, while she held him with her money, the business –"

"I believe you." Jemima spoke gently. "And I'm sure the police will, too."

A short while later, she was explaining it all to Pompey. The policeman, knowing the normally immaculate state of her hair and dress, was somewhat startled to be summoned to a private room at Arcangelo's by a Jemima Shore with her hair still in rollers and her elegant figure draped in a dove-grey Arcangelo's gown.

"I know, I know, Pompey," she said. "And for heaven's sake don't tell Mrs Portsmouth you've seen me like this. But the heat of the dryer I was under a few minutes ago gave me an idea. The time of Mr Clark's death was all-important, wasn't it? By heating the body under the dryer and setting the time switch for an hour, the murderer made the police think that he had been killed nearer ten or eleven than the actual seven or eight when he was struck down.

"As it happened, ten or eleven was very awkward for Mr Leo, ostensibly at the pub, but not noticed in the pub by anyone – I have a feeling that there may be an extra-marital relationship there, too. Mr Leo is still a very good-looking man. That's not our business, however, because Mr Leo didn't kill Mr Clark. Between eight and nine, he was in the Underground on the way home, and there we have many people to vouch for him. As for Epiphany, the girl at the box office verifies that she bought a ticket and the commissionaire that she was in the queue. The timing lets her out, lets them both out, but it lets in someone else – someone who kept the appointment she knew Mr Clark had made. The abandoned wife. Domenica.

"Domenica," Jemima went on sadly, "entertaining her sister-in-law from half-past nine onward. Sitting with her, chatting with her. Spending the rest of the long evening with her, pretending to wait for her husband. And all the time he was dead here in the salon. Domenica had worked at the salon – she helped her father build it up. She knew about the rubber gloves and the keys and the hand-dryers and the time switches on the stationary ones.

"Pompey," Jemima paraphrased Jason: "it's heavy being an abandoned wife. So in the end, Domenica decided to keep Epiphany's appointment. She even left her baby alone to do so – such was the passion of the woman. The woman scorned. It was she who cancelled all future appointments for Mr Clark, with a heavy blow of a hand-dryer."

A CASE OF COINCIDENCE

Ruth Rendell

Adapted for:

THE RUTH RENDELL MYSTERIES

(ITV, 1987–)

Starring: Keith Barron,

Ronald Pickup & Don Henderson

Directed by John Davies

Amidst the plethora of highly rated crime series on television in the nineties – Cracker with Robbie Coltrane, David Jason in Frost and John Thaw as Inspector Morse are just three that spring quickly to mind – one mystery writer has retained her status as "a Queen among the Queens of Crime", as she was described by the Observer in 1991: Ruth Rendell. The first adaptation of one of her stories, "Wolf to the Slaughter", which launched The Ruth Rendell Mysteries in August 1987, also introduced George Baker as Detective Chief Inspector

Wexford, and such was its appeal and that of its successors that she shows every sign of continuing to dominate the genre throughout the nineties. What has made her work so popular is her ability to write murder mysteries that constantly extend boundaries as well as display an insight into the minds of psychopaths, murderers and rapists, that is quite unmatched by her contemporaries. In this context, she has developed a second identity as "Barbara Vine" (from her middle name and her grandmother's maiden name, Vine) and her first pseudonymous novel, A Dark Adapted Eye *(1986) – the dramatic story of a war of attrition between two sisters and their niece over some dark family secrets – was recently adapted for television by BBC1, starring the excellent acting trio of Celia Imrie, Sophie Ward and Helena Bonham-Carter. The Barbara Vine tales, if they are all adapted, promise to earn the BBC the same kind of audiences that her real name has been gaining for ITV.*

The success of The Ruth Rendell Mysteries *is just one of many milestones in the career of Ruth Rendell (1930–) during the past thirty years since she switched roles from that of a rather unsuccessful local journalist in Essex to a novelist of international renown. The saga began with her first Wexford novel,* From Doon With Death *(1964), for which she was paid £75! The appeal of the rather dour Chief Inspector – who she admits is partly based on her father – has turned her into a cult figure, and Wexford is now unique among the "cops on the box", as the only English policeman to have a big following in Japan! Apart from the cases of Wexford and the "Barbara Vine" novels, several of Ruth's short stories have also been adapted for* The Ruth Rendell Mysteries, *notably "A Case of Coincidence" which was broadcast as a two-parter in March 1996. The account of a serial killer in the Cambridgeshire fens, it starred Keith Barron as the policeman Masters who has serious doubts that his colleague, Ronald Pickup, has actually arrested the right man when he brings in a suspect. It was an unforgettable adaptation that reads just as chillingly on the printed page . . .*

Of the several obituaries which appeared on the death of Michael Lestrange not one mentioned his connection with the Wrexlade murders. Memories are short, even journalists' memories, and it may be that the newspapermen who wrote so glowingly and so mournfully about him were mere babes in arms, or not even born, at the time. For the murders, of course, took place in the early fifties, before the abolition of capital punishment.

Murder is the last thing one would associate with the late Sir Michael, eminent cardiac specialist, physician to Her Royal Highness the Duchess of Albany, and author of that classic work, the last word on its subject, so succinctly entitled *The Heart*. Sir Michael did not destroy life, he saved it. He was as far removed from Kenneth Edward Brannel, the Wrexlade Strangler, as he was from the carnivorous spider which crept across his consulting room window. Those who knew him well would say that he had an almost neurotic horror of the idea of taking life. Euthanasia he had refused to discuss, and he had opposed with all his vigour the legalizing of abortion.

Until last March when an air crash over the North Atlantic claimed him among its two hundred fatalities, he had been a man one automatically thought of as life-enhancing, as having on countless occasions defied death on behalf of others. Yet he seemed to have had no private life, no family, no circle to move in, no especially beautiful home. He lived for his work. He was not married and few knew he ever had been, still fewer that his wife had been the last of the Wrexlade victims.

There were four others and all five of them died as a result of being strangled by the outsized, bony hands of Kenneth Edward Brannel. Michael Lestrange, by the way, had exceptionally narrow, well-shaped hands, dextrous and precise. Brannel's have been described as resembling bunches of bananas. In her study of the Wrexlade case, the criminologist Miss Georgina Hallam Saul, relates how Brannel, in the condemned cell, talked about committing these crimes to a prison officer. He had never understood why he killed those women, he didn't dislike women or fear them.

"It's like when I was a kid and in a shop and there was no one about," he is alleged to have said. "I had to take something, I couldn't help myself. I didn't even do it sort of of my own will. One minute it'd be on the shelf and the next in my pocket. It was the same with those girls. I had to get my hands on their throats. Everything'd go dark and when it cleared my hands'd be round their throats and the life all squeezed out . . ."

He was twenty-eight, an agricultural labourer, illiterate, classified as educationally subnormal. He lived with his widowed father, also a farm worker, in a cottage on the outskirts of Wrexlade in Essex. During 1953 he strangled Wendy Cutforth, Maureen Hunter, Ann Daly and Mary Trenthyde without the police having the least suspicion of his guilt. Approximately a month elapsed between each of these murders, though there was no question of Brannel killing at the full moon or anything of that sort. Four weeks after Mary Trenthyde's death he was arrested and charged with murder, for the strangled body of Norah Lestrange had been discovered in a ditch less than a hundred yards from his cottage. They found him guilty of murder in November of that same year, twenty-five days later he was executed.

"A terrible example of injustice," Michael Lestrange used to say. "If the M'Naughten Rules apply to anybody they surely applied to poor Brannel. With him it wasn't only a matter of not knowing that what he was doing was wrong but of not knowing he was doing it at all till it was over. We have hanged a poor idiot who had no more idea of evil than a stampeding animal has when it tramples on a child."

People thought it amazingly magnanimous of Michael that he could talk like this when it was his own wife who had been murdered. She was only twenty-five and they had been married less than three years.

It is probably best to draw on Miss Hallam Saul for the most accurate and comprehensive account of the Wrexlade stranglings. She attended the trial, every day of it, which Michael Lestrange did not. When prosecuting counsel, in his opening speech, came to describe Norah Lestrange's reasons for being in the neighbourhood of Wrexlade that night, and to talk of the Dutchman and the hotel at Chelmsford, Michael got up quietly and left the court. Miss Hallam Saul's eyes, and a good many other pairs of eyes, followed him with compassion. Nevertheless, she didn't spare his feelings in her book. Why should she? Like everyone else who wrote about Brannel and Wrexlade, she was appalled by the character of Norah Lestrange. This was the fifties, remember, and the public were not used to hearing of young wives who admitted shamelessly to their husbands that one man was not enough for them. Michael had been obliged to state the facts to the police and the facts were that he had known for months that his wife spent nights in this Chelmsford hotel with Jan Vandepeer, a businessman on his way from The Hook and Harwich to London. She had told him so quite openly.

"Darling . . ." Taking his arm and leading him to sit close beside her while she fondled his hand. "Darling, I absolutely have to have Jan, I'm crazy about him. I do have to have other men, I'm made that way. It's nothing to do with the way I feel about you, though, you do see that, don't you?"

These words he didn't, of course, render verbatim. The gist was enough.

"It won't be all that often, Mike darling, once a month at most. Jan can't fix a trip more than once a month. Chelmsford's so convenient for both of us and you'll hardly notice I'm gone, will you, you're so busy at that old hospital."

But all this came much later, in the trial and in the Hallam Saul book. The first days (and the first chapters) were occupied with the killing of those four other women.

Wendy Cutforth was young, married, a teacher at a school in Ladeley. She went to work by bus from her home in Wrexlade, four miles away. In February, at four o'clock dusk, she got off the bus at Wrexlade Cross to walk to her bungalow a quarter of a mile away. She was never seen alive again, except presumably by Brannel, and her strangled body was found at ten that night in a ditch near the bus stop.

Fear of being out alone which had seized Wrexlade women

after Wendy's death died down within three or four weeks.
Maureen Hunter, who was only sixteen, quarrelled with her
boyfriend after a dance at Wrexlade village hall and set off to
walk home to Ingleford on her own. She never reached it.
Her body was found in the small hours only a few yards from
where Wendy's had been. Mrs Ann Daly, a middle-aged
widow, also of Ingleford, had a hairdressing business in
Chelmsford and drove herself to work each day via Wrexlade. Her car was found abandoned, all four doors wide open,
her body in a small wood between the villages. An unsuccessful attempt had been made to bury it in the leaf mould.

Every man between sixteen and seventy in the whole of
that area of Essex was closely examined by the police.
Brannel was questioned, as was his father, and was released
after ten minutes, having aroused no interest. In May,
twenty-seven days after the death of Ann Daly, Mary Trenthyde, thirty-year-old mother of two small daughters and
herself the daughter of Brannel's employer, Mark Stokes of
Cross Farm, disappeared from her home during the course of
a morning. One of her children was with its grandmother,
the other in its pram just inside the garden gate. Mary
vanished without trace, without announcing to anyone that
she was going out or where she was going. A massive hunt
was mounted and her strangled body finally found at midnight in a disused well half a mile away.

All these deaths took place in the spring of 1953.

The Lestranges had a flat in London not far from the
Royal Free Hospital. They were not well off but Norah had a
rich father who was in the habit of giving her handsome
presents. One of these, for her twenty-fifth birthday, was a
Triumph Alpine sports car. Michael had a car too, the kind
of thing that is called an "old banger".

As frontispiece to Miss Hallam Saul's book is a portrait
photograph of Norah Lestrange as she appeared a few
months before her death. The face is oval, the features almost
too perfectly symmetrical, the skin flawless and opaque. Her
thick dark hair is dressed in the high fashion of the time, in
short smooth curls. Her make-up is heavy and the dark,

greasy lipstick coats the parted lips in a way that is somehow lascivious. The eyes stare with a humourless complacency.

Michael was furiously, painfully jealous of her. When, after they had been married six months, she began a flirtation with his best friend, a flirtation which soon developed into a love affair, he threatened to leave her, to divorce her, to lock her up, to kill Tony. She was supremely confident he would do none of these things. She talked to him. Reasonably and gently and lovingly she put it to him that it was he whom she loved and Tony with whom she was amusing herself.

"I *love* you, darling, don't you understand? This thing with Tony is just – fun. We have fun and then we say goodbye till next time and I come home to you, where my real happiness is."

"You promised to be faithful to me," he said, "to forsake all others and keep only to me."

"But I do keep only to you, darling. You have all my trust and my thoughts – Tony just has this tiny share in a very unimportant aspect of me."

After Tony there was Philip. And after Philip, for a while, there was no one. Michael believed Norah might have tired of the "fun" and be settling for the real happiness. He was working hard at the time for his Fellowship of the Royal College of Surgeons.

That Fellowship he got, of course, in 1952. He was surgical registrar at a big London hospital, famous for successes in the field of cardiac surgery, when the first of the Wrexlade murders took place. Wendy Cutforth. Round about the time the account of that murder and of the hunt for the Wrexlade strangler appeared in the papers, Norah met Jan Vandepeer.

Michael wasn't a reader of the popular press and the Lestranges had no television. Television wasn't, in those days, the indispensable adjunct to domestic life it has since become. Michael listened sometimes to the radio, he read *The Times*. He knew of the first of the Wrexlade murders but he wasn't much interested in it. He was busy in his job and he had Jan Vandepeer to worry about too.

The nature of the Dutchman's business in London was never clear to Michael, perhaps because it was never clear to Norah. It seemed to have something to do with commodity markets and Michael was convinced it was shady, not quite above board. Norah used to say that he was a smuggler, and she found the possibility he might be a diamond smuggler exciting. She met him on the boat coming from The Hook to Harwich after spending a week in The Hague with her parents, her father having a diplomatic post there.

"Darling, I absolutely have to have Jan, I'm crazy about him. It's nothing to do with us, though, you do see that, don't you? No one could ever take me away from you."

He used to come over about once a month with his car and drive down to London through Colchester and Chelmsford, spend the night somewhere, carry out his business the following day and get the evening boat back. Whether he stayed in Chelmsford rather than London because it was cheaper or because Chelmsford, in those days, still kept its pleasant rural aspect, does not seem to be known. It hardly matters. Norah Lestrange was more than willing to drive the forty or so miles to Chelmsford in her Alpine and await the arrival of her dashing, blond smuggler at the Murrey Gryphon Hotel.

Chelmsford is the county town of Essex, standing on the banks of the river Chelmer and in the midst of a pleasant, though featureless, arable countryside. The land is rather flat, the fields wide, and there are many trees and numerous small woods. Wrexlade lies some four miles to the north of the town, Ingleford a little way further west. It was some time before the English reader of newspapers began to think of Wrexlade as anywhere near Chelmsford. It was simply Wrexlade, a place no one had heard of till Wendy Cutforth and then Maureen Hunter died there, a name on a map or maybe a signpost till the stranglings began – and then, gradually, a word synonymous with fascinating horror.

Bismarck Road, Hilldrop Crescent, Rillington Place – who can say now, except the amateur of crime, which of London's murderers lived in those streets? Yet in their day they were names on everyone's lips. Such is the English sense of humour that there were even jokes about them. There were jokes, says Miss Hallam Saul, about Wrexlade, sick jokes for the utterance of one of which a famous comedian was banned by the BBC. Something on the lines of what a good idea it would be to take one's mother-in-law to Wrexlade . . .

Chelmsford, being so close to Wrexlade, became public knowledge when Mrs Daly died. She was last seen locking up her shop in the town centre and getting into her car. It was after this that Norah said to Michael: "When I'm in Chelmsford, darling, I promise you I won't go out alone after dark."

It was presumably to be a consolation to him that if she went out after dark it would be in the company of Jan Vandepeer.

Did he passively acquiesce, then, in this infidelity of hers? In not leaving her, in being at the flat when she returned home, in continuing to be seen with her socially, he did acquiesce. In continuing to love her in spite of himself, he acquiesced. But his misery was terrible. He was ill with jealousy. All his time, when he was not at the hospital, when he was not snatching a few hours of sleep, was spent in thrashing out in his mind what he should do. It was impossible to go on like this. If he remained in her company he was afraid he would do her some violence, but the thought of being permanently parted from her was horrible. When he contemplated it he seemed to feel the solid ground sliding away from under his feet, he felt like Othello felt – "If I love thee not, chaos is come again."

In June, on Friday, 19 June, Norah went down to Chelmsford, to the Murrey Gryphon Hotel, to spend the night with Jan Vandepeer.

Michael, who had worked every day without a break at the hospital for two weeks, had two days off, the Friday and the Saturday. He was tired almost to the point of sickness, but those two days he was to have off loomed large and glowing and inviting before him at the end of the week. He got them out of proportion. He told himself that if he could have those two days off to spend alone with Norah, to take Norah somewhere into the country and laze those two days away with her, to walk with her hand in hand down country lanes (that he thought with such maudlin romanticism is evidence of his extreme exhaustion), if he could do that, all would miraculously become well. He would explain and she would explain and they would listen to each other and, in the words of the cliché, make a fresh start. Michael was convinced of all this. He was a little mad with tiredness.

After she was dead, and they came in the morning to tell him of her death, he took time off work. Miss Hallam Saul gives the period as three weeks and she is probably correct. Without those weeks of rest Michael Lestrange would very likely have had a mental breakdown or – even worse to his way of thinking – have killed a patient on the operating table. So when it is said that Norah's death, though so terrible to him, saved his sanity and his career, this is not too far from the truth. And then, when he eventually returned to his work, he threw himself into it with total dedication. He had nothing else, you see, nothing at all but his work for the rest of his life that ended in the North Atlantic last March.

Brannel had nothing either. It is very difficult for the educated middle-class person, the kind of person we really mean when we talk about "the man in the street", to understand the lives of people like Kenneth Edward Brannel and his father. They had no hobbies, no interests, no skill, no knowledge in their heads, virtually no friends. Old Brannel could read. Tracing along the lines with his finger, he could just about make out the words in a newspaper. Kenneth Brannel could not read at all. These days they would have television, not then. Romantic town-dwellers imagine such as the Brannels tending their cottage gardens, growing vegetables, occupying themselves with a little carpentry or shoemaking in the evenings, cooking country stews and baking bread. The Brannels, who worked all day in another man's fields, would not have dreamt of further tilling the soil in the evenings. Neither of them had ever so much as put up a shelf or stuck a sole on a boot. They lived on tinned food and fish and chips, and when the darkness came down they went to bed. There was no electricity in their cottage, anyway, and no running water or indoor sanitation. It would never have occurred to Mr Stokes of Cross Farm to provide these amenities or to the Brannels to demand them.

Downstairs in the cottage was a living room with a fireplace and a kitchen with a range. Upstairs was old Brannel's room into which the stairs went, and through the door from this room was the bedroom and only private place of Kenneth Edward Brannel. There, in a drawer in the old, wooden-knobbed tallboy, unpolished since Ellen Brannel's death, he kept his souvenirs: Wendy Cutforth's bracelet, a lock of Maureen Hunter's red hair, Ann Daly's green silk scarf, Mary Trenthyde's handkerchief with the lipstick stain and the embroidered M. The small, square handbag mirror was always assumed to have been the property of Norah Lestrange, to be a memento of her, but this was never proved. Certainly, there was no mirror in her handbag when her body was found.

In Miss Hallam Saul's *The Wrexlade Monster* there were several pictures of Brannel, a snapshot taken by his aunt when he was ten, a class group at Ingleford Middle School (which he should properly have never, with his limitations, been allowed to attend), a portrait by a Chelmsford photographer that his mother had had taken the year before her death. He was very tall, a gangling, bony man with a bumpy, tortured-looking forehead and thick, pale, curly hair. The eyes seem to say to you: The trouble is that I am puzzled, I am bewildered, I don't understand the world or you or myself and I live always in a dark mist. But when, for a little, that mist clears, look what I do . . .

His hands, hanging limply at his sides, are turned slightly, the palms half-showing, as if in helplessness and despair.

Miss Hallam Saul includes no picture of Sir Michael Lestrange, MD, FRCS, eminent cardiac specialist, author of *The Heart*, Physician to Her Royal Highness the Duchess of Albany, professor of cardiology at St Joachim's Hospital. He was a thin, dark young man in those days, slight of figure and always rather shabbily dressed. One would not have given him a second glance. Very different he was then from the Sir Michael who was mourned by the medical elite of two continents and whose austere yet tranquil face with its sleek silver hair, calm light eyes and aquiline features appeared on the front pages of the world's newspapers. He had changed more than most men in twenty-seven years. It was a total metamorphosis, not merely an ageing.

At the time of the murder of his wife Norah he was twenty-six. He was ambitious but not inordinately so. The ambition, the vocation one might well call it, came later, after she was dead. He was worn out with work on 19 June 1953, and he was longing to get away to the country with his wife and to rest.

"But, darling, I'm sure I told you. I'm going to meet Jan at the Murrey Gryphon. I did tell you, I never have any secrets from you, you know that. *You* didn't tell me you were going to have two days off. How was I to know? You never seem to take time off these days and I do like to have *some* fun *some*times."

"Don't go," he said.

"But, darling, I want to see Jan."

"It's more than I can bear, the way we live," he said. "If you won't stop seeing this man I shall stop you."

He buried his face in his hands and presently she came and laid a hand on his shoulder. He jumped up and struck her a blow across the face. When she left for Chelmsford to meet Jan Vandepeer she had a bruise on her cheek which she did her best to disguise with make-up.

They had a message for her at the hotel when she got there, from her "husband" in Holland to say he had been delayed at The Hook. Hotels, in those days, were inclined to be particular that couples who shared bedrooms should at least pretend to be husband and wife. It was insinuated at Brannel's trial that Jan Vandepeer failed to arrive on this occasion because he was growing tired of Norah, but there was no evidence to support this. He was genuinely delayed and unable to leave.

Why didn't she go back to London? Perhaps she was afraid

to face Michael. Perhaps she hoped Vandepeer would still come, since the phone message had been received at four-thirty. She dined alone and went out for a walk. To pick up a man, insisted prosecuting counsel, though he was not prosecuting *her* and the Old Bailey is not a court of morals. Nobody saw her go and no one seems to have been sure where she went. Eventually, of course, to Wrexlade.

Brannel also went out for a walk. The long light evenings disquieted him because he could not go to bed and he had nothing to do but sit with his father while the old man puzzled out the words in the evening paper. He went first to his bedroom to look at and handle the secret things he kept there, the scarf and the lock of hair and the bracelet and the handkerchief with M on it for Mary Trenthyde, and then he went out for his walk. Along the narrow lanes, to stop sometimes and stand, to lean over a gate, or to kick a pebble aimlessly ahead of him, dribbling it slowly from side to side of the long, straight, lonely road.

Did Norah Lestrange walk all the way to Wrexlade or did someone give her a lift and for reasons unknown abandon her there? She could have walked, it is no more than two miles from the Murrey Gryphon to the spot where her body was found half an hour before midnight. Miss Hallam Saul suggests that she was friendly with a second man in the Chelmsford neighbourhood and, in the absence of Vandepeer, set off to meet him that evening. Unlikely though that seems, similar suggestions were put forward in court. It was as if they all said, a woman like that, a woman so immoral, so promiscuous, so lacking in all proper feeling, a woman like that will do anything.

Her body was found by two young Wrexlade men going home after an evening spent at the White Swan on the Ladeley–Wrexlade road. They phoned the police from the call box on the opposite side of the lane, and the first place the police went to, because it was the nearest habitation, was the Brannels' cottage. Norah Lestrange's body lay half-hidden in long grass on the verge by the bridge over the river Lade, and the Brannels' home, Lade Cottage, was a hundred yards the other side of the bridge. They went there initially only to ask the occupants if they had seen or heard anything untoward that evening.

Old Brannel came down in his nightshirt with a coat over it. He hadn't been asleep when the police came, he said, he had been awakened a few minutes before by his son coming in. The detective superintendent looked at Kenneth Edward Brannel, at his huge dangling hands, as he stood leaning against the wall, his eyes bewildered, his mouth a little open. No, he couldn't say where he had been, round and about, up and down, he couldn't say more.

They searched the house, although they had no warrant. Much was made of this by the defence at the trial. In Kenneth Brannel's bedroom, in the drawer of the tallboy, they found Wendy Cutforth's bracelet, Maureen Hunter's lock of red hair, Ann Daly's green silk scarf, and the handkerchief with M on it for Mary Trenthyde. The Wrexlade Monster had been caught at last. They cautioned Brannel and charged him and he looked at them in a puzzled way and said: "I don't think I killed the lady. I don't remember. But maybe I did, I forget things and it's like a mist comes up . . ."

Michael Lestrange was told of the death of his wife in the early hours of the morning. Their purpose in coming to him was to tell him the news and ask him if he would later go with them to Chelmsford formally to identify his wife's body. They asked him no questions and would have expressed their sympathy and left him in peace, had he not declared that it was he who had killed Norah and that he wanted to make a full confession.

They had no choice after that but to drive him at once to Chelmsford and take a statement from him. No one believed it. The detective chief superintendent in charge of the case was very kind to him, very gentle but firm.

"But if I tell you I killed her you must believe me. I can prove it."

"Can you, Dr Lestrange?"

"My wife was constantly unfaithful to me . . ."

"Yes, so you have told me. And you bore with her treatment of you because of your great affection for her. The truth seems to be, doctor, that you were a devoted husband and your wife – well, a less than ideal wife."

Michael Lestrange insisted that he had driven to Chelmsford in pursuit of Norah, intending to appeal to Jan Vandepeer to leave her alone. He had not gone into the hotel. By chance he had encountered her walking aimlessly along a Chelmsford street as he was on his way to the Murrey Gryphon.

"Mrs Lestrange was still having her dinner at the time you mention," said Chief Superintendent Masters.

"What does that matter? It was earlier or later, I can't be precise about times. She got into the car beside me. I drove off, I don't know where, I didn't want a scene in the hotel. She told me she had to get back, she was expecting Vandepeer at any moment."

"Vandepeer had sent her a message he wasn't coming. She didn't tell you that?"

"Is it important?" He was impatient to get his confession over. "It doesn't matter what she told me. I can't remember what we said."

"Can you remember where you went?"

"Of course I can't. I don't know the place. I just drove and parked somewhere, I don't know where, and we got out and walked and she drove me mad, the things she said, and I got hold of her throat and . . ." He put his head in his hands. "I can't remember what happened next. I don't know where it was or when. I was so tired and I was mad, I think." He looked up. "But I killed her. If you'd like to charge me now, I'm quite ready."

The chief superintendent said very calmly and stolidly, "That won't be necessary, Dr Lestrange."

Michael Lestrange shut his eyes momentarily and clenched his fists and said, "You don't believe me."

"I quite believe you believe it yourself, doctor."

"Why would I confess it if it wasn't true?"

"People do, sir, it's not uncommon. Especially people like yourself who have been overworking and worrying and not getting enough sleep. You're a doctor, you know what the psychiatrists would say, that you had a reason for doing violence to your wife so that now she's dead your mind has convinced itself you killed her, and you're feeling guilt for something you had nothing to do with.

"You see, doctor, look at it from our point of view. Is it likely that you, an educated man, a surgeon, would murder anyone? Not very. And if you did, would you do it in Wrexlade? Would you do it a hundred yards from the home of a man who has murdered four other women? Would you do it by strangling with the bare hands which is the method that man always used? Would you do it four weeks after the last strangling which itself was four weeks after the previous one? Coincidences like that don't happen, do they, Dr Lestrange? But people do get overtired and suffer from stress so that they confess to crimes they never committed."

"I bow to your superior judgement," said Michael Lestrange.

He went to the mortuary and identified Norah's body and then he made a statement to the effect that Norah had gone to Chelmsford to meet her lover. He had last seen her at four on the previous afternoon.

Brannel was found guilty of Norah's murder, for he was specifically charged only with that, after the jury had been out half an hour. And in spite of the medical evidence as to his mental state he was condemned to death and executed a week before Christmas.

For the short time after that execution that capital punishment remained law, Michael Lestrange was bitterly opposed to it. He used to say that Brannel was a prime example of someone who had been unjustly hanged and that this must never be allowed to happen in England again. Of course there was never any doubt that Brannel had strangled Wendy Cutforth, Maureen Hunter, Ann Daly and Mary Trenthyde. The evidence was there and he repeatedly confessed to these murders. But that was not what Michael Lestrange meant. People took him to mean that a man must not be punished for committing a crime whose seriousness he is too feeble-minded to understand. This is the law, and there can be no exceptions to it merely because society wants its revenge. People took Michael Lestrange to mean that when he spoke of injustice being done to this multiple killer.

And perhaps he did.

THE END OF AN ERA

Richard Levinson & William Link

Adapted for:

COLUMBO

(Universal TV, 1971–79; 1989–)

Starring: Peter Falk,

Patrick Bauchau & Fionnula Flanagan

Directed by Roland Kibbee

The advent of satellite and cable television has given a new lease of life to many of the classic crime series which are now being reshown to enthusiastic audiences of younger viewers. Among the crime fighters who have been particularly successful the second time around are The Saint *(1962–9), in which Roger Moore brought the exploits of Leslie Charteris's famous man-about-town sleuth, Simon Templer, to the screen; the long running saga of the man on the run,* The Fugitive *(1963–7), with David Janssen as Dr Richard Kimble forever on the track of the mysterious one-armed man in episodes which engrossed audiences on both sides of the Atlantic; and* Jason King *(1971–3) starring Peter Wyngarde as the flamboyant enemy of law-breakers who wore the most outlandish shirts and romanced every beautiful woman who crossed his path. Perhaps even more successful than these has been* Columbo *(1971–9), the cases of the rather down-at-heel Los Angeles Homicide Department detective who uses his mind instead of his gun to solve crimes, and has made its star, Peter Falk, into an international celebrity. The signs for the series were, in fact, auspicious right from the beginning when the first episode was directed by a rising young director named Steven Spielberg. Such an icon did* Columbo *become even after the series ended, that in 1989 Universal TV decided to bring him back in* New Columbo. *In the interim, however, nothing has changed about Columbo: he has the same eye for detail, the same taste in cheap cigars and the same crumpled raincoat. Peter Falk has confessed that there is a lot of himself in the character, and once revealed that he actually found his trademark coat in a cut-price store while escaping from the rain while waiting for shooting to begin – and then insisted on wearing it when the cameras began to roll. In that moment, the image of one of the most famous policemen created especially for television was set.*

Richard Levinson (1934–) and William Link (1937–) are two of the most respected writer-producers in American television, having created some of the most popular crime shows of recent years including Mannix *which starred Mike Connors,* McCloud *with Dennis Weaver, the long-running* Ellery Queen Mysteries *and* Murder She Wrote, *the recent triumph for Angela Lansbury. The partners have drawn the inspiration for these series from many sources; perhaps the most surprising being* Columbo *which Richard Levinson says was inspired by Porfiry Petrovich, the clever but unprepossessing police inspector in Dostoevsky's* Crime and Punishment *published in 1866! Like Petrovich, one of Columbo's most abiding qualities is his loyalty to the police force and his dedication to duty in the face of all manner of obstructions put in his way, not only by suspects. "The End of an Era" is a rare short story written by Levinson and Link for* Alfred Hitchcock's Mystery Magazine *in January 1962 and also features a devoted employee who gets caught up in crime.*

It was an absolute nuisance, something to be endured like a session in the dentist's chair. Mr Grubb found himself wishing he could close his ears with invisible plugs. They were talking about him, paying false tribute to his fifteen years with the firm, and the one thing he didn't want to do was listen. But he was forced to smile and nod, trying to look shy and grateful at the same time. He squirmed in his seat, consoling himself with the knowledge that it couldn't last much longer. And within forty-eight hours – he was delighted by the irony – they'd all see this little gathering in a totally different light.

"Those mornings by the water cooler," Miss Lemmon was saying. "Why, I'd just peek over at Mr Grubb behind his desk and I'd say to myself: 'There's the man for me.' But he never even gave me a tumble. Did you, Miles?"

There was laughter. Why shouldn't they laugh, he reflected; he was old enough to be her grandfather. The little flirt knew he was married, too, but that didn't stop her. She had to make a conquest of every man in the office, young or old, and he was no exception.

While they all laughed, he made himself smile the idiot grin of the good sport. Then Miss Lemmon sat down and there was a hush in the room as Mr Dougherty got ponderously to his feet. Well, here come the platitudes, thought Mr Grubb. The fifteen years of unswerving service to the firm, the feeling of personal loss at this particular retirement. Mr Grubb permitted himself a small smile. There'd be loss, all right, and much more personal than Dougherty expected. He settled back as his employer began to speak, wondering if they'd have the staggering effrontery to give him a wristwatch.

"I'll be brief," Mr Dougherty was saying, gazing out over his staff like a benevolent shepherd. "The end of an era is not a time for chatter, it's a time for thought. And when Miles Grubb leaves this office today it *will* be the end of an era, a moment for all of us here at Cumberland, Inc. to take stock of ourselves and our company."

Having promised to be brief, he launched into a lengthy oration. Mr Grubb, bored, cast his eye around the office. His co-workers were listening with the proper look of reverence; they sat behind their desks, completely absorbed, their thoughts no doubt winging to the day of their own retirement. He grunted under his breath. They were all such fools; their white collars were choking them and they didn't even know it. Well, it wasn't for him. He had intelligence and ambition; he intended to spend the last years of his life in unfettered luxury. And Mr Dougherty, poor, bumbling Mr Dougherty, would provide the means.

The speech ran down of its own sheer weight and Mr Grubb was asked to stand. "Miles," said his employer, "there's very little we can do to show our appreciation on this, your last day here at Cumberland." He held up a wrapped package. "But we hope this small gift will stand as a token of our esteem."

There was applause. Mr Grubb crossed the office, past the two buckets of iced champagne near the filing cabinets, past the desk where he had labored for fifteen years, and with just the right show of bashfulness he took the package from Dougherty's pink hands. "I'd like to thank –" he began.

"Open it," shouted Rudy Schmidt, the billing clerk.

"Yes, Miles, let's see," said Miss Lemmon.

Dutifully, he peeled away the layers of paper and opened the box. Inside was a matching lighter and ashtray set. A small card read: 'To Miles From The Gang At The Office.' He winced. "This is – this is very nice," he said. "Thank you."

Then everyone was standing around clapping him on the back. With twin pops the champagne corks were pulled and someone brought glasses from Mr Dougherty's private office. A toast was proposed, then another. Mr Grubb was compelled to drink to Miss Lemmon, to Cumberland, Inc., to the free enterprise system. It struck him that it would never do to get drunk; there was much to accomplish before the day was over. Fortunately, the big wall clock was inching toward six and a few people were already going for their coats.

Finally it was over. Mr Dougherty drove off in his limousine and the warehouse men came from the back to punch out. Mr Grubb stuffed his few belongings in his overcoat pockets, tucked the gift under his arm, and headed for the door. He was stopped by Alvin Griggle, the assistant comptroller.

"Gotta take you out and buy you a drink," said Alvin.

"Thanks, but I have to get home for dinner. The wife's expecting me."

Alvin's face drooped, then he brightened. "Yeah, guess so," he said. "But I'll miss you, buddy. You don't know how lucky you are, leaving this place." He shook his head. "I've been here ten years myself. And what does it get me? A hundred twenty-five less deductions. It isn't worth it, Miles. Look at you. Fifteen years. And you wind up with a lighter and a glass of champagne."

Mr Grubb was touched. The man seemed on the verge of tears. "I'll get by, Alvin," he said. Then he smiled. "I'll get by very well."

He left the office and went into a hotel across the street to phone his wife, telling her he'd be late for dinner. Then he bought a paper and read the news until seven-thirty. When it was dark outside he left the hotel and crossed the windy pavements to a bus terminal. There, in one of the wall lockers, he found the suitcase he had left that morning. Everything was fine, he told himself. Just fine.

It was almost eight o'clock when he let himself into the Cumberland office. The place was dark but he didn't need a flashlight; after fifteen years he could have moved around the desks and partitions blindfolded. He crossed to Mr Dougherty's office, went inside, and set down his suitcase, orientating himself. The safe was concealed by paneling to the left of the door. Mr Grubb chuckled. Its location was an open secret to everyone in the office.

He touched a hidden device to slide the panel aside, remembering quite clearly the day the safe had been delivered. Mr Dougherty had beamed proudly, instructing the workmen in the mechanics of its installation. Mr Grubb had come into the office to discuss an accounting error and had noticed, completely by accident, a slip of paper on his employer's desk. It contained in neat, ball-point lettering, the combination of the safe. Mr Grubb remembered those numerals. They had stayed in a corner of his brain for the past two years, always available and ready for use.

Now, with his fingers turning the dial, he felt a quiet touch of triumph. First the money, then the plane ticket resting in a drawer at home, and finally the flight to Hawaii, to Brazil, to some lush spot beyond extradition where he could sit on a beach and watch a hundred tropical suns come in and out with the tide.

All thanks to Mr Dougherty and his habit of keeping large amounts of cash on hand. Carefully, quietly, Mr Grubb opened the safe and lit a match. Ranged on the shelves before his eyes were neat stacks of currency in bank wrappers. He wouldn't even have to count them; each packet had its total value stamped on the wrapper. Mr Grubb brought his suitcase to the mouth of the safe and began removing the money. It was, he reflected, the last transaction he would ever perform for Cumberland, Inc.

The first thing his wife said when he came into the house was, "How was your party, dear?"

He examined her critically and decided he wouldn't miss her at all. In the beginning, when he was formulating his plan, he had hesitated for weeks over whether or not to take her with him. But now, looking at the wrinkled face, the gray hair and the vacant eyes, he was positive he had made the right choice. She didn't even ask him why he was carrying his suitcase; he had an excuse ready and waiting, but apparently all she could think of was the party.

"Very pleasant," he said. "They gave me a gift, a lighter and matching ashtrays."

"Oh, how lovely. Where are they?"

He suddenly remembered he had put them in the suitcase. "I have them," he said. "I'll show them to you later. Now I think I'd better wash up."

"Of course, dear."

She bustled into the kitchen and he went upstairs. In their bedroom he opened the suitcase and set the office gift on the dresser. Then he looked at the money for a long moment, trying to picture what would happen on Monday morning. Dougherty would be livid. Probably wouldn't even believe it at first. Not Miles Grubb. Not old, trustworthy, loyal Miles Grubb. How could he do such a thing? And after fifteen years with the firm.

He began loading a few essentials into the suitcase. He'd buy the rest, clothes and everything, when he reached his destination. Then he took the plane ticket from his drawer, went to the hall extension phone, and dialed the airlines. Flight 106 would be leaving for Hawaii on schedule? Eleven o'clock? Thank you very much. He closed the suitcase and went down to dinner.

The meal was uneventful. His wife chattered aimlessly and he only half listened while he ate. She was telling him that they could now enjoy the benefits of leisure. "You'll have all this time on your hands," she said. "So I was thinking . . . Dear? Did you hear me?"

"Yes. You were thinking."

"And I thought it might be nice if we took a drive across the country. You've always wanted to travel and we could stop by Cleveland and see my sister." The idea seemed to excite her. "We don't have to push it or anything. Just a slow, pleasant drive. After all, we're getting older, and we might not have the chance unless we do it soon."

She might be getting older, thought Mr Grubb, but he felt ageless. For a moment he was sorry for her; she'd live out the remainder of her days in this house, never once tasting, touching, or seeing, and death would come as a favor. He wondered how she'd feel when she found out he had betrayed her. Would she be angry, would she cry, would she condemn or defend him? No, she'd probably accept the whole thing with her usual passivity. Well, that was her problem, not his. She'd vanish from his memory the moment he got on the plane.

After dinner she went into the kitchen to do the dishes. Mr Grubb silently climbed to the bedroom, slipped the ticket into his breast pocket, and lifted the suitcase. He glanced around for the last time and was pleased to find that no chords were struck; there wasn't even a slight twinge of nostalgia. Smiling, he went downstairs and left the suitcase by the door. Then he strolled into the kitchen.

"I'm going to take a drive," he said. "Get some fresh air."

"All right dear. Bring back the paper when you come, will you?"

"Of course."

He bent to kiss the back of her neck. Then he left her there, arms plunged in soapy water, gray hair wispy in the steam. No, he decided, he wouldn't miss her at all.

Everything went smoothly at the airport. He left his car in the parking area with the keys in the ignition. It was a small gesture of kindness – now they wouldn't have to tow it away. Inside the terminal building he dropped his suitcase on the scales at the check-in counter and it was comfortably underweight. Well, money wasn't heavy, he reflected, at least not in the physical sense. He bought a few magazines and a box of cough drops, then browsed until loudspeakers began announcing his flight.

Settled on the plane, his seat belt fastened and his magazines on his lap, Mr Grubb sighed a sigh of contentment. He was safe; there hadn't been a single hitch in plans. Within a few minutes the motors would roar, they would taxi down the runway, and then, lifting, lifting, he'd be carried toward Hawaii and gilt-edged anonymity. He waited, his mind pleasantly occupied with thoughts of the things he would buy, for the propellers to grind into life.

And then the stewardess' voice was speaking over the PA system. "Ladies and gentlemen, due to mechanical difficulties we'll be unable to take off on schedule. We'd appreciate it if you'd leave by the rear door and go to the main waiting room until further notice."

There was a discontented murmur from the other passengers. Mr Grubb frowned. Always some idiotic fly in the ointment. And he had just been congratulating himself on how smoothly things were going. Well, they'd get it straightened out, whatever it was. He unfastened his seat belt and joined the others inching down the aisle.

As soon as he reached the waiting room he crossed to the check-in counter, "How long will 106 be delayed?" he asked.

"We don't know, sir," said the young man smoothly. "An hour, maybe more."

"What's the problem?"

"Just a few mechanical difficulties, sir. Nothing serious."

Mr Grubb found a chair and tried to read his magazine, but his eye was constantly drawn to the check-in counter. It seemed to be the meeting spot of a group of officials; they were talking animatedly among themselves, then one would hurry off and someone else would join the circle. He got up and moved closer to them, trying to overhear, but their voices were pitched too low. Finally, deciding it had nothing to do with his flight, he started back to his seat.

And then he saw the police officers, four of them, come into the building and move toward the desk. There was a hurried conference and they headed through double doors to the landing field.

He resisted a momentary impulse to run. But they couldn't be here after him. It was impossible. He made himself relax by an effort of will. No one would enter the Cumberland office until Monday morning. Then and only then would the police be interested in his whereabouts.

Mr Grubb paged through his magazine as time stretched on. His flight had been delayed a half hour now and he was growing nervous. The cluster at the check-in counter had dispersed and a new man – he seemed to be younger than the other, possibly new on the job – was weighing in luggage. Mr Grubb watched him for a moment. These airline people never tell you anything, he thought, but this fellow had the look of inexperience about him. Perhaps he could be bullied into parting with some information. Mr Grubb stood up and approached the counter.

"Look," he said in an angry voice, "we've been waiting here for thirty-five minutes. What's happening with 106 to Hawaii?"

"Just some minor diff –"

"I don't believe it," he snapped. "There's something else. Now do you tell me what it is or do I go to your superior?"

"Really, sir –"

"Don't 'really, sir' me! There were four police officers here a while ago. Why? What's going on?"

He continued to raise his voice and the young man looked uncomfortable.

"Well – if I tell you, sir, will you promise you won't tell the other passengers?"

"I promise."

The young man hesitated for a moment, then he said, "We got a crank call. You know, it happens every once in a while. Something about a bomb on the plane."

"A bomb?"

"No truth to it, of course. But we have to check. As soon as they're finished you'll be taking off."

Mr Grubb felt immensely relieved. Just a silly anonymous phone call. Some crank who hated the world. It had nothing to do with him at all. "I appreciate your telling me," he said, "and I'll keep quiet about it. How much longer will it take them?"

"Another ten, fifteen minutes, I guess. They have to search the luggage."

Mr Grubb stared at him. "Search the luggage?"

"Yes, sir. Just a normal precaution."

Mr Grubb felt his heart pumping abnormally. He reeled

away from the desk, just in time to see a police officer come through the double doors and start toward him.

The man held his suitcase in his hand.

"He wants you to call your family lawyer and come down to police headquarters right away," said the voice on the phone.

"But – I don't understand," said Mrs Grubb.

"Neither do we, lady. All we know is that he had a fortune in cash in that suitcase of his."

Mrs Grubb had difficulty speaking.

"We're at the airport," said the policeman. "We're leaving now and we'll be at the station house in twenty minutes."

"Is he – under arrest?"

"Yes, ma'am."

"Tell him – tell him I'll call Bill Moore and we'll both be down there right away. Tell him everything will be all right."

The police officer hung up and Mrs Grubb stood looking at the telephone for a long time. Then she dialed the airline terminal. When someone answered the phone she said, "I called you before, about that bomb on flight 106 to Hawaii."

"Who is this?" said the voice sharply.

"Never mind. I just wanted to say there isn't any bomb. You can leave now, if you want to."

"If you'd give me your name –"

"Tell them down there it was all a joke. That's all that it was. Just a joke."

She hung up, smiled, and began to dial the family lawyer.

MR BIG

Woody Allen

Adapted to:

MANHATTAN MURDER MYSTERY

(Tristar Pictures, 1994)

Starring: Woody Allen,

Diane Keaton & Alan Alda

Directed by Woody Allen

Parody has had a place in crime movies ever since Dashiell Hammett's Thin Man *series back in the Thirties about a husband-and-wife detective team, Nick and Nora Charles, who were played by William Powell and Myrna Loy. So popular did the idea prove that the pair of amateur sleuths who tackled everything from high society theft to murder have twice been revived on TV: in the late fifties with Peter Lawford and Phyllis Kirk, and then again in 1975 starring Craig Stevens and Jo Ann Pflug. The series was also the inspiration for Woody Allen's critically acclaimed 1994 film,* Manhattan Murder Mystery, *in which the gloomy comedian and Diane Keaton played a couple who suddenly begin to suspect they might be living next door to a murderer . . . and they had better do something about getting to the bottom of the mystery. Combining nail-biting Hitchcock-style suspense with comic moments of mistaken identity, it is another example of Woody's love for the crime genre − which he had already evidenced in his fiction and an earlier movie,* Bullets Over Broadway (1993), *a mad-cap thirties tale of gangsters and the theatre business.*

Woody Allen (1935−) the versatile director, screen-writer and comedy actor, was born in New York and made his early living writing jokes for newspaper columns and sketches for stage revues. His big break came in 1965, when he created the kind of cynical parody that has since become his trademark: What's New Pussycat?, *in which he was both the scriptwriter and a co-star with Peter Sellers. Woody scored his biggest critical and commercial success with* Annie Hall *(1977), which won him two Oscars as director and screenwriter. Apart from his high-profile movie career, he has also shown himself to be a fine short-story writer. "Mr Big" is one of the best examples of this side of his multi-faceted talent and again underlines his affection for the crime story genre. It is a first-person account of the life of a typical Los Angeles Private Eye − and, although written in 1981, is a story very much in the style of those great masters, Hammett and Chandler, who would doubtless have enjoyed its tribute to their work. "Mr Big" also makes an ideal finale to this journey through almost a century of crime movies and television series for the armchair detective . . .*

I was sitting in my office, cleaning the debris out of my thirty-eight and wondering where my next case was coming from. I like being a private eye, and even though once in a while I've had my gums massaged with an automobile jack, the sweet smell of green-backs makes it all worth it. Not to mention the dames, which are a minor preoccupation of mine that I rank just ahead of breathing. That's why, when the door to my office swung open and a long-haired blonde named Heather Butkiss came striding in and told me she was a nudie model and needed my help, my salivary glands shifted into third. She wore a short skirt and a tight sweater and her figure described a set of parabolas that could cause cardiac arrest in a yak.

"What can I do for you, sugar?"

"I want you to find someone for me."

"Missing person? Have you tried the police?"

"Not exactly, Mr Lupowitz."

"Call me Kaiser, sugar. All right, so what's the scam?"

"God."

"God?"

"That's right, God. The Creator, the Underlying Principle, the First Cause of Things, the All Encompassing. I want you to find Him for me."

I've had some fruit cakes up in the office before, but when they're built like she was, you listened.

"Why?"

"That's my business, Kaiser. You just find Him."

"I'm sorry, sugar. You got the wrong boy."

"But why?"

"Unless I know all the facts," I said, rising.

"Okay, okay," she said, biting her lower lip. She straightened the seam of her stocking, which was strictly for my benefit, but I wasn't buying any at the moment.

"Let's have it on the line, sugar."

"Well, the truth is – I'm not really a nudie model."

"No?"

"No. My name is not Heather Butkiss, either. It's Claire Rosensweig and I'm a student at Vassar. Philosophy major. History of Western Thought and all that. I have a paper due January. On Western religion. All the other kids in the course will hand in speculative papers. But I want to *know*. Professor Grebanier said if anyone finds out for sure, they're

a cinch to pass the course. And my dad's promised me a
Mercedes if I get straight A's."

I opened a deck of Luckies and a pack of gum and had one
of each. Her story was beginning to interest me. Spoiled
coed. High IQ and a body I wanted to know better.

"What does God look like?"

"I've never seen him."

"Well, how do you know He exists?"

"That's for you to find out."

"Oh, great. Then you don't know what he looks like? Or
where to begin looking?"

"No. Not really. Although I suspect he's everywhere. In
the air, in every flower, in you and I – and in this chair."

"Uh huh." So she was a pantheist. I made a mental note of
it and said I'd give her case a try – for a hundred bucks a day,
expenses, and a dinner date. She smiled and okayed the deal.
We rode down in the elevator together. Outside it was
getting dark. Maybe God did exist and maybe He didn't,
but somewhere in that city there were sure a lot of guys who
were going to try and keep me from finding out.

My first lead was Rabbi Itzhak Wiseman, a local cleric
who owed me a favor for finding out who was rubbing pork
on his hat. I knew something was wrong when I spoke to him
because he was scared. Real scared.

"Of course there's a you-know-what, but I'm not even
allowed to say His name or He'll strike me dead, which I
could never understand why someone is so touchy about
having his name said."

"You ever see Him?"

"Me? Are you kidding? I'm lucky I get to see my grand-
children."

"Then how do you know He exists?"

"How do I know? What kind of question is that? Could I
get a suit like this for fourteen dollars if there was no one up
there? Here, feel a gabardine – how can you doubt?"

"You got nothing more to go on?"

"Hey – what's the Old Testament? Chopped liver? How
do you think Moses got the Israelites out of Egypt? With a

smile and a tap dance? Believe me, you don't part the Red
Sea with some gismo from Korvette's. It takes power."

"So he's tough, eh?"

"Yes. Very tough. You'd think with all that success he'd
be a lot sweeter."

"How come you know so much?"

"Because we're the chosen people. He takes best care of us
of all His children, which I'd also like to someday discuss
with Him."

"What do you pay Him for being chosen?"

"Don't ask."

So that's how it was. The Jews were into God for a lot. It
was the old protection racket. Take care of them in return for
a price. And from the way Rabbi Wiseman was talking, He
soaked them plenty. I got into a cab and made it over to
Danny's Billiards on Tenth-Avenue. The manager was a
slimy little guy I didn't like.

"Chicago Phil here?"

"Who wants to know?"

I grabbed him by the lapels and took some skin at the same
time.

"What, punk?"

"In the back," he said, with a change of attitude.

Chicago Phil. Forger, bank robber, strong-arm man, and
avowed atheist.

"The guy never existed, Kaiser. This is the straight dope.
It's a big hype. There's no Mr Big. It's a syndicate. Mostly
Sicilian. It's international. But there is no actual head.
Except maybe the Pope."

"I want to meet the Pope."

"It can be arranged," he said, winking.

"Does the name Claire Rosensweig mean anything to
you?"

"No."

"Heather Butkiss?"

"Oh, wait a minute. Sure. She's that peroxide job with the
bazooms from Radcliffe."

"Radcliffe? She told me Vassar."

"Well, she's lying. She's a teacher at Radcliffe. She was mixed up with a philosopher for a while."

"Pantheist?"

"No. Empiricist, as I remember. Bad guy. Completely rejected Hegel or any dialectical methodology."

"One of those."

"Yeah. He used to be a drummer with a jazz trio. Then he got hooked on Logical Positivism. When that didn't work, he tried Pragmatism. Last I heard he stole a lot of money to take a course in Schopenhauer at Columbia. The mob would like to find him – or get their hands on his textbooks so they can resell them."

"Thanks, Phil."

"Take it from me, Kaiser. There's no one out there. It's a void. I couldn't pass all those bad checks or screw society the way I do if for one second I was able to recognize any authentic sense of Being. The universe is strictly phenomenological. Nothing's eternal. It's all meaningless."

"Who won the fifth at Aqueduct?"

"Santa Baby."

I had a beer at O'Rourke's and tried to add it all up, but it made no sense at all. Socrates was a suicide – or or so they said. Christ was murdered. Neitzsche went nuts. If there was someone out there, He sure as hell didn't want anybody to know it. And why was Claire Rosenweig lying about Vassar? Could Descartes have been right? Was the universe dualistic? Or did Kant hit it on the head when he postulated the existence of God on moral grounds?

That night I had dinner with Claire. Ten minutes after the check came, we were in the sack and, brother, you can have your Western thought. She went through the kind of gymnastics that would have won first prize in the Tia Juana Olympics. After, she lay on the pillow next to me, her long blond hair sprawling. Our naked bodies still intertwined. I was smoking and staring at the ceiling.

"Claire, what if Kierkegaard's right?"

"You mean?"

"If you can never really *know*. Only have faith."

"That's absurd."

"Don't be so rational."

"Nobody's being rational, Kaiser." She lit a cigarette. "Just don't get ontological. Not now. I couldn't bear it if you were ontological with me."

She was upset. I leaned over and kissed her, and the phone rang. She got it.

"It's for you."

The voice on the other end was Sergeant Reed of Homicide.

"You still looking for God?"

"Yeah."

"An all-powerful Being? Great Oneness, Creator of the Universe? First Cause of All Things?"

"That's right."

"Somebody with that description just showed up at the morgue. You better get down here right away."

It was Him all right, and from the looks of Him it was a professional job.

"He was dead when they brought Him in."

"Where'd you find Him?"

"A warehouse on Delancey Street."

"Any clues?"

"It's the work of an existentialist. We're sure of that."

"How can you tell?"

"Haphazard way how it was done. Doesn't seem to be any system followed. Impulse."

"A crime of passion?"

"You got it. Which means you're a suspect, Kaiser."

"Why me?"

"Everybody down at headquarters knows how you feel about Jaspers."

"That doesn't make me a killer."

"Not yet, but you're a suspect."

Outside on the street I sucked air into my lungs and tried to clear my head. I took a cab over to Newark and got out and walked a block to Giordino's Italian Restaurant. There, at a back table, was His Holiness. It was the Pope, all right.

Sitting with two guys I had seen in half a dozen police line-ups.

"Sit down," he said, looking up from his fettucine. He held out a ring. I gave him my toothiest smile, but didn't kiss it. It bothered him and I was glad. Point for me.

"Would you like some fettucine?"

"No thanks, Holiness. But you go ahead."

"Nothing? Not even a salad?"

"I just ate."

"Suit yourself, but they make a great Roquefort dressing here. Not like at the Vatican, where you can't get a decent meal."

"I'll come right to the point, Pontiff. I'm looking for God."

"You came to the right person."

"Then He does exist?" They all found this very amusing and laughed. The hood next to me said, "Oh, that's funny. Bright boy wants to know if He exists."

I shifted my chair to get comfortable and brought the leg down on his little toe. "Sorry." But he was steaming.

"Sure He exists, Lupowitz, but I'm the only one that communicates with him. He speaks only through me."

"Why you, pal?"

"Because I got the red suit."

"This get-up?"

"Don't knock it. Every morning I rise, put on this red suit, and suddenly I'm a big cheese. It's all in the suit. I mean, face it, if I went around in slacks and a sports jacket, I couldn't get arrested religion-wise."

"Then it's a hype. There's no God."

"I don't know. But what's the difference? The money's good."

"You ever worry the laundry won't get your red suit back on time and you'll be like the rest of us?"

"I use the special one-day service. I figure it's worth the extra few cents to be safe."

"Name Claire Rosensweig mean anything to you?"

"Sure. She's in the science department at Bryn Mawr."

"Science, you say? Thanks."

"For what?"

"The answer, Pontiff." I grabbed a cab and shot over the George Washington Bridge. On the way I stopped at my office and did some fast checking. Driving to Claire's apartment, I put the pieces together, and for the first time they fit. When I got there she was in a diaphanous peignoir and something seemed to be troubling her.

"God is dead. The police were here. They're looking for you. They think an existentialist did it."

"No, sugar. It was you."

"What? Don't make jokes, Kaiser."

"It was you that did it."

"What are you saying?"

"You, baby. Not Heather Butkiss or Claire Rosensweig, but Doctor Ellen Shepherd."

"How did you know my name?"

"Professor of physics at Bryn Mawr. The youngest one ever to head a department there. At the mid-winter Hop you get stuck on a jazz musician who's heavily into philosophy. He's married, but that doesn't stop you. A couple of nights in the hay and it feels like love. But it doesn't work out because something comes between you. God. Y'see, sugar, he believed, or wanted to, but you, with your pretty little scientific mind, had to have absolute certainty."

"No, Kaiser, I swear."

"So you pretend to study philosophy because that gives you a chance to eliminate certain obstacles. You get rid of Socrates easy enough, but Descartes takes over, so you use Spinoza to get rid of Descartes, but when Kant doesn't come through you have to get rid of him too."

"You don't know what you're saying."

"You made mincemeat out of Leibnitz, but that wasn't good enough for you because you knew if anybody believed Pascal you were dead, so he had to be gotten rid of too, but that's where you made your mistake because you trusted Martin Buber. Except, sugar, he was soft. He believed in God, so you had to get rid of God yourself."

"Kaiser, you're mad!"

"No, baby. You posed as a pantheist and that gave you access to Him – *if* He existed, which he did. He went with you to Shelby's party and when Jason wasn't looking, you killed Him."

"Who the hell are Shelby and Jason?"

"What's the difference? Life's absurd now anyway."

"Kaiser," she said, suddenly trembling. "You wouldn't turn me in?"

"Oh yes, baby. When the Supreme Being gets knocked off, *somebody's* got to take the rap."

"Oh, Kaiser, we could go away together. Just the two of us. We could forget about philosophy. Settle down and maybe get into semantics."

"Sorry, sugar. It's no dice."

She was all tears now as she started lowering the shoulder straps of her peignoir and I was standing there suddenly with a naked Venus whose whole body seemed to be saying, Take me – I'm yours. A Venus whose right hand tousled my hair while her left hand had picked up a forty-five and was holding it behind my back. I let go with a slug from my thirty-eight before she could pull the trigger, and she dropped her gun and doubled over in disbelief.

"How could you, Kaiser?"

She was fading fast, but I managed to get it in, in time.

"The manifestation of the universe as a complex idea unto itself as opposed to being in or outside the true Being of itself is inherently a conceptual nothingness or Nothingness in relation to any abstract form of existing or to exist or having existed in perpetuity and not subject to laws of physicality or motion or idea relating to non-matter or the lack of objective Being or subjective otherness."

It was a subtle concept but I think she understood before she died.